# Quarrels
## That Have Shaped
## the Constitution

EDITED BY JOHN A. GARRATY

# Quarrels That Have Shaped the Constitution

*HARPER & ROW, PUBLISHERS*
*NEW YORK, EVANSTON, AND LONDON*

FIRST EDITION

LIBRARY OF CONGRESS CATALOG CARD NUMBER: 64-18054

G-O

# Contents

v

# Introduction

"The judicial power of the United States shall be vested in one Supreme Court, and in such inferior courts as the Congress may from time to time ordain and establish." So begins Article III of the United States Constitution. This simple sentence provides the authorization for the entire structure of the federal judiciary. The Supreme Court, unique, prestigious, but controversial, is the crown of the system. Beyond question it is the best-known and most powerful judicial body in the world. Designed chiefly as a court to settle arguments between the states, matters involving foreign ambassadors, and other quarrels beyond the scope of state courts, it has from the time of John Marshall to that of Earl Warren added to its power by slow accretion, until today its influence affects every aspect of American life. Troops deploy, great corporations dissolve, little children march past jeering mobs to school because nine black-robed justices in Washington have discovered new meanings in an old and hallowed document.

The Constitution has endured because of its flexibility. The Founding Fathers knew better than to pin down their descendants too closely. Basic principles rather than petty details were what they sought to establish at the Philadelphia Convention in 1789. Even so, anticipating future growth, they provided (Article V) an orderly process for amending the Constitution, and, of course, this process has been frequently put to use.

In 1791 the ten amendments that make up the Bill of Rights were added, and over the years other important changes and additions have been made, such as the Thirteenth Amendment abolishing slavery, the Sixteenth giving Congress the right to levy taxes on incomes, the Nineteenth providing for women's suffrage, and the Twenty-second limiting Presidents to two terms in office.

The amendment process was wisely made complicated and time-consuming in order to discourage ill-considered changes and petty alterations of the nation's fundamental law. To allow for necessary minor adjustments, the Founding Fathers counted upon the Supreme Court, which, they reasoned, could interpret the Constitution and thus clarify doubtful points when important cases came before it.

However, the Fathers really expected the Supreme Court to preserve, rather than to change, the Constitution. For partisan or other reasons, Congress might be tempted to exceed the powers granted it, but the Court, magisterial, conservative, and aloof, could be counted upon to cleave to first principles. Although nowhere does the Constitution state explicitly that the Court has the right to void unconstitutional laws, this power was clearly understood to exist. Alexander Hamilton put it most plainly in the 78th *Federalist*:

> The courts were designed to be an intermediate body between the people and the legislature, in order, among other things, to keep the latter within the limits assigned to their authority. . . . Whenever a particular statute contravenes the Constitution, it will be the duty of the judicial tribunals to adhere to the latter and disregard the former.

In practice it has not worked out entirely as the Constitution-makers expected. The Court has many times protected the Constitution against the illegal acts of Congress and the state legislatures, but it has also repeatedly altered the document itself by its decisions, modifying the fundamental frame of government more extensively in this manner than have all the amendments taken together. The very broadness and generality of the Constitution have permitted —indeed required—that the justices expand, explain, and elaborate upon its terse phraseology. The famous "necessary and proper" clause, the due process of law provision of the Fourteenth Amendment, and many other parts of the Constitution have been time and again explicated in decisions of immense importance. To try to understand the modern Constitution without a knowledge of these judicial landmarks would be like trying to comprehend Christianity without reading the Bible.

The elaboration of the Constitution by judicial interpretation has added greatly to its flexibility and durability, but it has left its evolution partly in the hands of chance. Amendments have always been carefully considered and debated before passage. The nature of the process, requiring, in addition to initial approval by either two-thirds of both houses of Congress or of two-thirds of the states, final ratification by three-quarters of the states, has made this inevitable. Only one amendment, the Eighteenth, prohibiting the manufacture and sale of alcoholic beverages, has ever been repealed, and few of the others have been seriously criticized after ratification by thoughtful students of government.[1]

However, constitutional changes resulting from judicial interpretation have come about in far more casual and unplanned fashion. The Supreme Court can only explain what the Constitution says and thus reshape its meaning when specific cases are brought to it for settlement. The Constitution declares that Congress can "regulate Commerce . . . among the several States," but only when Aaron Ogden sued Thomas Gibbons because he was operating a ferry between New York and New Jersey did Chief Justice John Marshall have the opportunity to explain that this phrase meant every kind of "intercourse" and not merely the movement of goods across state lines. Even legislative acts plainly in violation of the Constitution remain in force until some actual suit comes before the courts for decision. If Congress should abolish trial by jury, for example, nothing could be done about it until someone convicted without a jury trial appealed to the judiciary to obtain his rights.

Thus, constitutional questions of tremendous significance often depend upon the actions of individuals totally unconcerned with broad legal issues. In the hypothetical case just mentioned, the man convicted without a jury trial might be a great reformer unjustly persecuted, but he might just as well be a tramp convicted of stealing a chicken. Constitutionally, it would not matter.

In the following pages, a number of historians examine the personal conflicts, many of them extremely petty, that have led the Supreme Court to hand down some of its most important decisions. In each instance, attention has been focused on the actual controversies and the men whose antagonisms gave the justices the opportunity to act. The cast of characters in these dramas include men of every sort: smugglers and black slaves, bankers and butchers, ferryboat captains, rebels, sweated workers, and great tycoons. Yet in every case the authors have also pointed out the significance of the controversy.

William Marbury wanted to get back his commission as a justice of the peace for the District of Columbia, snatched almost literally from his hand by Thomas Jefferson, but by making the effort he

[1] The Twenty-second Amendment (1951) is the major exception to this generalization.

established once and for all the right of the Supreme Court to declare acts of Congress unconstitutional. The trustees of Dartmouth College were trying to prevent New Hampshire from making the college a state university, but their suit resulted in the Court severely restricting the power of all the states to control corporations. When William McCulloch refused to pay a state tax he was hoping to save his bank from destruction, but in effect he was broadly expanding the power of the federal government vis-à-vis the states. Such trivial arguments begun by men concerned only with their own interests have often resulted in decisions that have shaken the foundations of American society. No doubt this is illogical and perhaps even against the national interest. Nevertheless, it is part of American history, and a particularly absorbing part because its basic elements are conflict, surprise, and human passions.

I wish to thank the authors of the following chapters for their cooperation and understanding in dealing with their subjects from the particular point of view required by the approach outlined above. With minor editing the pieces in this book by John A. Garraty, Richard N. Current, George Dangerfield, Bruce Catton, C. Peter Magrath, Alan F. Westin and C. Vann Woodward first appeared in *American Heritage,* The Magazine of History. *Heritage* editors Oliver Jensen and Robert L. Reynolds have been especially helpful both in working out the general scheme of this book and in editing some of the chapters. Margaret Butterfield of Harper & Row has also made many important editorial suggestions. My son, John A. Garraty, Jr., provided valuable assistance in preparing the manuscript for publication.

J. A. G.

Columbia University
*January, 1964*

# Quarrels
## That Have Shaped
## the Constitution

# The Case of the Missing Commissions

I

BY JOHN A. GARRATY

(*Marbury* v. *Madison,* 1 Cranch 137)

*Paradoxically, the first of our controversies and in some respects the
most important rose from by far the least significant of causes and
the meanest of motives. It is a tale of narrow partisanship, clashing
ambitions, and a man seeking the humble office of justice of the
peace for the District of Columbia.*

It was the evening of March 3, 1801, his last day in office,
and President John Adams was in a black and bitter mood. Assailed
by his enemies, betrayed by some of his most trusted friends, he and
his Federalist party had gone down to defeat the previous November
before the forces of Thomas Jefferson. His world seemed to have
crumbled about his doughty shoulders.

Conservatives of Adams' persuasion were deeply convinced that
Thomas Jefferson was a dangerous radical. He would, they thought,
in the name of individual liberty and states' rights, import the worst
excesses of the French Revolution, undermine the very foundations
of American society, and bring the proud edifice of the national
government, so laboriously erected under Washington and Adams,
tumbling to the ground. Jefferson was a "visionary," Chief Justice
Oliver Ellsworth had said. With him as President, "there would be
no national energy." Ardent believers in a powerful central government like Secretary of State John Marshall feared that Jefferson
would "sap the fundamental principles of government." Others went
so far as to call him a "howling atheist."

Adams himself was not quite so disturbed as some, but he was
deeply troubled. "What course is it we steer?" he had written
despairingly to an old friend after the election. "To what harbor are
we bound?" Now on the morrow Jefferson was to be inaugurated,

1

and Adams was so disgruntled that he was unwilling to remain for the ceremonies, the first to be held in the new capital on the Potomac. At the moment, however, John Adams was still President of the United States, and not yet ready to abandon what he called "all virtuous exertion" in the pursuit of his duty. Sitting at his desk in the damp, drafty, still unfinished sandstone "palace" soon to be known as the White House, he was writing his name on official papers in his large, quavering hand.

The documents he was signing were mostly commissions formally appointing various staunch Federalists to positions in the national judiciary, but the President did not consider his actions routine. On the contrary: he believed he was saving the Republic itself. Jefferson was to be President and his Democratic Republicans would control Congress, but the courts, thank goodness, would be beyond his control. As soon as the extent of Jefferson's triumph was known, Adams had determined to make the judiciary a stronghold of Federalism. Responding enthusiastically to his request for expansion of the courts, the lame-duck Congress had established sixteen new circuit judgeships (and a host of marshals, attorneys, and clerks as well). It had also given Adams blanket authority to create as many justices of the peace for the new District of Columbia as he saw fit, and—to postpone the evil day when Jefferson would be able to put one of his sympathizers on the Supreme Court—it provided that when the next vacancy occurred it should not be filled, thus reducing the Court from six justices to five.[1]

In this same period between the election and Jefferson's inauguration, Chief Justice Ellsworth, who was old and feeble, had resigned, and Adams had replaced him with Secretary of State Marshall. John Marshall was primarily a soldier and politician; he knew relatively little of the law. But he had a powerful mind, and, as Adams reflected, his "reading of the science" was "fresh in his head." He was also but forty-five years of age, and vigorous. Clearly a long life lay ahead of him, and a more forceful opponent of Jeffersonian principles would have been hard to find.

Marshall had been confirmed by the Senate on January 27, and

[1] The Constitution says nothing about the number of justices on the Court; its size is left to Congress. Originally six, the membership was enlarged to seven in 1807, and to nine in 1837. Briefly during the Civil War the bench held ten; the number was set at seven again in 1867 and in 1869 returned to nine, where it has remained.

without resigning as Secretary of State he had begun at once to help Adams strengthen the judicial branch of the government. Perforce they had worked rapidly, for time was short. The new courts were authorized by Congress on February 13; within two weeks Adams had submitted a full slate of officials for confirmation by the Senate. The new justices of the peace for the District of Columbia were authorized on February 27; within three days Adams had submitted for confirmation the names of no less than forty-two justices for that sparsely populated region. The Federalist Senate had done its part nobly too, pushing through the necessary confirmations with great dispatch. Now, in the lamplight of his last night in Washington, John Adams was affixing his signature to the commissions appointing these "midnight justices" to office.

Working with his customary puritanical diligence, Adams completed his work by nine o'clock, and went off to bed for the last time as President of the United States, presumably with a clear conscience. The papers were carried to the State Department, where Secretary Marshall was to affix the Great Seal of the United States to each, and see to it that the documents were then dispatched to the new appointees. But Marshall, a Virginian with something of the Southerner's easygoing carelessness about detail, failed to complete this routine task. All the important new circuit judgeships were taken care of, and most of the other appointments as well. But in the bustle of last-minute arrangements, the commissions of the new District of Columbia justices of the peace went astray. As a result of this trivial slip-up, and entirely without anyone's having planned it, a fundamental principle of the Constitution—affecting the lives of countless millions of future Americans—was to be forever established. Because *Secretary of State* Marshall made his last mistake, *Chief Justice* Marshall was soon to make his first—and in some respects the greatest—of his decisions.

It is still not entirely clear what happened to the missing commissions on the night of March 3. To help with the rush of work, Adams had borrowed two State Department clerks, Jacob Wagner and Daniel Brent. Among his other tasks that fateful night, Brent prepared a list of the forty-two new justices and gave it to another clerk, who "filled up" the appropriate blank commissions. As fast as batches of these were made ready, Brent took them to Adams' office, where he turned them over to William Smith Shaw, the

President's private secretary. After they were signed, Brent brought them back to the State Department, where Marshall was supposed to attach the Great Seal. Evidently he did seal these documents, but he did not trouble to make sure that they were delivered to the appointees. As he later said: "I did not send out the commissions because I apprehended such . . . to be completed when signed & sealed." Actually, he admitted, he would have sent them out in any case "but for the extreme hurry of the time & the absence of Mr. Wagner who had been called on by the President to act as his private secretary."

March 4 dawned and Jefferson, who does not seem to have digested the significance of Adams' partisan appointments at this time, prepared to take the oath of office and deliver his brilliant inaugural address. His mood, as the speech indicated, was friendly and conciliatory. He even asked Chief Justice Marshall, who administered the inaugural oath, to stay on briefly as Secretary of State while the new administration was getting established.

That morning it would still have been possible to deliver the commissions. As a matter of fact, a few actually were delivered, although quite by chance. Marshall's brother James (whom Adams had just made Circuit Judge for the District of Columbia) was disturbed by rumors that there was going to be a riot in Alexandria in connection with the inaugural festivities. Feeling the need of some justices of the peace in case trouble developed, he went to the State Department and personally picked up a batch of the undelivered commissions. He signed a receipt for them, but "finding that he could not conveniently carry the whole," he returned several, crossing out the names of these from the receipt. Among the ones returned were those appointing William Harper and Robert Townshend Hooe. By failing to deliver these commissions, Judge James M. Marshall unknowingly enabled Harper and Hooe, obscure men, to win for themselves a small claim to legal immortality.

The new President was eager to mollify the Federalists, but when he realized the extent to which Adams had packed the judiciary with his "most ardent political enemies," he was justly indignant. Adams' behavior, he said at the time, was an "outrage on decency," and some years later, when passions had cooled a little, he wrote sorrowfully: "I can say with truth that one act of Mr. Adams' life, and only one, ever gave me a moment's personal displeasure. I did consider his last appointments to office as personally unkind." When he discovered the J.P. commissions in the State Department, he decided at once not to allow them to be delivered.

James Madison, the new Secretary of State, was not yet in Washington. So Jefferson called in his Attorney General, a Massachusetts lawyer named Levi Lincoln, whom he had designated Acting Secretary. Giving Lincoln a new list of justices of the peace, he told him to put them "into a general commission" and notify the men of their selection.

In truth, Jefferson acted with remarkable forbearance. He reduced the number of justices to thirty, fifteen each for Washington and Alexandria Counties. But only seven of his appointees were new men; the rest he chose from among the forty-two names originally submitted by Adams. (One of Jefferson's choices was Thomas Corcoran, father of W. W. Corcoran, the banker and philanthropist who founded the Corcoran Gallery of Art.) Lincoln prepared the general commissions, one for each county, and notified the appointees. Then, almost certainly, he destroyed the original commissions signed by Adams.

For some time thereafter Jefferson did very little about the way Adams had packed the judiciary. Indeed, despite his much criticized remark that officeholders seldom die and never resign, he dismissed relatively few persons from the government service. For example, the State Department clerks, Wagner and Brent, were permitted to keep their jobs. The new President learned quickly how hard it was to institute basic changes in a going organization. "The great machine of society" could not easily be moved, he admitted, adding that it was impossible "to advance the notions of a whole people suddenly to ideal right." Soon some of his more impatient supporters, like John Randolph of Roanoke, were grumbling about the President's moderation.

But Jefferson was merely biding his time. Within a month of the inauguration he conferred with Madison at Monticello and made the basic decision to try to abolish the new system of circuit courts. Aside from removing the newly appointed marshals and attorneys, who served at the pleasure of the Chief Executive, little could be done until the new Congress met in December. Then, however, he struck. In his annual message he urged the "contemplation" by Congress of the Judiciary Act of 1801. To direct the lawmakers' thinking, he submitted a statistical report showing how few cases the federal courts had been called upon to deal with since 1789. In January, 1802, a Repeal Bill was introduced; after long debate it passed early in March, thus abolishing the jobs of the new circuit judges.

Some of the deposed jurists petitioned Congress for "relief," but their plea was coldly rejected. Since these men had been appointed for life, the Federalists claimed that the Repeal Act was unconstitutional, but to prevent the Supreme Court from quickly so declaring, Congress passed another bill abolishing the June term of the Court and setting the second Monday of February, 1803, for its next session. By that time, the Jeffersonians reasoned, the old system would be dead beyond resurrection.

This powerful assault on the courts thoroughly alarmed the conservative Federalists; to them the foundations of stable government seemed threatened if the "independence" of the judiciary could be thus destroyed. No one was more disturbed than the new Chief Justice, John Marshall, nor was anyone better equipped by temperament and intellect to resist it. Headstrong but shrewd, contemptuous of detail and of abstractions but a powerful logician, he detested Jefferson, to whom he was distantly related, and the President fully returned his dislike.

In the developing conflict Marshall operated at a disadvantage that a modern Chief Justice would not have to face. The Supreme Court had none of the prestige and little of the accepted authority it now possesses. Few cases had come before it, and none of these were of any great importance. Before appointing Marshall, Adams had offered the chief justiceship to John Jay, the first man to hold the post, as an appointee of President Washington. Jay had resigned from the Court in 1795 to become Governor of New York. He refused the appointment, saying the Court lacked "energy, weight, and dignity." A prominent newspaper of the day referred to the chief justiceship, with considerable truth, as a "sinecure." One of the reasons Marshall had accepted the post was his belief that it would afford him ample leisure for writing the biography of his hero, George Washington. Indeed, in the grandiose plans for the new capital, no thought had been given to housing the Supreme Court, so that when Marshall took office in 1801 the judges had to meet in the office of the Clerk of the Senate, a small room on the first floor of what is now the North Wing of the Capitol.

Nevertheless, Marshall struck out at every opportunity against the power and authority of the new President; but the opportunities were pitifully few. In one case, he refused to allow a Presidential message to be read into the record on the ground that this would bring the President into the Court in violation of the principle of separation of powers. In another, he ruled that Jefferson's action in a ship seizure case was illegal. But these were matters of small importance. When he tried to move more boldly, his colleagues would not sustain him. He was ready to declare the Judicial Repeal Act unconstitutional, but none of the deposed circuit court judges would bring a case to court. Marshall also tried to persuade his associates that it was unconstitutional for Supreme Court justices to ride the circuit, as they must again do since the lower courts had been abolished. But although they agreed with his legal reasoning, they refused to go along because, they said, years of acquiescence in the practice lent sanction to the old law requiring it. Thus frustrated, Marshall was eager for any chance to attack his enemy, and when a case that was to be known as *Marbury* v. *Madison* came before the Court in December, 1801, he took it up with gusto.

William Marbury, a forty-one-year-old Washingtonian, was one of the justices of the peace for the District of Columbia whose commissions Jefferson had held up. Originally from Annapolis, he had moved to Washington to work as an aide to the first Secretary of the Navy, Benjamin Stoddert. It was probably his service to this staunch Federalist that earned him the appointment by Adams. Together with one Dennis Ramsay and Messrs. Harper and Hooe, whose commissions James Marshall had *almost* delivered, Marbury was asking the Court to issue an order (a writ of mandamus) requiring Secretary of State Madison to hand over their "missing" commissions. Marshall willingly assumed jurisdiction and issued a rule calling upon Madison to show cause at the next term of the Supreme Court why such a writ should not be drawn. Here clearly was an opportunity to get at the President through one of his chief agents, to assert the authority of the Court over the executive branch of the government.

This small controversy quickly became a matter of great moment both to the administration and to Marshall. The decision to do away with the June term of the Court was made in part to give Madison more time before having to deal with Marshall's order. The abolition of the circuit courts and the postponement of the next Supreme Court session to February, 1803, made Marshall even more determined to use the Marbury case to attack Jefferson. Of course, Marshall was embarrassingly involved in this case, since his carelessness was the cause of its very existence. He ought to have disqualified himself, but his fighting spirit was aroused, and he was in no mood to back out.

On the other hand, the Jeffersonians, eager to block any judicial investigation of executive affairs, used every conceivable mode of obstruction to prevent the case from being decided. Madison ignored Marshall's order. When Marbury and Ramsay called on the Secretary to inquire whether their commissions had been duly signed (Hooe and Harper could count on the testimony of James Marshall to prove that theirs had been attended to), he gave them no satisfactory answer. When they asked to *see* the documents, Madison referred them to the clerk, Jacob Wagner. He, in turn, would only say that the commissions were not then in the State Department files.

Unless the plaintiffs could prove that Adams had appointed them their case would collapse. Frustrated at the State Department, they turned to the Senate for help. A friendly Senator introduced a motion calling upon the Secretary of the Senate to produce the record of the action in executive session on their nominations. But the motion was defeated after an angry debate, on January 31, 1803. Thus tempers were hot when the Court finally met on February 9 to deal with the case.

In addition to Marshall, only Justices Bushrod Washington and Samuel Chase were on the bench, and the Chief Justice dominated the proceedings. The almost childishly obstructive tactics of administration witnesses were no match for his fair but forthright management of the hearing. The plaintiffs' lawyer was Charles Lee, an able advocate and brother of "Light-Horse Harry" Lee; he had served as Attorney General under both Washington and Adams. He was a close friend of Marshall, and his dislike of Jefferson had been magnified by the repeal of the Judiciary Act of 1801, for he was another of the circuit court judges whose "midnight" appointments repeal had canceled.

Lee's task was to prove that the commissions had in fact been completed by Adams and Marshall, and to demonstrate that the Court had authority to compel Madison to issue them. He summoned Wagner and Brent, and when they objected to being sworn because "they were clerks in the Department of State, and not bound to disclose any facts relating to the business or transactions in the office," he argued that in addition to their "confidential" duties as agents of the President, the Secretary and his deputies had duties "of a public nature" delegated to them by Congress. They must testify about these public matters, just as, in a suit involving property, a clerk in the land office could be compelled to state whether or not a particular land patent was on file.

Marshall agreed and ordered the clerks to testify. They then disclosed many of the details of what had gone on in the President's "palace" and in the State Department on the evening of March 3, 1801, but they claimed to be unsure of the fate of the particular commissions of the plaintiffs.

Next Lee called Attorney General Levi Lincoln. He too objected strenuously to testifying. He demanded that Lee submit his questions in writing so that he might consider carefully his obligations both to the Court and to the President before making up his mind. He also suggested that it might be necessary for him to exercise his constitutional right (under the Fifth Amendment) to refuse to give evidence that might "criminate" him. Lee then wrote out four questions. After studying them, Lincoln asked to be excused from answering, but the justices ruled against him. Still hesitant, the Attorney General asked for time to consider his position further, and Marshall agreed to an overnight adjournment.

On the next day, the tenth of February, Lincoln offered to answer all Lee's questions but the last: What had he done with the commissions? He had seen "a considerable number of commissions" signed and sealed, but could not remember—he claimed—whether the plaintiffs' were among them. He did not know if Madison had ever seen these documents, but was certain that *he* had not given them to him. On the basis of this last statement, Marshall ruled that the embarrassing question as to what Lincoln had done with the commissions was irrelevant; he excused Lincoln from answering it.

Despite these reluctant witnesses, Lee was able to show conclusively through affidavits submitted by another clerk and by James Marshall that the commissions had been signed and sealed. In his closing argument he stressed the significance of the case as a test of the principle of judicial independence. "The emoluments or the dignity of the office," he said, "are no objects with the applicants." This was undoubtedly true; the positions were unimportant and two years of the five-terms had already expired. As Jefferson later pointed out, the controversy itself had become "a moot case" by 1803. But Marshall saw it as a last-ditch fight against an administration campaign to make lackeys of all federal judges, while Jefferson looked at it as an attempt by the Federalist-dominated judiciary to usurp the power of the executive.

In this controversy over principle, Marshall and the Federalists were of necessity the aggressors. The administration boycotted the hearings. After Lee's summation, no government spokesman came forward to argue the other side, Attorney General Lincoln coldly announcing that he "had received no instructions to appear." With his control over Congress, Jefferson was content to wait for Marshall to act. If he overreached himself, the Chief Justice could be impeached. If he backed down, the already trifling prestige of his court would be further reduced.

Marshall had acted throughout with characteristic boldness; quite possibly it was he who had persuaded the four aggrieved justices of the peace to press their suit in the first place. But now his combative temperament seemed to have driven him too far. As he considered the Marbury case after the close of the hearings, he must have realized this himself, for he was indeed in a fearful predicament. However sound his logic and just his cause, he was on very dangerous ground. Both political partisanship and his sense of justice prompted him to issue the writ sought by Marbury and his fellows, but what effect would the mandamus produce? Madison almost certainly would ignore it and Jefferson would back him up. No power but public opinion could make the Executive Department obey an order of the Court. Since Jefferson was riding the crest of a wave of popularity, to issue the writ would be a futile act of defiance; it might even trigger impeachment proceedings against

Marshall that, if successful, would destroy him and reduce the Court to servility.

Yet what was the alternative? To find against the petitioners would be to abandon all principle and surrender abjectly to Jefferson. This a man of Marshall's character could simply not consider. Either horn of the dilemma threatened utter disaster; that it was disaster essentially of his own making could only make the Chief Justice's discomfiture the more complete.

But at some point between the close of the hearings on February 11 and the announcement of his decision on the twenty-fourth, Marshall found a way out. It was an inspired solution, surely the cleverest of his long career. It provided a perfect escape from the dilemma, which probably explains why he was able to persuade the associate justices to agree to it despite the fact that it was based on the most questionable legal logic. The issue, Marshall saw, involved a conflict between the Court and the President, the problem being how to check the President without exposing the Court to his might. Marshall's solution was to state vigorously the justice of the plaintiffs' cause and to condemn the action of the Executive, but to deny the Court's power to provide the plaintiffs with relief.

Marbury and his associates were legally entitled to their commissions, Marshall announced. In withholding them Madison was acting "in plain violation" of the law of the land. But the Supreme Court could not issue a writ of mandamus because the provision of the Judiciary Act of 1789 authorizing the Court to issue such writs was unconstitutional. In other words, Congress did not have the legal right to give that power to the Court!

So far as it concerned the Judiciary Act, modern commentators agree that Marshall's decision was based on a very weak legal argument. The Act of 1789 stated (section 13) that the Supreme Court could issue the writ to "persons holding office under the authority of the United States." This law had been framed by experts thoroughly familiar with the Constitution, including William Paterson, who now sat by Marshall's side on the Supreme Bench. The Justices had issued the writ in earlier cases without questioning section 13 for a moment. But Marshall now claimed that the Court could not issue a mandamus except in cases that came to it *on appeal* from a lower court, since, under the Constitution, the Court was specifically granted original jurisdiction only over "cases affecting ambassadors, other public ministers and consuls, and those in which a state shall be a party." The Marbury case had *originated* in the Supreme Court; since it did not involve a diplomat or a state, any law that gave the Court the right to decide it was unauthorized.

This was shaky reasoning because the Constitution does not say the Court may exercise original jurisdiction *only* in such cases, but Marshall was on solid ground when he went on to argue cogently the theory that "the constitution controls any legislative act repugnant to it," which he called "one of the fundamental principles of our society." The Constitution is "the *supreme* law of the land," he emphasized. Since it is "the duty of the judicial department to say what the law is," the Supreme Court must overturn any law of Congress that violates the Constitution. "A law repugnant to the constitution," he concluded flatly, "is void." By this reasoning section 13 of the Act of 1789 simply ceased to exist and without it the Court could not issue the writ of mandamus. By thus denying himself authority, Marshall found the means to flay his enemies without exposing himself to their wrath.

Although this was the first time the Court had declared an act of Congress unconstitutional, its right to do so had not been seriously challenged by most authorities. Even Jefferson accepted the principle, claiming only that the executive as well as the judiciary could decide questions of constitutionality. Jefferson was furious over what he called the "twistifications" of Marshall's gratuitous opinion in *Marbury* v. *Madison,* but his anger was directed at the Chief Justice's stinging criticisms of his behavior, not at the constitutional doctrine Marshall had enunciated.

Even in 1803, the idea of judicial review, which Professor E. S. Corwin has called "the most distinctive feature of the American constitutional system," had had a long history in America. The concept of natural law (the belief that certain principles of right and justice transcend the laws of mere men) was thoroughly established in American thinking. It is seen, for example, in Jefferson's statement in the immortal Declaration that men "are endowed by their Creator" with "unalienable" rights. Although not a direct precedent for Marshall's decision, the colonial practice of "disallowance," whereby various laws had been ruled void on the ground that local legislatures had exceeded their powers in passing them, illustrates the American belief that there is a limit to legislative power and that courts may determine when it has been overstepped.

More specifically, Lord Coke had declared early in the seventeenth century that "the common law will controul acts of Parliament." One of the chief legal apologists of the American Revolution, James Otis, had drawn upon this argument a century and a half later in his famous denunciation of the Writs of Assistance, and in the 1780's courts in New Jersey, New York, Rhode Island, and North Carolina had exercised judicial review over the acts of local legislatures. The debates at the Constitutional Convention and some of the *Federalist Papers* (especially No. 78) indicated that most of the Founding Fathers accepted the idea of judicial review as already established. The Supreme Court, in fact, had considered the constitutionality of an act of Congress before—when it upheld a federal tax law in 1796—and it had encountered little questioning of its right to do so. All these precedents, when taken together with the fact that the section of the Act of 1789 nullified by Marshall's decision was of minor importance, explain why no one paid much attention to this part of the decision.

Thus the "Case of the Missing Commissions" passed into history, seemingly a fracas of but slight significance. When it was over, Marbury and his colleagues disappeared into the obscurity whence they had arisen.[2] In the partisan struggle for power between Marshall and Jefferson, the incident was of secondary importance. The real showdown came later in the impeachment proceedings against Justice Chase and the treason trial of Aaron Burr. In the long run, Marshall won his fight to preserve the independence and integrity of the federal judiciary, but generally speaking, the Courts have not been able to exert as much influence over the appointive and dismissal powers of the President as Marshall had hoped to win for them in *Marbury* v. *Madison*. Even the enunciation of the Court's power to void acts of Congress wrought no immediate change in American life. Indeed, it was more than half a century before another federal law was overturned.

Nevertheless, this trivial squabble over a few petty political plums was of vital importance for later American history. For with the expansion of the federal government into new areas of activity in

[2] Marbury became president of a Georgetown bank in 1814 and died in 1835.

more recent times, the power of the Supreme Court to nullify acts of Congress has been repeatedly employed, with profound effects upon our social, economic, and political life. At various times income tax, child labor, wage and hours laws, and many other types of legislation have been thrown out by the Court, and always, in the last analysis, its right to do so has depended upon the decision John Marshall made to escape from a dilemma of his own making. The irony is that in 1803 no one—not even the great Chief Justice himself—realized how tremendously significant the case of the missing commissions would one day become.

# The Dartmouth College Case

BY RICHARD N. CURRENT

*(Trustees of Dartmouth College v. Woodward, 4 Wheaton 518)*

*John Marshall's brilliant handling of* Marbury v. Madison *marked the opening of his long service as Chief Justice, a period of thirty-four years during which he dominated the Court as no other Justice has in its history. In more than a thousand decisions rendered during his reign, he found himself in the minority only eight times, and this despite the fact that Jefferson and his Republican successors were able gradually to replace all the Federalist justices with men of their own choosing. Repeatedly he enunciated decisions strengthening the national government at the expense of the states and buttressing the position of the property interests of the country. In* Fletcher v. Peck *(1810), his Court threw out a Georgia law rescinding large land grants even though it was proved that many members of the legislature that had made the original grants had been bribed by speculators. A contract, once agreed to, could not be summarily broken, Marshall decreed. Even more momentous was his handling of a controversy involving the clash of federal and state authority which was settled in 1819. This quarrel concerned the charter of Dartmouth College. Richard N. Current, Professor of History at the University of Wisconsin, has written a biography of Daniel Webster, who figured prominently in the case, and many other books.*

Spring had found its way to the valley of the upper Merrimack, and petals were falling from the apple trees, lately in full bloom. The streets of Concord, New Hampshire, were no longer full of soldiers, the three years of war with Great Britain and Canada having ended that winter. Instead, the capital was beginning to bustle with the usual June crowd of men from out of town. Lawmakers and their hangers-on were arriving, to meet from day to day in the long, low, cupolaed wooden building that doubled as a town house and a state house.

This year—1815—they came together in an atmosphere that was unusually tense, despite the return of both spring and peace. State politics was beginning to be stirred by a campus quarrel brought over from the village of Hanover. Before long, this quarrel was to attract attention far beyond the boundaries of New Hampshire, and after dragging on for nearly four years, it was to leave its mark indelibly upon the Constitution of the United States.

The trouble arose from the sinister scheming of a few men—if a certain anonymous pamphlet, going the rounds in Concord that June, was to be believed. This pamphlet made more exciting reading than was suggested by the wordy title: *Sketches of the History of Dartmouth College . . . with a Particular Account of Some Late Remarkable Proceedings of the Board of Trustees from the Year 1779 to the Year 1815*. From these eighty-eight pages, pedantically yet vigorously written, it appeared that the wicked trustees were interfering with the work of the virtuous president. Worse, they were misapplying college funds. Worse still, they were plotting somehow to extend their tyranny to the entire state.

The anonymous author of the *Sketches* was present in Concord, among the legislators and lobbyists. Over sixty but still very erect, he walked with slow and measured steps and with exaggerated dignity. He wore the old-fashioned outfit of dun-colored coat, knee breeches with buckles, white stockings, and three-cornered beaver hat. From time to time he lifted his hat and bowed and smiled. He could be gracious enough, in his way, but he was not here for a social visit. John Wheelock, president of Dartmouth, was here to launch a fight to the finish against his rebellious professors and trustees.

Wheelock expected to need legal as well as legislative aid. To help him in court, he counted on the services of a young man of growing reputation, a thirty-three-year-old Congressman and lawyer named Daniel Webster, now living in Portsmouth. Wheelock had sounded him out, and Webster had promised to be in Concord. Wheelock kept an eye out for his prospective attorney.

Wheelock and other older people of Dartmouth and Hanover could recall Webster from the day of his arrival, back in 1797, to enroll as a student at the college. He was dressed in homespun which his mother had made and dyed; he had ridden through a hard rain, and the color had run. As he dismounted at the Hanover Inn, the bystanders smiled at his streaked and mottled appearance. They also wondered at his swarthy complexion. Surely this boy, Black Dan, must be an Indian whom Wheelock, after a lapse of several years during which the college enrolled none of the aborigines for whom it presumably had been founded, had finally brought in!

To Webster, as to the townspeople and to other students, Wheelock himself was a figure no less memorable. Often enough they had observed him as he made his way, slowly, stiffly, across the college green. The boys would snicker and repeat their stock joke: Wheelock's profile, with that tremendous nose, they said, made a perfect quadrant.

In the chapel, when he officiated, they found additional cause for amusement. He possessed no training as a minister, and he prayed in unconventional ways. One day, after having attended a chemistry experiment, he fervently addressed the ceiling: "We thank thee, O Lord, for the oxygen gas; we thank thee, O Lord, for the hydrogen gas; we thank thee, O Lord, for the nitrogen gas and for all the gases." (He spoke in a sanctimonious falsetto, which young Webster learned to mimic perfectly.)

Wheelock taught history and theology to the seniors. In the classroom he would ask, textbook in hand, "What does the author say on such and such a page?" If a curious boy raised questions of his own, Wheelock would shut him up with sarcasm. In his office, students invariably discovered him with a tome he had been poring over; he was the most indefatigable reader that Webster ever saw. Covetous of his time, Wheelock would dispose of the student's business as quickly as possible, then inquire: "Will you sit longer, or will you go now?" It is not recorded that any boy ever sat longer.

This caricature of a college president had inherited his job. His father, Eleazar Wheelock, was Dartmouth's founder and first president. By the terms of the charter he had gotten from King George III in 1769, Eleazar could name his own successor, who was to hold office "until such appointment" should be "disapproved by the trustees." He named his son John.

When Eleazar died, the trustees hesitated to approve John's appointment. John was only twenty-five, a devil-may-care army officer. Though a Dartmouth graduate, he hardly seemed to qualify as a Dartmouth president. But the trustees could not very well pick and choose. They had not the wherewithal to provide a salary, and the younger Wheelock, like the elder, was willing to serve (at least for the time being) without pay.

At the time he took over, in 1779, John Wheelock must have sensed, deep inside, a feeling of inadequacy and insecurity. He was scarcely older or more distinguished than the college boys themselves. Desperately eager to command the respect that his new office required, he went too far. He introduced rules compelling the students to remove their hats in his presence and to remain standing until he told them to sit. He took to reading, or at least to looking at printed pages, at all hours of the day and night, so as to give the appearance of diligent scholarship. And he put on a stiff formality of speech and manner.

Wheelock came to act as if he owned the college—and the village too. Well, he did own them, practically. From his father he had inherited, along with his job, a sizable estate. Through marriage to a well-to-do woman he had acquired additional property. By lending money at steep rates, and foreclosing without mercy, he got still more. He could, and did, contribute much to the material support of the college.

Dartmouth continued to be pretty much a one-man show for nearly thirty years, until 1809. Then, after the passing, one by one, of older trustees who deferred to Wheelock, the board acquired a majority of newer members who chose to defy him. These men were disgusted by, among other things, the president's pertinacity in quarreling with the parishioners of the Hanover church, who resisted his efforts to impose an unwanted minister upon them. By vetoing his nominations to the college faculty, the newer trustees soon had most of the professors and tutors on their side.

After several years of forced retreat, Wheelock took the offensive. At the board meeting in November, 1814, he made a proposal which he thought would put his opponents in a dilemma. A part of his back salary, amounting to about $8,000 with interest, had never been paid. He now offered this sum as a gift to endow two professorships—but only on the condition that he be allowed to appoint the two professors. In case the trustees should reject his offer, he would have to demand immediate payment of the $8,000.

His opponents were infuriated. Their first impulse was to demand his resignation. Still, with the college owing him so much money, they hesitated to do that. Perhaps, by humiliating him, they could obtain his resignation without coming out and demanding it. Accordingly, they passed a resolution that, "to relieve the President of some portion of the burdens" weighing heavily upon him, he hereby "be excused from hearing the recitations of the Senior Class" in the theology course. This was considerately worded, yet well calculated to sting the Wheelock pride. The day before, he had met the seniors, as usual, to query them on such matters as the freedom of the will; the day after, he was absent, and another man was in his place.

Humiliated though he was, Wheelock had no intention of resigning. He prepared to strike back, put down the trustees, and regain control of the college, and when spring came he was ready. Whether he sued the trustees or not, Wheelock was determined to appeal to the sovereign people and to their representatives in the legislature. So he wrote his *Sketches of the History of Dartmouth College*, got the pamphlet printed, and sent bundles of copies to Isaac Hill, editor of the Concord *New Hampshire Patriot*, with instructions in an unsigned letter to see that each member of the legislature received a copy. Then, in plenty of time for the 1815 session, Wheelock set out for Concord.

A majority of the legislators, though a very small majority, belonged to the Federalist party, and so did Governor John T. Gilman. The Federalists sponsored theocracy and aristocracy, if one was to believe their rivals, the Jeffersonian Republicans. These men itched to overthrow the Federalist rule and, along with it, the arrangement by which public taxes went to the support of the Congregational Church.

The Jeffersonians had a shrill but effective journalist in the youthful hunchback Isaac Hill (who in years to come was to devote his invective talents to the service of Andrew Jackson). With Hill and the *Patriot* in the forefront, they took up the cause of Wheelock. In it they saw, or pretended to see, the cause of religious and political liberty. Now Wheelock was in fact no libertarian of any kind. He was a good Calvinist and a conservative Federalist. With Hill and the rest of his new-found friends he really had nothing in common—except to the extent that they, for whatever reason, were willing to help him recover his authority at Dartmouth.

When the legislature met, Wheelock got at least a part of what he had come for. He had stolen a march on the trustees: they were not prepared to launch organized opposition to him. Before a sympathetic committee, with no one to refute him, he stated his case, charging the trustees with misusing college funds, overpaying professors, infringing on the president's prerogatives, and conspiring to subvert popular liberties! He asked the legislature to look into Dartmouth's affairs. The legislature agreed, meanwhile endorsing neither Wheelock nor his opponents.

While in Concord, Wheelock also succeeded in finding Webster, who said he would be happy to provide professional assistance.

Several weeks later, at home in Hanover, Wheelock received notice that the investigating committee of the legislature would meet in Hanover on August 16. He could not be sure what tack the committee might take. Promptly he wrote to Webster, enclosing twenty dollars and requesting him to come at once. Wheelock waited, with growing impatience. By August 16 Webster had not appeared and had not answered. So Wheelock faced the committee without him. The committee only tried to patch up a truce. Failing in that, the members withdrew and composed a report—which turned out to be more critical of Wheelock than of his foes.

About a week after the committee hearing, the board of trustees held its annual meeting in Hanover. The eight majority members, "the Octagon," were in no mood to temporize. They voted to remove Wheelock immediately from his positions as president, professor, and trustee. Then they named as the new president the Reverend Francis Brown, thirty-one years old, of Yarmouth, Maine.

Having regained the initiative, the men of the Octagon pressed on to confirm and justify what they had done, publishing a *Reply* to Wheelock's *Sketches* and collecting affidavits to show that he had been incompetent as Dartmouth's head. None of the eight was more active than William W. Thompson, of Concord. Thompson, a United States Senator, was a friend of Representative Webster, and during Congressional terms the two roomed in the same Washington house.

Before Wheelock could recover from the trustees' blow, he received another shock when he saw what Trustee Thompson had written to one of the Dartmouth professors. Thompson's letter must have been opened and copied in the Hanover Post Office; apparently Wheelock had an ally there. Thompson had written: "I have had a long conversation with Mr. D. W., by which it appears that a strong desire prevails that the *Reply*, with the *Committee's Report*, should effectually put down a certain man." From this and other sentences, Wheelock could not mistake the unhappy fact. Instead of helping *him*, Mr. D. W. obviously was taking a big part in the strategy talks of the opposing camp!

A friend of Wheelock's wrote to Webster to protest. Back came the reply that Webster had heard from Wheelock too late to go to Hanover and aid him at the legislative committee's hearing. Anyhow, Webster now said, "I regard that as no professional call." Coldly, if disingenuously, he explained: "On the subject of the dispute between the president and the trustees, I am as little informed as any reading individual in society; and I have not the least inclination to espouse either side, except in proceedings in which my services may be professional." Webster's meaning in this bit of double talk and his motivation in changing sides in the battle are as obscure today as they must have been to Wheelock himself.

Throughout the ensuing autumn and winter the New Hampshire papers argued the Dartmouth question back and forth. The Jeffersonian Republicans made Wheelock a martyr and Dartmouth a leading issue in the state elections of March, 1816. In that year, for the first time in history, the voters chose a Republican governor, William Plumer, and a predominantly Republican legislature. The trustees and their friends, including Webster, expected a strong counterattack from the now strategically placed Wheelock forces. It was not long in coming.

This was the year without a summer. In June, 1816, while the legislature was meeting, snow fell in Concord, the ground froze, and the young corn was killed. Addressing the legislators in the chill State House, Governor Plumer condemned the Dartmouth charter as one that "emanated from royalty" and contained, as was to be expected, "principles congenial to monarchy." It had no reason for existence in a republic like the United States.

Proud of his message, Plumer sent a copy to his party's founder and patron saint, then in retirement at Monticello. "It is replete with sound principles, and truly republican," Thomas Jefferson replied. He went on to condemn those "lawyers and priests" who believed that "the earth belongs to the dead, and not to the living."

The Republicans in Concord were as much impressed as Jefferson. In response to the Governor's message, they passed a law to lift the dead hand of the past and supersede the royal charter—and give control back to Old John Wheelock. The law changed the name of Dartmouth College to "Dartmouth University," increased the number of trustees from twelve to twenty-one, and provided for a board of overseers with a veto over the decisions of the trustees. The law gave the Governor and his council the power to appoint the additional trustees and the overseers. In effect, it transformed Dartmouth from a private college to a state university.

Governor Plumer called the enlarged board of trustees, the university board, together at Hanover, in August. It was still cold, and morning after morning there was frost on the ground. The Hanover reception for the new Plumer trustees was as chilly as the weather. Somehow no one could find the key to the library room where the board customarily met, and when the meeting was called to order in a college office, none of the eight anti-Wheelock trustees was there. Without a quorum present, the Plumer men could do nothing.

The men of the Octagon could not do much either. They had lost the college charter, seal, records, and account books. These were in the hands of the treasurer of the board, and he was an old crony of Wheelock's named William H. Woodward. He was, of course, on the side of the new university.

With this deadlock the first phase of the public controversy, the strictly political one, came to an end. The second, the legal and constitutional (as well as political), phase was to begin after a lull of several months.

In February, 1817, Governor Plumer renewed his attack. He called a second meeting of the university board, this time in Concord, not in Hanover. No longer could the anti-Wheelock trustees frustrate the proceedings by staying away. The legislature had reduced the quorum so that the new Plumer appointees would suffice. At its Concord meeting the university board removed President Brown, two professors, and three of the Octagon trustees. The board then restored Wheelock to the presidency and named his son-in-law William Allen to a professorship.

To Wheelock, who had remained in Hanover, all this was gratifying, though it had come a little late. He now lay in bed, propped up on pillows, coughing his life away. He took some consolation, however, from writing his last will and testament. In it he bequeathed property worth $20,000 to Dartmouth University and made clear that the bequest would be void if, in place of the university, the old college should ever be restored. Too weak to perform the duties of his office, he let his son-in-law serve as acting president.

That same February the college trustees, refusing to accept the new state of affairs, took the advice of Webster and other friends and resorted to a lawsuit. They undertook an action in trover, an action based upon the common-law principle (the opposite of "finders keepers") that one who finds goods must return them to the owner on demand. In this case the trustees called upon their deserting treasurer, William H. Woodward, to return to them the college charter, seal, records, and account books, and to pay $50,000 damages besides. Woodward himself was judge of the Court of Common Pleas of Grafton County, before which the action was brought, and so the case was transferred directly to the New Hampshire Superior Court at Exeter.

While the college trustees were trying to recover the items that Woodward had "found," they lost another big one: the Dartmouth plant itself. The spring term of the college—or was it the university? —was scheduled to begin on March 3. A few days ahead of time three "superintendents of buildings," representing the university, called upon President Brown of the college and asked for a set of keys. He refused to give them up. So the university men enlisted a mason and a carpenter and went the rounds of Dartmouth Hall, the chapel, and the rest of the buildings, forcing the doors and installing new locks.

"There were several boys with them, and among others," the waggish *Dartmouth Gazette* reported, "some or all of the aborigines who are in this place for the purpose of acquiring civilized habits."

When the term opened, the university had the buildings, but the college had the students, all but one of them! These stalwarts met in borrowed rooms in the village. They were summoned to classes by a cow horn instead of a bell, since the university forces commanded the belfry.

The term passed quietly enough. When Wheelock finally died, in April, he was duly mourned by a large crowd, including many of his old opponents, at the funeral in the meetinghouse. But the controversy did not die with him; he was merely replaced by his son-in-law as university president. When, in July, President James Monroe arrived in Hanover on the way from Boston, where even the Federalists had hailed him for bringing an "Era of Good Feelings," he was awarded *two* honorary degrees, one from the college and another from the university.

At the beginning of the fall term, in September, the college numbered ninety-five students, the university fourteen. The campus calm continued until November, when news came that the state Superior Court had decided in favor of Woodward and against the college trustees. Only one student now shifted from the college to the university, but the university students, few though they were, dared to attempt a coup.

Earlier the university had taken over the college library, with its approximately four thousand volumes. The college boys had managed, however, to hold on to the quarters of the two literary societies, the Social Friends and the United Fraternity, on the second floor of Dartmouth Hall. Together, these societies owned as many books as the library, and newer and better ones.

On the night of November 11, after bedtime, a band of university students and villagers, along with university Professor Nathaniel H. Carter, sneaked into Dartmouth Hall. At the entrance to the room of the Social Friends, they bunched together and crashed into the door. They could not move it. So one of them took an ax to the door and cut a hole big enough to crawl through.

The noise awakened some of the college boys. They arrived in time to arm themselves with sticks of firewood from the hallway and to trap the enemy inside the Social Friends' room. "It appears to me we are in a cursed poor scrape," the village shoemaker, one of those inside, was heard to say. "I had rather be in a nest of hornets than among the college boys when they get mad and roused up."

Finally the university forces capitulated. In token of their abject surrender, they were made to file out beneath the crossed clubs of the college boys, lined up in two rows. From this indignity, Professor

Carter was excused. He was shaking with fright and was complaining that he had lost his cane; besides, he had once given the Social Friends fifteen dollars for books, which he now wanted back. Two of the college boys led him home.

Saving the society's books did not save the college. The college trustees could appeal from the Superior Court of New Hampshire to the Supreme Court of the United States, but if they did so, the prospects were most uncertain. Writing contemptuously of "Brown & Co.," Governor Plumer said: "I think they can have no rational grounds to hope for success in the National Court."

The trustees needed money to resume legal action. As they pointed out in a circular soliciting contributions, the annual income from the Dartmouth endowments amounted to barely more than $1,500—only about half the endowment income of Phillips Exeter Academy. Even this $1,500 was not available to the college, since Treasurer Woodward controlled the funds. The college managed to keep going only because loyal parents continued to pay tuition fees and generous alumni and friends rallied with gifts.

Daniel Webster, Dartmouth '01, was not moved to contribute. If an appeal should be carried to the Supreme Court, he was expected, for a fee, to represent the college, and Joseph Hopkinson—famous as a Baltimore lawyer and even more famous as the author of "Hail, Columbia!"—was being mentioned as a suitable associate. On November 15, Webster, now living in Boston, wrote to President Brown to inquire about the college's plans. "I am aware that there must be great difficulty in obtaining funds on this occasion," he said. "I think that I would undertake, for a thousand dollars, to go to Washington and argue the case, and get Mr. Hopkinson's assistance also. I doubt whether I could do it for a much less sum." A thousand-dollar gift to the college made it possible for the trustees to hire Webster and Hopkinson.

Already Webster was thoroughly familiar with the case. He had followed it from the beginning, and he had joined with Jeremiah Mason and Jeremiah Smith to present the college's argument before the New Hampshire court at Exeter. Their brief contended that the legislators, in reorganizing the college as a university, had gone beyond their rightful powers in these three respects:

1. They had violated an accepted legal principle: only the courts, not the legislature, could take away a vested right.

2. They had violated the constitution of New Hampshire, which provided that no person should be deprived of his property except by the "law of the land," meaning the common law and not a legislative act.

3. They had violated the Constitution of the United States, which provided that no state should pass any law "impairing the obligation of contracts."

Only on the third of these contentions, as Webster knew, could the case properly be reargued before the Supreme Court, and he thought the point weak and unconvincing. To hedge the case, and to bring in the whole range of arguments, he persuaded the trustees to lease Dartmouth properties to Vermont residents and then arrange for the lessees to sue. These suits, involving citizens of two states, would go directly to the federal courts.

Before any of these synthetic cases reached the Supreme Court, however, the case of the *Trustees of Dartmouth College* v. *Woodward* was taken up, on appeal. Webster opened for the trustees on the morning of March 10, 1818. The Court still sat in a rented house, for the Capitol, left burned and blackened by the British invaders of Washington during the War of 1812, had not yet been restored. The temporary courtroom was small, and it was jammed.

Among those who had crowded in were representatives of other colleges, which might lose their independence if Dartmouth lost hers. Chauncey A. Goodrich, professor of oratory at Yale, was present in Yale's behalf. It was a good thing he was there; otherwise, his colorful account of Webster's performance would never have been recorded for posterity.

For more than four hours, on past noon, Webster spoke in a calm and conversational tone, as if dealing with propositions everyone knew and accepted. For more than three of the hours he dealt in irrelevancies, cleverly bringing in all the arguments that had been used before the New Hampshire court. He also hinted strongly, for the benefit of Chief Justice Marshall, the arch-Federalist, that the college was a victim of political machinations by the Jeffersonians.

Webster took plenty of time, however, to elaborate upon the one relevant point. What, he asked, was the full meaning of the clause in the United States Constitution prohibiting the states from "impairing the obligation of contracts"? The Supreme Court itself, he answered, had decided in the case of *Fletcher* v. *Peck,* involving land grants by the State of Georgia, that "a *grant* is a contract." The Dartmouth charter, he went on, "is embraced within the very terms of that decision," for "a grant of corporate powers and privileges is as much a *contract* as a grant of land."

At the end of his formal argument, as Professor Goodrich afterward recalled, Webster stood silent for a time. Then, addressing Chief Justice John Marshall, he said:

"This, sir, is my case. It is the case not merely of that humble institution; it is the case of every college in our land. . . . It is more. It is, in some sense, the case of every man who has property of which he may be stripped, for the question is simply this: Shall our state legislature be allowed to take that which is not their own, to turn it from its original use, and apply it to such ends or purposes as they, in their discretion, shall see fit?"

Webster pulled out the stops and continued: "Sir, you may destroy this little institution. It is weak. It is in your hands. I know it is one of the lesser lights in the literary horizon of the country. You may put it out. But if you do so, you must carry through your work. You must extinguish, one after another, all those great lights of science which, for more than a century, have thrown their radiance over our land. It is, sir, as I have said, a small college, and yet *there are those that love it.*"

Here Webster, the consummate actor, pretended to break down. His lips quivered, his voice choked, his eyes filled with tears. From this spectacle Professor Goodrich turned to observe the judges. Marshall bent his tall, gaunt figure forward as if straining to catch every word. His eyes seemed wet. Joseph Story still sat, pen in hand, as if to take notes, which he never took. The rest of the justices, too, appeared to be transfixed.

But the show had to go on. Other attorneys had to be heard—the two for Woodward that afternoon and the next day, and Hopkinson for the trustees on the third day. After Hopkinson had concluded, Marshall announced that some of the justices could not make up their minds and that the case therefore would be continued to the next term. This meant postponing the decision for a year or so.

Webster and other advocates of the college cause put the interim to good use. On the day after the postponement he guessed that, of the seven judges then on the Court, two sided with the college, two were opposed, and three were wavering. The trustees and their counsel faced the delicate task of bringing over to their side at least two of the doubtful three.

"Public sentiment has a great deal to do in affairs of this sort, and it ought to be well founded," the Chief Justice of Massachusetts wrote to Webster in April, 1818. "That sentiment may even reach and affect a court; at least, if there be any members who wish to do right, but are a little afraid, it will be a great help to know that all the world expects they will do right." The Massachusetts judge was responding to a gift from Webster—a printed copy of Webster's argument in Washington. The judge urged that it be "extensively circulated." It was.

Of all the various state judges, much the most influential was James Kent, the Chancellor (the highest judicial officer) of New York. In July, while on a tour by chaise with his wife, Kent stopped in Hanover and in neighboring Windsor, Vermont. He visited with university but not with college officials, and in conversation he casually implied approval of the New Hampshire decision in favor of Woodward.

This worried the college officials, especially President Brown. They quickly sent a copy of Webster's brief to Kent. In September Brown went to Albany and called on him. Kent now came out unequivocally for the college. He agreed to talk with William Johnson, one of the wavering federal justices. Johnson, a dissenter in the case of *Fletcher* v. *Peck,* had held that a grant of land was *not* a contract, and so he found it hard to believe that a grant of corporate powers could be one. But Kent convinced him and drafted an opinion for him.

That summer, while the struggle for judicial minds was going on, the defendant in the case, William H. Woodward, quietly died in Hanover, at the age of forty-three.

By the time the Supreme Court reconvened, in February, 1819, five of the Justices favored the college, one was still opposed, and one was absent. The university officials, having hired the impressive William Pinkney of Baltimore as their new attorney, hoped to have the case reopened and reargued, but Marshall ignored Pinkney and calmly read his magisterial opinion. A grant of corporate powers, Marshall opined, was indeed a contract within the meaning of the Constitution; a state legislature had no power to void it.

Of all his opinions, this was to be one of the most often cited. As the nation's leading magazine, the *North American Review,* remarked about a year afterward: "Perhaps no judicial proceedings in this country ever involved more important consequences." The Dartmouth case enhanced the prestige of John Marshall and the Supreme Court. It extended the national power at the expense of state power. It confirmed the charter rights not only of Dartmouth College but of all private colleges. It protected and encouraged business corporations as well as nonprofit corporations. And, incidentally, it brought Daniel Webster to the top of the legal profession.

Poor old John Wheelock! He could have had no idea what he was starting, back in 1815, when he took his problems into politics.

# The Bank Cases III

BY BRAY HAMMOND

*(McCulloch* v. *Maryland,* 4 Wheaton 316;
*Osborn* v. *Bank of the United States,* 9 Wheaton 738)

*Although the Dartmouth College case was very important, it did not finally lay to rest the knotty problem of federal versus state power. Equally epoch-making and even more bitterly contested were two cases rising out of the efforts of Maryland and Ohio to drive a federal corporation, the Bank of the United States, from their territories. Bray Hammond is former Assistant Secretary of the Federal Reserve Board and author of* Banks and Politics in America from the Revolution to the Civil War, *which was awarded the 1958 Pulitzer Prize in History.*

## I

In Baltimore on a day early in May, 1818, an informer named John James mounted the stairs to the floor above the Union Bank where the local office of the Bank of the United States was maintained. His call was formal. He had come for legal evidence that the Bank and James W. McCulloch, its local cashier, were violating the law.

Back in February, the Maryland Assembly had enacted a statute which gave the Baltimore office of the Bank the hard choice of buying stamped paper from the state, on which notes issued by the office were to be printed, of paying the state $15,000 a year, or of going out of business. The law was to come into effect the first day of May. That day had now passed, with no sign that the law was to be obeyed. So Maryland, whose motto, roughly translated from the Italian, is that deeds are for men and words are for women, was taking prompt action. There was a penalty of $100 for each note

30

issued on unstamped paper since the effective date of the law, one-half for the state and one-half for the informer; but if John James expected to leave the Bank richer than he came he was certainly stupid, for the tax was prohibitive, as he must have known, and not intended to provide revenue but to force the office to close. Maryland chartered banks for her people herself, and she wanted the Bank of the United States, chartered by the federal government, to leave her sovereign soil and stay off it.

McCulloch, the cashier, could not have been surprised by his visitor. He acknowledged that notes were being issued by him in defiance of Maryland's law. He refused to pay the penalty demanded by John James. And he presumably let the latter depart with an impression that the Bank considered Maryland's law nugatory and that it intended to remain in business in Balitmore without either buying stamped paper or paying the $15,000 tax.

The state at once brought suit, and judgment against McCulloch —that is, against the Bank—was given by the Baltimore County Court. The Bank took the case to the Maryland Court of Appeals, which affirmed the lower court's judgment, and thence by writ of error to the United States Supreme Court. In the appeals to both the higher Maryland court and the Supreme Court the two parties to the case agreed upon the facts, so that the only questions to be decided were whether the federal law chartering the Bank and the state law taxing it were in conflict and if so which was constitutional and overrode the other.

Maryland's action was the first which several states in the Southern and Western parts of the country were taking against the Bank. Tennessee, Georgia, North Carolina, Kentucky, and Ohio authorized measures to the same end, the Bank having one or two offices in each of these states; the tax was $50,000 for each of the two offices in Ohio and $60,000 for each of the two in Kentucky. Similar measures were being advocated elsewhere. Illinois and Indiana, where the Bank had no offices, forbade the establishment of any.

## II

There were three things that in general counted most heavily with the public against the Bank. One was a strong traditional hatred of all banks and especially of the biggest one. Banks were enemies of the farmer and of all other common folk. This was an orthodox principle of the Republicans, as the Jeffersonians then called themselves, and though there was a split over it within the party, what was probably a majority maintained an agrarian fear of banking and a passionate will to curb or forbid it. Years later, in 1852, there were no incorporated banks in seven of the thirty-one states—Arkansas, California, Florida, Illinois, Iowa, Texas, and Wisconsin—none in the two organized territories shortly to become states—Minnesota and Oregon—and none in the District of Columbia. They were kept out either by bans in the states' constitutions or by steadfast legislative refusal to enact charters. In Indiana and Missouri banking was a state-controlled monopoly; in still other states banks undoubtedly would have been prohibited but for the fear that prohibition would aggravate the evil. The effort to stamp out banking resembled in some respects the attempt a century later to stamp out the consumption of alcoholic beverages.

The second force working against the Bank of the United States in 1818, also political and an orthodox Republican tenet dating back thirty years to formation of the Union, was the idea that the federal Constitution was a compact by which the states had created a collective government and delegated certain powers to it but reserved to themselves (or to the people) the powers not delegated. Since the power to issue corporate charters had not been delegated, the corporate charter of the United States Bank was considered unconstitutional and the Bank had no legal standing.

The third force inimical to the Bank was the self-interest of the banks which the individual states had chartered. These state institutions found the federal Bank oppressive and monopolistic; and they got the ready sympathy of their customers, to whom they explained that if it were not for the big Bank, lending would be much easier. Times were hard and bankers, like other debtors, were trying to avoid paying what they owed their depositors and note-holders. The federal Bank had been set up for the direct purpose of making the state banks resume payments in specie. This the state banks called oppression.

The difference between those persons who hated all banks and those—the state bankers with their borrowers—who hated merely the federal Bank, was readily compounded; each party thought that it could destroy the other once the big Bank was done for.

## III

The Bank, paradoxically, owed its charter to the Republicans, who as a party had from the first opposed banking in principle and denied that the federal government was permitted by the Constitution to share with the states the power to grant corporate charters. For these reasons the Republicans had denounced the present Bank's predecessor, established in 1791 at Alexander Hamilton's instance and over Thomas Jefferson's sharp protests. But between 1791 and 1818 the two parties had altered greatly. The Federalists had lost power with the election of Jefferson in 1800 and were plaintively approaching their extinction. The Republicans had flourished, holding their original agrarian core but also gaining the major part of the business community, which, thanks to the industrial revolution, now comprised many entrepreneurs, engaged in manufacturing as well as commerce, in transportation by turnpike and canal, in banking and brokerage, and in feverish speculation. Being recruited mostly from farm families, retaining agrarian dislike of the old mercantile aristocracy—which equally disliked them as smelly, freckled upstarts—they found the principles of the Declaration of Independence as congenial to enterprise as to farming. This change gave the Republican party two wings, which, years later when it adopted the name Democratic, were distinguished within the party as "Democrats in principle" and "Democrats by trade."

In 1811, early in James Madison's administration, the two had joined in letting the federal Bank expire, the agrarians for orthodox reasons, the enterprisers and state bankers because the Federalist management of the old relic, stubbornly conservative, was interfering with easy money. But five years later, still in Madison's administration, the party leadership decided after all that a government bank was necessary. The Treasury was in a desperate situation in consequence of monetary disorder, weak fiscal policy, and the general peace which in 1815 ended a long period of wars. In its legal and proper aspect the Bank was fiscal agency of the government, public depository, and regulator of the currency and of the commercial banks' lending powers. It was what is now called a central bank. It had a capital of $35 million—a foolishly large sum for its purposes—and was by far the largest corporation in America and one of the largest anywhere. It was inspected by the Treasury, to which it reported. One-fifth of its shares were owned by the federal government, and one-fifth of its directors were appointed by the President of the United States with the approval of the Senate. Its home office was in Philadelphia. When it came before the Supreme Court in 1819, the Bank had eighteen branch offices in as many cities, ranging from Portsmouth and Boston in the Northeast to Savannah and New Orleans in the South and to Louisville and Cincinnati in the West. Louisiana, Mississippi, and Illinois were then the westernmost states of the Union. The Bank's various offices were located where business was considerable and the federal Treasury's receipts and expenditures could be most conveniently handled.

## IV

The Bank had its good angels and its bad.

Among its better angels was the Madison administration itself, including particularly the Secretary of the Treasury, William Crawford of Georgia. As a Senator years before, he had been, with Albert Gallatin, one of the few Republicans actively advocating renewal of the first Bank's charter. Another was the cast-iron John C. Calhoun of South Carolina, also Republican, under whose strenuous and inexorable leadership the new charter had been enacted in 1816.

Prominent among the Bank's darker angels was General Samuel Smith of Baltimore, long a member of Congress, a former Federalist but now a Republican, a rich trader, and the senior partner in the Baltimore firm of S. Smith and Buchanan, which John Quincy Adams called "one of the greatest commercial establishments in the United States." The firm was especially active in the export of silver to India and to that extent obstructed the return of the banks to a specie basis. General Smith had been a tireless, aggressive enemy of the old Bank and a prominent sponsor of the new one. His partner, James Buchanan, was president of the new Bank's Baltimore office, which, it came out a year later, he and another director, with the help of the cashier, James McCulloch, had been busy looting for a year or more. The General, who was to be distracted and put to bed by the disclosure, had his rank from military service in the Revolution, the Whiskey Rebellion, and his more recent defense of Baltimore from the British. He was active in public life, a man of distinguished appearance, an uncle by marriage to that forsaken beauty, Betsy Patterson of Baltimore, whose star-crossed marriage to Prince Jerome Bonaparte, brother of the Emperor, had been imperiously annulled. "The moral, political, and commercial character" of Baltimore, wrote John Quincy Adams, then Secretary of State, "has for twenty-five years been formed, controlled, and modified almost entirely by this house of Smith and Buchanan. . . . It may be added that there is not a city in the Union which has had so much apparent prosperity or within which there has been such complication of profligacy."

The Bank's directors were in two camps paralleling its sponsors. Stephen Girard of Philadelphia and John Jacob Astor of New York were both Republicans, but conservative. Girard had early complained of several directors whom he plainly considered fly-by-nights. He intended, he said, to use all his "activity, means, and influence to change and replace the majority of directors with honest independent men." Instead, he had given up and resigned. The majority had chosen for president of the Bank a former merchant of Philadelphia, William Jones, who, having gone through bankruptcy, became a Republican politician. He had served as Secretary of the Navy and Acting Secretary of the Treasury. Jones informed Secretary Crawford that he was not disposed to follow the conservative example of the former Bank of the United States, whose policy he thought "less enlarged, liberal, and useful" than it should have been. Men like him filled positions throughout the Bank.

McCulloch, the Baltimore cashier, also thought the "timid and faltering course" of the former Bank should not be emulated. Neither did George Williams, a director both of the Baltimore branch and of the home office in Philadelphia. How "enlarged and liberal" his ideas were is illustrated by his ingenuity in getting around a complex restriction in the Bank's charter which limited to thirty the number of shares that any shareholder might vote, no matter how many he owned. He, McCulloch, and the Smith and Buchanan partnership purchased among themselves over four thousand of the Bank's shares, using money "borrowed" from the Baltimore office, and had each share registered in a different name, with themselves, severally, designated to vote all the shares as attorneys. So together they were able to vote four thousand shares or more instead of the mere 120 that was the maximum any four shareholders might vote otherwise. Williams later explained that he had gone into the market and bought names "at eleven pence each." This practice became so common in Baltimore and Philadelphia that according to Professor Catterall, the Bank's historian, a clique of speculators in the two cities "controlled the Bank as soon as it was organized," those from Baltimore alone casting close to a majority of all the votes at the first election of directors.

The directors so chosen favored speculation and encouraged lending on the Bank's own shares. This was done on such loose terms that the Bank was supplying the money for much of its own capital and financing a rash speculative advance in the market price of the shares. But finding even this "enlarged and liberal" policy insufficiently enlarged and liberal for their ambitions, Williams, Smith and Buchanan, and McCulloch lent themselves still more, McCulloch as cashier arranging advances through discounts and overdrafts without adequate security and without reporting them honestly. The net loss sustained by the Bank as a result of these shenanigans in the end was estimated to be in excess of $1.4 million, which in those days was a fairly large sum. Though McCulloch achieved legal immortality from his byplay with the informer John James, he seems to have been a mere clerk to his partners, useful because he controlled the office records and could lend them money freely without letting it be known—or so they fancied.

Though all this was slow in coming to light, enough had got about to whet existing antagonism to the Bank and to make Congress order an investigation in October, 1818. Maryland's demand through John James had by then been refused, the suit had gone successfully through two state courts, and the Bank's appeal was on the Supreme Court's docket. There was already much talk of the Bank's surrendering its charter, but Secretary Crawford would not listen to it. He rallied the Madison administration to help the Bank in its plea to the Supreme Court and encouraged the Bank's directors to speed their housecleaning. Attorney General William Wirt joined the Bank's counsel in preparing for the Supreme Court hearing. The Congressional committee's report, though severe on the Bank, recommended it be continued minus its abuses. In January, Jones was forced out of the presidency and an able lawyer from Charleston, Langdon Cheves, was engaged to replace him. Resignations were obtained from incompetent directors and officers, and suits were filed against defaulters. Half the branch office directors, it was estimated, resigned. It was pretty late to be resorting to soap and water, but the Bank was going to come before the Court with its hands as clean as possible.

## V

The hearing opened February 22, 1819 and continued till March 3. The Bank was represented by Daniel Webster, who as a Federalist Congressman three years before had opposed the bill chartering it, by William Pinkney of Baltimore, and by Attorney General Wirt. Maryland was also represented by distinguished counsel, Joseph Hopkinson and Walter Jones, of Philadelphia and Washington respectively, and Luther Martin, who had been an active dissident in the Constitutional Convention of 1787. In the battle over ratification of the Constitution, Martin had cried out against the chains being forged for "his country," meaning Maryland, and its subjection to the new federal authority. Now, thirty years later, Martin was protesting for "his country" against the reality that he had foreseen.

But the argument that most impressed the Court was that of Pinkney, who spoke for three days, attaining heights of eloquence and persuasiveness that Justice Joseph Story found brilliant and overwhelming. The decision was given by Chief Justice Marshall March 6. It affirmed the constitutionality of the Bank's charter, and it was unanimous—a circumstance galling to Thomas Jefferson and other orthodox Republicans, for of the seven justices only two were Federalists. The other five were appointees of Jefferson and Madison. Marshall's opinion followed the same line of reasoning as Pinkney's in his argument and as Alexander Hamilton's in his exposition of the problem in 1791.

Hamilton, while Secretary of the Treasury in that early period following organization of the federal government under the Constitution, had recommended measures to Congress of which one was the chartering of a government bank. The proposal had immediately aroused sharp differences of opinion in Congress about the nature of the federal government and its relation to the individual states, but it had been adopted. President Washington, who was so far uncommitted, had then faced the question if he should approve or veto the charter Congress had enacted. He had consulted Thomas Jefferson, the Secretary of State, and Edmund Randolph, the Attorney General, both of whom roundly condemned the measure as unconstitutional. Jefferson had argued that the federal government had not been given the power to grant charters of incorporation. Washington had then consulted Hamilton, who had held that the federal government, though not endowed with all powers, was supreme and sovereign with respect to those it did possess. He had contended that every power vested in the federal government "is in its nature sovereign and includes, by force of the term, a right to employ all the means requisite" to make the power effective, unless the means were specifically forbidden by the Constitution, were immoral, or were inexpedient. Congress had decided the services of a bank were requisite to the government's discharge of its services, and Congress was competent to make that decision. Therefore the act was constitutional. Washington had sided with Hamilton and approved the charter February 25, 1791.

His choice was not the popular one. The Republicans, becoming the political majority, rested their case against the Bank on the Ninth and Tenth Amendments to the Constitution, and on the Kentucky and Virginia resolutions of 1798. In the two amendments it was declared in effect, as contended by Jefferson, that the federal government had only those powers delegated to it by the Constitution and that those not delegated remained with the states and the people. The resolutions, though only a statement of political principle, affirmed the sovereignty of the states and the limitation on the powers of the federal government.

By 1819 these affirmations had gained in popular support, especially in the West. The government in Washington through the federal judiciary had tentacles penetrating every state, and through the federal Bank it had still others penetrating half of them. Popular resentment was intensified by hard times, which made both the federal courts and the local offices of the Bank instruments of oppression. For the Bank, following the "enlarged and liberal" policy of William Jones, had led men into debt by offering easy credit, and now, under the conservative Cheves and with the federal courts' assistance, it was taking their property from them. It seemed to people as Thomas Jefferson had said: a strong, consolidated government was crushing them and their liberties.

So in *McCulloch* v. *Maryland*, 1819, when the controversy of 1791, never dead, flared up violently, the Supreme Court defied a strong drift toward a weak Union. Marshall, reverting to the argument of Hamilton, affirmed the implied powers of the federal government —and by further implication the subordination to them of the powers of the individual states—in words pregnant with significance for subsequent American history. "Let the end be legitimate," he said, "let it be within the scope of the Constitution, and all means which are appropriate, which are plainly adapted to that end, which are not prohibited, but consist with the letter and spirit of the Constitution, are constitutional."

A loud popular outcry arose. Congress could establish a bank and the bank could spread its branches into the individual states without leave. The states, it seemed, could only submit. For perhaps most of the public, the Court's decision appeared revolutionary. The masses could understand the Tenth Amendment but not the subtleties of Hamilton and Marshall, according to whom the Constitution meant yes when it said no. A week after the decision was announced, Hezekiah Niles wrote in his popular *Weekly Register* that "every person must see" in the courts' validation of the Bank's charter "a total prostration of the states' rights and the loss of the liberties of the nation." Niles was convinced "that the welfare of the union has received a more dangerous wound than fifty Hartford conventions, hateful as that assemblage was, could inflict." Still deeper than this dismay, which was rational, whether right or wrong, lay the unsophisticated conviction that the Court should not ignore moral considerations and blandly imply, in silence, an unquestioning approval of the Bank, whose reputation was already bad and was soon to grow still worse.

## VI

Anger at the Court's decision was especially strong in Ohio, where the ravage produced by speculation and aggravated by the federal Bank was sensational. After a burst of lending, the Bank had had to turn to a rigorous contraction which through foreclosures drew an immense amount of Cincinnati property into its hands. The bitterness of the public was intense. In February, 1819, the month before *McCulloch* v. *Maryland* was decided, the legislature enacted the law levying prohibitive taxes—$50,000 each—on the local offices in Cincinnati and Chillicothe. The legislature declared it "just and necessary that such unlawful banking while continued should be subject to the payment of a tax." It authorized the state auditor to demand payment, to ransack the premises for cash if refused, and when the money was found to take it and deliver it to the state treasury. The tax was to be due in September.

Early in March the Ohio officials concerned were made uneasy by the Supreme Court's decision in *McCulloch* v. *Maryland*. They hesitated to carry out the legislature's authorization, for they might find themselves landed in prison by federal court action no matter what the Ohio Legislature said. But in May it was disclosed that funds of the Bank's Baltimore office had been embezzled by McCulloch and his two associates, George Williams and James Buchanan.

Langdon Cheves, the new president, who had taken office back in March the day before announcement of the decision for the Bank in *McCulloch* v. *Maryland,* had got on the trail of the Baltimore speculators within a week. It was not till May that the investigation was complete; McCulloch was dismissed and his two associates had to resign. All three were brought to court—but not General Smith, who apparently was left unmolested on the ground that he was but a sleeping partner, a hero absorbed in public affairs and unaware of what his junior was doing.

Ohio's excuse for holding firm despite the Supreme Court's decision had been that the case was collusive and not managed by Maryland in a way that fairly presented Ohio's interest. Maryland had been too polite; by agreeing with the Bank as to the facts, it had tamely laid the case in the Court's lap to be decided. This dissatisfied Ohio; now, after the Baltimore disclosures, the state had still greater reason to act. The Baltimore affair did not show the Bank to be a victim of thieves but a den of them. Resolute politicians urged resort to the crowbar law to assure collection of the taxes due in September.

The Bank, apprehending what would be attempted, obtained a federal court order to prevent it. However, the state auditor, Ralph Osborn, was informed by legal counsel that the order was defective and lacked the force of an injunction. So he instructed his deputy, John L. Harper, with assistants, to enter the Chillicothe office and get the money. They arrived just before closing time on September

17, 1819. According to the report of the Chillicothe cashier to Secretary Crawford, Harper and his party "suddenly entered the office and in a ruffian-like manner, jumped over the counter," and took possession of the vault. Harper asked the cashier if he was going to pay the tax. The cashier said no; he tried to force the intruders from the vault, warned them not to touch the Bank's property, and waved the court order at them. In spite of his efforts, they gathered up specie and banknotes amounting to $120,425, and moved it over to the Bank of Chillicothe with the wagon and horses they had left hitched outside. The state allowed Harper to keep $2,000 as his fee, returned $20,425 to the Bank as overpayment, and retained $98,000 as the net tax in the hands of H. M. Curry, the state treasurer.

There ensued a long period of abortive struggle to clear up the conflict of duty and jurisdiction. Harper and an assistant were sued for having taken the Bank's money, were kept in prison four months for want of bail, and were then released on a technicality. Osborn the auditor and Curry the treasurer were sued for recovery of the money, which, however, the treasurer could not give up without a warrant, which the auditor could not issue without legislative appropriation, which, of course, the legislature would not authorize.

Meanwhile a joint committee of the legislature reviewed the whole problem of state and federal sovereignties, the Ninth and Tenth Amendments, the Kentucky and Virginia resolutions of 1798, and the question of federal court jurisdiction in matters involving a state. The report of the committee was prepared by Charles Hammond, one of Ohio's foremost lawyers, who thought the principles of the McCulloch decision "not worth refutation." The report vigorously denounced the pretensions of the federal judiciary. Ohio's sovereignty, it declared, should not be sacrificed by the "inadvertence or connivance" of Maryland in its suit against the Bank. "This case dignified with the important and high-sounding title of 'McCulloch v. the State of Maryland,' when looked into, is found to be an ordinary *qui tam* action of debt, brought by a common informer of the name of John James. . . ." It was "throughout an agreed case," the report said, "manufactured in the summer of the year 1818 and passed through the county court of Baltimore county and the court of appeals of the state of Maryland in the same season, so as to be got upon the docket of the Supreme Court of the United States for adjudication at their February term, 1819. It is only by the management and concurrence of the parties that causes can be thus expeditiously brought to a final hearing in the Supreme Court." The report recommended that an agreement be negotiated whereby Ohio would return to the Bank the $100,000 taken from it and the Bank would withdraw from the state. As an inducement for the Bank to leave, Ohio should outlaw it, forbidding the state's courts, judges, jailors, notaries, and other agencies to serve or protect it. The report, which also recommended that Ohio formally approve the Kentucky and Virginia resolutions, was adopted by the legislature in December, 1820, and its recommendations were enacted.

The proposal for negotiations leading to return of the $100,000 upon the Bank's closing its local offices came to naught. Instead, in September, 1821, after continued skirmishing, the Bank obtained a federal court order for return of the money outright. The state's treasurer, a new incumbent named Sullivan, disregarded the order; he was arrested by federal officers, lodged in prison, and deprived of his keys, with which the state's vault was opened, and the money, which had lain there intact for two years, was put back in the Bank.

Ohio was in an uproar. Whose state was this? When would the encroachments of the federal courts on state sovereignty be curbed? These encroachments had been growing from the organization of the federal government. Ohio was now the victim; she had "to complain of the imprisonment of the treasurer, the taking from his pockets the keys of the treasury whilst so imprisoned, and the entry into the treasury and violent seizure of monies therein contained, the property of the state! ! ! If our sister states patiently look on and permit scenes of this kind to be acted in broad daylight, we may well despair of the Republic." Largely on questions of jurisdiction, Ohio took her complaint to the Supreme Court, against the will of her more ardent citizens who wished to snub that presumptuous body.

## VII

The sister states to whom Ohio had appealed differed in opinion. Several were sympathetic but hesitant. They denounced the federal courts but stopped short of flouting them. Kentucky had started to assert her liberties and then deferred to a federal court injunction, as Ohio had not. But in South Carolina, where nullification was to be attempted ten years later, and in New England, where five years before, the Hartford convention had advocated defense by the individual states of their sovereignties and the liberties of their people, Ohio's action was condemned. No state followed her example.

Least of all Maryland. Ohio had already denounced *McCulloch* v. *Maryland* as a collusive case, "manufactured" for a quick decision favorable to the Bank. Now, cheek by jowl with the Bank she had pretended to sue for not paying her tax, Maryland was helping the Bank to prosecute, in her courts, three victims of its wrath.

But fortunately for the three, Maryland, still in the main an agrarian community, had as yet no statute against embezzlement, and though the Bank's charter authorized punishment for counterfeiting the Bank's notes, it too was mute about embezzlement. There was doubt if the accused had committed an indictable offense. Maryland had a law against larceny, a simple crime as obvious as murder, and had the three men robbed a bank other than their own, they could have been dealt with readily. But how could one steal something of which he had lawful possession? The three, after considerable delay, were charged with conspiracy, an ancient form of wrongdoing well known to the law, and indicted "for being evil disposed and dishonest persons and wickedly devising, contriving, and intending, falsely, unlawfully, fraudulently, craftily, and unjustly, and by indirect means to cheat and impoverish" the stockholders of the Bank. William Pinkney, who had represented the Bank before the Supreme Court in *McCulloch* v. *Maryland*, was now counsel for the "traversers" (as the accused were styled "in criminal cases less than felony"); William Wirt, the Attorney General, was counsel for the Bank throughout.

At their first trial, in April, 1821, judgment was given for the traversers, thanks to the county court's conclusion, on the basis of a statute of King Edward I enacted nearly two centuries before Columbus discovered America, that the offense charged was not punishable in Maryland. The case was carried to the State Court of Appeals, which held to the contrary. In an opinion ranging over precedents from the reign of Edward I to that, just closed, of George III, it held that under the common law inherited by Maryland from the mother country the offense charged was a punishable one. Accordingly, in December, 1821, it returned the case to the county court for retrial. But to no purpose. Though the traversers were charged with an offense that the higher court said was indictable and punishable, they were again found not guilty by the lower court.

They had in their favor the rising sympathy for men of enterprise. They were exemplars of what was already recognized in America as the "almost universal ambition to get forward." The entrepreneur was crowding up alongside the farmer as an ideal American figure. He too was in his origins typically humble, born on a farm, but by hard work, ingenuity, ambition, and force of character he was advancing himself, rising in the world, developing his country's resources, arousing emulation in his fellows, and making America great.

The defense for the traversers made much of this new trend. What they had done was not denied but was said to have turned out badly through the mistakes of others. They had "relied too strongly upon the hopes and calculations in which the whole community indulged"; and "the failure of their stock speculations was rather to be pitied as a misfortune than condemned as a crime." England was to blame for it because her investors had lent money to France that they might have bought Bank stock with instead; France was to blame because she had borrowed the money which the English might have invested in Bank stock; and the Bank itself was to blame because it had been poorly managed. These things had depressed the value of the Bank's shares and ruined the traversers' projects. If, instead, the Bank's shares had risen in value, then the traversers "would have been looked upon as nobles, as the architects of their fortunes . . . and lauded to the skies as possessing spirits fraught with enterprise."

This attitude toward success in business, as achieved notably by "self-made men" was to become popular later in the century with a host of Americans and unpopular with another host of them. Already in 1823 it helped the Baltimore conspirators, though it is impossible to measure its influence besides that of animosity toward the Bank and of technical deficiencies in the law. The men being again acquitted, the prosecution ceased, though the dissenting judge averred that the traversers had in fact "taken from the funds of the office a large sum of money, which they converted to their own use," and that they had "failed to return to the Bank a cent of their spoil."

## VIII

Meanwhile, the Ohio case, *Osborn* v. *the Bank of the United States*, was pending on the Supreme Court docket; it was heard in March, 1824. The court may well have indulged in delay in order to let Ohio calm down, which she did when business began to improve and her citizens could become preoccupied with returning prosperity. The Court was sensitive about popular charges of "encroachment" by the federal judiciary, and in hearing the Ohio case it had the question of jurisdiction reargued. Ohio's counsel was Charles Hammond and the Bank's was Henry Clay. In the reargument Daniel Webster and John Sergeant joined Clay, and Hammond was joined by Ethan Allen Brown, a former governor of Ohio. The Court reaffirmed its decision in *McCulloch* v. *Maryland* summarily but gave lengthy consideration to the Federal Circuit Court's jurisdiction, which it affirmed. The case died quietly, with none of the excitement of its beginning. Time, prosperity, and federal firmness had quietened things, for a while.

A generation later, though, the quarrel of Ohio and other states with the federal government broke out again, in different circumstances which nevertheless involved the same constitutional issue as in the Bank cases. The Fugitive Slave Act of 1850 authorized infamous procedure, in free states, against Negros alleged to be escaped slaves and against their protectors. Ohio revolted and, citing her measure of 1820 outlawing the Bank as a precedent, refused the use of state jails and the aid of state officers and agencies in the enforcement of the hated federal statute. Her courts checkmated the federal courts; and her people, in the Oberlin-Wellington rescue, in the attempt to save Margaret Garner, and in other similar actions defied the federal government and the slave-catchers with every extreme of violence, ruse, and litigation. Members of the new Republican party, in repugnance to the South's "peculiar institution" and the behavior of Southern politicians, accepted the example of the South Carolina nullifiers less than thirty years before, finding it "the only sound, logical, and tenable position, unless we give up everything to the sweep of centralization." It was much the same in other states, east and west. In 1855 the Massachusetts Legislature had declared the Fugitive Slave Act "a direct violation of the Xth amendment," as the charter of the Bank of the United States had been called in 1819. In 1859 the Wisconsin Supreme Court pronounced the same act unconstitutional, and the state legislature supported the court, denouncing the act as a federal usurpation, violating both the Tenth Amendment and "the compact" between the states.

## IX

In the North, emotions over slavery and the South's success in Washington during the 1850's certainly helped to weaken the force of John Marshall's opinions, but it is doubtful if the principles affirmed in *McCulloch* v. *Maryland* and reiterated in *Osborn* v. *the Bank of the United States* had ever been heartily accepted by most people. The popular aversion to a Hamiltonian or strong central government grew rather than diminished in the following decades. It had been nourished on agrarianism; it now throve on business enterprise democratized, as described so admiringly in 1823 in the Baltimore conspiracy cases. By the time of Andrew Jackson's election in 1828 there had evolved a business class very different in size and character from the merchant class which had constituted the entire business community in early Federalist days. The industrial revolution had diversified business enterprise, had made it dynamic and democratic. For other than tariff matters, these new businessmen turned more readily to their familiar state authorities than to Washington. It was the states that taxed, regulated, and promoted enterprise. So, except to maintain the Bank of the United States for a few years, the McCulloch decision had little force until the Civil War.

When the Bank's charter was renewed by Congress in 1832, Jackson vetoed it, saying among other things that it was unconstitutional. He believed the President had as much right to decide what was constitutional as the Supreme Court had. *His* decision, in 1832, was greeted with popular enthusiasm; and the Jeffersonian and Jacksonian doctrine of a strictly limited federal sovereignty preponderated till the Civil War. It purposed and achieved a limitation of federal powers that is amazing in contrast with what those powers have since become.

Yet this implied no corresponding disrespect for the national government. Quite the contrary. No one was more devoted to the Union than Andrew Jackson. The Americans, in a world that had been shaken by revolutionary menaces and torn by Napoleonic wars from the time they formed their Union till long after, had sense enough to recognize that a federation afforded better military protection than could a growing number of small, separate sovereignties; that it was acquiring for them more and more continental territory; and that it enabled them to boast of citizenship in no small nation. Otherwise the federal Union was held in esteem much the way contemporary woman was, and revered affectionately so long as it kept within its sphere, which was important but modest.

The Civil War brought about a revolutionary change. Besides forcing the federal government to assume powers "to the very verge of the Constitution" and even beyond, it made the Union, in the eyes of the North, a beneficent power fighting slavery and secession and eventually worthy of all sorts of responsibilities, economic, paternal, conservatory, corrective, educational. First the farmers, its original enemies, and then labor, became its suppliants. By their votes they have multiplied its powers. It taxes, it regulates, and it affords security to a degree unpracticed and undreamt in 1819. Its spirit is not Hamiltonian but its structure and its operations are.

There is no older issue in American politics than that of the relation between the federal government's powers and those of the individual states, each side of which got its classical statement in 1791, by Hamilton and Jefferson respectively. The differences of opinion then expressed as to means have never been reconciled, though sides have changed. Seventy years after the issue arose and despite Marshall's opinion in 1819, it produced a ghastly Civil War; seventy-five years after that the welfare state arose—an innovation as far from Hamilton's purpose as from Jefferson's, or farther —yet involving the same constitutional questions that separated them.

At no time have the differences subsided into more than uneasy sleep. The issue is one bound to beset confederations of groups unwilling on the one hand to lose their individual sovereignties and on the other to forgo the incontestable advantages of union. It has troubled Canada, it now troubles Western Europe. It is an issue tempting to interests—economic, political, social, religious— which see advantages now from one side, now from the other. And these characteristics give it a history, in the United States at least, in which motives become curiously mixed.

The conventional contrast between Hamilton and Jefferson, for example, is that Hamilton was materialistic and a spokesman for wealth and privilege; and that Jefferson was humane and a champion of the neglected interests of the common man and the lowly. But the weapons, like those of Hamlet and Laertes, have somehow got exchanged. At this moment it is a federal government, conformed to principles urged first by Hamilton and reaffirmed by Marshall in *McCulloch* v. *Maryland,* that is combating discrimination—political, social, economic—against the Negro; and it is states conforming still to Jeffersonian principles of local sovereignty that are loudly resisting, as Maryland and Ohio did nearly a century and a half ago. With respect to responsibility for employment, security, and welfare in general, it is the posterity of Jefferson's party who thankfully acclaim a strong federal government and the posterity of Hamilton's who shrink away from its alleged hypertrophy.

# The Steamboat Case

BY GEORGE DANGERFIELD

(*Gibbons* v. *Ogden,* 9 Wheaton 1)

*As the country expanded in the early nineteenth century, efficient transportation became increasingly necessary, for unless men and goods could circulate freely from section to section the United States could scarcely hope to remain a single nation. Once again, however, uncertainties over the extent of federal and state authority caused quarrels that hampered development. These could only be settled by the Supreme Court. The great landmark in this area rose out of a fight between rival steamboat operators in New York Harbor. George Dangerfield is the author of the Pulitzer Prize winning* Era of Good Feelings *and of a biography of Robert R. Livingston, a pioneer in the development of the steamboat.*

The famous case of *Gibbons* v. *Ogden,* decided on March 2, 1824, was, with its preceding litigation, ultimately concerned with a single question: the power of Congress to regulate interstate as well as foreign commerce. It produced a triumph for nationalism, in the most generous and constructive sense of that term, and its influence has been immense. Its immediate effect, however, was to release from monopoly, like a genie from a bottle, a sooty, romantic, and useful servant to the American people—the steamboat.

One cannot altogether understand this aspect of *Gibbons* v. *Ogden* without considering the origins and consequences of the Livingston-Fulton steamboat monopoly, and the personalities involved in them: personalities of considerable determination and marked eccentricity, one of them brushed with genius, and all displaying a strong desire to move to some location more favorable to themselves that neighborly landmark which lies between *meum* and *tuum*.

The actual inaugurators of the American steamboat—John Fitch, James Rumsey, perhaps Oliver Evans—were also its innocent victims; they could make it run, but they could not make it run economically, nor could they raise sufficient funds to enable them, by research and experiment, to overcome this problem. One still sees them, nobly (and in Fitch's case somewhat drunkenly) silhouetted against the pale dawn of the Age of Steam, gesticulating in vain to the inattentive financier, the jocose and sceptical public. From their valiant dust springs *Gibbons* v. *Ogden*.

The great case may be taken back to March 27, 1798, when the New York Legislature repealed an exclusive privilege to run steamboats on state waters, which it had conferred on John Fitch, and bestowed it instead upon Robert R. Livingston, Chancellor of the state. Livingston had what Fitch conspicuously lacked—social status, political influence, wealth, credit. He resembled Fitch only in one respect: he was an enthusiast. An amateur scientist, he believed that nature might at any moment yield one of her tremendous secrets to some chance experiment or happy flash of insight. The building of grist mills on a novel principle which should eliminate friction between the stones; the crossing of cows with the elk in his park at Clermont on the Hudson; the manufacture of paper out of river weed locally known as frog's spit—such schemes occupied his leisure hours. His spirit, one might almost say, dwelt more and more apart on the farthest and most airy borders of rational speculation; almost but not quite. He was a progressive farmer, for example, whose work was of the first importance. And there was a hard, practical element in his singular composition—he was, after all, of Scottish and Dutch descent—which made it unlikely that he would throw good money after bad. To his great credit, he had perceived that the steamboat had a future: and although steamboat legislation, like Vulcan among the gods, excited the immortal laughter of the New York Legislature, Livingtson was quite impervious to mockery of this sort.

His experiments with John Stevens (one of the fathers of the railroad) and Nicholas J. Roosevelt proved abortive, and when he left for France in 1801, where as American Minister he plunged into those complex and exasperating negotiations which ultimately led to the purchase of Louisiana, it was presumed that no more would be heard of the steamboat. But in Paris he met the one man who could give his schemes what they needed—precision, economy, practicability.

Robert Fulton, darkly handsome, supremely self-confident, the very embodiment of energy, had been raised as an artisan in Lancaster, Pennsylvania. He had been a locksmith, a gunsmith, a draftsman, a portrait painter; he had gone to England to study under Benjamin West; and in England he had first conceived what was to become a permanent preoccupation with submarines and submarine torpedoes. Of Fulton it might indeed be doubted whether his lifelong purpose was to put boats upon the water or to blow them out of it. One thing, however, was certain. He had, supremely, the faculty of coordination. Other men's original ideas, in the realm of steamboats, existed only to be borrowed: "All these things," he said airily, "being governed by the laws of nature, the real invention is to find [such laws]." To him, it was all a matter of exact proportions, of nicely calculated relations. Where the steamboat was concerned, it was Fulton's destiny, and his genius, to find a commotion and to turn it into a revolution.

Fulton and Livingston put an experimental steamboat upon the Seine; its performance satisfied them, and Fulton left for England, to cajole out of the British Government a Boulton & Watt engine built to his own specifications. The engine was claimed by Fulton from the New York customs house on April 23, 1807; it was placed in a boat built at the Charles Brownne shipyards at Paulus Hook; and on August 17, 1807, *The Steamboat* (she seems never to have been called the *Clermont*)[1] made her triumphant voyage from New York to Albany.

On her maiden night, as she passed through the darkling Highlands of the Hudson, a plangent volcano, *The Steamboat* excited great terror among the pious dwellers beside the banks of that river. One rustic is said to have raced home, barred the doors, and shouted that the Devil himself was going up to Albany in a sawmill.

---

[1] Fulton variously referred to the vessel as the *North River Steamboat of Clermont*—after Livingston's Hudson estate—the *North River Steamboat*, or the *North River*. On her first voyage, she seems simply to have been *The Steamboat*. But the public came to call her the *Clermont*, and the name stuck.

Here he was, perhaps understandably, wrong. It was not a demon, it was a most useful spirit, which had been released by Fulton and Livingston; the trouble was that, having released it, they at once imprisoned it again. Fulton did indeed take out two United States patents—perhaps more interesting as essays than valid as claims—but it was not upon these that he and Livingston relied; their great support was restrictive state legislation.

On April 6, 1808, the New York Legislature extended their privilege up to a limit of thirty years, and imposed thumping penalties upon anyone who should dare, without a license from the monopoly, to navigate upon any of the waters of New York. In 1809, a sister to *The Steamboat,* the *Car of Neptune,* was built; in 1810, the *Paragon* appeared; on April 9, 1811, the New York Legislature passed a monopoly act even more stringent in its penalties than the one enacted in 1808. And in April, 1811, the Legislature of the Territory of Orleans conferred upon Livingston and Fulton privileges fully as extensive as those granted by New York. Thus they controlled two of the greatest commercial waterways in the United States.

Although they had shown true vision in their estimate of the steamboat's future, Livingston and Fulton had been somewhat less perceptive in gauging the reaction of their countrymen. They had not supposed that their monopoly would be unpopular, still less that it would be seriously resisted. From the outset, however, obloquy and litigation became their portion. The litigation reached its climax in 1811, when twenty-one enterprising gentlemen of Albany started a rival steamboat, the *Hope,* upon the Albany-New York run, and threatened to follow her up with a sister ship, not inaptly to be called the *Perseverance.*

The monopolists, of course, fought back in the courts, and in March, 1812, New York Chief Justice James Kent issued a permanent injunction against the *Hope.* Kent's very learned opinion may be reduced to this simple proposition: either the New York steamboat acts violated the federal Constitution or they did not. A stern supporter of states' rights, Kent ruled that they did not. Obviously, he said, where a national and a state law are aimed against each other, the state law must yield. But this was not the case here, since all commerce within a state was exclusively within the power of that state. Supported by Kent, one of the most respected jurists in the nation, the monopoly had certainly become respectable. When Robert R. Livingston, full of years and honors, died in 1813, when Robert Fulton followed him into the shades in 1815, they left to their heirs and assigns an inheritance as rich and safe as state laws could make it.

Nonetheless, the contentious atmosphere which had clouded the monopoly from the beginning seems to have been increased rather than diminished by the decision of Kent. New Jersey had already passed a retaliatory act in 1811; in the course of time her example was followed by Connecticut and by Ohio. Massachusetts, Georgia, New Hampshire, Vermont, and Pennsylvania bestowed exclusive rights upon their own favored monopolists. Elsewhere, unlicensed steamboats blew their lonely, defiant whistles upon remote lakes and waterways, and pale denizens of the uncharted wilderness crept down to watch and wonder. The development of the steamboat was a great adventure, but it was threatening to turn into that gravest of evils, a commercial civil war—unless, indeed, someone could break the Livingston-Fulton grip upon Louisiana and New York. In the former state, by 1819, there were distinct signs of rebellion; but the latter, the cradle of the whole restrictive movement, would undoubtedly prove to be the more dramatic and decisive scene for some abrupt reversal of this ominous trend. . . .

In May, 1819, John R. Livingston of New York brought suit in the Chancery Court of that state against Aaron Ogden and Thomas Gibbons of New Jersey. Mr. Livingston, a younger brother of Robert R. Livington, was a wealthy merchant, who had dedicated his youth to making what he called "something clever" out of the Revolution, and who had thereafter devoted his energies to the single-minded pursuit of material advantage. In 1808, for the extremely stiff price of one-sixth of his gross proceeds, he had purchased from his brother's monopoly the exclusive right to navigate steamboats "from any place within the city of New York lying south of the State Prison, to the Jersey shore and Staten Island, viz: Staten Island, Elizabethtown Point, Amboy and the Raritan up to Brunswick, but to no place or point north of Powles Hook." (The location of Powles or Paulus Hook may be determined by drawing a line from the southernmost tip of Manhattan Island due west to the Jersey shore.) He was certain to extract from this hard-bought concession whatever there was to be extracted—and thus arose his suit against Ogden and Gibbons.

Aaron Ogden, finding his own legislature unwilling to support him in his claim to run steamboats on his own, had reluctantly yielded to the monopoly in 1815, and had purchased from Mr. Livingston, its assignee, the right to run a steamboat ferry from Elizabethtown Point to New York. A Revolutionary soldier who had fought at Yorktown, a former Governor of New Jersey, and one of the state's leading lawyers and most prominent Federalists, Ogden was a man of an impressive physique, a craggy and truculent countenance, and a character to match. He bore the monopoly no goodwill; and in the course of time he acquired in Thomas Gibbons a partner even more truculent than himself.

Gibbons was a wealthy lawyer from Georgia, who had been a Loyalist during the Revolution, thereby (since his brother and father were both patriots) saving the Gibbons plantation from both British vandalism and anti-Loyalist revenge. His was not exactly a happy record, but he survived it, to acquire at length a reputation, notable even in Georgia, for some of the more opprobrious and quarrelsome forms of political intermeddling. "His soul," said one enemy, "is faction and his life has been a scene of political corruption." In 1811 he acquired a home at Elizabethtown, New Jersey.

The partnership between Ogden and Gibbons, instituted in 1817, was no doubt doomed from the start. In October, 1818, Ogden obtained an injunction against Gibbons in the New York Chancery Court, presumably because that oblique personage could not resist the temptation to cheat his partner by running a steamboat on his own account from Powles Hook to New York. Nonetheless, when John R. Livingston brought suit against the pair in 1819, their partnership was still uneasily alive and upon the following terms: Ogden ran passengers from New York to Elizabethtown Point in his steamboat *Atalanta.* At Elizabethtown Point, the passengers changed into Gibbons' *Bellona,* for which (as for his smaller steamboat the *Stoudinger*) Gibbons had taken out a United States coasting license. The passengers were then carried to New Brunswick, whence they proceeded overland to Trenton and Philadelphia.

John R. Livingston, whose steamboat *Olive Branch* ran regularly from New York to New Brunswick, claimed that the Ogden-Gibbons partnership constituted a single voyage, in defiance of his exclusive right. He also showed that the partners had a common booking agent in New York, by the name of William B. Jaques. Livingston petitioned for an injunction restraining them from navigating their two boats, except from New York to Elizabethtown Point. Since Ogden had already enjoined Gibbons from doing any such thing, this meant that in future the *Atalanta* would have to transfer her passengers, not into Gibbons' *Bellona,* but into Livingston's *Olive Branch.*

Both Gibbons and Ogden disclaimed any partnership or any knowledge of Mr. Jaques. Both insisted that the ports and harbors of Elizabethtown Point and New Brunswick were within the jurisdiction of New Jersey, as were the waters lying between them; and both asserted that the agreement between the monopoly and John R. Livingston gave the latter no right whatsoever to navigate between a port in New York and one in New Jersey. Gibbons had other arguments, but the chief of them—and this in time became the crux of the whole matter—was that under his national coasting license he had a perfect right to navigate between one point in New Jersey and another.

The reigning Chancellor of New York was now none other than James Kent who, as Chief Justice, had delivered the decisive opinion in the case of the *Hope* in 1812. That he would reverse in the Court of Chancery a decision he had delivered in the Court of Errors was not to be expected. In a complicated decision that adds nothing to his fame as a jurist, he held that Ogden could continue to steam between New York and Elizabethtown Point in the *Atalanta,* but that Gibbons' *Bellona* could not operate between the Point and New Brunswick.

If the temperaments of Ogden and Gibbons had been more compatible, they might have continued the fight together. The New York law, claiming jurisdiction all the way to the Jersey shore, was clearly preposterous, and simple justice should have compelled the partners to stand together for their common rights. But Ogden decided to content himself with Kent's decision. No doubt he contemplated the discomfiture of Gibbons with a certain amount of ill-concealed complacency.

The result was the final break between Gibbons and Ogden.

Gibbons was justifiably angry and full of fight. Since Kent had ignored his federal coasting license argument, he planned to bring the case to the United States Supreme Court. Meanwhile he hoped to stir up trouble in the New Jersey Legislature; and he proposed to be a thorn in the side of the monopoly by breaking the New York statute wherever and whenever he could.

For this latter project he had ready, in the rude person of Cornelius Vanderbilt, master of the *Bellona* (who feared no man, and in whom one may detect even in this early stage of his memorable career a characteristic admixture of talent, forthrightness, and low cunning), precisely the instrument he needed. Together they invented many ingenious ways of outwitting the monopoly. One of the finest of these was to run passengers in the *Bellona* out of Elizabethtown Point and transship them, in Jersey waters, to the *Nautilus* of Daniel D. Tompkins, who had acquired from the monopoly the ferry rights between Staten Island and New York. Tompkins was an old opponent of the Livingston faction in the New York Republican party and was not unwilling to make a little mischief. The physical risks of transshipment were far from negligible, but Americans were made of stern stuff in those days, the fare of fifty cents a head was undeniably attractive, and all was going beautifully—one might say swimmingly, except that no one fell overboard—until brought to a halt by the decision of Chancellor Kent in *Ogden* v. *Gibbons* of December 4, 1819.

The web of litigation was already tangled. Ogden had earlier sued Gibbons before Kent on October 6, 1819, on the grounds that Gibbons was running his two steamboats between New Jersey and New York, in open defiance of the monopoly rights that Ogden had purchased from Livingston, and on this occasion Gibbons had at least wrung from Kent what he most needed, and that was a ruling upon the scope of national coasting licenses. Nobody could deny that an act of Congress of February 18, 1793, permitted vessels of over twenty tons' burden to be enrolled and licensed. The question was: did this national license permit a vessel to trade, not only between port and port of one state, but between the port of one state and the port of another? If it did, it was clear that there would be little comfort thereafter for the Livingston-Fulton monopoly.

Chancellor Kent, however, was now ready with an ingenious reply. A national license, he said, merely conferred upon any given vessel a national character, freeing it from those burdensome duties which were imposed upon foreign vessels if they attempted to engage in the coasting trade. That it was a license to trade, still less to trade in waters restricted by a state law, he steadfastly denied. Was it likely, he asked, that the New York steamboat acts, every one of which had been written and passed subsequent to the Act of Congress, would have been written and passed at all if it could have been held that the Act of Congress had annihilated them all in advance?

This argument was certainly forcible, but whether it cast more darkness upon New York legislation than light upon the Act of Congress must remain in some doubt. Gibbons, of course, appealed from Kent's ruling to the New York Court of Errors; the appeal was heard in January, 1820; and Gibbons' counsel now contended that the licensing act was derived from the eighth section of the first article of the federal Constitution—from the power of Congress, that is, to regulate commerce among the several states. Thus in *Gibbons* v. *Ogden* in the New York Court of Errors there dawned what was afterward to become the high nationalist noonday of *Gibbons* v. *Ogden* in the Supreme Court of the United States. Justice Jonas Platt, pronouncing the decision of the Court of Errors, upheld Chancellor Kent; and against this decision Gibbons appealed to the Supreme Court.

The times, if not necessarily the law, were now certainly on Gibbons' side. With the passing of the War of 1812, a new light seemed to fall upon the map of the United States. The nation, now figuratively facing westward, began to think of its lamentable roads, its lack of canals, the primitive counterclockwise motion of its exchange of staples for manufactures as that exchange moved down the Ohio and the Mississippi, up the Atlantic coast, and back across the Appalachians. That the steamboat might do much to reverse this process, nobody now doubted; but the steamboat, a strange but sufficient symbol of nationalism, was struggling in the grip of a monopoly, dubiously bottomed upon the doctrine of states rights.

Nor was this all. The contest between state-conferred steamboat monopolies, the clash of state retaliatory laws, threatened to reduce the nation's commerce to that particularist chaos which the Constitution itself had been providentially designed to avert. And here the indefatigable Thomas Gibbons was not backward. He persuaded the New Jersey Legislature to pass a new retaliatory act, and on February 20, 1820, it did so. By this act, any nonresident of New Jersey who enjoined a New Jersey citizen, in the Chancery Court of New York, from navigating by steamboat any of the waters between the "ancient" shores of New Jersey, could in turn be enjoined by the Chancery Court of New Jersey from navigating between those "ancient" shores. Moreover—and this was the sting—he could be made liable for all damages, *with triple costs,* in any action for trespass or writ of attachment which he had obtained against a New Jersey citizen in the New York court.

Thus John R. Livingston, to his dismay, discovered that his *Olive Branch* had been detained and attached in New Brunswick to answer for damages alleged to have arisen from the injunction he had won against Gibbons in May, 1819. Threatened with successive attachments and prohibitive costs, he had at one time withdrawn the *Olive Branch* from service. In *Livingston* v. *D. D. Tompkins* (June 1, 1820), *Livingston* v. *Gibbons* (August 26, 1820), and *Livingston* v. *Gibbons, impleaded with Ogden* (May 8, 1821), one may trace his efforts, on behalf of Ogden as well as himself, to wriggle out of this predicament. But, alas there was in Livingston's character just a touch of Sir Giles Overreach; he succeeded only in arousing the wrath of Chancellor Kent, a high-minded gentleman, who cared little for the stratagems of entrepreneurs, but much for the dignity of the law.

Actually, Chancellor Kent had now thrown in the sponge. He had done his best for the rights and dignity of his state and his court; he might talk about State reprisals and jurisdictions until the very walls of his courtroom reverberated with his declamations; but he was, after all, one of the first jurists in the nation; and there had been growing upon his shuddering inner vision, feature by feature, like some Cheshire cat's, the implacably smiling visage of the Commerce Clause of the Constitution. In the meantime, he had left the quarrel between Ogden and Gibbons in a state of armed neutrality, and Gibbons and Vanderbilt continued, by one device or another, to keep the *Bellona* steaming between New Jersey and New York until such time as the Supreme Court should rule upon Gibbons' appeal from the New York Court of Errors.

This appeal had been docketed with the Supreme Court in 1820, dismissed for technical reasons in 1821, docketed again in 1822, and continued from term to term until February, 1824. By that time and in that political climate, with nationalism and states' rights opposed on many fronts, it was already a famous case. Eminent counsel had been briefed on both sides: Daniel Webster and Attorney General William Wirt for Gibbons; Thomas J. Oakley and Thomas Adis Emmet for the monopoly.

One might have supposed, since the nationalist John Marshall was Chief Justice and the Court was supposedly "Marshall's Court," that a decision in favor of Gibbons was a foregone conclusion. But the assertion that Congress could actually regulate interstate trade was in those days a very daring one; and although John Marshall was a bold man, many people doubted if he would be as bold as all that. Nor could one be sure that, in this instance, he would be supported by a majority of his brethren.

The legal questions were extremely complicated and Gibbons' able lawyers exploited every possible argument. Wirt, for example, reasoned that the monopoly laws conflicted with certain acts of Congress, and were therefore void. Webster, however, who opened for Gibbons, went boldly to the heart of the matter by claiming that it was of no moment whether or not the New York statutes were in conflict with an act of Congress. The constitutional authority of Congress was such that it had the power exclusively to regulate commerce in all its forms upon all the navigable waters of the United States. Afterward he said—whatever Webster's faults, self-depreciation was not among them—that Marshall took in his words "as a baby takes in his mother's milk." This was not quite the case. The truth seems to be that the two men thought very much alike on the question, but that it required all Marshall's gifts to weave into a more prudent form the arguments so vehemently presented by Webster.

The pleadings consumed four and a half days, and it was generally conceded that every one of the counsel had surpassed himself —in learning, in subtlety, in eloquence. Nearly a month passed before Marshall delivered the Court's opinion. It was one of the most statesmanlike he had ever penned, and, in a legal point of view, one of his soundest. (There was only one dissent, Justice William Johnson's, and that uttered doctrine more extreme than

Marshall's.) And one should always remember, as Justice Frankfurter says, that when Marshall applied the Commerce Clause in *Gibbons* v. *Ogden* "he had available no fund of mature or coherent speculation regarding its implications." Like the steamboat itself, the decision which freed the steamboat was a pioneer.

Marshall began by defining "commerce," not in the strict sense of "buying and selling" (as Ogden's counsel had urged), but (this was Wirt's definition) as "intercourse," and this of course included navigation; and it comprehended also the power to prescribe rules for carrying on that intercourse. ("I shall soon expect to learn," wrote Henry Seawall to Thomas Ruffin, "that our fornication laws are unconstitutional.")

This being the case, one had then to ask whether the power of Congress, under the Commerce Clause, invalidated the monopoly statutes of the State of New York. Here Marshall ruled that the coasting license Act of 1793, dealing with the subject matter of that clause, was superior to a state law dealing with the same subject matter. Thus Gibbons' license did not merely confer upon his vessel an American character; it also permitted that vessel to trade between the port of one state and the port of another; nor did the fact that it was a *steamboat* have any relevance. Marshall's majestic reasoning struck down the monopoly in twenty words: "The laws of Congress, for the regulation of commerce, do not look to the principle by which vessels are moved."

Congress, in short, has power over navigation "within the limits of every State" so far as navigation may be, in any way, connected with foreign or interstate trade. (It should be remarked, in passing, that it took two more suits in the New York courts to determine whether or not the Livingston-Fulton monopoly was valid for purely *intrastate* commerce; and that when Chief Justice Savage in the Court of Errors—*North River Steamboat Co.* v. *John R. Livingston,* February, 1825—declared that it was not, both Justice Woodworth and a handful of state senators felt obliged to dissent.)

The subtleties, the complexities, the mass of subsequent legal glossing, the vexed questions of state taxing and state police powers —all these are irrelevant to this bare narrative; the point is that Marshall's great decision, which has been called "the emancipation proclamation of American commerce," has substantially survived the erosions of time and of change. Its immediate effect was to set the steamboat free on all the waters of the United States. Its more distant effects were beyond the scrutiny of Marshall and his contemporaries; the railroad, the telegraph, the telephone, the oil and the gas pipe lines, the airplane, as they moved across state borders, all came under the protection of *Gibbons* v. *Ogden*.

The decision was the only popular one which Marshall ever rendered. And yet there were many dissidents. Slaveowners, for example, were deeply alarmed for the future of the interstate slave trade. Others, more selfless and high-minded—and of these Thomas Jefferson was the first and greatest—saw in *Gibbons* v. *Ogden* only a despotic extension of the powers of the federal government. What Gibbons and Ogden had to say has not been recorded for the instruction of posterity. One might however add, by way of postscript, that Ogden died a bankrupt and Gibbons a millionaire. Since Ogden was undoubtedly the more estimable of the two, one must leave it to the reader to decide whether the tendency of this essay is on the whole to emphasize the injudiciousness of yielding to a monopoly or the advantage of breaking the law.

# The Charles River Bridge Case

## V

BY HENRY F. GRAFF

*(Charles River Bridge v. Warren Bridge, 11 Peters 420)*

*The safeguarding of property rights, one of John Marshall's major objectives, was a necessary condition of rapid economic growth. However, by making property too sacrosanct, some of Marshall's decisions threatened to slow up progress by hindering the development of new enterprises. This story, which came to its climax only after Marshall's death in 1835, involved the claims and counterclaims of rival bridgebuilders in Boston, Massachusetts. It produced a decision as epochal as many of Marshall's greatest. Professor Graff is chairman of the Columbia University History Department. He is the co-author of* The Modern Researcher, *and has written other works in the field of American history.*

Bridges and the rivers they span have always been the subjects of romancers as well as of engineers. And whether at San Luis Rey or over the Kwai or where Horatius stood alone, the drama inevitably revolves about the tension a bridge creates between, on the one hand, its own brave existence and, on the other, the magical changes it brings to the lives of the people who use it.

Every bridge, real no less than fictional, is *sui generis*—in design, in impact, in meaning.

At least one American bridge lives in assured immortality. It is the one that the descendants of the Massachusetts Puritans put across the Charles River at Boston in 1786. An ordinary bridge by some standards of judgment, its draw swayed in the strong winter wind and its broad planks froze over badly when the weather was cold and the spray from the river was high. But it became in time the symbol of a powerful dispute between two conceptions of government's role in the economy, and ultimately a "case" enshrined in our constitutional history. Its impress on the history of American transportation, on the history of antitrust actions, and on American free capitalism itself has been abiding.

The circumstances of the "Charles River Bridge case" are deeply embedded in New England's history. They began on October 17, 1640, when the General Court of the Massachusetts Bay Colony, then only seventeen years old, generously bestowed on Harvard College the right to operate a ferryboat across the Charles River between Boston and Charlestown. Over the years the tolls from this enterprise fluctuated, but the profits were never large. After 1701 the ferry franchise was sublet, but returns still remained modest because the cost of maintaining the ferry and the ferry slip was frequently high. It was not until the War of Independence was over and the river traffic had increased markedly that the promise of higher profits seemed close to fulfillment—a significant fact in the life of an impecunious liberal arts college like Harvard.

In the year 1785, though, the Commonwealth of Massachusetts took a bold step that its leading men believed would keep Massachusetts abreast of the times. It incorporated as the "Proprietors of the Charles River Bridge," a group of entrepreneurs which included, among other well-known figures, that old friend of enterprise and progress, the merchant John Hancock. The Proprietors were empowered to replace the Boston-Charlestown ferry with a bridge. For the "income of the ferry which they might have received had not said bridge been erected," Harvard College was to be reimbursed during the next forty years in the amount of two hundred pounds annually, equivalent to $666.66. At the end of that time a reasonable sum would be paid to Harvard College as final compensation.

The new bridge, a remarkable example of the engineering skills of the day, was opened on June 17, 1786—a glorious way to mark the eleventh anniversary of the Battle of Bunker Hill. Standing 1,470 feet long and 42 feet wide, it defied the lugubrious predictions that the tidal currents or the breaking up of the ice on the Charles would certainly smash its footings and carry it away. The designer of this masterpiece was the gifted artisan, Lemuel Cox, whose labors earned him now something of an international reputation.

At the jubilant celebration of the opening, his appreciative fellow citizens paid Cox tribute in a poem which contained the lines:

> Now Boston, Charlestown, nobly join,
> And roast a fatted Ox;
> On noted Bunker Hill combine,
> To toast our patriot, Cox.

Among the twenty thousand people who were present on that bright occasion, no one could have foreseen the long legislative and legal battles that would make the name of the bridge legendary. In 1786 there was simply rejoicing. Such a splendid example of American technology must surely be only a foretaste of other marvels to come. At the time, there were 150 shares of the capital stock of the bridge, worth at par $333.33 each.

Within a few years, as the prosperity that accompanied the establishment of the Constitution continued, a petition was offered in the state legislature to build another bridge—this one to stretch across the Charles River between Boston and Cambridge. The Proprietors of the Charles River Bridge and the spokesmen for Harvard College (often difficult to tell apart) were understandably distressed, and they argued vehemently that the loss of revenue on the Charles River Bridge in consequence of the building of a new span would be substantial. But the committee of the legislature before which the matter had come took the position that the Proprietors had never been granted a monopoly on the crossing of the river. This stand carried the day. As a result, authorization to build the new bridge was approved by the General Court. The grantees, nevertheless, had to agree to pay an annuity as compensation to Harvard. Furthermore, the annuity payable to the college by the Charles River Bridge was extended from forty to seventy years, that is, to the year 1856.

John Hancock, who was now Governor of Massachusetts, might well have vetoed the bill. The interested speculators, however, had drawn his fangs and made the merest talk of a veto a suspicious thing by inserting in a local paper an advertisement for the sale of shares, which began: "As *all* citizens have an *equal* right to propose a measure that may be beneficial to the public or advantageous to themselves, and as no body of men have an *exclusive* right to take to themselves such a privilege, a number of gentlemen have proposed to open a new subscription for the purpose of a bridge from West Boston to Cambridge, at such a place as the General Court may be pleased to direct."

Although Hancock, who was always attentive to the public voice, did not have the audacity to withhold his approval from the bill, he had not been helpless to protect his self-interest. He had used his influence to have the bridge established "near the Pest House" on the Boston side, and he arranged to have the proprietors of the new bridge pay Harvard three hundred pounds—a hundred pounds more than his own was paying! The principal proprietor of the new venture, Francis Dana, who had served during the Revolution as the first American Minister to Russia, did not find the location as objectionable as his adversaries had hoped, because the Pest House was at the point nearest to Cambridge. However, Dana protested strenuously the one-hundred-pound difference between his obligation and that of Hancock, and he succeeded in having this annuity payment reduced to two hundred pounds.

Opened on November 23, 1793, Dana's West Boston Bridge was hailed for its beauty immediately. Some regarded it as a structure that outshone and outclassed by far the Charles River Bridge. The *Columbian Centinel* asserted exuberantly that the "elegance of workmanship" and "the magnitude of the undertaking are perhaps unequalled in the history of enterprises." The first man to travel across this wonderwork was the patriot, Elbridge Gerry, who had been one of the signers of the Declaration of Independence and would later be Vice President of the United States.

The Boston community was now enjoying the convenience of two bridges, and Harvard College was enjoying the use of four hundred pounds annually in compensatory payments. As the traffic on both bridges increased, the tolls poured in and the value of the stock grew apace. How fascinating it was that so much money could be made out of the transit of people and goods from one side of the Charles to the other! By 1805 the value of a share of the Charles River Bridge stock had risen to $1,650. A few years later the cautious overseers of Harvard bought two shares at $2,080 each and considered them a prudent investment for the college.

But changing times shortly made their judgment seem questionable. The simple truth was that new outlooks were forming and a new world was in the making. Perceptive men, by the 1820's, were being persuaded that charters which tended to be exclusive in practice like the one granted to the Charles River Bridge Proprietors hindered rather than aided the growth of business. These emerging leaders had not yet become fully convinced that competition was "the life of trade," but they were tending in that direction. For the moment their resentment took the form of an angry conviction that the Charles River Bridge monopoly was a costly bottleneck in the circulation of people and goods in the busy city of Boston. This kind of public irritation seems to have grown parallel with the spirit of Jacksonian democracy, which ultimately destroyed the greatest monopoly of all: the Bank of the United States.

As early as 1823 a petition was introduced in the Massachusetts legislature to build another bridge over the Charles, this one for foot passengers, which was to be wholly free of toll. Comparable petitions followed at subsequent sessions, each time being rejected. The Charles River Bridge Proprietors argued solemnly that the building of a new bridge would flagrantly damage their property interest. Estimating the value of it at $280,000, they declared, in obvious answer to the charge that their bridge had paid back its original shareholders many times over, that the majority of the stock "is holden by persons who have purchased the stock within the last ten or fifteen years—by widows, by orphans, by literary and charitable institutions. The erection of another bridge from Charlestown to Boston would annihilate at once two-thirds of this property." Besides, the Proprietors regarded a new span across the Charles as quite unnecessary. Advocates of it were interested, they said, not in *another* bridge but in a *free* one. The Proprietors pointed out in a pamphlet: "Scarcely a man . . . would be in favour of a new bridge if the charter contained a provision for taking a foot toll."

By the end of the 1820's, though, the tone of the remonstrances for a new bridge became more strident and, in fact, the general atmosphere of the discussion was changing. The easy confidence that the law would unfailingly protect charters in their exclusivity was no longer inviolate. The issue was being dragged into the political arena, with the Democrats arrayed on the side of permitting the new bridge and the Whigs, strengthened and emboldened by the involvement of revered Harvard College, firmly committed to opposing it.

For the Whigs, nothing less than the good faith of government seemed now to be at stake in the controversy. In 1827, vetoing a proposal for a new bridge, Governor Levi Lincoln said it this way: "To the interest and confidence of private associations we must look for investment of funds in the prosecution of valuable and useful objects, and it is only from a firm reliance on the most scrupulous regard to rights under acts of incorporation that they will be encouraged to action." Lincoln's eyes were fixed not only on the plight of his alma mater but also on the canals and new steam railroads just being developed and the possibilities they opened for revolutionizing transportation. Only the year before, the first railroad had been incorporated in Massachusetts. It was a small one—designed to carry granite from the quarries of Quincy to the Neponsit River—but the handwriting was on the wall, and, to him, clear: if men were to be encouraged to invest in railroads, railroad charters must be sacrosanct. Two questions cried out for answering: Could the state destroy the equity of a corporation it had once solemnly helped to create? And yet, could the state disregard the current requirements and interests of its citizens by holding them to be less important than contracts drawn in an earlier day when public needs were different?

These questions could not easily be settled with justice to all parties. Events, however, have an insistent way of forcing solutions. The growing size of Boston helped to hasten the day of reckoning. The population of the city had leaped from 39,000 in 1810 to 54,000 in 1820. The census of 1830 would show it to be over 85,000. The city's economy, already exerting enormous pressure on its seams, would not be restrained by the sophistries and tortuous reasoning of bridge-toll collectors. Is it any wonder that there was talk of a free bridge over the Charles, and that—in 1827—it became an issue in the state's gubernatorial election?

The advocates of change were sorely pressing the Charles River Bridge Proprietors. These in turn buckled under the attack, and in panic talked of surrendering their property to the state for a sum to be agreed upon by impartial commissioners. Failing that, they said they would surrender their bridge without payment of any kind after eight more years of operation. Expressing confidence in the intention of Massachusetts to defend their rights, they declared their desire to be relieved of the necessity to argue their case periodically before committees of the legislature, or ultimately in the courts.

In a manner of speaking, the issue was between the old and the new. But it partook also of a tug-of-war between urban and rural Massachusetts. The rural portion was contending for the right to enter Boston free of charge; the city fathers, being more solicitous of property rights, defended the toll collectors. The legislature, showing no more determination to hold itself against the force of public sentiment than do most servants of the people, on March 12, 1828, approved a charter for a new span to be known as the Warren Bridge, in honor of the hero of Bunker Hill.

The Proprietors of the Warren Bridge, under the charter's terms, would collect tolls until the cost of construction plus 5 percent had been recovered. After that there would be no charge for passage across the bridge. In any event, the term of toll-collecting was not to exceed six years. Until the bridge became free, its proprietors agreed to assume one-half of the annuity of $666.66 required to be paid to Harvard College by the Charles River Bridge. Despite a vigorous protest by a number of the leading citizens of Massachusetts—for the most part, alumni of Harvard—Governor Lincoln signed the enactment. Thus the saga of the Warren Bridge began.

Immediately upon the passage of the act, the Proprietors of the Charles River Bridge sought a preliminary injunction against the building of the proposed bridge. Counsel for the Charles River Bridge were the incomparable Daniel Webster, and Lemuel Shaw, later Chief Justice of the Massachusetts Supreme Court. Of immediate concern to the Proprietors was the estimate that the Warren Bridge would easily absorb two-thirds of the traffic over the river. At the Charlestown end the new bridge, when completed, would be only 260 feet away from the Charles River Bridge; at the Boston end the distance would be only 916 feet. The roads leading from them would come within 26 feet of one another. Clearly, the traffic —and the tolls—on the Charles River Bridge would cease altogether when the Warren Bridge reverted to the state in six years. To show the extent of their equity at stake, the Proprietors offered in court the fact that from 1786 to 1827 the Charles River Bridge had collected $824,798 in tolls. Although the court did not grant the preliminary injunction, it left the door open for future litigation. The opinion was rendered by Chief Justice Isaac Parker, who until a year and a half before had held the Royall Professorship at the Harvard Law School.

In anticipation of the opening of the Warren Bridge on Christmas Day, 1828, the stockholders of the Charles River Bridge reckoned anew the anticipated loss in tolls. Harvard College could feel itself a particularly aggrieved victim. When the new bridge should become free in 1834, Harvard stood to lose an annuity of $666.66 which had twenty-three more years to run; and it stood to lose the value of its Charles River Bridge stock, which would, of course, become virtually worthless.

In a supplemental bill, the Charles River Bridge Proprietors asserted that the creation of the new company violated their charter and in so doing violated also the contract clause of the United States Constitution. The bill declared further that to be deprived of property without compensation was a violation of the Massachusetts Constitution.

The defendants filed their answers early in December, 1828, even before they had collected their first toll; and the titanic court battle was thus joined. Their strategy was to seek delay until the successful operation of their bridge drew public sentiment to their side. Not until more than a year later—January 12, 1830—were the opinions rendered. The court proved to be evenly divided: two of the justices declared the statute creating the new bridge unconstitutional and two upheld it. Chief Justice Parker, in attacking the law, expressed the interesting view that the high profits earned over the years by the Charles River Bridge had willy-nilly affected adversely the case for indemnifying its Proprietors. He observed that if the Warren Bridge had been authorized without appropriate compensation in 1787 when the Charles River Bridge was only a year old, "the opinion of the injustice would have been universal."

On the other side was the stern view of Judge Marcus Morton. He simply declared that to accept the arguments of the Charles River Bridge Proprietors meant that "no improved road, no new bridge, no canal, no railroad, can be constitutionally established. For I think, in the present state of our country, no such improved channel of communication can be opened without diminishing the profits of some old corporation." The court was keenly aware that railroad interests were watching the outcome closely. Until the extent of charter rights could be ascertained, potential investors would view with questioning eyes the railroad securities now beginning to appear throughout the country.

Morton, for many years an overseer of Harvard, was also a Jacksonian who may be said to have been uttering the anticorporation sentiments of his political constituents. He ran for governor on the Democratic ticket in every election year from 1828 to 1843, not stepping down from the bench until he was finally elected in 1839!

Without delay, the issue was taken to the United States Supreme Court. It was set to be argued in the following year. This final drama would be inseparably interwoven, as the whole question had been from the first, with the name of Harvard College. The Supreme Court, presided over by the aging John Marshall, included Joseph Story, who in 1829 had been appointed the Dane Professor at the Harvard Law School. A brilliant letter writer, he kept his family and friends in Cambridge fully informed about the arguments presented in those five crowded days in March, 1831, when the case was heard. Like a tennis match, the pleadings held the charm for him not only of competition carried to a conclusion, but of a gladiatorial spectacle delicious for its own sake. Yet his keen personal sympathies for the Charles River Bridge cause were always apparent.

Chief counsel for the Charles River Bridge was Daniel Webster, without a peer among the lawyers of his day. At Webster's side was Warren Dutton, another prominent attorney, who had a personal interest in the Charles River Bridge. The Warren Bridge was represented by William Wirt, as chief counsel, who had been Attorney General under Monroe and John Quincy Adams, and by Walker Jones, a District of Columbia lawyer of repute. Wirt, who earlier in his career had served as prosecuting attorney in Aaron Burr's trial for treason, was a master of courtroom techniques. Story, deeply moved by the intellectual excitement of the trial, wrote in fascination to a Harvard colleague:

We . . . have heard the opening counsel on each side in three days. Dutton for the plaintiffs made a capital argument in point of matter and manner, lawyerlike, close, searching and exact; Jones on the other side was ingenious, metaphysical, and occasionally strong and striking. Wirt goes on to-day and Webster will follow tomorrow.

But for all the brilliance of the argument, the court was not yet ready to decide. Owing to the illness, indisposition, and death of several of the justices, it was to be another six years before the verdict was rendered. A decision of this importance, it seemed, ought not to be made with less than the full court in attendance. Meanwhile, the cast of characters was significantly altered.

Marshall died in 1835. (We will never be certain where he stood on the issue, although it might be inferred from the Dartmouth College case that he would have defended as inviolable the rights conferred by the Charles River Bridge charter.) Two other members of the court also died. So did William Wirt, chief counsel for the Warren Bridge, on February 14, 1834. The case, patently, would have to be reargued before a reconstituted court by a reorganized defense.

When at last President Jackson filled the vacancies on the Supreme Bench, the membership included a new Chief Justice, Roger B. Taney of Maryland. Taney was the product of a different political tradition than Marshall's. His career measured the road over which the new country had traveled in the generation that separated him from his great predecessor. Born in Maryland, he came of a family of wealthy slaveowners who raised tobacco. Entering politics after graduation from Dickinson College, he became a staunch Federalist. He broke with his party's leadership when it opposed the War of 1812, but not yet with the party itself. That rupture did not come until 1824, when he committed his political future to the Jacksonians by supporting their man for President. In 1831 he became Jackson's Attorney General. Then, as the third in the line of Secretaries that Jackson appointed, Taney showed the necessary loyalty to his chief when he obeyed the President's order to remove the government's deposits from the Bank of the United States.

In 1835 at the age of fifty-eight, Taney had been designated by Jackson to be an associate justice of the Supreme Court. Marshall had personally approved of the appointment, but an angry Senate had rejected it. The membership and the mood of the Senate changed quickly, however, and the following year it confirmed Taney as Marshall's successor. A New York newspaper commented sourly: "The pure ermine of the Supreme Court is sullied by the appointment of that political hack." This was a partisan statement, with arguable justification, for Taney had a good legal mind and was a man of conviction.

Taney's chief fault was that on economic matters he faced the future. The first Supreme Court chief to wear trousers instead of knee breeches, he was an obvious threat to the past. It was misleading to judge him by his gentle mien, to which deep-set, collie-like eyes lent an almost melancholy air; his manner was leonine and his purpose was firm. More important, Taney had formulated his position on one of the principal questions of the day, namely the role in society of the corporation which performs public services—what we today would call the public utility. In an opinion written in 1832 as Attorney General, Taney had said that corporations engaged in providing services to the community, such as the building and maintaining of roads and bridges, bore special responsibilities. He explained the bounds of such corporations as he understood them. Charters, he said, can "never be considered as having been granted for the exclusive benefit of the corporators. Certain privileges are given to them, in order to obtain a public convenience; and the interest of the public must, I presume, always be regarded as the main object of every charter for a toll-bridge or a turnpike road."

Like Marshall, a commanding personality, Taney was now going to write *his* economic views into the Constitution and hope to have them prevail in his generation. The Charles River Bridge case could not help but appeal to Taney as the first case he would hear. Not only were its issues made to order, but the impact of the decision would be considerable. Because of the long delay, the case had turned into a festering sore of Massachusetts politics. Indeed, in the half-dozen years since it was first argued, the situation had changed so significantly that further delay was indefensible.

By 1837 the commuters of Boston had put the *Warren* Bridge under attack! Its very success had brought this about. The bridge had paid for itself within two years of its completion, and this had led almost immediately to a general cry that its use be made free immediately. The legislature could not permit this, lest an unfavorable decision by the Supreme Court in the Charles River

Bridge case impose heavy damages and consequent financial liabilities on the Warren Bridge Proprietors.

Annually, therefore, the collection of tolls was extended. In 1835, however, the legislature took from the Proprietors of the Warren Bridge all further interest in the tolls, and it provided that subsequent collections would have to be earmarked to be used exclusively in the maintenance and repair of the bridge, and for "such sums of money as may be recovered by the proprietors of Charles River Bridge in any suit in law or equity." When the Warren Bridge became free of tolls at last in April, 1836, Charlestown held a joyful celebration. Robert Rantoul, the reformer, whose legal arguments and victory on behalf of labor in the case of *Commonwealth v. Hunt* a few years hence established a towering landmark in the history of unionization in America, was publicly thanked for his unceasing efforts, now rewarded. Gloomily, the Proprietors of the Charles River Bridge opened their draw and suspended operations.

The Harvard College Corporation was discomfited thoroughly. With the Warren Bridge free, the annuity from it had ceased to be payable. Furthermore, since the Charles River Bridge stock was now practically valueless, the Proprietors halted the payment of the annuity to which they were pledged.

This was the situation when, at the end of January, 1837, the case was reargued. For the Charles River Bridge the imposing counsel were once again Daniel Webster, the senior Senator from Massachusetts, and Warren Dutton; and for the Warren Bridge, the Proprietors engaged Simon Greenleaf, holder of the Royall Professorship at the Harvard Law School, and John Davis, the junior Senator. It is, perhaps, worth noting that Charles Sumner, destined also to sit in the Senate for Massachusetts and then just turned twenty-six, substituted for Greenleaf at the Harvard Law School in the weeks of Greenleaf's absence in Washington. It is a shining tribute to Harvard that it gave Greenleaf permission to defend the Warren Bridge side of the issue. Greenleaf had inquired simply whether the Harvard Corporation would permit him to engage in the practice of law as his predecessor had. The Harvard authorities, undoubtedly with full knowledge of the nature of the "moonlighting" in which their professor was engaged, gave no indication of that fact in granting him permission to be absent for two weeks "for the purpose of arguing an important cause before the Supreme Court of the United States."

Still sitting like the conscience of old New England, pained but gripped in this hour when Massachusetts men were turned upon one another with the welfare of Harvard and society at stake, was Joseph Story of the class of 1798. He wrote his son in a description of the proceedings:

We have been for a week engaged in hearing the Charles River Bridge cause. It was a glorious argument on all sides, strong and powerful and apt. Mr. Greenleaf spoke with great ability and honored Dane College— Mr. Webster pronounced one of his greatest speeches. Mr. Dutton was full of learning and acute remarks, and so was Governor Davis—"Greek met Greek."

And a few days later Story was writing to Sumner: "On the whole it was a glorious exhibition for old Massachusetts; four of her leading men brought out in the same cause, and none of them inferior to those who are accustomed to the lead here."

The decision, then, could not fail, one way or another, to be a triumph for honorable men. But not, as it turned out, for Harvard. In a powerful decision rendered on February 12, 1837, Taney spoke for the majority of a court split 7-2. He arrayed himself unequivocally on the side of "progress," declaring that grants by state legislatures such as the charter for the Charles River Bridge might not be construed as exclusive unless specifically stated to be so. His language seemed crystal-clear:

The whole community are interested in this inquiry and they have a right to require that the power of promoting their comfort and convenience, and of advancing the public prosperity, by providing safe, convenient, and cheap ways for the transportation of produce and the purposes of travel, shall not be construed to have been surrendered or diminished by the state unless it shall appear by plain words that it was intended to be done.

And what, he asked, would happen if the Court took an opposite position and permitted an exclusive right for the Charles River Bridge? In that event, he predicted, America would "find the old turnpike corporations awakening from their sleep and calling upon this court to put down the improvements which have taken their place." The building of canals and railroads would be arrested and the country would have to wait until the old turnpike companies had been satisfied and were ready to permit Americans "to avail themselves of the lights of modern science, and to partake of the benefit of those improvements which are now adding to the wealth and prosperity, and the convenience and comfort, of every other part of the civilized world." Story in his eloquent dissent stood where he had always stood in decrying any "encroachment upon the rights and liberties of the citizens, secured by public grants [of charter rights]. I will not consent to shake their title deeds by any speculative niceties or novelties."

Webster testily predicted that the decision would be overturned. But he proved to be wrong. Instead, as the construction of railroads went forward in the next decades, it became the basis for limiting the rights granted in their charters. The effect on the railways themselves was not always salutary. Ruinous competition often enervated roads financially, and left them with inadequate rolling stock and roadbeds.

Fears, though, that the courts were weakening in their defense of property rights proved completely illusory and foolish. Not so the defense of monopoly. Charles Warren, the distinguished historian of the Supreme Court, regarded the Charles River Bridge case as one of the two (the other being *Gibbons* v. *Ogden*) great antitrust cases of our early national history, creating precedents that have been followed over and over again in our own day.

For a generation the implications of Taney's decision for the Commonwealth of Massachusetts itself continued to reverberate. The Massachusetts Legislature in 1837 appointed a joint committee to examine the question of compensation for the Charles River Bridge Proprietors. There seemed slim likelihood of such indemnification. But in 1841 the issue was resolved with the payment of $25,000 for the surrender to the state of all rights held by the Proprietors. The Charles River Bridge was now opened to travel again, after having been closed for about five years, and a toll was once more charged. The same act of the legislature, moreover, made the Warren Bridge a toll bridge again! And in 1847 the State of Massachusetts compensated Harvard College for the annuities it had lost by awarding it the sum of $3,333.30. Harvard's treasurer recorded: ". . . it is agreeable to see the disposition manifested by the state, once more to do something for education at Cambridge after the lapse of so long an interval in her patronage. . . ."

Tolls on the bridges were removed at the end of 1843. Except for a short time between 1854 and 1858, they remained free ever after. In 1887 the right and title to the Charles River Bridge was transferred to the City of Boston. This opened the way, when the Boston Transit Commission made ready to build a still newer form of transportation—a subway—to demolish the old bridge and build a new one, of steel and stone, called the Charlestown Bridge. Just as the nineteenth century was drawing to a close the last of the Charles River Bridge was hauled away, victim of disrespectful demolition crews and the cruel passage of time. Yet in its fashion it still stands, a shining and indestructible monument to the dogged struggle between property rights and human needs that once assailed the New England conscience.

# The Dred Scott Case VI

BY BRUCE CATTON

(*Dred Scott* v. *Sandford*, 19 Howard 393)

*Constitutional questions relating to the rights of Negroes began to attract the attention of American courts as early as the era of the American Revolution. In the early 1780's, a Massachusetts man, Nathaniel Jennings, was indicted for attacking a Negro, Quock Walker. His defense was that Walker was his slave, but the Massachusetts Supreme Court ruled (1783) that "slavery is inconsistent with our . . . [State] Constitution," thus effectively abolishing the institution in the Commonwealth. Other Northern courts followed this Massachusetts precedent.*

*However, the federal Constitution recognized the "peculiar institution" as a matter for state control and in Article IV included an authorization for a national Fugitive Slave Law. Congress passed such a law in 1793. In the case of* Prigg v. *Pennsylvania (1842), the Supreme Court upheld the constitutionality of this act, and eight years later, as part of the Compromise of 1850, Congress passed a very stringent Fugitive Slave Act which denied jury trials to accused fugitives apprehended in free states.*

*A still more important constitutional question was that of the power of Congress to regulate slavery in the territories. For decades this power was assumed. The Ordinance of 1787 banned the institution from the old Northwest Territory, and the Missouri Compromise of 1820 outlawed it in the Louisiana Territory north of 36 degrees, 30 minutes North Latitude, except for the State of Missouri. Some Southerners, however, most notably John C. Calhoun of South Carolina, argued that Congress was bound by the Constitution to maintain slavery in the territories, since its abolition in these regions discriminated against one class of citizens, those who owned property in the form of slaves. Of course, nearly all Northerners objected violently to this doctrine. The Supreme Court took it upon itself to settle this argument in the case described by Bruce Catton, author of* The Centennial History of the Civil War *and many other well-known books on the period.*

Dred Scott was nobody in particular. A slave born of slave parents, unable to read or write, physically frail, he was a man without energy, who for a full decade drifted about in St. Louis as an errand boy and general odd-jobs factotum, an unremarkable bondsman on whom the burden of servitude rested rather lightly. Nobody directly concerned with him wanted him as a slave. As a chattel he was a liability rather than an asset, and in any case his various owners seem to have been antislavery people. Yet his unsuccessful legal battle to become free left an enduring shadow on the history of the United States and was an important factor in the coming of the Civil War.

He is remembered because in March, 1857, the Supreme Court of the United States handed down its decision in the case of *Dred Scott* v. *Sandford.* (That last name, by the way, was misspelled and should be Sanford: one minor mistake in a case clouded by larger errors.) The Chief Justice asserted that Scott and all men like him neither were nor ever could be citizens. This ruling was upset a few years later by marching armies, at the cost of much bloodshed, but the reversal came too late to be of any help to Dred Scott because he died before the Civil War began.

It is hard to feel that Scott was the prime mover in this momentous case that shook the entire nation. He unquestionably wanted very much to be free, and as his struggle progressed he appears to have enjoyed the backhanded sort of fame which it brought to him, but his part was chiefly that of a pawn. He was a counter played in a tense and ominous game, and the fact that this particular counter was played just when and as it was played was one of the reasons why the game at last broke up in a furious fight. Yet the whole of it touched Scott himself only indirectly.

Dred Scott was born in Southampton County, Virginia, somewhere around 1795, the property of a man named Peter Blow. In 1827, Blow moved to St. Louis, taking his family and his chattels with him. Four years later Peter Blow died, and Scott became the property of Blow's daughter Elizabeth, who in 1833 sold him to Dr. John Emerson, an army surgeon. In 1834 Dr. Emerson was transferred to duty at Rock Island, Illinois, and some time after that he was transferred again to Fort Snelling, which lay farther up the Mississippi River in what was then Wisconsin Territory. Dr. Emerson took Scott with him as a body servant during all of this time, so that for approximately five years Scott lived on free soil. At the end of 1838 Dr. Emerson returned to St. Louis, taking Scott along, and soon after this Dr. Emerson died, leaving Scott to his widow, Mrs. Irene Sanford Emerson.

For some time Mrs. Emerson did what many slaveowners did in those days—hired her chattel out to various families who needed servants. Then, in the mid-1840's, she moved to New York, and she did not take Dred Scott with her. Instead, she left him in St. Louis in the charge of the two sons of Scott's original owner, Henry and Taylor Blow. It was at about this time that the seeds of what was to become one of America's most famous court cases were planted.

Henry Blow was then in his thirties, a lawyer and businessman of some wealth and prominence. He was head of a railroad, active in developing lead-mining properties in southwestern Missouri; active also in the Whig party, beginning to be known as an opponent of the extension of slavery. (A few years later Henry Blow helped organize the Free-Soil movement in Missouri, and eventually he became a Republican.) As an antislavery man, Blow wanted Scott freed, and in 1846 he helped finance a suit in the Missouri courts to have Scott declared free. Scott himself appears to have been a little hazy as to what this was all about, but he willingly signed his mark to the necessary papers, and the lawsuit was on.

At this point it becomes obvious that the real point to this proceeding was not so much to win freedom for Scott personally as to win a legal point in the broad fight against slavery as an institution. Mrs. Emerson obviously did not want to retain Scott as her slave, and she apparently was no believer in slavery—a few years later she became the wife of Calvin Clifford Chaffee, a radical antislavery Congressman from Massachusetts. When she moved to New York she could easily have executed papers of manumission to give Scott his freedom. She did not do that; instead, she left him with the Blows, and when his lawsuit began she was technically the defendant—the case was listed formally as "Scott, a Man of Color, v. Emerson." The case is just a little mysterious, but it seems clear that what everyone wanted was a definite ruling about the status of a slave whose master took him into free territory.

This was beginning to be an important point. The Western country was opening up for settlement, and the law said that north of the Missouri Compromise line of 36 degrees, 30 minutes, the new territory was free soil. Exactly what would happen if a slaveowner took his slaves with him when he moved into such territory?

Lawyers for Dred Scott argued that his five-year sojourn on free soil had ended his bondage and that on his return to Missouri the state court should make formal declaration of his freedom. The lower court ruled in Scott's favor, but an appeal was taken—what everybody wanted, obviously, was a high-level finding that would stand as some sort of landmark—and the State Supreme Court eventually reversed the lower court, holding that Missouri law still applied and that Scott, as a resident of Missouri, must remain a slave.

The law's delays were as notorious then as they are now, and the case dragged on for six years; the ruling of the State Supreme Court was not handed down until 1852. During this time Scott remained under the nominal control of the county sheriff, who hired him out here and there for five dollars a month. Scott was in limbo, everybody's slave and nobody's slave; if he had any thoughts about this interminable process of determining his future, they were never recorded.

Meanwhile, things had been happening—not to Scott, but to the country that countenanced the institution that held him in slavery. The Mexican War had been fought and won, and the United States came into possession of a vast new area running all the way to the golden shores of California, one of the immediate results being that the whole slavery controversy became a dominant issue in national politics. Until now there had been a slightly unstable equilibrium, with the Missouri Compromise decreeing that new territories created from Louisiana Purchase lands lying north of the line that marked the southern boundary of Missouri should be free soil. This equilibrium vanished when the immense acquisitions of the Mexican War made it obvious that sooner or later many new states would be created, and the issue was pointed up when Congressman

David Wilmot of Pennsylvania unsuccessfully tried to get Congress to pass a law providing that slavery be excluded from all the land that had been taken from Mexico. The question of slavery in the territories, by the early 1850's, had become the great, engrossing question in American politics.

It became important because the way this issue was settled would determine whether the institution of slavery could continue to expand or must be limited to the areas where it already existed. On the surface, it might seem to make very little difference to a planter in Alabama or a farmer in Ohio whether slaves could or could not be held in some such faraway place as New Mexico; actually, the future of slavery itself was at stake, and everybody knew it.

The Compromise of 1850 brought a temporary easing of the tension. Under this arrangement, California came in as a free state, a stronger Fugitive Slave Law was enacted, and it was agreed that when new territories were organized out of the empty lands that had been taken from Mexico the inhabitants of those territories would themselves decide whether slavery was to be permitted or prohibited. This was the famous principle of popular sovereignty; it looked like a fair, democratic way to settle things, and for a short time the nation relaxed.

It did not relax very long. Senator Stephen A. Douglas of Illinois in 1854 brought in his Kansas-Nebraska Act, a measure to organize the new territories of Kansas and Nebraska. This area had been acquired through the Louisiana Purchase, and it lay north of the Missouri Compromise line of 36 degrees, 30 minutes, and hence these territories must be free soil. But Douglas was a Democrat, in a Democratic Congress, and the Democratic party was largely dominated by Southerners, who were most unlikely to consent to the creation of two new free territories which would presently become free states. So Douglas, a firm believer in the principle of popular sovereignty, decided to extend that principle to Kansas and Nebraska. His act, which passed Congress after most heated debate, wiped out the Missouri Compromise line and provided that the settlers of Kansas and Nebraska could say whether slavery might exist there. Meanwhile, slaveowners and their chattels were free to move in.

When he introduced this bill Douglas commented that it would "raise [a] hell of a storm." He was entirely right. It did; and the slavery controversy returned to the center of the stage, never to leave it until the papers were signed at Appomattox Courthouse.

Of all of this Dred Scott knew nothing. He continued to shift back and forth on the little jobs for which he was now and then farmed out, totally unaware of the new currents that were swirling about him. But he suddenly became an important person because of that old lawsuit. Missouri slaveowners were moving into Kansas, taking their slaves with them; antislavery people from the North were also moving in, taking their antislavery convictions with them; and there were bitter clashes, with gunfire and bloodshed to focus national attention on the situation. The old question about the status of a slave whose owner took him into an area which the old Missouri Compromise called free soil had become a matter of vast consequence.

It was time, in other words, to get a ruling from the Supreme Court of the United States. The original lawsuit was revived, Mrs. Emerson transferred title to Scott to her brother, John F. A. Sanford of New York, and in 1854 the case, now known as *Dred Scott v. Sandford,* got on the docket in the Federal Circuit Court for Missouri.

It was a bit complicated. If Scott was to sue Sanford in a federal court he had to show that he was a citizen of Missouri—that is, a federal case had to involve an action between citizens of different states. Sanford's lawyers argued that as a Negro slave Scott was not a citizen of Missouri and that the federal court therefore lacked jurisdiction. The circuit court eventually ruled that way, and Scott's lawyers took the case to the Supreme Court on a writ of error. In 1856 the Supreme Court heard the arguments.

Bear in mind, again, that what happened to Scott in all of this was of no especial importance to anybody except the man himself. What everybody wanted was a final ruling from the highest court in the land—a finding which (it was innocently hoped) would settle once and for all the disturbing question of slavery in the territories.

Three issues were involved. Was Scott actually a citizen of Missouri and so entitled to sue in a federal court? Did his residence on free soil give him a title to freedom which Missouri was bound to respect? Finally, was the Missouri Compromise itself, which had made Wisconsin Territory free soil, constitutional? (That is, did Congress actually have the power to prohibit slavery in a territory?)

A final ruling on all of these points might have much to do with the question of slavery in Kansas.

So the Supreme Court had been given a very hot potato to handle, and the rising tumult in Kansas made it all the hotter. So did the Presidential election of 1856, in which the new Republican party—a sectional Northern party, dedicated chiefly to the theory that slavery must not be allowed to expand—showed enormous growth and came respectably close to electing John C. Frémont President of the United States. The whole argument over slavery, which was fast becoming too explosive for American political machinery to handle, had come to center on this question of slavery in the territories, and the Dred Scott case brought the question into sharp relief.

The Supreme Court could have avoided most of the thorns in this case simply by declaring that it lacked jurisdiction. A somewhat similar case had been handled so in 1850, and in the beginning most of the justices seem to have been disposed to follow that precedent. Justice Samuel Nelson prepared such an opinion: Missouri law controlled Scott's status, Missouri law said that he was still a slave, and as a slave he could not sue in the federal courts. Yet the pressures were too great for such an easy solution. The justices at last concluded to handle all of the issues. A brief glance at the makeup of the Court is in order.

Of the nine justices, five came from slave states: Chief Justice Roger B. Taney of Maryland, and Justices James M. Wayne of Georgia, John Catron of Tennessee, Peter V. Daniel of Virginia, and John A. Campbell of Alabama. Seven of the nine were Democrats—these five plus two Northerners, Nelson of New York and Robert C. Grier of Pennsylvania. Justice John McLean of Ohio was a Republican, and Justice Benjamin R. Curtis of Massachusetts was a Whig. All nine were men of integrity and repute, but everything considered, it might be hard for them to be completely objective about the issues that were presented to them.

It might be hard; and indeed it proved quite impossible for these men to limit themselves to the basic question about Scott's actual status. They had to say something, not just about one slave, but about all slaves.

To begin with, it soon became apparent that Justices McLean and Curtis were prepared to write dissenting opinions setting forth their views about the Missouri Compromise and the power of Congress to legislate about slavery in the territories. (They held that Scott had properly been made free by his sojourn on free soil, and that Congress had a constitutional right to outlaw slavery in the territories.) If these two dissenters were going to air their views on this latter point, those who disagreed with them would obviously do the same. In addition, many of the justices honestly believed that it was necessary to hand down a broad, definitive ruling that would stand as a landmark, settling the territorial problem once and for all. Finally, Mr. James Buchanan exerted a little pressure of his own.

James Buchanan was elected President in the fall of 1856, and during the following winter—after the arguments had been heard, but before the Court had handed down its opinion—he was composing the address which he would deliver when he took the oath of office on March 4. He was bound to say something about popular sovereignty, and the issue was a tough one for a brand-new President to discuss, especially a President who owed his nomination and election largely to the fact that he had never been directly involved in the furious arguments over the territorial question. It occurred to him that it would be excellent if in his inaugural he could say that the question of Congress' constitutional power to legislate on slavery in the territories would very shortly be decided by the Supreme Court and that all good citizens might well stop agitating the issue and prepare to abide by the Court's ruling.

In February the President-elect wrote a letter to Justice Catron, setting forth his desire to say that the Supreme Court would presently settle this question. A bit later he wrote to Justice Grier in the same vein. Mr. Buchanan, clearly, was skirting the edge of outright impropriety; he was not exactly telling the justices what he wanted the Court to say, but he was making it clear that he wanted the Court to say *something,* and Justice Catron finally assured him that the Court would handle the matter and that Buchanan could safely say that the country ought to wait for its decision.

This Mr. Buchanan proceeded to do. In his inaugural address he remarked that the whole question of legalizing or prohibiting slavery in the territories was "a judicial question, which legitimately belongs to the Supreme Court of the United States, before whom it is now pending and will, it is understood, be speedily and finally settled. To their decision, in common with all good citizens, I shall cheerfully submit, whatever this may be."

This set the stage. Two days later—on March 6, 1857—the Court handed down its decision, the gist of which was that Dred Scott was a slave and not a citizen, and hence could not sue in federal court, and that the Missouri Compromise was unconstitutional because Congress had no power to prohibit slavery in the territories. To these basic findings there were just two dissents, those of Justices McLean and Curtis.

Thus the Supreme Court had (to use a police-court colloquialism) thrown the book at Dred Scott. But the case was most complicated. Each of the nine justices wrote an opinion; and although the majority agreed on the basic findings, they gave different reasons for their beliefs, and some of them remained silent on points which others considered highly important. In effect, the Court went beyond both Scott and the authority of Congress and discussed the whole rationale of slavery and the status of the Negro, and in all of this the sectional and political backgrounds of the Justices were sharply emphasized. As Allan Nevins sums it up in *The Emergence of Lincoln:*

> Three Southern judges declared that no Negro of slave ancestry could be entitled to citizenship; five Southern judges, with Nelson of New York, decided that Dred's status depended upon the laws of Missouri; five Southern judges, with Grier of Pennsylvania, maintained that any law excluding slavery from a territory was unconstitutional; and two Northern judges, McLean and Curtis, held that Dred was a citizen, that Missouri law did not control his status, and that Congress had a constitutional right to pass laws debarring slavery from any territory.

It was Taney's opinion that reverberated across the land like a thunderclap. Not only was Taney the Chief Justice; he was a man of immense prestige and learning, a veteran of Andrew Jackson's famous fight with the Bank of the United States, named Chief Justice by Jackson in 1835 as successor to John Marshall, one of the most impressive figures in American life. Taney was eighty now, shrunken, wispy, with a heavy shock of iron-gray hair framing a deeply lined face. Fires burned in him, but he was physically frail, and as he read his momentous opinion his voice was so low that many of the people in the courtroom could not catch his words. Nevertheless, what he said was heard all across the country.

The Chief Justice addressed himself to the question of the constitutional power of Congress over the territories. It had been argued, he noted, that federal authority over the territories came from a clause permitting Congress to make rules and regulations for the government of the territories; but this, he held, was a mere emergency provision applying only to the lands ceded to the Confederation by the original states and did not apply to lands acquired after 1789. Properly, Congress had only those powers associated with the right to acquire territory and prepare it for statehood; it had no internal police authority, and while it might organize local territorial government it could not "infringe upon local rights of person or rights of property."

The right to hold slaves was a property right; since Congress could not interfere with a man's property rights, it could not prohibit slavery in the territories: "And no word can be found in the Constitution which gives Congress a greater power over slave property, or which entitles property of that kind to less protection, than property of any other description." To exclude slavery would violate the due-process clause of the Fifth Amendment. Congress had nothing more than the power—"coupled with the duty"—to protect the owner in his property rights. Thus all territorial restrictions on slavery were dead.

Therefore the Missouri Compromise was unconstitutional. Its provision prohibiting slavery north of the 36 degree, 30 minute line was "not warranted by the Constitution" and thus void. It was idle to argue that Dred Scott's residence on free soil had made him a free man, because slavery had not lawfully been excluded from Wisconsin Territory in the first place.

But that was not all. As a Negro of slave origins (said Taney) Scott could not be a citizen of the United States anyway. He and all people like him were simply ineligible. The Founding Fathers who wrote the Declaration of Independence and framed the Constitution had been thinking only of white men. At the time the Constitution was adopted, and for a long time before that, there was general agreement that Negroes were "beings of an inferior order, and altogether unfit to associate with the white race, either in social or political relations; and so far inferior that they had no rights which the white man was bound to respect."

It is clear enough now that in making this remark the Chief

Justice was in no sense laying down a rule of law for his own day; he was simply expressing what he believed was the prevailing opinion of Americans in the latter part of the eighteenth century. But his use of these words, embedded in an opinion which antislavery people were going to object to in any case, was in the highest degree unfortunate. To many people in the North it seemed that the Chief Justice had officially declared that the colored man had no rights which the white man was bound to respect. President Buchanan's pious hope that all good citizens would willingly accept the Court's finding in the Dred Scott case was bound to run onto this reef if on no other.

Only two other justices, Wayne and Daniel, joined with Taney in the opinion that no Negro could be a citizen. Justices Curtis and McLean dissented vigorously, and the remainder kept silent on this particular question. This made very little difference. The Missouri Compromise was unconstitutional—the first act of Congress to be declared unconstitutional since the famous *Marbury* v. *Madison* case in 1803—and Dred Scott was still a slave; the net effect of the decision was to give an immense impetus to the furious arguments over slavery and to help materially to make this issue so acute and so emotion-laden that it became too explosive for political settlement.

To the rising Republican party the ruling was a challenge to renewed struggle. This party was dedicated to the conviction that slavery must not be allowed to expand; now the High Court was formally saying that there was no legal way by which it could be excluded from the territories. Congress could not do it; a territorial legislature, as a creature of Congress, could not do it either. Only when the people of a territory drafted a constitution and prepared to enter the Union as a state could they adopt an effective antislavery law. To many Northerners it seemed that, logically, the next step would be for the Court to declare that no state could outlaw slavery and that the institution must be legalized all across the country.

Free-soil adherents in the North promptly accepted the challenge which they found implicit in the decision. They expressed profound contempt for the Court itself, asserting that it was wholly biased in favor of the Southern sectional interest and that its decision in the Dred Scott case had no moral substance and could not be permanently binding. For the moment, to be sure, the ruling was legally valid, but in effect the antislavery people of the North defied the Court. Instead of taking the territorial issue out of politics, the Court had put itself squarely and disastrously into politics. Never before had there been such a deep and widespread revulsion against a finding of the nation's highest judicial tribunal.

To the Northern wing of the Democratic party—the wing that followed Senator Douglas—the ruling was equally disturbing, because it knocked the props out from under the doctrine of popular sovereignty. Douglas, to be sure, defended the Court against Republican criticism, declaring that "whoever resists the final decision of the highest judicial tribunal aims a deadly blow at our whole republican system of government," and expressed the conviction that the decision must not be made a political issue. But he was breaking with the Buchanan administration on the Kansas issue—the administration was accepting a rigged election which would give Kansas a constitution permitting slavery even though a majority of the voters obviously were antislavery. Douglas was fighting hard for popular sovereignty, and the Dred Scott decision simply accentuated this issue by driving the Northern and Southern wings of the Democratic party farther and farther apart.

For while the Douglas Democrats in the North continued to rely on popular sovereignty as the answer to the territorial problem, the Southern Democrats were led by this decision to press forward in complete opposition to popular sovereignty. Now they demanded positive protection of the slaveowner's right to take his chattels with him when he moved into a territory. The decision said that nobody could outlaw slavery in a territory; the Southerners felt it was only logical that the federal government act to protect slavery there by formal legislation. The Northern and Southern wings of the party could never agree on any such formula. In substance, the Court's decision was a weighty factor in determining that no Democrat who had any chance to carry the North could also carry the South, which meant that the Presidential election of 1860 would be won by the Republicans, after which the discordant sections would find themselves at the parting of the ways. The irreconcilable sectionalism which would bring the country to civil war was accentuated by this ruling of the High Court.

Perhaps the real trouble with the decision was that the general trend of events was moving in the other direction. The New York *Herald,* on March 9, 1857, summed it up:

The Washington politicians who believe that it [the Dred Scott decision] settles anything must be afflicted with very severe ophthalmia indeed. For while these venerable judges are discoursing on theoretical expansions of slavery to North and West, free labor is marching with a very tangible step into the heart of the strongest slaveholds of slavery. Chief Justice Taney lays out on paper an infinitude of new slave states and territories; he makes all the states in a measure slave states; but while the old gentleman is thus diverting his slippered leisure, free carpenters and blacksmiths and farmers with hoe, spade and plough are invading Missouri, Kentucky, Delaware, Maryland and Virginia, and quietly elbowing the slaves further South. It will take a good many Supreme Court decisions to reverse a law of nature such as we here see in operation.

All in all, the Dred Scott decision did the Court profound and lasting harm. Many years later Chief Justice Charles Evans Hughes remarked that it was a case in which the Court suffered from a self-inflicted wound, and characterized the ruling as a "public calamity." More than a century after the decision was handed down, a historian of the Court wrote of it as a "monumental indiscretion." The Court's prestige suffered immensely, and Justice Felix Frankfurter once remarked that after the Civil War justices of the Supreme Court never mentioned the Dred Scott case, any more than a family in which a son had been hanged mentioned ropes and scaffolds.

In the end, the profound majority of people in the North, who, regardless of party labels, believed that slavery's expansion into the territories must be checked, agreed that while the Court's finding was binding it must eventually be reversed. A new administration would give the Court new justices and a new background, and in the course of time it would be shown that a nation whose majority did not want slavery to expand would be able to make its wish good. There was just one point on which Republicans, Northern Democrats, and Southern Democrats all agreed: Dred Scott was still a slave.

Their legal efforts to have him declared free having failed, Dred Scott's owners manumitted him a few weeks after the Court's decision. On September 17, 1858, he died, in St. Louis, of tuberculosis. Henry Blow paid his funeral expenses.

# The Case of the Copperhead Conspirator

BY ALLAN NEVINS

(*ex parte Milligan*, 4 Wallace 2)

*In a sense the Civil War represented an attempt by the Southern states to erase the gloss that the Supreme Court had placed upon the Constitution during the first half of the nineteenth century. Secession could be justified legally only by restoring to the states much of the authority that John Marshall's powerful decisions had assigned to the national government. Thus the defeat of the Confederacy permanently established the Marshall view of the Constitution, although it by no means ended the debate over the exact limits of federal and state authority.*

*The war also brought new constitutional issues to the fore, the most important being the power of the government to restrict civil liberties in time of national crisis. Early in the conflict Lincoln authorized the suspension of the writ of habeas corpus under certain circumstances. In May, 1861, a citizen of Baltimore, John Merryman, was arrested and imprisoned by the military without trial or formal charge. He petitioned Chief Justice Taney for a writ ordering his captors to bring him into Federal Circuit Court for a hearing. Taney granted this plea, but the local commander, General George Cadwalader, refused to obey, citing Lincoln's order. Taney then filed an opinion, ex parte Merryman, denying the right of the President to suspend habeas corpus. Only Congress could do this, he argued. However, lacking executive support, Taney was unable to free the prisoner, although eventually Merryman was turned over to the civilian courts and released without being brought to trial.*

*During the remainder of the Civil War practices such as that adopted in the Merryman affair continued to be employed by the military authorities. Taney died in 1864 without ever having been vindicated. But the issue remained. It was finally settled by the case described here by Allan Nevins, Senior Research Fellow at the Henry E. Huntington Library and author of the multi-volumed study,* The Ordeal of the Union.

On an August day in 1835 a group of young men in St. Clairsville, the seat of Belmont County in eastern Ohio, passed the rudimentary examination in law required of them and were admitted to the bar. One was destined to write his name high in the annals of the nation: Edwin McMasters Stanton, later Secretary of War under Lincoln and Andrew Johnson. Another was to take a different road to fame—or infamy; the road of disunion activities and subversive conspiracy that narrowly missed, if it did not reach, treason. His name was Lambdin P. Milligan, and although he is now forgotten by all but students of civil liberties, he was briefly a national celebrity. The paths of Stanton and Milligan were later to cross in dramatic fashion.

Within a dozen years both men removed to new fields, Stanton settling in Pittsburgh and Milligan in Huntington County in northeastern Indiana. Stanton was soon securely established as one of the nation's leading attorneys. For a time Milligan also did well, although handicapped by ill health. Records speak vaguely of spinal meningitis, and when he finally stood military trial he asked for special consideration on the ground of bodily ailment. However, by the time that Stanton won his famous victory in preventing the erection of a bridge over the Ohio at Wheeling as certain to obstruct Pennsylvania steamboats, Milligan was one of the more distinguished Indiana lawyers. He was interested in railroad promotion, and the scrappy, uncertain accounts of his antebellum years indicate that he was counsel for short Indiana lines later incorporated in the Wabash and Erie systems.

In the 1850's, if not before, Milligan began to cherish political ambitions. He was a zealous Democrat, an admirer of Thomas Jefferson and in lesser degree Andrew Jackson, and a fervent states' rights man. He brought to politics certain gifts. He was generously hospitable, giving dinners to fellow attorneys, railroad men, and politicians all the way from Fort Wayne to Indianapolis. He was an interesting conversationalist, entertaining hearers by his wit, legal lore, and anecdotes of party leaders. A devout Catholic, he was a man of integrity and principle. But it is plain from the cloudy facts preserved upon him that as the Civil War approached he became grimly fanatical. Indiana had been settled largely by Southerners descending the Ohio or crossing from Kentucky, and part of it was a hotbed of Southern feeling. All Milligan's sympathies lay with the South, and with the measures of Franklin Pierce and James Buchanan friendly to slave-state interests. He did not carry his predilections as far as Jesse D. Bright, the Indiana leader who owned slaves on Kentucky soil and was expelled from the Senate in 1861 for writing Confederate President Jefferson Davis a letter recommending a friend for employment. But he carried them as far as the demagogue Daniel Voorhees, "the tall sycamore of the Wabash," who would cheerfully have made Kansas the fifteenth slave state, and was willing to accept secession; in fact, a good deal further.

Nobody ever thought Milligan a great or important man. He and his friends hoped in 1864 that he might be nominated for governor, but he was not of sufficient caliber. He was merely a disturbing zealot, a rider of the wave of sectional passion. It is not the man who merits attention, but the terribly perilous situation which, in the midst of the Civil War, created the dramatic case of which he was the center.

I

The fierce conflict between North and South no sooner gained headway, straining the old-time fealties of countless men, than the government in Washington had to meet two crucial questions: How should the nation be safeguarded against traitors? And just what should be regarded as treasonable conduct? Inevitably, radical opinion on these issues differed from conservative opinion as night from day.

After four months of Lincoln's administration, declared the New York *Daily News* on July 1, 1861, civil liberties were prostrate. The sacred privilege of habeas corpus had been thrust aside; homes were illegally entered and searched; the private papers of citizens were seized without warrant; men were arrested without legal process, and held behind bars without a hearing. "Almost every right which American citizens have been taught to consider sacred and inalienable," this proslavery daily asserted, "has been trampled upon by Mr. Lincoln and his Administration." Yet at the same time some Republican editors, some members of Congress, and many military commanders believed that the government was grossly negligent in ferreting out traitors and that its mildness imperiled the life of the Republic.

Late in April, 1861, Lincoln had authorized General Winfield Scott to suspend the writ of habeas corpus in the communications zone between Philadelphia and Washington, and Scott had deputed this power to his principal subordinates. Military arrests began immediately. The Constitution provided that the writ might be suspended if, in time of rebellion or invasion, the public safety demanded it. A few dim precedents existed. During the Revolution the Pennsylvania authorities had suspended the writ, and in 1815 Andrew Jackson had put New Orleans under martial law and arrested a judge who tried to intervene. Lincoln believed that he rather than Congress had the power and boldly exercised it. He had to deal promptly with men trying to stop the vital movement of troops from the north to the capital, and majority opinion in the critical weeks after Sumter upheld him.

In due course Lincoln made his theoretical approach to the field of disloyalty, martial arrests, and civil liberties perfectly clear. He felt a tremendous anxiety for the safety of the government he had sworn to protect and uphold. The preservation of the Union seemed to him far more important than the uninterrupted maintenance of privileges and immunities which could later be restored. As he put it, a limb might well be amputated to save a life, but a life ought never to be sacrificed to save a limb. "I felt that measures, otherwise unconstitutional, might become lawful by becoming indispensable to the preservation of the Constitution, through the preservation of the nation."[1] As a broad guiding rule, most people in the North apparently (we cannot be sure) regarded his statement

---

[1] According to one member of his Cabinet, Lincoln's difficulty was his inability to administer this policy effectively. "The President . . . wishes well to his country, but lacks the faculty of control, the *will* to punish the abuses of his power, which, rampant and unrebuked, are rapidly bringing him and this good cause to sorrow and shame." Edward Bates to James O. Broadhead, August 13, 1864.

as sound. They were willing to let the military authorities arrest suspected traitors in an endangered area, throw them into jail, and hold them behind bars until the danger was past.

Nevertheless, so deeply ingrained in Americans was their attachment to the principles of civil liberty as laid down by Magna Carta and subsequent Anglo-American declarations that the first military arrests aroused deep uneasiness. The imprisonment of heads of the Baltimore police force, secessionist members of the Maryland Legislature, and others troubled thoughtful observers. For one reason, some of the officers who ordered arrests were mere whippersnappers; one a major of New York militia, another a militia captain. For another reason, the grounds offered were often weak; General Banks, in immuring the Baltimore police commissioners, merely alleged that they entertained "some purpose not known to the government" but supposedly inimical to its safety. Senator Pearce of Maryland declared in July, 1861, that citizens had been imprisoned "upon intimations conveyed by base and unprincipled men, who, to gratify private malignity and personal or political hostility, have rendered persons far more respectable than themselves, and quite as loyal too, the victims of this tyrannous oppression." At the same time, officers like Ben Butler, one of the first to lead national troops through Maryland, thought the government all too gentle.

When Congress met at Lincoln's call just before Bull Run, the debate showed how sensitive and difficult was the issue. Senator Pearce questioned not the suspension of the habeas corpus but the unguarded nature of the step, and the more arbitrary of the acts committed under its shelter. He recalled how reluctant Great Britain had been to use martial law in the Jacobite revolts of 1715 and 1745 and the stormiest period of the French wars, and how carefully the British Government had limited the period during which persons arrested for treason might be held without bail or mainprise. When the Senate Judiciary Committee proposed a bill to authorize, define, and regulate the use of martial law, angry comment came from two quarters, its proponents and opponents.

Everybody agreed that in suppressing rebellion the military authorities needed large powers in imperiled districts, and would certainly take them; no general would let his forces be hamstrung. But to define these powers was a difficult matter. Some feared the definition would not go far enough; others that it would go too far. Senator Edgar Cowan of Pennsylvania saw "difficulty environing us everywhere." Senator Lyman Trumbull of Illinois pleaded eloquently for a cautious measure as a safeguard. "I think that the idea that the rights of the citizen are to be trampled upon, and that he is to be arrested by military authority, without any regulation by law whatever, is monstrous in a free government," he said. Conservative members pointed out that loyal and disloyal men were inextricably mingled in some communities, and that suspicion often fell upon the wrong persons. Radicals argued for severity because loyalty oaths meant nothing to scoundrels, and because in some places military tribunals would be more trustworthy than the civil courts.

In the end Congress dropped the Judiciary Committee bill. It contented itself with passing a mild Conspiracies Act, punishing any plot to overthrow the government or levy war against it by a fine not exceeding $5,000 and imprisonment for not more than six years. Trumbull, a staunch defender of civil liberties, urged its passage. Eight border Senators, however, signed a protest declaring that its vagueness as to indictments and evidence offered a dangerous latitude to improper prosecutions. The sphere of military control remained vaguely defined, primarily because some Congressmen wanted a broad grant of powers, while others insisted upon a very narrow delimitation. The sequel of this failure to set clear bounds around the authority of the government and army to deal with alleged disloyalists offers one of the unfortunate chapters of wartime history.

## II

Arbitrary arrests became a commonplace of Northern life. Not only did no plain law exist; the administration made matters worse by failing to create a careful, well-organized, and responsible machinery for operating in the twilight zone. The Justice Department could not assume the task, partly because Attorney General Edward Bates was too old, slow, and erratic, and partly because he was outspokenly hostile to military arrests. ("I am resolved," Bates wrote in 1864, "that the records of my office shall bear testimony that at least *one* member of the Government did, sometime, resist capricious power and the arbitrary domination of armed forces.") Lincoln at first deputed the labor to William H. Seward. The Secretary of State was able, prompt, and shrewd, but he had all he could really manage in conducting foreign affairs, and was often distressingly casual, circuitous, and flippant in his methods. History will never forget his remark that whenever he wanted an offender seized, he tapped a little bell on his desk, and the man was soon in durance. As the complexity of the problem of disloyalty increased, and Seward found the burden insupportable, Lincoln took advantage of the appointment of Stanton to the War Department early in 1862 to hand him the responsibility. This was by executive order on February 14, 1862.

Theoretically, much could be said for giving the civilian head of the war machine responsibility for military arrests. Practically, however, this transfer of functions was open to grave objections. Of all the members of the Cabinet Stanton had the least judicial mind, and was the most prone to violent and unfair acts. His handling of the lamentable case of Brigadier General Charles P. Stone at once illustrated his worst qualities. Congressional radicals who controlled the Committee on the Conduct of the War mistakenly held Stone responsible for the Ball's Bluff disaster of October, 1861, in which more than half of a seventeen-hundred-man Union force was killed or captured in a battle on the Potomac upstream from Washington. Stanton ordered Stone's arrest, kept him in Fort Lafayette for more than six months on charges never specified, gave him no real trial, and finally released him without acquittal. Stone's career was blasted, and he had later to rebuild it under the Egyptian flag. Few grosser breaches of civil liberty in our history can be found than his long and causeless confinement. Other acts by Stanton were equally arbitrary.

The total of arrests continued to grow as 1861 passed into 1862. Meanwhile, few cases—far too few—came into court for a hearing. The situation produced so much irritation that in the session of 1861-62 Lyman Trumbull introduced a resolution calling on the executive to report the total number of alleged disloyalists held in prison, and to state under just what law they had been detained.

Various colleagues expostulated with him. Henry Wilson, chairman of the Senate Committee on Military Affairs, declared that Lincoln had done quite right in making an example of leading subversionists, that "the turning of the doors of Fort Lafayette and Fort Warren on their hinges silenced innumerable traitors in the loyal States." Dixon of Connecticut asserted that if Lincoln and Seward had not seized the dangerous men undermining the federal government, *they* would have been guilty of treason—at any rate, "moral treason."

However, powerful editors ranged themselves on Trumbull's side. William Cullen Bryant of the *Evening Post* denounced methods which savored of the old *lettres de cachet*. "For months we have read of arrests without a single cause of them having been specified." Horace Greeley had a *Tribune* correspondent hand Seward a letter declaring that whenever the government arrested decent citizens without strong reason, "you tear the whole fabric of society." And the editor of the Washington *National Intelligencer* wrote (February 12, 1862): "The neglect to bring a single person to trial when so many have been arrested, does not authorize any very satisfactory inference with regard to the efficiency of the government in ferreting out real traitors, or in preserving the innocent accused from the unlawful detention."

It was to Lincoln's credit that early in 1862, when General McClellan was about to advance upon Richmond and hopes of an early victory ran high, he ordered that all political prisoners in military custody be released upon parole and granted an amnesty for past offenses. Extraordinary arrests by the military authorities would continue; all spies, secret agents, and conspirators whom the Secretary of War regarded as dangerous to the public safety would be taken up and kept in custody. But the old slate was wiped clean. And it was to Stanton's credit that he adopted a sensible course for sifting the great body of prisoners held on various charges, and releasing most of them. He appointed John A. Dix and Edwards Pierrepont as commissioners to examine those held in the New York area and render a quick verdict. Visiting Fort Lafayette and other prisons, by April, 1862, they had practically finished their work. The judge advocate of the Army for the Washington area was empowered to dispose of prisoners arrested in the Federal District and adjacent Virginia. Governor David Tod of Ohio was authorized to use a special agent to investigate cases, with a promise that any prisoner would be released on his recommendation.

Early in 1863, however, after the bloody disaster at Fredericksburg, discontent and disloyalty rose to new heights, and nowhere more threateningly than in the Middle West. Lincoln's Emancipation Proclamation became final on New Year's Day. It not only angered friends of the South, but aroused fears that a host of liberated Negroes would inundate Ohio, Indiana, and Illinois. Losses on Mississippi Valley battlefields were heavy, and Democratic families bore their full share. A great many voters who had supported the struggle while it was simply a national war for the Union took a hostile attitude when it seemed to become a Republican war to destroy slavery, establish a strong central government, and hold the South in subjection.

Nor were very real economic grievances wanting. Astute farmers of the middle West saw plainly that the new high tariffs which enriched industry were injurious to agriculture, for they limited the ability of Europe to buy farm products. Daniel Voorhees delivered resentful speeches in the House on the subject. Western agrarians perceived also that while they suffered from a glut of grain and rising freight and elevator charges, Eastern manufacturers got most of the fat war contracts, and Eastern capitalists pocketed the large profits made by banks and railroad lines.

Naturally a cry for peace went up in many quarters. Early in 1863 the Democratic central committee in Indiana published an address which urged the "great duty of pacification or honorable adjustment," and advocated "compromise." Naturally, too, volunteering sank, and as Army morale declined many soldiers went absent without leave. "Desertions [are] occurring daily, and encouraged at home," wrote General Lew Wallace. Union enthusiasts demanded more arrests. When the impetuous General Burnside took command of the Department of the Ohio (which included Indiana) early in 1863, he issued a general order asserting that he would not tolerate declarations of sympathy for the enemy, or any other form of "express or implied treason." Implied treason was something new to the jurisprudence of English-speaking countries.

The stage was being set for the arrest of the Ohio copperhead

Clement L. Vallandigham—and for the case *ex parte Milligan.* For Milligan was coming under suspicion for his supposed connection with what was later termed the great Northwestern Conspiracy. Beyond doubt a conspiracy to array large groups in the Old Northwest against the war did take form in 1862-63. But how formidable was it?

## III

From the beginning of the war many Southerners had cherished a hope that, once Confederate victories bred a spirit of defeatism in the North, Indiana, Illinois, Missouri, and possibly Iowa would desert the struggle. Some Northern copperheads, sharing the hope, laid plans to realize it. How could this colossal defection be accomplished? By the formation of a Northwestern Confederacy.

"All people will recollect," wrote Stephen A. Douglas' old-time lieutenant, James A. Sheahan, in his Chicago *Post* of July 12, 1864, a paper for war Democrats,

[that the Northwestern Confederacy] was a common topic of conversation in the spring of 1862 among "Northern men of Southern principles," who scouted the idea that Grant would take Vicksburg as they are now pooh-poohing the idea that he will take Richmond. In all the larger cities of the Northwest, and in many of the smaller ones, these Northwestern Confederacy disunionists were bold in avowing and vociferous in advocating the traitorous scheme, whenever it could be done without personal danger. It was even supported in the columns of Mr. Vallandigham's shameless newspaper in this city [Sheahan meant Wilbur F. Storey's Chicago *Times*], and the subject was not allowed to drop until the fall of Vicksburg re-opened the Mississippi, and put an end to all immediate hopes of its realization.

Later it was revived.

Milligan, as a Northerner with Southern principles, violently detested the warlike Governor of Indiana, Oliver P. Morton. He opposed Morton's successful effort in 1861-62 to maintain a state arsenal for supplying Indiana regiments with ammunition. He was outraged by the movement of Grant's troops into Kentucky, and the capture of Forts Henry and Donelson. When Lincoln, in the summer of 1862, after McClellan's failure, called for 300,000 more troops, and Governor Morton worked valiantly to fill Indiana's quota of 31,350 recruits, Milligan did everything in his power to discourage enlistments. The patriotic Indianapolis *Daily Journal* castigated him, along with Voorhees and Thomas A. Hendricks, in burning terms. These seditionists cheered for Jeff Davis, it declared; they gloated over Union losses; they plotted to obstruct volunteering; and while weeping for slavery, they had not a single tear for the death of brave Union boys.

By 1863 government policy was more severe. Liberalized in the first half of 1862, it became stringent during the second half. As successive Northern defeats and the rebirth of fears for the safety of Washington made disloyalty bolder, the administration felt less inclined to take risks. Moreover, the first limping draft law in the summer of 1862 resulted in an ebullition of evasion and resistance which the War Department thought it had to repress by the use of extraordinary powers. Any man who left his community to escape conscription, or encouraged or abetted such evasion, was subject to abrupt military arrest. Public sentiment generally approved the apprehension of "skeedaddlers," forty of whom were caught in a single day at Rouses Point on the Canadian boundary. Yet when a number of prominent Democratic politicians were jailed for their denunciations of the war and administration policy, angry protests arose. Horatio Seymour of New York and Vallandigham of Ohio were particularly vocal.

Lincoln made matters worse by a most unfortunate proclamation of September 24, 1862, announcing that "all Rebels and Insurgents, their aiders and abettors within the United States, and all persons discouraging volunteer enlistments, resisting militia drafts, or guilty of any disloyal practise . . . shall be subject to martial law and liable to trial and punishment by Courts Martial or Military Commission." This was going far, indeed, in overriding the civil courts. Moreover, as it came two days after the Emancipation Proclamation, it seemed to offer a threat of overcoming all opposition to that measure by harsh punitive arrests.

Meanwhile, Milligan's bitter opposition to the war in 1862-63 attracted nearly as much attention in Indiana as Vallandigham's activities in Ohio. General Burnside, determined to punish "Implied treason," had failed in his effort to extend martial law over

Indiana, but federal agents followed Milligan closely, noting his actions, taking down his speeches, and watching for any support he gave to plans for a Northwestern Confederacy. They found evidence, according to subsequent allegations, that on or about October 1, 1863, he conspired with William A. Bowles, Andrew Humphreys, Stephen Horsey, and other Indiana copperheads to overthrow the government, and for this purpose helped organize a secret society, the Order of American Knights, or Order of Sons of Liberty—"erected on the dissolved fragments of the Knights of the Golden Circle," which had become discredited. One conspirator identified by government agents was a Kentuckian, Joshua F. Bullitt, and another a Missourian, J. A. Barrett, suggesting that the group might be formulating a broad Northwestern plan. They met in Indianapolis in complete secrecy.

Federal agents also gathered evidence that about a month later the group distributed arms to various malcontents for resisting the draft. They further alleged that the plotters held another meeting in Indianapolis on or about May 16, 1864, for flagrantly disloyal purposes. This time Milligan, Bowles, and others crossed the line of treason, for they communicated details of their scheme for an armed uprising later in the year to the Confederates, and asked for the cooperation of Confederate forces.

With this evidence in hand, the military authorities took action. They went further than with Vallandigham, whose seizure on flimsy grounds by General Burnside in May, 1863, had caused Lincoln so much embarrassment, and had ended merely in temporary deportation. On October 5, 1864, they arrested Milligan at his home, under orders of General Alvin P. Hovey, commanding in Indiana. Keeping him in close confinement, Hovey brought him on October 21 before a military commission in Indianapolis. This body found him guilty of inciting insurrection and giving aid and comfort to the enemies of the United States, and sentenced him to be hanged on May 19, 1865. Milligan, expert in law, at once petitioned the Federal Circuit Court for the District of Indiana to be discharged from what he termed his unlawful imprisonment; and in due course the case came before the Supreme Court in Washington.

The rigor shown by General Hovey, and the celerity with which the military tribunal imposed a death sentence, owed much to the fact that just before the arrest and trial the so-called Northwestern Conspiracy had come to a head. The plot, as given final form, had fantastic scope. It was nothing less than a plan to use the Sons of Liberty to seize federal and state arsenals in Ohio, Indiana, and Illinois; to release the prisoners of war held in Camp Douglas (Chicago), Camp Morton (Indianapolis), Camp Chase (Columbus, Ohio), and on Johnson's Island in Lake Erie; to arm these prisoners from the arsenals; and after creating terror by arson and pillage, to march against the Union troops in Missouri and Kentucky, where Confederate forces would be ready to lend assistance.

The boldness of the scheme was impressive; but how much support did it have in men and money? Apparently a good deal, for Confederate leaders and Eastern copperheads were actively involved. Jacob Thompson, a Mississippian who had been Secretary of the Interior under Buchanan, C. C. Clay, former Senator from Alabama, and Ben Wood, Congressman from New York, owner of the New York *Daily News* and brother of Fernando Wood, were all participants. The summer of 1864 found this trio in Canada. They hoped that the Northwestern uprising and a New York outbreak akin to the Draft Riots might be timed to occur simultaneously. This fact is revealed in a letter, hitherto unpublished, which Clay sent Jacob Thompson on August 3, 1864, from St. Catherine's in Canada:

I have just parted from Ben Wood, who expected to see you in Toronto. He knows nothing more of our speculations than he knew before meeting me. He had an impression of the storm impending and about to burst in the West, and expressed a willingness to see it and even to help it rage. He says there is a large body of laboring men in New York who can be commanded any day to aid in throwing off the yoke of the tyrant, if they had the arms. He thinks these can easily be obtained. If there be insurrection in the West, a riot in New York would checkmate any effort to suppress it. You will understand without fuller explanation.

Ben Wood was doubtless revolving plans for getting the needed weapons by sacking arms shops and breaking into regimental armories. Thompson was perfecting a pleasant scheme, later put into effect, for setting fires in New York hotels. Money was not a problem, for Clay went on to explain to Thompson that he had plenty from rebel sources. According to federal agents, the Confederacy had supplied half a million dollars.

"Holcombe arranges with me," Clay continued (Judge J. P. Holcombe of Virginia being a Confederate commissioner in Canada),

that we can invest twenty thousand dollars in New York with profit especially to assist the other operation in the West. The former will secure the fruits of the latter. I sent ten thousand dollars to X according to his and Holcombe's understanding with you. I have advanced to Captain C. [John B. Castleman of Kentucky] $250 for the purpose on which you sent him to the Falls. . . . If you see Ben Wood you can confide more than I have done to him, I think, for he is among the staunchest and boldest of our friends.

A full history of this sinister but utterly impracticable Northwestern Conspiracy, of the work of the officers detailed from the Southern Army to assist it—Colonel St. Leger Grenfell and Captain T. H. Hines being the chief—of the attempts to capture the U.S.S. *Michigan,* a little vessel of eighteen guns stationed on Lake Erie, and of the gathering of desperate men in Chicago, would require more space than it is worth; for it all came to naught. General Basil W. Duke declared later that "visionary and desperate" as the scheme appeared, "it was in reality very nearly the last hope the South had of prolonging the war." Grant's hammer blows in Virginia were plainly bringing the conflict close to its end. The conspirators' plan was to time the outbreak for the Democratic National Convention meeting in Chicago the last week in August, 1864.

"August 28th," writes the author of a sensational account of the conspiracy, "dawned upon at least a hundred thousand strangers in Chicago, both gentlemen of the Convention and the ruffians of the Sons of Liberty." Their numbers had been swollen by fugitives from the draft. Some were well armed, a few even possessing muskets. Weapons for at least ten thousand men, according to another sensational record, had been smuggled into the city. But Colonel B. J. Sweet, commandant at Camp Douglas, had obtained ample warning of the plot, and was watching suspicious characters like a sharp-taloned hawk. Guards at the camp and garrisons elsewhere in the Northwest had been reinforced. As the Sons waited for orders, word reached their leaders that a government agent, Felix G. Stidger, had wormed his way into the central recesses of the Sons of Liberty, obtained full particulars of their designs, and carried them to Union headquarters. They saw at once that the game was up. While the Democratic Convention still continued, they told their followers that the precaution of the military authorities made any attack impossible.

The frustrated Sons hastily left Chicago, some for home, some for Canada, and some for the border states, but all uttering threats of vengeance. Colonel Grenfell and a few others remained in the city, totally impotent. The Northwestern Conspiracy, in which Milligan was undoubtedly implicated—though nobody knows how far—had proved an utter fiasco. But as the press learned a good deal about it, while army officers knew more, it had an influence on the stern action of the military commission which condemned Milligan and two others to death. Fortunately for Milligan, the war ended before the date of his execution. After Lincoln's assassination, President Andrew Johnson first respited him, and then commuted his sentence to life imprisonment.

## IV

The issue which came before the Supreme Court in April, 1866, in *ex parte Milligan,* was simple. It was the question whether the government had the power, in an area free from invasion or rebellion, and not a theater of military operations—an area where the civil courts were in full discharge of their duties—to suspend the constitutional immunities of a citizen, and consign him to a military commission for arrest, trial, and sentence. The guilt or innocence of Milligan was not in question. What was challenged was the right of a military commission, deriving its powers entirely from martial law, to try and punish him. Lincoln had declared in his proclamation of September 24, 1862, that all insurgents with their aiders and abettors should be subject to martial law. Was this declaration valid in places where ordinary grand jury presentments and jury trials were still available, or was it valid only where this system of justice was paralyzed?

Four distinguished men, James A. Garfield, Jeremiah S. Black, Joseph Ewing McDonald, and David Dudley Field, appeared for Milligan. The logical force and eloquence of their pleas, the interest of the precedents they cited, and the far-reaching import of the Court's decision, combined to make the case one of the most memorable in our history. Milligan's personal record, however heinous, could be set aside. The all-important question was the nature of the line to be drawn around the powers of government in internal war, and the limits of the line protecting civil liberties. In the published proceedings, the opening plea of the government attorneys, James Speed, Henry Stanbery, and Benjamin F. Butler, occupies less than eight pages. The plea of Garfield, however, fills twenty-seven pages, that of Black twenty-six, and that of Field sixty pages. Ben Butler then made a reply of fourteen pages.

The weight as well as the volume of the arguments was heavily against the government. Field showed that when the military trial began, no known enemy in arms could be found in the State of Indiana; none within hundreds of miles. He showed that on the day set for Milligan's execution as an act of military necessity, Confederate resistance had ceased, and all was submission from the Rio Grande to Katahdin. Black recalled that when Washington called out troops to quell the Whiskey Rebellion, he never thought of suspending constitutional guarantees in Pennsylvania. The court was reminded that liberal members of the House of Representatives, late in the war, had attached to an appropriation bill an amendment declaring that, except for military personnel or alleged spies, "no person shall be tried by court-martial or military commission in any State or Territory where the courts of the United States are open," and when Congressmen objected, these liberals defeated the appropriation rather than recede.

Particularly telling were the precedents from Anglo-American history which Garfield cited. He showed that in 1745 a Lieutenant Frye serving on the British warship *Oxford* in the West Indies was ordered by his superior to arrest another officer; but doubting the legality of the action, he demanded a written directive. For this he was himself arrested and tried by a naval court which sentenced him to fifteen years' imprisonment and debarred him forever from the royal service. He at once brought an action in a civil court in England against the president of the naval tribunal. This court awarded him one thousand pounds for illegal detention and sentence, and informed him that he might arrest and sue *any* member of the naval tribunal. The incensed Frye promptly had two more members arrested.

At this, fifteen naval officers headed by a rear admiral met and formally declared it a gross insult to the British Navy that any civil officer, however highly placed, should cause the arrest of a naval officer for any of his official acts. Thereupon Lord Chief Justice Willes had all fifteen men arrested and brought before him. Despite their efforts to enlist the King, this courageous judge persevered so energetically in his determination to maintain the supremacy of the civil authority that after two months' examination the fifteen signed a humble letter of apology. This letter the Lord Chief Justice placed in the Remembrance Office "as a memorial to the present and future ages, that whoever set themselves up in opposition to the laws, or think themselves above the law, will in the end find themselves mistaken."

Still more impressive, as cited by Garfield, was the case of Governor Joseph Wall of the African colony of Goree. In 1782 the brutal Wall, suspecting that the garrison was about to mutiny, assembled five hundred British soldiers on parade, held a hasty consultation with some officers, and ordered Private Benjamin Armstrong, a supposed ringleader, seized, stripped, tied to an artillery wheel, and given eight hundred lashes with a one-inch rope. Armstrong died. Some years later Governor Wall was brought before the most august civil tribunal in England to answer for the murder of the poor private. Three eminent jurists listened to the pleas. Wall's counsel argued that as governor and military commander at Goree he held the power of life and death in time of mutiny, and was the sole judge of the necessities of the case. After a patient hearing, the jurists decisively vindicated the supremacy of the civil system of justice. They found Wall guilty of murder, sentenced him to death, and saw that he was executed.

The decision of the majority of the Supreme Court in *ex parte Milligan,* as read by Chief Justice Chase on April 3, 1866, was decisive. It declared that since the civil courts had been open in Indiana, and the state far removed from the battlefront, the military commission had possessed no legal jurisdiction for trying and sentencing Lambdin P. Milligan. Of course, no judicious person had any sympathy with the zealot who had apparently wished to see the Confederacy triumph, the Union riven asunder, and the institution of slavery preserved. He (like many others) had been severely penalized, by his long illegal imprisonment while the

Supreme Court was waiting to rule on the constitutionality of military arrests and trials; but in view of the impediments he had offered the prosecution of the war, he got off rather lightly. He had a certain compensation, too, in the immortality he received in the lawbooks and constitutional histories; in the fact that, as Chief Justice Warren declared in 1962, his case was a landmark which firmly established the principle that "when civil courts are open and operating, resort to military tribunals for the prosecution of civilians is impermissible."

Many observers then and later believed with John W. Burgess of Columbia University that the decision drew too rigid a line around the powers of the government in dealing with disloyalty in time of war or civil commotion. Radical leaders in Reconstruction days hotly denounced it. "That decision," said Thaddeus Stevens on January 3, 1867, "although in terms not as infamous as the Dred Scott decision, is yet far more dangerous in its operation upon the lives and liberties of the loyal men of this country." His view was that only military tribunals could protect carpetbaggers and Negroes against seditious enemies of the national government in some parts of the South. In the First Reconstruction Act of 1867, Congress provided for military jurisdiction and for trial by military commissions of the precise kind that the Milligan decision had stigmatized as illegal. Although such trials were clearly unconstitutional, efforts to prevent the enforcement of the military provisions by injunction suits broke down when the Supreme Court, intimidated by Congress, dismissed the suits as outside its competence.

But the Milligan decision nevertheless represented a great triumph for the civil liberties of Americans in time of war or internal dissension. The cautious Supreme Court might temporarily sidestep its implications, but it stood. No less respected a historian than William A. Dunning declared that Lincoln's proclamation of September 12, 1862, upon martial law and military arrests had offered "a perfect platform for a military depotism." So it had; and although Lincoln was the last man in the world to make himself such a despot, he might conceivably have a successor some day who, unless a clear line were drawn, would permit the erection of a martial autocracy. The line was now emphatically delineated. The Supreme Court established the rule that, no matter how grave the emergency, and no matter how high the public excitement, the civil authority is supreme over military authority; that wherever such civil authority is established and its ordinary judicial procedures are operating, its protections of the citizen shall remain absolute and unquestionable. The heart of this decision is the heart of the difference between the United States of America and Nazi Germany or Communist Russia.

# The Case of the Unscrupulous Warehouseman

VIII

BY C. PETER MAGRATH

(*Munn v. Illinois,* 94 U.S. 113)

*American businessmen have never opposed government activity in the economic area per se. Indeed, ever since Hamilton's day "propertied" interests have looked to the government for aid, advocating protective tariffs, land grants for railroads, and other forms of assistance. However, as the economy grew more complex, the need for government regulation of some aspects of the economy became manifest, and this businessmen have been far less eager to accept. Inevitably, their resistance to regulation brought constitutional questions to the fore. What were the limits of the government's power to control economic development? Professor C. Peter Magrath of the Political Science Department of Brown University discusses the controversy which more than any other provided an answer to this question. Professor Magrath is the author of a biography of Chief Justice Morrison R. Waite, whose Court decided this important case.*

One fine November day in 1848 a railroad locomotive christened the "Pioneer" chugged westward out of Chicago a distance of eight miles. It pulled only a single coach, a baggage car temporarily outfitted to carry a handful of prominent Chicagoans being treated to one of the first runs of the Galena & Chicago Union Railroad. Spotting a farmer driving an oxen wagon filled with wheat and hides toward Chicago, two of the passengers purchased the goods and transferred them to the baggage car. The train then returned to its home city. This simple event foreshadowed the future course of Chicago's development: within twenty years the modest railroad comprising ten miles of track became the giant Chicago & North Western, one of the roads that made Illinois the nation's leader in railroad mileage and, the city, which numbered 30,000 in 1848, grew tenfold. The inflow which had begun when that one-car train hauled a few bushels of wheat amounted by 1868 to tens of millions of bushels annually.

"Let the golden grain come, we can take care of it all," cried a Chicago newspaper of the 1850's. And come it did. Illinois was a major grain producer and Chicago—"the New York of the West" —enjoyed a strategic location that made it the key transfer point for transcontinental trade. Systems like the Chicago & North Western and the Illinois Central funneled in wheat, corn, and barley from the immense cereal carpet that lay to the city's west and northwest. During the sixties it became one of the world's primary grain markets; through the wonder of the telegraph fluctuations in the Chicago market were communicated to the rest of the world, affecting prices in New York and faraway Liverpool. At the center of these transactions stood the Chicago Board of Trade, the focal point for the buying and selling of grains, flour, and other foodstuffs. A contemporary called the Board "the Altar of Ceres," and the label was apt. Grain, or rather the money it might bring, was indeed a goddess to be worshiped by the restless merchants of the Board of Trade.

To accommodate the quantities of grain which flowed in and out of Chicago there developed a most lucrative business, that of storing the grain in warehouses until it was sold and shipped East. These warehouses or grain elevators were huge skyscrapers capable of holding 500,000 to 1,000,000 bushels in elongated perpendicular bins which were mechanically loaded by dump buckets fastened to conveyor belts. Warehousemen facilitated sales to merchants and speculators by issuing them receipts to represent the grain in storage. These receipts were regarded as stable tokens of value comparable to bank bills; and presumably a warehouseman, like a banker, held a position of public trust demanding a high level of integrity. The presumption, however, often proved to be quite unjustified.

The history of the great Chicago grain elevators is reflected in the rise and fall of Munn & Scott, a firm founded in Spring Bay, Illinois, in 1844. The two partners, Ira Y. Munn and George L. Scott, ran a small (about 8,000 bushels capacity) warehouse, located on the Illinois River, which served the north central part of the state. Munn, who was the firm's driving spirit, soon expanded his operations. Taking advantage of the opportunities presented by the growing commercial ascendancy of Chicago, he established a 200,000-bushel grain elevator there in 1856 under the name of Munn, Gill & Company. Two years later it became Munn & Scott, one of thirteen firms in Chicago with a combined storage capacity of over four million bushels.

The next decade was enormously prosperous for Munn & Scott. They expanded to four elevators with a total capacity of 2,700,000 bushels; their warehouses could daily receive as much as 300,000 bushels and ship out twice that amount. With success came power and prestige. Ira Munn emerged as a leading Chicago businessman; he was prominent in the affairs of the Board of Trade, serving as its president in 1860 and as president of the city's Chamber of Commerce in 1868. During the Civil War he participated conspicuously in activities supporting the Union cause. At the same time, good capitalist that he was, Munn diversified his enterprises by engaging in wholesale grain speculation and by investing in newspapers and banks.

On the surface all seemed well for Munn & Scott, but prosperity brought its problems. These, in large measure, were of the company's own making; the age of enterprise was also an age of corruption, and the Chicago warehousemen were not at war with the spirit of their age. By 1868 Munn & Scott and four other firms dominated the field. They were interlocked in a pool, each owning a part interest in the others' businesses. In consequence they could administer prices and force farmers, who had to store their grain prior to sale, to pay high storage fees. There were also cruder forms of chicanery. The warehousemen commonly made deals with the railroads whereby they were assured of receiving all the grain carried by a particular line, regardless of the shipper's consignment. Munn & Scott, for instance, received most of their grain from the Chicago & North Western. Another practice was to misrepresent the quality of grain by mixing inferior grains with superior ones. The warehouses also systematically issued bogus receipts not backed by actual grain. Yet another favorite trick, performed in league with allied speculators, was to spread false rumors that the grain was spoiling; unsuspecting merchants would hasten to unload their grain receipts at depressed prices, thus setting up a juicy profit for the warehousemen.

While this sophisticated graft pleased the profiteers, it aroused its victims. As early as 1857 Chicago's grain merchants, acting through the Board of Trade, sought to impose a system of self-regulation upon the grain elevator owners. Their aim was to get impartial inspectors into the warehouses whose presence would prevent improper mixing of grades and who could report on the condition and the quantity of the grain in storage. A related objective was to make the Board a central registration agency which would record the receipt of grain and validate its sale so as to eliminate the practice of issuing bogus receipts. The warehousemen naturally resisted, claiming that as private owners they had an inherent right to exclude outside parties from their property. Since the elevator proprietors also had representation on the Board of Trade, they were usually able to turn the regulatory proposals into meaningless compromises. The upshot was the semblance but not the substance of regulation: grain weighers who were in the employ of the warehousemen; inspectors whose admission into the elevators depended upon the owner's goodwill and who were vulnerable to bribes; and unverifiable reports filed by the warehousemen, which were as worthless as many of their grain receipts.

The Munn & Scott firm was both notoriously unscrupulous in its business practices and a leader in the fight against effective control by the Board. In 1861, after warehouse "wheat doctors" had camouflaged a huge quantity of spoiled grain by mixing it with good grades, open charges of fraud were voiced. The Board appointed an investigating committee, but by tacit agreement its report was suppressed. When Joseph Medill's crusading Chicago *Tribune* suggested that the report was shelved because it incriminated many elevator men, Munn & Scott succeeded in getting *Tribune* reporters expelled from Board meetings. Similar newspaper charges hinting at Munn & Scott frauds appeared in 1865; another public furor followed, but the lax inspection procedures remained unchanged.

Four years later almost all of Chicago's receivers, shippers, and dealers of grain united in demanding a system of real inspection. The immediate cause of these renewed demands was a rise in storage rates and the imposition of an extra charge for grain that spoiled while in storage. New Board regulations designed to eliminate fraudulent issues of grain receipts were adopted early in 1870; once again the warehousemen, including Munn & Scott, asserted their right to control matters within their own elevators. The fight intensified. Elections for Board of Trade officers in the spring of 1870 split the membership into two factions—one supported the warehousemen; the other, which won most of the offices, insisted that their power be broken.

Businessmen are not customarily champions of governmental regulation, but the warehouse situation had become intolerable. The conduct of complex business relationships, after all, depends in significant part on mutual trust. Unable to control the warehousemen, the Board of Trade turned to the state, asking that Illinois subject them to public regulation. It was necessary, declared the Board president in 1870, to destroy "a monopoly highly detrimental to every interest in the city." Joseph Medill, whose newspaper made warehouse regulation its cause, put it more colorfully when he described the warehousemen as "rapacious, blood sucking insects." These demands went before the state's constitutional convention of 1869-70, then in session. The result was one of those strange yet almost typical alliances of American politics: a temporary pact between two normally opposed interests, the grain merchants and the grain producers. Together they induced the convention to adopt constitutional articles which the state's voters overwhelmingly ratified; these authorized public regulation of warehouses and railroads.

The farmer-merchant alliance was an unusually strange one for 1870 because that year found the Midwestern farmer in bitter revolt against the forces of capitalism. The reasons were rooted in the economic depression which gripped agricultural America. Beyond a doubt, the economic balance of the post-Civil War period was heavily weighted against the American farmer. Between 1861 and 1865 he had rapidly expanded production to meet burgeoning needs, but the postwar market could absorb only part of his increased output of wheat, corn, and other grains. The farmer, moreover, sold in an unprotected world market at a time of falling prices; wheat, which sold at $1.45 a bushel in 1866, fell to seventy-six cents a mere three years later. As prices dropped, the value of money appreciated and the farmers, who had borrowed in the wartime flush of inflationary optimism, had to meet debts with a scarce and hard-earned currency. Manufacturers by contrast were protected by a high tariff which pushed up the cost of the farmers' tools and domestic necessities.

The farmers of the West and Midwest had yet another grievance which became the focus of all their discontents—the great railroad systems whose shiny rails crisscrossed the farm country. No one had welcomed the coming of the railroad more than Western farmers since it opened up new markets for their products and made farming feasible in otherwise remote areas. Many had mortgaged their property to buy railroad securities; others had cheerfully accepted high local taxes to finance the bonds that lured the iron horse into their territory. Unfortunately, the harvest was a bitter one. Once established, the railroads treated their clientele with disdain. Company officials were overbearing; freight rates were high and discriminated in favor of large shippers who received special discounts. Precisely because the railroads were so essential, they could act arrogantly; in any one area a single line usually enjoyed a monopoly and thus had the power to raise rates as high as, or even higher than, the traffic would bear. The railroads of course defended their charges as moderate, sufficient only to compensate for the immense speculative risks that they had taken.

The farmers were unimpressed. To them the dominant fact was that freight costs ate up a frightful percentage of their income, so that they were often reduced to burning their corn as fuel rather than shipping it to market. Almost inevitably their profound discontent found an organized outlet. Oddly, what became the major vehicle for agrarian protest had its start as a fraternal order intended to provide isolated farmers with social and educational opportunities. In 1867 an idealistic government clerk in Washington, Oliver Hudson Kelley, founded the National Grange of the Patrons of Husbandry. At first his organization existed more on paper than in reality, but Kelly was an indefatigable worker—and also a shrewd observer. He broadened the Grange's appeal by making its primary objective cooperative purchasing and control of monopolies. These tactics paid off, and the Grange spread like prairie wildfire. It soon blanketed the nation, reaching its peak in 1874 when representatives of 800,000 farmers convened in St.

Louis to proclaim "the art of agriculture" as "the parent and precursor of all arts, and its products the foundation of all wealth."

Although the term "Granger" became a synonym for all the agrarian movements of the seventies, there were other highly vocal farmer associations which intervened in their states' politics throughout the Midwest. Many antedated the Patrons of Husbandry, but all shared the same goals: elimination of the middleman's profits, lowered interest charges, and, most insistently, railroad rate regulation. "We were all grangers," a farmer later recalled. "I never belonged to the order but I was a granger just the same." What he and his fellow farmers wanted had been well summarized by a Granger publicist who wrote simply and directly: "We want cheap coal, cheap bread, cheap transportation, cheap clothing."

In Illinois the farmers scored one of their first victories when they joined with Chicago's merchants in getting the state's constitutional convention to authorize railroad and warehouse regulation. Like the Board of Trade, Illinois farmers had just cause for wanting to see the elevators controlled. Typically, a farmer might ship a thousand bushels of wheat to Chicago, receiving a warehouse receipt for 950. After paying costly storage charges he might be told that his grain was "heating," and that, to avoid a complete disaster, he should sell his receipt back to the warehouseman at a loss of ten cents per bushel. Later, the hapless farmer would learn that his grain, perfectly sound, had been sold at a nice profit. But beyond their joint desires to clean up a dirty business, the farmers were interested in comprehensive regulation. The Board of Trade merely wanted to make normal business relationships based on supply and demand possible; the farmers wanted a stringent limitation on the rates charged by railroads and warehouses.

Acting in response to these pressures, the 1871 legislature forbade railroad discriminations and prescribed maximum freight and passenger rates. The warehousemen's fraudulent practices were outlawed, storage rates were limited, and a Railroad and Warehouse Commission was created to enforce the regulations. Enforcement, however, was not easy; the warehousemen claimed that the law was unconstitutional and ignored its requirements. Munn & Scott refused to take out the license required by the law and denied the state-appointed registrar of grain access to their elevators. The state then sued the firm, but the trial proceedings were delayed because of the mass destruction of records by Chicago's Great Fire of 1871. In July, 1872, the state won a judgment of $100; Munn & Scott promptly appealed to the Illinois Supreme Court.

Meanwhile, a series of related events brought the downfall of Munn & Scott. Despite the state regulation (which at first had no practical impact), the Board of Trade continued to seek inspection of the warehouses during 1871 and 1872. Some elevators cooperated with Board inspectors in measuring their grain, but Munn & Scott remained defiant. Finally, in 1872, the firm consented to admit inspectors. It requested, however, that its elevators be inspected last in order to give it time to consolidate its grains and to avoid any implication that Munn & Scott were particularly distrusted. The Board agreed. The firm used this reprieve to floor over the tops of several bins in its Northwestern elevator, covering the false bottoms with grain so as to give the illusion of full bins. The inspectors were fooled until an employee divulged the secret; then it came out that Munn & Scott grain receipts totaled 300,000 bushels more than the actual grain in their elevators.

Deplorable as the corruption was, its revelation merely confirmed what had long been suspected. More immediately damaging were Munn & Scott's financial misadventures in the summer of 1872. Along with three other speculators the firm attempted to corner all the wheat pouring into Chicago, hoping to dictate its ultimate price in world markets. For a while the corner worked; the price of wheat rose to $1.40 a bushel. Then, however, as it rose still further, farmers marketed all their reserves. This was the crucial point and it destroyed the corner. Unable to raise a million-dollar loan from Chicago's banks, the speculators had to stop buying. Their scheme collapsed, and wheat prices plummeted forty-seven cents in a twenty-four-hour period. Munn & Scott were ruined, their grain receipts thoroughly discredited. To avoid a complete panic, the powerful George Armour & Company bought up the Munn interests and quietly set about purchasing grain to make its receipts good. Munn and Scott themselves went into bankruptcy; the ensuing court proceedings, as summarized in newspaper headlines, told the story of the Chicago elevator business:

Ira Y. Munn on Stand Lays Bare Elevator Combination—Profits Divided —Agreement in 1866—Included Northwestern Elevators, West Side Elevators, Galena and Wheeler & Munger—A General Pool—History of Contracts with Northwestern Railway Beginning in 1862 and Renewed in 1866.

On December 3, 1872, Munn & Scott were expelled from the Board of Trade.

Although Ira Munn and George Scott thus passed into oblivion, the regulatory impulse that they and their fellow warehousemen had helped trigger continued unabated. The year 1873 was one of economic panic; grain prices dropped further and a severe shortage of credit forced numerous mortgage foreclosures. The Granger movement reached floodtide, and its political power was felt in all the Midwestern states. Granger votes elected legislators, governors, and judges pledged to lowering railroad rates; as the Governor of Minnesota inelegantly phrased it, "It is time to take robber corporations by the scruff of the neck and shake them over hell!"

The period was indeed a hellish one for the railroads. Illinois strengthened its regulatory laws, creating the nation's first "strong" railroad commission. Unlike "weak" commissions with purely advisory powers such as existed in Rhode Island and Massachusetts, the Illinois Commission could set maximum rates, eliminate discriminations, and initiate court actions. Iowa and Minnesota adopted legislation akin to that of Illinois, and Wisconsin enacted unusually harsh legislation, the Potter Law, which lowered freight rates radically (25 percent, the railroads exaggeratedly claimed).

The Granger laws, cursed as communistic in Eastern business and financial circles, were a tribute to the political power of organized farmers. But the objects of their wrath—they might be described as the Patrons of Capital—soon showed why they were renowned for skill and resourcefulness. Having failed to prevent this legislation, they retaliated with a variety of weapons. Railroad agents fought to appeal or weaken the laws and to convince the public of their undesirability. They insisted that regulation was against the farmers' best interests and threatened that it would discourage further construction—an effective point, for even the bitterest foes of "the octopus" wanted increased railroad service at a fair price.

Resistance took other forms as well. In some cases the roads aimed to make the laws unpopular; because of technical loopholes they were able to equalize their rates (thus formally ending discriminations) by raising them as much as 50 percent in areas where they had been low. In other cases they reduced service and forecast its complete abandonment. Wisconsin customers, for example, were treated to dilapidated cars and erratic service—"Potter cars, Potter rails, and Potter time"—that the railroads suavely blamed on the new law. Alternatively, the railroads pretended the laws were non-existent. The president of the Chicago, Burlington & Quincy ordered his subordinates to ignore Iowa's "mousing RR commrs." "We have and shall pay no attention to the Iowa law," he told them. "We shall increase our rates on certain kinds of freight so as to make any reductions we are compelled to make good, and probably something more."

Mostly, however, the corporations put their faith in the judiciary, not the elective state courts where decisions were likely to mirror popular desires, but the United States Supreme Court. For the railroads were confident that rate regulation, no matter how moderate, violated the Constitution in at least three ways. First of all, the laws contravened the federal contract clause by impairing their right to set rates, a right which they declared had been granted by the states' charters of incorporation. Here the railroads cited the Dartmouth College doctrine of 1819. (They conveniently overlooked the Supreme Court's later ruling in the *Charles River Bridge Case*. Furthermore, the railroads' charters had been issued under state constitutions granting the legislatures the authority to amend such franchises.) Second, the corporations claimed that the laws tampered with interstate transportation, thereby impinging on Congress' plenary power over interstate commerce. And lastly, they argued that public rate-setting was a radical innovation unknown to the American experience. It was, they contended, an illegal confiscation of private property which violated the Fourteenth Amendment's prohibition against depriving persons of property without due process of law.

This resistance quickly led to specific cases in the state and federal courts. Wisconsin produced four, *Stone* v. *Wisconsin; Chicago, Milwaukee, & St. Paul* v. *Ackley; Lawrence* v. *Chicago & North Western;* and *Piek* v. *Chicago & North Western.* The Piek and Lawrence cases, which had been arranged at a New York meeting of the Chicago & North Western's directors, were carefully planned bondholders' and shareholders' suits against the Potter

Law. From Iowa came the case of *Chicago, Burlington & Quincy* v. *Iowa,* which involved another powerful line. At a conference in Boston the Burlington's principal attorney, the capable Orville Hickman Browning, who had served in President Andrew Johnson's Cabinet, persuaded its directors that their proper course was to deny absolutely any state power to set rates, no matter how reasonable the rates might be. The Supreme Court, argued Browning, "must decide in our favor." His confidence was echoed by James M. Walker, the Burlington's president, who was "certain" that the Iowa and Illinois laws would fall because according to their original charters "the railroad Companies have the exclusive right to fix rates of transportation." Minnesota gave rise to *Winona & St. Peter* v. *Blake* and *Southern Minnesota Railroad* v. *Coleman.*

The Illinois Railroad Act became bogged down in jurisdictional squabbles. However, *Munn* v. *Illinois* was litigated. The Chicago warehousemen who had succeeded to the Munn & Scott properties had continued to defy the Warehouse Act, unsuccessfully carrying their case to the State Supreme Court. The state, declared the Illinois judges, might regulate all subjects "connected with the public welfare" in order "to promote the greatest good of the greatest number."

Despite this and other reverses in the lower courts, the business interests were confident of ultimate victory. The assurances of their high-priced lawyers were soothing. An advisory opinion prepared for the Chicago & North Western by three distinguished attorneys, including former Supreme Court Justice Benjamin R. Curtis, pronounced Wisconsin's Potter Law unconstitutional. The prestigious *American Law Review* featured numerous articles during 1874 and 1875, all of them agreeing that the "assault upon private property" embodied in the Granger laws would be turned back. Well might the chairman of the Burlington line, John N. Denison, conclude that "we shall be annoyed very much," but "happily we have the law on our side." Thus convinced, the corporations appealed their cases; in 1873 and 1874 *Munn* v. *Illinois* and seven railroad cases, which became known as the *Granger Railroad Cases,* all made their way to the United States Supreme Court.

The confidence of the railroad leaders, however, was grossly misplaced; the Court of the 1870's did not regard itself as the judicial handmaiden to entrepreneurial capitalism. Its Chief Justice, Mor-

rison Remick Waite, was a moderate whose deep faith in representative democracy made him tolerant of legislative experimentation.
His predisposition to trust the people had been shaped in frontier Ohio, where he had settled in 1838. As a lawyer who practiced in Toledo, Waite was active in local and state affairs. His
politics were solidly Republican, but his experiences in a close-
knit community where personal honesty and character mattered as
much as business acumen made Waite a typical member of the
antebellum class of professional and mercantile men to whom
wealth was not an end in itself.

Ironically, this honest man owed his appointment as Chief Justice
to the tawdry maneuverings of the Grant era. President Grant's
blundering efforts to please his malodorous entourage after a
vacancy had occurred in the chief justiceship in 1873 created a
nine-month national scandal that saw three dubious candidates
considered for the post. The muddled President finally selected
Waite, whose respectability assured his confirmation. An unassum-
ing, middle-aged man of medium height, his face clothed in one
of those ample beards that were then the style, Waite proved an
excellent Chief Justice. While his intelligence was keen, Waite's
most valuable assets were an amiable personality and a knack for
leading men. "Policy" and "diplomacy" were his self-proclaimed
guidelines. In seeking to influence men, he once wrote, it was better
to move slowly rather "than jumping at once to the lead without
having built behind."

These qualities served him well because Waite's associates on
the Court were men of uncommon ability; their vanities and ambitions could easily have mired the Court in a morass of personal
conflicts. Unquestionably the best mind and the most learned jurist
on the Waite Court was Joseph P. Bradley. A self-made man,
Bradley enjoyed a successful career representing some of New
Jersey's leading railroads until put on the Court in 1870 by President Grant. Once on the bench, he showed marked independence
of the corporate interests he had formerly defended, frequently
upholding economic regulation. Another Court giant was Samuel
Freeman Miller. Beginning as a poor Kentucky farm boy, Miller
had two careers, one as a country doctor and, after studying law
on his own, another as a rural attorney. Moving to Iowa in 1850,
he fast became a leader of the Western bar and was active in Re-

publican politics. Appointed by Lincoln in 1862, Miller's judicial philosophy stressed the importance of personal liberties and reflected a hostility to corporate and financial wealth. Blunt, self-confident, somewhat vain, Miller was a dominant figure on the postwar Court.

Ward Hunt, Noah H. Swayne, Nathan Clifford, and David Davis, four of the tribunal's lesser lights, generally followed Waite's lead in economic regulation cases. Like Waite, all of them had grown to maturity in Jacksonian America, and they retained democratic faith which made them favorably disposed to laws passed by the people's representatives. Most of them had been attorneys for corporations, yet had not tied themselves to any single interest. Their image of what America should be remained essentially Jacksonian; Waite and the majority valued property rights, but had no real commitment to the immense concentrations of financial and corporate property which emerged in the post-Civil War years. To this general characterization there were two exceptions, William Strong, a conservative judge sympathetic to corporate claims, and Stephen J. Field. A transplanted New Englander, who prided himself on being a rugged Californian, Field was tactless, querulous, and given to fits of self-righteous moralizing. Yet, for all his faults, this "War Democrat," whom Lincoln had placed on the Court in 1862, was a remarkable judge. Through a service of nearly thirty-five years Field outspokenly defended the claims of American business—a bench of nine Stephen Fields would have handsomely rewarded the railroads' initiative in bringing their grievances before the Supreme Court.

Judicial processes are rarely speedy, and the Court of the seventies moved with majestic deliberation. Overburdened with a lengthy docket, it usually required about three years to reach decisions. The first Granger case to be considered, a challenge to Minnesota's rate law, arrived in October, 1873, and the Illinois, Iowa, and Wisconsin cases were docketed the next year. Oral arguments occupied two sessions during the 1875 term; the *Granger Railroad Cases* were heard in October, 1875, and *Munn* v. *Illinois,* the elevator case, was argued early in 1876. For the oral arguments the business interests marshaled the elite of the nation's bar. William M. Evarts, Orville H. Browning, David Dudley Field (Justice Field's brother), and Frederick M. Frelinghuysen were among the assembled legal talent. They contended that the laws unconstitutionally confiscated property, impaired the obligation of contracts, and interfered with interstate commerce. To these constitutional arguments they added the charge that, except for certain minor categories, rate regulation was unheard of in America. Almost hysterically, they described the Granger laws as forerunners to the total confiscation of private property, "the beginning of the operations of the [Paris] commune in the legislation of this country." In reply, the state attorneys defended the laws as reasonable measures to protect the general welfare against the exactions of uncurbed monopolies whose businesses had in effect become public.

Despite the brilliance of the railroad attorneys and the eloquence of their arguments, seven of the justices cast their votes for the Granger laws. Only Field and Strong dissented when, on November 18, 1876, all eight cases were decided together. Chief Justice Waite assigned himself the opinions, well aware of their importance; this was the Supreme Court's first major statement on the constitutionality of regulating the new industrial capitalism. He chose the elevator case, *Munn* v. *Illinois,* for his main opinion. Unlike the companies involved in the *Granger Railroad Cases,* Munn & Scott were unincorporated partners and their business was not interstate transportation. Their case therefore presented the crucial issue of rate regulation in pure form, uncomplicated by the contract and commerce questions raised in the other disputes.

The Chief Justice devoted the winter to preparing the opinions, later remarking that "they kept my mind and hands at work all the time." He wrote at home, sitting at a long and cluttered library table in his private study where he worked in the morning's early hours and often into the night. Admittedly "old-fashioned," Waite spurned secretaries and the newfangled typewriters, writing his drafts in longhand. A glimpse of his labors on the *Munn* opinion is preserved on a lined sheet of paper on which he jotted down earlier illustrations of American business regulation:

MILLS
1. Ohio regulated tolls from 1799 until present time—No distinction between water & steam mills—
Ferries—same—any stream
Auctions

TAVERNS—
> In New Jersey—County Court was authorised to fix rates of charge
> Revision of 1821 P. 281.

LICENSES BY CITIES IN OHIO
> Ferries
> Shows
> Hawkers & Peddlers
> Venders of Gunpowder
> Taverns
> Hucksters
> Vehicles
> Undertakers
> Pawn Brokers

TAVERNS.
> County Courts fix rates in Mississippi—
> Dig Stat Miss. 7 397—Pub. in 186

These references to historical practice, some of which appeared in the final opinion, were pertinent. Those challenging the Granger laws had strongly contended that regulation was alien to America; to demolish their claim Waite naturally referred to the state he knew best, citing numerous precedents drawn from Ohio history.

As Waite prepared the *Munn* opinion, he turned for assistance to Justice Bradley, his closest collaborator on the Court. Bradley, in fact, deserves recognition as co-author, for he prepared a lengthy "Outline of my views on the subject of the Granger Cases" from which the Chief Justice freely borrowed. In refuting the business arguments, Bradley, a confirmed legal antiquarian, dug up an obscure seventeenth-century English legal treatise, *De Portibus Maris*. Written by Lord Chief Justice Hale, it justified regulation of the fees charged by enterprises in public ports with the following language: "For now the wharf and crane and other conveniences are affected with a publick interest, and they cease to be *juris privati* only." Waite quoted the statement and so introduced the public-interest doctrine into American constitutional law. Late in February he circulated the draft opinions among the brethren for final approval. Bradley, the former railroad attorney, responded enthusiastically: "terse, correct, & safe." Miller found the opinions "equal to the occasion which is a very great one."

With these endorsements, the Court released its opinions on

March 1, 1877, ruling that the Constitution sanctioned economic regulation in the public interest. Waite's opinion in *Munn* v. *Illinois* began by stressing the power of the Chicago grain elevators which, standing at the gateway of commerce to the East, "take toll from all who pass." Their business, he argued citing Lord Hale, "tends to a common charge, and is become a thing of public interest and use" subject to state control. Noting earlier instances of American price regulation, Waite summarily dismissed the contention that such laws unconstitutionally destroyed private property. Underlying these conclusions was the root assumption of *Munn* v. *Illinois*—that popularly accountable legislatures should be the judges of the wisdom of regulatory laws. "For protection against abuses by legislatures the people must resort to the polls, not to the courts," Waite wrote, thus enunciating one of the Supreme Court's major declarations in favor of judicial self-restraint in economic-regulation cases.

With the Warehouse Act sustained, the *Granger Railroad Cases* fell easily into place. In brief opinions Waite disposed of them by relying on the *Munn* public-interest doctrine. He rejected the commerce-clause argument, finding that none of the regulations extended to commerce beyond state lines. Waite found the claim that the rate laws impaired contract rights to be equally without merit; the states' constitutions had reserved the power to amend charters. Justice Field wrote a fiery dissent labeling the *Munn* decision "subversive of the rights of private property," and he predicted that its reasoning implied an almost unlimited scope for the regulatory power: "If the power can be exercised as to one article, it may as to all articles, and the prices of everything, from a calico gown to a city mansion, may be the subject of legislative direction."

Although Field's gloomy prediction that property rights would be destroyed proved false, he was essentially correct in calling attention to the broad implications of the *Munn* decision. In modern-day America the scope of governmental regulation is immense; no one doubts that "the prices of everything"—even calico gowns and city mansions—may be regulated. And this intervention by government in economic affairs finds much of its constitutional sanction in *Munn* v. *Illinois* and the line of cases which are its progeny. During the seventies and eighties, the years when Waite and his majority sat on the Court, the public-interest doctrine and the underlying assumption that legislative acts are valid unless completely arbitrary led to further expansions of regulatory power. State railroad regulations were repeatedly upheld, as were laws setting the rates charged by water companies, outlawing businesses that engaged in the liquor trade or operated lotteries, and scaling down the interest and principal owed to the holders of state bonds. Congress' power to regulate federally chartered corporations was similarly upheld in the *Sinking Fund Cases* of 1879, a decision which infuriated corporation and financial leaders.

Later, roughly between 1895 and 1937, judges far more committed to industrial capitalism than Waite, Bradley, and Miller often found in the general prohibitions of the due-process clauses of the Fifth and Fourteenth Amendments reasons for invalidating economic regulations. *Munn* v. *Illinois* was never overruled, but its public-interest doctrine was radically reinterpreted. In the 1920's the Taft Court decided that only a narrow category of businesses— enterprises traditionally regulated and large monopolies—were affected with a public interest, and it struck down a number of state regulatory laws as unconstitutional.

All this came to an end in the next decade. In the 1934 case of *Nebbia* v. *New York,* sustaining a comprehensive scheme of state milk-price regulation, the Supreme Court returned to a sweeping view of the public-interest doctrine. "A state," Justice Roberts announced in words that Waite would have approved, "is free to adopt whatever economic policy may reasonably be deemed to promote the public welfare, and to enforce that policy by legislation adapted to its purpose." Three years later in the case of *NLRB* v. *Jones & Laughlin Steel Corporation,* when the justices began the process of upholding the economic regulation of the New Deal, the permissive spirit of Waite's *Munn* opinion again triumphed. For now his insistence on judicial toleration of legislation regulating economic relationships was the supreme law of the land.

This, then, is the ultimate meaning of *Munn* v. *Illinois*—one of the landmark pronouncements of American constitutional law on the subject of economic regulation. But the case also had a more contemporary impact. The proprietors of the city's grain elevators, the Chicago *Tribune* reported a few days after the

Supreme Court's decision, "are thoroughly reconstructed. They bow to the inevitable." They lowered their rates and began co-operating fully with the state's Railroad and Warehouse Commission. Two decades of arrogance by the warehousemen had come to an end; not only were their opponents politically dominant, but the elevator business itself was in a period of relative decline. Competing grain centers at Milwaukee and Minneapolis, and especially the growing practice of shipping grain directly through Chicago, weakened the warehousemen's power. In 1876 13 percent of the grain arriving in Chicago was not stored; by 1885 the figure had jumped to 57 percent, though the volume of grain handled by the elevators was still impressive.

The state's railroads also complied with the *Munn* decision. Many of the Midwestern states, responding to powerful railroad lobbies, repealed or drastically loosened their regulatory laws. Illinois, however, remained a leader in strong railroad regulation; the farmers' influence prevented the repeal of the laws, which were sustained by the state's highest court in 1880 and by the Supreme Court in 1883.

A few final words on the parties whose behavior and maneuverings contributed to *Munn* v. *Illinois* are appropriate, for the case well illustrates the many ironies of constitutional litigation in America. By 1877 the Patrons of Husbandry, which had provided much of the political pressure behind the regulatory laws, was but a shadow of its onetime strength. Organizational dissensions and the collapse of its cooperative enterprises sharply reduced membership and destroyed its political influence. In fact, the Grange gradually reverted to its original social purposes and is today a thriving fraternal order.

The unsavory firm of Munn & Scott was also no longer a factor in 1877. It had long since passed out of existence, bankruptcy forcing the dispersal of its properties. Eventually three of its four elevators came under the control of Munger, Wheeler & Company, a firm which enjoyed a near-monopoly of the Chicago grain-storage business.

Chicago's Board of Trade, having finally curbed the warehousemen, had second doubts about the wisdom of public control. Through the seventies and eighties its leaders vigorously, though unsuccessfully, sought to return the power of regulating the warehouses to their hands. Other businessmen, too, had cause for regret. As the decisions of 1877 showed, the warehousemen who succeeded to Munn & Scott, and particularly the railroad leaders who deliberately forced the *Granger Railroad Cases* to a final decision, had disastrously miscalculated the Court's judicial position.

But ultimately more significant than the immediate results and the conflicting motives of the many participants was the constitutional residue left by the struggles of the seventies: the clear announcement that legislatures might regulate business on behalf of the public interest, a principle that received additional vitality from Chief Justice Waite's assertion that the Court should be reluctant to upset regulatory laws passed by the people's representatives. This was the meaning of *Munn* v. *Illinois,* and it provided a leading precedent for the day when the Patrons of Capital would find themselves under effective and continuing governmental regulation.

# The Case of the Prejudiced Doorkeeper

BY ALAN F. WESTIN

(*U.S.* v. *Singleton,* etc., [*The Civil Rights Cases*] 109 U.S. 3)

*The Civil War, caused in part by Chief Justice Taney's dictum in the Dred Scott case that Congress could not bar slavery from the territories, resulted, of course, in destroying slavery. The Thirteenth Amendment formally abolished the institution. The Fourteenth and Fifteenth Amendments, which the defeated Southern states were forced to ratify in order to get back into the Union, made Negroes citizens, prohibited the states from depriving "all persons" of life, liberty, or property without due process of law, and made it illegal to deny anyone the right to vote "on account of race, color, or previous condition of servitude."*

*For a time, backed by federal bayonets, former slaves in the South were able to exercise their civil rights fairly effectively. But the dominant white element in the former Confederacy resisted every effort to grant them real freedom and equality, and with the passage of time the determination of Northerners to force Southern whites to do so began to flag. Gradually the Negro slipped back into a state of second-class citizenship.*

*Naturally Negroes resisted this trend, calling upon the courts to protect them against discrimination. How the Supreme Court reacted in this situation is described below. Alan F. Westin, Associate Professor of Public Law and Government at Columbia University, is editor of* Freedom Now! The Civil Rights Struggle in America. *He is at present working on a biography of Justice John Marshall Harlan, the hero of this tale.*

On November 22, 1879, Messrs. Poole and Donnelly, managers of the Grand Opera House in New York City, were looking forward to a well-attended Saturday matinee. The Thanksgiving season was on, and Edwin Booth, the famous tragedian and brother of the late John Wilkes Booth, was in the middle of a record-breaking, four-week engagement. His *Hamlet, Othello,* and *Richelieu* had been lauded by the critics, and the attempt of a madman to shoot him during a performance of *Richard II* a few months earlier had made the actor a center of attention. "I am jamming the Grand Opera House," he wrote happily to a friend on November 16, and turned to putting the final touches on his scheduled Saturday appearance in Victor Hugo's *Ruy Blas.*

One person who had decided to see Booth that Saturday was William R. Davis, Jr., a tall, handsome and well-spoken man of twenty-six. He was the business agent of the *Progressive-American,* a weekly newspaper in New York City. This happened to be a Negro newspaper, and Davis happened to be a Negro, born a slave in South Carolina in 1853. At ten o'clock Saturday morning, Davis' girl friend, described by the press as "a bright octoroon, almost white," purchased two reserved seats at the box office of the Opera House. At 1:30 P.M., Davis and his lady presented themselves at the theater, only to be told by the doorkeeper, Samuel Singleton, that "these tickets are no good." If he would step out to the box office, Singleton said, Davis could have his money refunded.

That Davis was either surprised or dismayed by Singleton's action is unlikely. In 1875, shortly after passage of the federal Civil Rights Act forbidding racial discrimination in places of public accommodation, William R. Davis, Jr. had been refused a ticket to the dress circle of Booth's Theater in New York. He had sworn out a warrant against the ticket seller but a federal grand jury had refused to return an indictment, apparently because Davis' witnesses failed to show up at the hearing. In light of this earlier episode, Davis' appearance at the Grand Opera House this Saturday in 1879 could well have been a deliberate test of Messrs. Poole's and Donnelly's admission policies. There is more than a slight possibility that this was so, for the 1870's were unique years of testing for race relations in America.

During the 1870's, no state in the Union, whatever its relation to the Mason-Dixon line, had laws requiring separation of whites and Negroes in places of public accommodation. Admission and

arrangement policies were generally a matter of choice for individual owners. In the North and West, many theaters, hotels,
restaurants, and public carriers served Negro patrons without hesitation or discrimination. Others accepted Negroes for second-class
accommodations, such as smoking cars on railroads or balconies
in theaters; here, Negroes sat beside white customers who could
not afford first-class tickets. Some Northern and Western establishments refused Negro patronage entirely.

The situation was much the same in the larger cities of the
border states and in the Deep South. Most establishments admitted
Negroes to second-class facilities. Some gave first-class service to
Negroes with high social status, such as federal and state public
officials, army officers, newspapermen, and traveling clergymen. On
the other hand, many places, particularly in rural areas, were
closed to Negroes whatever their wealth or status.

From 1865 through the 1870's, the general trend in the nation
was toward wider acceptance of Negro patronage. The federal
Civil Rights Act of 1866, with is guarantee to Negroes of the "equal
benefit of the laws" had set off a flurry of test suits—for denying
sleeper accommodations to Negroes on a Washington–New York
train; for refusing to sell theater tickets to Negroes in Boston; for
restricting Negroes to the front platforms of Baltimore streetcars;
and for barring Negro women from the waiting rooms and parlor
cars of railroads in Virginia, Illinois, and California. Ratification
of the Fourteenth Amendment in 1868 had spurred on the challenges, and three Northern states had passed laws making it a
crime for owners of public-accommodation businesses to discriminate. Similar laws were enacted during the Reconstruction period
in several Southern states. Most state and federal court rulings
on these statutes between 1865 and 1880 held in favor of Negro
rights, and the rulings served as a steady pressure on owners to
relax racial bars.

Laws were not the only pressure. In many communities, Negroes
won recognition of their legal rights through direct action. A
typical campaign took place in Louisville, Kentucky, during the
spring of 1871. Although Negroes paid the same five-cent fare
as white passengers on the horse-drawn streetcars of Louisville,
the companies did not permit them to sit inside; they had to stand
on the open platforms at the front of the cars. Company officials

were encouraged to maintain this policy by anti-Negro Democratic administrations in the city of Louisville and the State of Kentucky.

In April of 1871, a Negro man named Robert Fox entered the Walnut Street car, deposited his nickel in the fare box, and attempted to take a seat. He was put off forcibly by the driver. Fox sued the company in Federal District Court for assault and battery, and the presiding judge instructed the jury that under federal law the company was obligated as a public carrier to serve passengers without regard to color. The jury awarded Fox $15, plus $72.80 in legal costs.

Armed with this legal precedent, and encouraged by the local white Republican leadership, Louisville Negroes began what today would probably be termed a "ride-in." At 7:00 P.M. on May 12, 1871, near the Willard Hotel, a young Negro boy paid his fare and took a seat. Following company policy adopted after the Fox decision, the driver did not try to eject him but simply stopped the car, refusing to drive on until the Negro got out. A large crowd gathered swiftly, including the governor, the city chief of police, and other prominent citizens, as well as many white teen-agers. The police were under orders not to intervene.

As the crowd grew, cries of "Put him out," "Hit him," "Kick him," and "Hang him" were heard. White teen-agers climbed into the car and shouted in the face of the Negro boy, who sat quietly in his seat. Then they dragged him out by force. He was pushed away from the car and beaten until he finally turned and began to fight back. At this point, two policemen seized the boy and took him to jail.

The "ride-in" demonstrators were prosecuted immediately in Louisville City Court for disorderly conduct. The judge ruled that there was no common-law duty commanding streetcar companies to carry Negroes inside the cars and that all federal legislation passed since 1865 to guarantee Negro rights was "clearly unconstitutional," whatever other federal and state judges may have said to the contrary. The defendants were fined and warned that further attempts would result in jail sentences.

By now, the nation was watching, and Northern newspapers carried full accounts of the final round of the Louisville contest. Negroes returned to the "ride-ins." For several days, violence erupted sporadically. Some Negroes were forced from the cars by groups of white newsboys. One Negro was thrown out of a car window. On several occasions, in various parts of the city, Negroes stayed on the cars, the drivers got off, and the Negro passengers drove to their destination, accompanied by cheers from Negro spectators. As the situation approached riot proportions, Kentucky newspapers warned of another "Bloody Monday" such as Louisville had experienced in the 1850's between Know-Nothing and Catholic groups.

The Negroes' determination and the support they received from federal officials proved decisive. The streetcar company managers met and agreed that "it was useless to try to resist or evade the enforcement by the United States authorities of the claim of the Negroes to ride in the cars." To "avoid serious collisions," the company would allow all who paid their nickels to take seats. The Louisville press during the 1870's records no history of violence following this integration. In fact, the peaceful way in which the two races occupied the streetcars was cited by many observers as proof that, once facilities were opened, "Southern mores" could accommodate successfully. Never again would Louisville streetcars be segregated.

Despite civil rights laws and test cases, stories of exclusion or separation were a steady diet in the press during the early 1870's. The rulings of a substantial minority of state and federal courts that there was no duty to serve Negroes created a cloudy legal atmosphere, and the United States Supreme Court did not pass on this issue during the decade. To settle the question "once and for all" and to harvest the political benefits of this "final protection" for the new freedmen, Congressional Republicans led by Senator Charles Sumner pressed for a new statute. Democrats and conservative Republicans warned in the debates that such a law would violate states' rights and would never be upheld by the Supreme Court, a view which was echoed by influential journals such as the *New York Times* and the *Nation*. Sumner had the votes, however. On March 1, 1875, "An Act to Protect all Citizens in their Civil and Legal Rights" went into force. Its preamble declared that "the appropriate object of legislation [was] to enact great fundamental principles into law," and such principles were involved here:

[I]t is essential to just government [that] we recognize the equality of all men before the law, and . . . it is the duty of government in its dealings with the people to mete out equal and exact justice to all, of whatever nativity, race, color, or persuasion, religious or political.

Section 1 declared that "all persons within the jurisdiction of the United States shall be entitled to the full and equal enjoyment of the accommodations . . . of inns, public conveyances on land or water, theaters and other places of public amusement; subject only to the conditions and limitations established by law, and applicable alike to citizens of every race or color." Section 2 provided that any person violating the Act could be sued in federal court for a penalty of $500, could be fined $500 to $1,000, or could be imprisoned from thirty days to one year. Other provisions provided for jurisdiction by the lower federal courts and review by the Supreme Court regardless of the amount in controversy. An additional section forbade racial discrimination in the selection of juries.

Reaction to the law was swift—and varied. Several hotels in Baltimore and Alexandria closed temporarily. In Chattanooga, some hotels turned in their licenses and filed to become private boardinghouses. A group of Negroes was refused admission to the orchestra of the Public Library Hall in Louisville. (They were offered balcony seats and all but one accepted these. The lone holdout walked over to Macauley's Theater, where he and a friend were sold tickets to the dress circle and sat through the play among the white patrons without incident.) But in Washington, D.C., two Negroes were served at the bar of the Willard Hotel, and in Chicago a black man was admitted for the first time to McVicker's Theater.

In other episodes, Negroes were not successful. Several visited restaurants and barbershops in Richmond, Virginia, two days after the Act became law, but were refused service at each establishment. In Montgomery, Alabama, a party of Negroes was refused admission to the dress circle to see Cal Wagner's Minstrels. In New Orleans, a Negro man and his wife were refused accommodations on the steamboat *Seminole*. Suits were filed in many cities. A few of the resulting court cases were dismissed, with comments by federal commissioners or district judges that the Civil Rights Act was unconstitutional. Other cases resulted in verdicts against the owners, as in Galveston, Texas, where the manager of the Tremont Opera House was fined $500 for refusing to admit a Negro. In both types of situation, appeals began their slow march upward through the federal courts.

This was the situation in 1879, when William R. Davis, Jr. was turned away from the Grand Opera House. Convinced that the operators of the theater were acting out of "prejudice against his race," he had no intention of pocketing a refund and walking away. Seeing a small white boy standing on the sidewalk near the theater, Davis gave him a dollar, plus ten cents for his trouble, and had him purchase two more tickets to the matinee. When Davis presented himself, his lady, and these tickets to Samuel Singleton, the lady was admitted, "perhaps because her complexion deceived the doorkeeper," as the press speculated. But Davis was again told that his ticket "was no good." Singleton ordered him to move out of the entrance, and when the Negro argued with him, a policeman was called. The officer told Davis that Messrs. Poole and Donnelly did not admit colored persons to the Opera House. "Perhaps the managers do not," Davis retorted, "but the laws of the country [do]." He announced that he would see to their enforcement at once.

On Monday, November 24, Davis filed a criminal complaint and on December 9, Singleton was indicted. The press described this as the first criminal proceeding under the Act to go to trial in New York. When the case was heard, on January 14, 1880, counsel for Singleton, Louis Post, adopted the position that the Act of 1875 was invalid. "It interferes with the right of the State of New York to provide the means under which citizens of the State have the power to control and protect their rights in respect to their private property." Assistant United States Attorney Fiero replied that such a conception of states' rights had been "exploded and superseded long ago." It was unthinkable, he argued, that "the United States could not extend to one citizen of New York a right which the State itself gave to other of its citizens—the right of admission to places of public amusement." The presiding judge referred the constitutional question to the Circuit Court at its February term. Justice Samuel Blatchford of the Supreme Court, assigned to the Southern District of New York, and District Judge William Choate reached opposite conclusions on the issue and certified it to the United States Supreme Court "on division of opinion between the judges."

Perhaps a hundred such cases were tried and appealed during the late 1870's and early 1880's. Federal judges in Pennsylvania, Texas, Maryland, and Kentucky, for example, ruled the Act constitutional; in North Carolina, New Jersey, and California, the Act was held invalid. In New York, Tennessee, Missouri, Kansas, and other states, divided federal circuit courts certified the issue to the Supreme Court for decision.

The Supreme Court was in no hurry to settle the issue, however. Two cases reached the Supreme Court in 1876 and a third in 1877. The Attorney General of the United States, Charles Devens, filed a brief in 1879 defending the constitutionality of the Act. Yet the Court simply continued the cases on its docket. In 1880, three additional cases were filed and the Solicitor General of the United States filed a new brief in 1882. The Court's ruling did not come down until late in 1883. Even though they were badly delayed on their docket in the 1880's, it is difficult to resist the conclusion that the justices preferred to accumulate the civil rights act cases and let them "ripen" a while before decision.

William R. Davis, Jr.'s case reached the Supreme Court in 1880, under the title of *U.S.* v. *Singleton.* Four similar cases accompanied it. *U.S.* v. *Stanley* involved the refusal of Murray Stanley in 1875 to serve a meal at his hotel in Topeka, Kansas, to Bird Gee, a Negro. *U.S.* v. *Nichols* presented the refusal in 1876 of Samuel Nichols, owner of the Nichols House in Jefferson City, Missouri, to accept a Negro named W. H. R. Agee as a guest. *U.S.* v. *Ryan* involved the conduct of Michael Ryan on January 4, 1876, as doorkeeper of Maguire's Theater in San Francisco, in denying a Negro named George M. Tyler entry to the dress circle. In *U.S.* v. *Hamilton,* James Hamilton, a conductor on the Nashville, Chattanooga & St. Louis Railroad, on April 21, 1879, had denied a Negro woman with a first-class ticket access to the ladies' car and had restricted her to "a dirty disagreeable coach known as the smoking car." These five cases all were criminal prosecutions and presented as their issues the constitutionality of the Act of 1875.

The sixth case had a different setting. On the evening of May 22, 1879, Mrs. Sallie J. Robinson, a Negro woman twenty-eight years old, purchased two first-class tickets at Grand Junction,

Tennessee, for a trip to Lynchburg, Virginia, on the Memphis & Charleston Railroad. Shortly after midnight, she and her nephew, Joseph C. Robinson, described as a young Negro "of light complexion, light hair, and light blue eyes," boarded the train and started into the parlor car. The conductor, C. W. Reagin, held Mrs. Robinson back ("bruising her arm and jerking her roughly around," she alleged) and pushed her into the smoking car. He called her "girl" and when asked why he refused them entry, replied brusquely, "Why do you people try to force yourselves in that car?" A few minutes later, when Joseph informed the conductor that he was Mrs. Robinson's nephew and was a Negro, the conductor looked surprised. He said that in that case they could go into the parlor car at the next stop. The Robinsons finished the ride in the parlor car, but they filed complaints with the railroad about their treatment and then sued for $500 under the Act of 1875. At the trial, Reagin testified that he had thought Joseph to be a white man with a colored woman, and his experience was that such combinations were "for illicit purposes." Couples of this sort usually "laughed, drank, smoked and acted disorderly, and were objectionable to other passengers" in the parlor car.

Counsel for the Robinsons objected to Reagin's testimony, on the ground that his actions were based on race and constituted no defense. The railroad admitted the constitutionality of the Act for purposes of the trial, but contended that the action of its conductor did not fall within the statute. The district judge ruled that the motive for excluding persons was the decisive issue under the Act; if the jury believed that the conductor had acted because he thought Mrs. Robinson "a prostitute travelling with her paramour," whether "well or ill-founded" in that assumption, the exclusion was not because of race and the railroad was not liable. The jury found for the railroad, and the Robinsons appealed.

The brief that Solicitor General Samuel F. Phillips submitted for the United States in 1882 was a strong presentation. It reviewed the cases involved, described the history of the war amendments and civil rights laws, and stressed the importance of equal access to public accommodation facilities. Four times since 1866, Phillips noted, a Congress led by men who had fought in the Civil War and had framed the war amendments had enacted civil rights legislation. These men knew that "[e]very rootlet of slavery has an individual vitality, and, to its minutest hair, should be anxiously followed and plucked up."

They knew also that if Negroes were denied accommodations "by persons who notably are sensitive registers of local public opinion," and if the federal government allowed this to continue, the warning of Junius would be applicable, that "What upon yesterday was only 'fact' will become 'doctrine' tomorrow."

On the afternoon of October 15, 1883, Justice Joseph Bradley disposed of five of the six cases with an opinion holding the Act of 1875 to be unconstitutional. (One case, *U.S.* v. *Hamilton,* was denied review on a procedural point.) Bradley, who was the spokesman for eight members of the Court, was probably the most powerful intellect among the justices, a disciplined craftsman in his opinions, a tough-minded constitutional logician, and, despite his background as a leading lawyer for New Jersey railroads and insurance companies, a justice who supported liberal values. He had originally been a Whig in New Jersey politics of the 1850's, had struggled for a North-South compromise in the darkening months of 1860–61, and had swung to a strong Unionist position with the firing on Fort Sumter. He ran for Congress on the Lincoln ticket in 1862, and in 1868 he headed the New Jersey electors for Grant. He had given firm support to the Thirteenth and Fourteenth Amendments when they were adopted, and his appointment to the Supreme Court by Grant in 1870 drew no criticism from friends of the Negro.

Those who joined Bradley in the majority position were an uncommonly talented group of justices. Chief Justice Morrison Waite, underrated today, was a good judge and a courageous spokesman for Jacksonian values in the Gilded Age. Samuel Miller was a sophisticated constitutional lawyer who left issues glowing clearly after he had written on them. Stephen J. Field had the power and arrogance of an Old Testament prophet, and his pounding opinions forged American constitutional law in a *laissez-faire* pattern in these decades. Horace Gray was a tower of erudition and master of legal procedure. William Woods, Stanley Matthews, and Samuel Blatchford, while lesser men, were still better-than-average justices. All except Field were Republicans, and even he had been appointed by Lincoln. All had made their careers in Northern, Mid-western, or Western states.

Bradley's opinion had a tightly reasoned simplicity. The Thirteenth Amendment forbade slavery and involuntary servitude, Bradley noted, but its protection against reinstituting the incidents of slavery could not fairly be stretched to cover "social" discriminations such as those involved here. As for the Fourteenth Amendment, it was addressed specifically to *state* deprivations of liberty or equal protection and did not encompass private acts of discrimination. Thus there was no source of constitutional power in the war amendments to uphold Congress' attempt to control private actions in the Act of 1875. Even as a matter of policy, Bradley argued, the obvious intention of the war amendments to aid the newly freed Negro had to have some limits. There must be a point at which the Negro ceased to be "the special favorite of the laws" and took on "the rank of mere citizen."

When Bradley finished reading his opinion, Justice John Marshall Harlan of Kentucky—the Court's only Southerner, a former slaveholder, and a bitter critic of the war amendments in the 1860's—announced that he did not agree with his colleagues. Without summarizing his reasons for the onlookers, he stated he would file a dissent later.

At the Atlanta Opera House that evening, the end man of Haverly's Minstrels interrupted the performance to announce the decision. The entire orchestra and dress circle audience rose and gave three cheers. Negroes sitting in the balcony kept their seats, "stunned" according to one newspaper account. A short time earlier, a Negro had been denied entrance to the dress circle at the Opera House and had filed criminal charges against the management under the Act of 1875. Now, his case—their case—was dead.

In Washington, D.C., Frederick Douglass, the noted Negro publicist, lashed out at the decision. Southerners are gloating, he said, that they have now got the Negro "just where they want him."

They can put him in a smoking car or baggage car . . . take him or leave him at a railroad station, exclude him from inns, drive him from all places of amusement or instruction, without the least fear that the National Government will interfere for the protection of his liberty.

Most of the nation's press supported the Court. Newspapers like the *New York Times,* Chicago *Tribune,* Washington *Post,* and Louisville *Courier-Journal* found the opinion well reasoned and wise, a salutary restoration of "constitutional government" after years of "Congressional excess." Those newspapers that disagreed with the majority ruling, such as the New York *World* and the Chicago *Interocean*, commented that the nation was awaiting Justice Harlan's dissent with intense interest.

Harlan's odyssey from slave supporter to civil rights champion makes a fascinating chronicle. Like Bradley, he had entered politics as a Whig and had tried to find a middle road between secessionist Democrats and antislavery Republicans. Like Bradley, he sought compromise between North and South in the months of indecision after Lincoln's election. Like Bradley, the firing on Fort Sumter sent him without hesitation into the Union camp. Here the parallels end. Although Harlan entered the Union Army, he was totally opposed to freeing the slaves, and his distate for Lincoln and the "Radicals" was complete. Between 1863 and 1868, he led the Conservative party in Kentucky, a third-party movement which supported the war but opposed pro-Negro and civil rights measures as "flagrant invasions of property rights and local government."

By 1868, however, Harlan had become a Republican. The resounding defeat of the Conservatives in the 1867 state elections convinced him that two-party politics were finally emerging in Kentucky. Harlan had moved from the Democratic, anti-Negro city of Frankfort to the more cosmopolitan atmosphere of Louisville, center of such urbane and talented Republicans as Benjamin Bristow, with whom Harlan entered into a law partnership. Harlan's antimonopoly views and his general ideas about economic progress conflicted directly with state Democratic policies. Thus, when the Republicans nominated his field commander, Ulysses S. Grant, in 1868, Harlan was one of the substantial number of conservatives who joined the GOP.

He changed his views on Negro rights also. The wave of "vigilantism" against white Republicans and Negros which swept Kentucky in 1868-70, convinced Harlan that federal guarantees were essential. He watched Negroes in Kentucky move with dignity and skill to become useful citizens, and his devout Presbyterianism led him to adopt a "brotherhood-of-man" outlook in keeping with the position of his church. That sixty thousand Kentucky Negroes would become voters in 1870 was not lost on Harlan as a realistic political leader of the Republicans.

Thus a "new" Harlan took the stump in 1871 as Republican gubernatorial candidate. He opened his rallies by confessing that he had formerly been anti-Negro. But "I have lived long enough," he said, "to feel that the most perfect despotism that ever existed on this earth was the institution of African slavery." The war amendments were necessary "to place it beyond the power of any State to interfere with . . . the results of the war." The South should stop agitating the race issue, and should turn to the rebuilding of the region on progressive lines. When the Democrats laughed at "Harlan the Chameleon" and read quotations from his earlier anti-Negro speeches, Harlan replied: "Let it be said that I am right rather than consistent."

Harlan became an influential figure in the Southern Republican wing, and when President Hayes decided to appoint a prominent Southern Republican to the Supreme Court in 1877, Harlan was a logical choice. Even then, the Negro issue rose to shake Harlan's life again. His confirmation was held up because of doubts by some Senators as to his "real" civil rights views. Only after Harlan produced his speeches between 1871 and 1877 and party leaders supported his firmness on this question was he approved.

Once on the Supreme Court, Harlan could have swung back to a conservative position on civil rights. Instead, he became one of the most intense and uncompromising defenders of Negro rights of his generation. Perhaps his was the psychology of the convert who defends his new faith more passionately, even more combatively, than the born believer. Harlan liked to think he changed because he knew the South, and realized that any relaxation of federal protection of the rights of Negroes would encourage the "white irreconcilables" to acts of discrimination and then of violence, destroying all hope of racial accommodation.

This was Harlan's odyssey on civil rights. When he sat down in October of 1883 to write his dissent in the *Civil Rights Cases,* he hoped to set off a cannon of protest. But he simply could not get his thoughts on paper. He worked late into the night, and even rose from half-sleep to write down ideas that he was afraid would elude him in the morning. "It was a trying time for him," his wife observed. "In point of years, he was much the youngest man on the Bench; and standing alone, as he did in regard to a decision which the whole nation was anxiously awaiting, he felt that . . . he must speak not only forcibly but wisely."

After weeks of drafting and discarding, Harlan seemed to reach a dead end. The dissent would not "write." It was at this point that Mrs. Harlan, bred in an abolitionist New England household, contributed a dramatic touch to the history of the *Civil Rights Cases*.

When the Harlans had moved to Washington in 1877, the Justice had acquired from a collector the inkstand which Chief Justice Roger Taney had used in writing all his opinions. Harlan was fond of showing this to guests and remarking that "it was the very inkstand from which the infamous *Dred Scott* opinion was written." Early in the 1880's, however, a niece of Taney, who was engaged in a collection of her uncle's effects, visited the Harlans. When she saw the inkstand she asked Harlan to contribute it to this reconstruction, and the Justice agreed. The next morning, Mrs. Harlan noted her husband's reluctance to part with his most prized possession, so without telling him, she arranged to have the inkstand "lost." She hid it away and the Justice was forced to make an embarrassed excuse to Taney's niece.

Now, on a Sunday morning, probably early in November of 1883, after Harlan had spent a sleepless night working on his dissent, Mallie Harlan remembered the inkstand. While the Justice was at church, she retrieved it from its hiding place, filled it with a fresh supply of ink and pen points, and placed it on the blotter of his upstairs desk. When the Justice returned from church, she told him, with an air of mystery, that he would find something special in his study. Harlan was overjoyed to recover his symbolic antique. It broke his writer's block at once. As Mrs. Harlan explains:

> The memory of the historic part that Taney's inkstand had played in the Dred Scott decision, in temporarily tightening the shackles of slavery upon the negro race in those ante-bellum days, seemed, that morning, to act like magic in clarifying my husband's thoughts in regard to the law . . . intended by Summer to protect the recently emancipated slaves in the enjoyment of equal "civil rights." His pen fairly flew on that day and, with the running start he then got, he soon finished his dissent.

How directly the recollection of Dred Scott pervaded Harlan's dissent is apparent to anyone who reads the opinion. Harlan noted that the pre-Civil War Supreme Court had upheld, by *implication* from the Constitution, Congressional laws forbidding individuals to interfere with recovery of fugitive slaves. To strike down the Act of 1875 meant that "the rights of freedom and American citizenship cannot receive from the Nation that efficient protection which heretofore was unhesitatingly accorded to slavery and the rights of masters."

Harlan argued that the Act of 1875 was constitutional on any of several grounds. The Thirteenth Amendment had already been held to guarantee "universal civil freedom"; Harlan stated that barring Negroes from facilities licensed by the state and under legal obligation to serve white persons without discrimination restored a major disability of slavery days and violated that civil freedom. As for the Fourteenth Amendment, its central purpose had been to extend national citizenship to the Negro, reversing the rule of *Dred Scott;* the final section of the Fourteenth Amendment gave Congress power to pass appropriate legislation to enforce that affirmative grant as well as the section barring state action which denied liberty or equality. Now the Supreme Court was deciding what legislation was appropriate and necessary for those purposes, although that role belonged to Congress, not the federal judiciary.

Even under the "state action" clause of the Fourteenth Amendment, he continued, the Act was constitutional; it was well settled that "railroad corporations, keepers of inns and managers of places of public accommodation are agents or instrumentalities of the State." Finally, Harlan attacked the majority's unwillingness to uphold the public carrier section of the Act under Congress' power to regulate interstate trips. That was exactly what was involved in Mrs. Robinson's case, he reminded his colleagues, and it had never been true before that Congress had to recite the section of the Constitution on which it relied.

In a closing peroration, Harlan replied to Bradley's comment that Negroes had been made "a special favorite of the laws." The war amendments had been passed not to "favor" the Negro but to include Negro men and women as "part of the people for whose welfare and happiness government is ordained."

Today, it is the colored race which is denied, by corporations and individuals wielding public authority, rights fundamental in their freedom and citizenship. At some future time, it may be that some other race will fall under the ban of race discrimination. If the constitutional amendments be enforced, according to the intent with which, as I conceive, they were adopted, there cannot be in this republic, any class of human beings in practical subjection to another class.

One of the major results of the *Civil Rights Cases* was predicted by one of Harlan's friends from Kentucky shortly after the decision. "I greatly fear the Court's action will invite assaults upon the colored people from the worst class of whites in the country," John Finnell speculated. The Southern states would give Negroes no legal protection against discrimination. "As long as it was understood that the Federal Government felt bound to protect the Negro, there was a healthy fear of the Federal Government by these poor whites. The Negro, except in certain localities in the far South, was getting along passably well." Now, the "patriotic vagabonds of the South" will move against the Negro.

Actually, the *Civil Rights Cases* ruling did two things. First, it destroyed the delicate balance of federal guarantee, Negro protest, and private enlightenment which was producing a steadily widening area of peacefully integrated public facilities in the North and South during the 1870's and early 1880's. Second, it had an immediate and profound effect on national and state politics as they related to the Negro. By denying Congress power to protect the Negro's rights to equal treatment, the Supreme Court wiped the issue of civil rights from the Republican party's agenda of national responsibility. At the same time, those Southern political leaders who saw anti-Negro politics as the most promising avenue to power could now rally the "poor whites" to the banner of segregation.

If the Supreme Court had stopped with the *Civil Rights Cases* of 1883, the situation of Negroes would have been bad but not impossible. Even in the South, there was no immediate imposition of segregation in public facilities. During the late 1880's, Negroes could be found sharing places with whites in many Southern restaurants, streetcars, and theaters. But increasingly, Democratic and Populist politicians found the Negro an irresistible target. As Solicitor General Phillips had warned the Supreme Court, what had been tolerated as the "fact" of discrimination was now being translated into "doctrine": between 1887 and 1891, eight Southern states passed laws requiring railroads to separate all white and Negro passengers. The Supreme Court upheld these laws in the 1896 case of *Plessy* v. *Fergu-*

*son.*[1] Then in the Berea College case of 1906, it upheld laws forbidding private schools to educate Negro and white children together. Both decisions aroused Harlan's bitter dissent. In the next fifteen or twenty years, the chalk line of Jim Crow was drawn across virtually every area of public contact in the South.

Today, as this line is slowly and painfully being erased, we may reflect on what might have been in the South if the Act of 1875 had been upheld, in whole or in part. Perhaps everything would have been the same. Perhaps forces were at work between 1883 and 1940 too powerful for a Supreme Court to hold in check. Perhaps Sumner's law was greatly premature. Yet the notion that total, state-required segregation was inevitable in the South after the 1880's is hard to credit. If the Supreme Court had taken the same *laissez-faire* attitude toward race relations that it took in economic affairs in these decades, voluntary integration would have survived as a counter-tradition to Jim Crow and might have made the transition of the 1950's less painful than it was. At the very least, one cannot help thinking that Harlan was a better sociologist than his colleagues, a better Southerner than the "irreconcilables." American constitutional history has a richer ring to it because of the protest that John Marshall Harlan finally put down on paper from Roger Taney's inkwell, in 1883.

[1] See Chapter X, *The Case of the Louisiana Traveler.*

# The Case of the Louisiana Traveler X

BY C. VANN WOODWARD

(*Plessy* v. *Ferguson,* 163 U.S. 537)

*Despite the discouraging decision in the* Civil Rights Cases, *not all American Negroes stood by idly while the country undid the progress that had been made during the Civil War and Reconstruction. C. Vann Woodward, Professor of History at Yale University and author of many important books, including* The Strange Career of Jim Crow, *describes some of these efforts, culminating in one of the most important cases in the history of the Supreme Court.*

In the spring of 1885, Charles Dudley Warner, Mark Twain's friend, neighbor, and onetime collaborator from Hartford, Connecticut, visited the International Exposition at New Orleans. He was astonished to find that "white and colored people mingled freely, talking and looking at what was of common interest," that Negroes "took their full share of the parade and the honors," and that the two races associated "in unconscious equality of privileges." During his visit he saw "a colored clergyman in his surplice seated in the chancel of the most important white Episcopal church in New Orleans, assisting the service."

It was a common occurrence in the 1880's for foreign travelers and Northern visitors to comment, sometimes with distaste and always with surprise, on the freedom of association between white and colored people in the South. Yankees in particular were unprepared for what they found and sometimes estimated that conditions below the Potomac were better than those above. Segregation was, after all, a Yankee invention. It had been the rule in the

North before the Civil War and integration the exception. In the South slavery and, afterward, its heritage of caste had so far served to define the Negro's "place" in the eyes of the dominant whites. There was discrimination, to be sure, but that was done on the responsibility of private owners or managers and not by requirement of law. As Alan Westin points out in the previous chapter, after the Supreme Court's decision in the *Civil Rights Cases* federal law gave no protection from such private acts.

Where discrimination existed it was often erratic and inconsistent. On trains the usual practice was to exclude Negroes from first-class or "ladies'" cars but to mix them with whites in second-class or "smoking" cars. In the old seaboard states of the South, however, Negroes were as free to ride first class as whites. In no state was segregation on trains complete, and in none was it enforced by law. The age of Jim Crow was still to come.

The first genuine Jim Crow law requiring railroads to carry Negroes in separate cars or behind partitions was adopted by Florida in 1887. Mississippi followed this example in 1888, Texas in 1889, Louisiana in 1890, Alabama, Arkansas, Georgia, and Tennessee in 1891, and Kentucky in 1892. The Carolinas and Virginia did not fall into line until the last three years of the century.

Negroes watched with despair while the foundations for the Jim Crow system were laid and the walls of segregation mounted around them. Their disenchantment with the hopes based on the Civil War amendment and the Reconstruction laws was nearly complete by 1890. The American commitment to equality, solemnly attested by three amendments to the Constitution and elaborate civil rights acts, was virtually repudiated. What had started as a retreat in 1877, when the last Federal troops were pulled out of the South, had turned into a rout. Northern radicals and liberals had abandoned the cause; the courts had rendered the Constitution helpless; the Republican party had forsaken the cause it had sponsored. A tide of racism was mounting in the country unopposed. Negroes held no less than five national conventions in 1890 to consider their plight, but all they could do was to pass resolutions of protest and confess their helplessness.

The colored community of New Orleans, with its strong infusion of French and other nationalities, was in a strategic position to furnish leadership for the resistance against segregation. Among these people were men of culture, education, and some wealth, as well as a heritage of several generations of freedom. Unlike the great majority of Negroes, they were city people with an established professional class and a high degree of literacy. By ancestry as well as by residence they were associated with Latin cultures at variance with Anglo-American ideas of race relations. Their forebears had lived under the Code Noir decreed for Louisiana by Louis XIV, and their city faced out upon Latin America.

When the Jim Crow car bill was introduced in the Louisiana Legislature, New Orleans Negroes organized to fight it. Negroes were still voting in large numbers, and there were sixteen colored senators and representatives in the Louisiana General Assembly at that time. On May 24, 1890, that body received "A Protest of the American Citizens' Equal Rights Association of Louisiana Against Class Legislation," an organization of colored people. The Association protested that the pending separate-car bill was "unconstitutional, unamerican, unjust, dangerous and against sound public policy." It would, declared the protest, "be a free license to the evilly-disposed that they might with impunity insult, humiliate, and otherwise maltreat inoffensive persons, and especially women and children who should happen to have a dark skin."

Nevertheless, on July 10, 1890, the Assembly passed the bill, the Governor signed it, and it became law. Entitled "An Act to promote the comfort of passengers," the new law required railroads "to provide equal but separate accommodations for the white and colored races." Two members of the Equal Rights Association, L. A. Martinet, editor of the New Orleans *Crusader,* and R. I. Desdunes, placed heavy blame on the sixteen colored members of the Assembly for the passage of the bill. According to Martinet, "they were completely the masters of the situation." They had but to withhold their support for a bill desired by the powerful Louisiana Lottery Company until the Jim Crow bill was killed. "But in an evil moment," he added, "our Representatives turned their ears to listen to the golden siren," and voted for the lottery bill "for a 'consideration.' "

Putting aside recriminations, the *Crusader* declared: "The Bill is now a law. The next thing is what we are going to do?" The editor spoke testily of boycotting the railroads, but concluded that "The next thing is . . . to begin to gather funds to test the constitutionality of this law. We'll make a case, a test case, and bring it before the Federal Courts."

On September 1, 1891, a group of eighteen men of color, all but three of them with French names like Esteves, Christophe, Bonseigneur, and Labat, including Desdunes and Martinet, formed a "Citizens' Committee to Test the Constitutionality of the Separate Car Law." Money came in slowly at first, but by October 11 Martinet could write that the committee had already collected $1,500 and that more could be expected "after we have the case well started." Even before the money was collected, Martinet had opened a correspondence about the case with Albion Winegar Tourgée, of Mayville, New York, and on October 10 the Citizens' Committee formally elected Tourgée "leading counsel in the case, from beginning to end, with power to choose associates."

This action called back into the stream of history a name prominent in the annals of Reconstruction. Albion Tourgée was in 1890 probably the most famous surviving carpetbagger. His fame was due not so much to his achievements as a carpetbagger in North Carolina, signficant though they were, as to the six novels about his Reconstruction experience that he had published since 1879. Born in Ohio, of French Huguenot descent, he had served as an officer in the Union Army, and moved to Greensboro, North Carolina, in 1865 to practice law. He soon became a leader of the Radical Republican party, took a prominent part in writing the Radical Constitution of North Carolina, and served as a judge of the superior court for six years with considerable distinction. On the side he helped prepare a codification of the state law and a digest of cases.

Tourgée's enemies questioned his public morals and his political wisdom, but never his courage or his intelligence. Although he entitled his most successful Reconstruction novel *A Fool's Errand,* he had by no means lost the convictions that inspired his crusade for the freedmen of North Carolina, and he brought to the fight against segregation in Louisiana a combination of zeal and ability that the citizens' Committee of New Orleans would have found it hard to improve on. They had reason to write him, "We know we have a friend in you & we know your ability is beyond question." He was informed that the committee's decision was made "spontaneously, warmly, & gratefully."

Tourgée's first suggestion was that the person chosen for defendant in the test case be "nearly white," but that proposal raised some doubts. "It would be quite difficult," explained Martinet, "to have a lady *too* nearly white refused admission to a 'white' car." He pointed out that "people of tolerably fair complexion, even if unmistakably colored, enjoy here a large degree of immunity from the accursed prejudice. . . . To make this case would require some tact." He would volunteer himself, "but I am one of those whom a fair complexion favors. I go everywhere, in all public places, though well-known all over the city, & never is anything said to me. On the cars it would be the same thing. In fact, color prejudice, in this respect, does not affect me. But, as I have said, we can try it, with another." An additional point of delicacy was a jealousy among the darker members of the colored community, who "charged that the people who support our movement were nearly white, or wanted to pass for white." Martinet discounted the importance of this feeling, but evidently took it into account. The critics, he said, had contributed little to the movement.

Railroad officials proved surprisingly cooperative. The first one approached, however, confessed that his road "did not enforce the law." It provided the Jim Crow car and posted the sign required by law, but told its conductors to molest no one who ignored instructions. Officers of two other roads "said the law was a bad and mean one; they would like to get rid of it," and asked for time to consult counsel. "They want to help us," said Martinet, "but dread public opinion." The extra expense of separate cars was one reason for railroad opposition to the Jim Crow law.

It was finally agreed that a white passenger should object to the presence of a Negro in a "white" coach, that the conductor should direct the colored passenger to go to the Jim Crow car, and that he should refuse to go. "The conductor will be instructed not to use force or molest," reported Martinet, "& *our* white passenger will swear out the affidavit. This will give us our *habeas corpus* case, I hope."

On the appointed day, February 24, 1892, Daniel F. Desdunes, a young colored man, bought a ticket for Mobile, boarded the Louisville & Nashville Railroad, and took a seat in the white coach. All went according to plan. Desdunes was committed for trial to the Criminal District Court in New Orleans and released on bail. On

March 21, James C. Walker, a local attorney associated with Tourgée in the case, filed a plea protesting that his client was not guilty
and attacking the constitutionality of the Jim Crow law. He wrote
Tourgée that he intended to go to trial as early as he could.

Between the lawyers there was not entire agreement on procedure.
Walker favored the plea that the law was void because it attempted
to regulate interstate commerce, over which the Supreme Court
held that Congress had exclusive jurisdiction. Tourgée was doubtful.
"What we want," he wrote Walker, "is not a verdict of not guilty,
nor a defect in this law but a decision whether such a law can be
legally enacted and enforced in any state and we should get everything off the track and out of the way for such a decision." Walker
confessed that "It's hard for me to give up my pet hobby that the
law is void as a regulation of interstate commerce," and Tourgée
admitted that he "may have spoken too lightly of the interstate
commerce matter."

However, the discussion was ended abruptly and the whole approach altered before Desdunes' case came to trial by a decision of
the State Supreme Court handed down on May 25. In this case,
which was of entirely independent origin, the court reversed the
ruling of a lower court and upheld the Pullman Company's plea
that the Jim Crow law was unconstitutional insofar as it applied
to interstate passengers.

Desdunes was an interstate passenger holding a ticket to Alabama,
but the decision was a rather empty victory. The law still applied
to intrastate passengers, and since all states adjacent to Louisiana
had by this time adopted similar or identical Jim Crow laws, the
exemption of interstate passengers was of no great importance to
the Negroes of Louisiana and it left the principle against which they
contended unchallenged. On June 1, Martinet wired Tourgée on
behalf of the committee saying, "Walker wants new case wholly
within state limits," and asked his opinion. Tourgée wired his agreement.

One week later, on June 7, Homer Adolph Plessy bought a ticket
in New Orleans, boarded the East Louisiana Railroad bound for
Covington, Louisiana, and took a seat in the white coach. Since
Plessy later described himself as "seven-eighths Caucasian and one-
eighth African blood," and swore that "the admixture of colored
blood is not discernible," it may be assumed that the railroad had

been informed of the plan and agreed to cooperate. When Plessy refused to comply with the conductor's request that he move to the Jim Crow car, he was arrested by Detective Christopher C. Cain, and charged with violating the Jim Crow car law. Tourgée and Walker then entered a plea before Judge John H. Ferguson of the Criminal District Court for the Parish of New Orleans, arguing that the law Plessy was charged with violating was null and void because it was in conflict with the Constitution of the United States. Ferguson ruled against them. Plessy then applied to the State Supreme Court for a writ of prohibition and certiorari and was given a hearing in November, 1892. Thus was born the case of *Plessy* v. *Ferguson.*

The court recognized that neither the interstate commerce clause nor the question of equality of accommodations was involved and held that the sole question was whether a law requiring "separate but equal accommodations" violated the Fourteenth Amendment. Citing numerous decisions of lower federal courts to the effect that accommodations did not have to be identical to be equal, the court, as expected, upheld the law. "We have been at pains to expound this statute," added the court, "because the dissatisfaction felt with it by a portion of the people seems to us so unreasonable that we can account for it only on the ground of some misconception."

Chief Justice Francis Tillou Nicholls, who presided over the court that handed down this decision in 1892, had signed the Jim Crow act as Governor when it was passed in 1890. Previously he had served as the "Redeemer" Governor who took over Louisiana from the carpetbaggers in 1877 and inaugurated a brief regime of conservative paternalism. In those days Nicholls had denounced race bigotry, appointed Negroes to office, and attracted many of them to his party. L. A. Martinet wrote Tourgée that Nicholls in those years had been "fair & just to colored men" and had, in fact, "secured a degree of protection to the colored people not enjoyed before under Republican Governors." But in November, 1892, the wave of Populist radicalism was reaching its crest in the South, and the course of Nicholls typified the concessions to racism that conservatives of his class were making in their efforts to divert poor-white farmers from economic reforms.

At a further hearing Judge Nicholls granted Plessy's petition for a writ of error that permitted him to seek redress before the Supreme Court of the United States. The brief that Albion Tourgée submitted to the Supreme Court in behalf of Plessy breathed a spirit of equalitarianism that was more in tune with his carpetbagger days than with the prevailing spirit of the mid-nineties. And it was no more in accord with the dominant mood of the Court than was the lone dissenting opinion later filed by Justice John Marshall Harlan, which echoed many of Tourgée's ringing phrases.

At the very outset, however, Tourgée advanced an argument in behalf of his client that unconsciously illustrated the paradox that had from the start haunted the American attempt to reconcile strong color prejudice with equalitarian commitments. Plessy, he contended, had been deprived of property without due process of law. The "property" in question was the "reputation of being white." It was "the most valuable sort of property, being the master-key that unlocks the golden door of opportunity." Intense race prejudice excluded any man suspected of having Negro blood "from the friendship and companionship of the white man," and therefore from the avenues to wealth, prestige, and opportunity. "Probably most white persons if given the choice," he held, "would prefer death to life in the United States as colored persons."

Since Tourgée had proposed that a person who was "nearly white" be selected for the test case, it may be presumed that he did so with this argument in mind. Of course, this was not a defense of the colored man against discrimination by whites, but a defense of the "nearly" white man against the penalties of color. From such penalties the colored man himself admittedly had no defenses. The argument, whatever its merits, apparently did not impress the Court.

Tourgée went on to develop more relevant points. He emphasized especially the incompatibility of the segregation law with the spirit and intent of the Thirteenth and Fourteenth Amendments, particularly the latter. Segregation perpetuated distinctions "of a servile character, coincident with the institution of slavery." He held that "slavery was a caste, a legal condition of subjection to the dominant class, a bondage quite separable from the incident of ownership." He scorned the pretense of impartiality and equal protection advanced in defense of the "separate but equal" doctrine. "The object of such a law," he declared, "is simply to debase and distinguish against the inferior race. Its purpose has been properly interpreted by the general designation of 'Jim Crow Car' law. Its object is to separate the Negroes from the whites in public conveyances for the gratification and recognition of the sentiment of white superiority and white supremacy of right and power." He asked the members of the Court to imagine the tables turned and themselves ordered into a Jim Crow car. "What humiliation, what rage would then fill the judicial mind!" he exclaimed.

The clue to the true intent of the Louisiana statute was that it did not apply "to nurses attending the children of the other race." On this clause he observed:

The exemption of nurses shows that the real evil lies not in the color of the skin but in the relation the colored person sustains to the white. If he is a dependent, it may be endured: if he is not, his presence is insufferable. Instead of being intended to promote the *general* comfort and moral well-being, this act is plainly and evidently intended to promote the happiness of one class by asserting its supremacy and the inferiority of another class. Justice is pictured blind and her daughter, the Law, ought at least to be color-blind.

Looking to the future, Tourgée asked, "What is to prevent the application of the same principle to other relations" should the separate-car law be upheld? Was there any limit to such laws?

Why not require all colored people to walk on one side of the street and whites on the other? . . . One side of the street may be just as good as the other. . . . The question is not as to the equality of the privileges enjoyed, but *the right of the State to label one citizen as white and another as colored* in the common enjoyment of a public highway.

The Supreme Court did not get around to handing down a decision in *Plessy* v. *Ferguson* until 1896. In the intervening years the retreat from the commitment to equality and the Fourteenth Amendment had quickened its pace in the South and met with additional acquiescence, encouragements, and approval in the North. New segregation laws had been adopted. Lynching had reached new peaks. Frightened by Populist gains in 1892 and 1894, Southern conservatives raised the cry of Negro Domination and called for White Solidarity. Two states had already disfranchised the Negro, and several others, including Louisiana, were planning to take the same course. In 1892 Congress defeated the Lodge Bill to extend federal protection to elections, and in 1894 it wiped from the federal statutes a mass of Reconstruction laws for the protection of equal rights. And then, on September 18, 1895, Booker T. Washington delivered a famous speech embodying the so-called "Atlanta Compromise," which was widely interpreted as an acceptance of subordinate status for the Negro by the foremost leader of the race.

On May 18, 1896, Justice Henry Billings Brown, of Michigan residence and Massachusetts birth, delivered the opinion of the court on the case of *Plessy* v. *Ferguson*. His views upholding the separate-but-equal doctrine were in accord with those of all his brothers, with the possible exception of Justice Brewer, who did not participate, and the certain exception of Justice Harlan, who vigorously dissented. In approving the principle of segregation, Justice Brown was also in accord with the prevailing climate of opinion and the trend of the times. More important for purposes of the decision, his views were in accord with a host of state judicial precedents, which he cited at length, as well as with unchallenged practice in many parts of the country, North and South. Furthermore, there were no federal judicial precedents to the contrary.

Whether Brown was well advised in citing as his principal authority the case of *Roberts* v. *City of Boston* is another matter. The fame of Chief Justice Lemuel Shaw of the Massachusetts Supreme Court was undoubtedly great, and in this case he unquestionably sustained the power of Boston to maintain separate schools for Negroes and rejected Charles Sumner's plea for equality before the law. But that was in 1849, twenty years before the Fourteenth Amendment, which, as Tourgée pointed out, should have made a difference. More telling was Brown's mention of the action of Congress in establishing segregated schools for the District of Columbia, an action endorsed by Radical Republicans who had supported the Fourteenth Amendment and sustained in regular Congressional appropriations ever since. Similar laws, wrote Brown, had been adopted by "the legislatures of many states, and have been generally, if not uniformly, sustained by the courts."

The validity of such segregation laws, the Justice maintained, depended on their "reasonableness." And in determining reasonableness, the legislature "is at liberty to act with reference to the established usages, customs, and traditions of the people, and with a view to the promotion of their comfort, and the preservation of the public peace and good order."

In addition to judicial precedent and accepted practice, Justice Brown ventured into the more uncertain fields of history, sociology, and psychology for support of his opinion. The framers of the Fourteenth Amendment, he maintained, "could not have intended to abolish distinctions based upon color, or to enforce social, as distinguished from political, equality." The issue of "social equality" was hardly in question here, but there were certainly grounds for maintaining that the framers of the amendment were under the impression that they intended to abolish all legal distinctions based on color.

The sociological assumptions governing Justice Brown's opinion were those made currently fashionable by Herbert Spencer and William Graham Sumner, but the dictum of Chief Justice Shaw in 1849, that prejudice "is not created by law, and probably cannot be changed by law," can hardly be attributed to the influence of either of those theorists. "We consider the underlying fallacy of the plaintiff's argument," said Brown,

to consist in the assumption that the enforced separation of the two races stamps the colored race with the badge of inferiority. If this is so, it is not by reason of anything found in the act, but solely because the colored race chooses to put that construction upon it. . . . The argument also assumes that social prejudices may be overcome by legislation, and that equal rights cannot be secured by the negro except by an enforced commingling of the two races. We cannot accept this proposition. . . . Legislation is powerless to eradicate racial instincts, or to abolish distinctions based upon physical differences, and the attempt to do so can only result in accentuating the difficulties of the present situation. If the civil and political rights of both races be equal, one cannot be inferior to the other civilly or politically. If one race be inferior to the other socially, the constitution of the United States cannot put them upon the same plane.

The most fascinating paradox in American jurisprudence is that the opinions of two sons of Massachusetts, Shaw and Brown, should have bridged the gap between the radical equalitarian commitment of 1868 and the reactionary repudiation of that commitment in 1896; and that a Southerner should have bridged the greater gap between the repudiation of 1896 and the radical rededication of the equalitarian idealism of Reconstruction days in 1954. For the dissenting opinion of Justice Harlan, embodying many of the arguments of Plessy's ex-carpetbagger counsel, foreshadowed the court's eventual repudiation of the *Plessy* v. *Ferguson* decision and the doctrine of "separate but equal" more than half a century later.

John Marshall Harlan is correctly described by Robert Cushman as "a Southern gentleman and a slaveholder, and at heart a conservative." His famous dissent in the *Civil Rights Cases* of 1883 had denounced the "subtle and ingenious verbal criticism" by which "the substance and spirit of the recent amendments of the Constitution have been sacrificed." In 1896 the "Great Dissenter" was ready to strike another blow for his adopted cause.

Harlan held the Louisiana segregation law in clear conflict with both the Thirteenth and Fourteenth Amendments. The former "not only struck down the institution of slavery," but also "any burdens or disabilities that constitute badges of slavery or servitude." Segregation was just such a burden or badge. Moreover, the Fourteenth Amendment "added greatly to the dignity and glory of American citizenship, and to the security of personal liberty," and segregation denied to Negroes the equal protection of both dignity and liberty. "The arbitrary separation of citizens, on the basis of race, while they are on a public highway," he said, "is a badge of servitude wholly inconsistent with the civil freedom and the equality before the law established by the constitution. It cannot be justified upon any legal grounds."

Harlan was as scornful as Tourgée had been of the claim that the separate-car law did not discriminate against the Negro. "Every one knows," he declared, that its purpose was "to exclude colored people from coaches occupied by or assigned to white persons." This was simply a poorly disguised means of asserting the supremacy of one class of citizens over another. The Justice continued:

But in view of the constitution, in the eye of the law, there is in this country no superior, dominant, ruling class of citizens. There is no caste here. *Our constitution is color-blind,* and neither knows nor tolerates classes among citizens. In respect of civil rights, all citizens are equal before the law. The humblest is the peer of the most powerful. The law regards man as man, and takes no account of his surroundings, or of his color when his civil rights as guaranteed by the supreme law of the land are involved. . . . We boast of the freedom enjoyed by our people above all other peoples. But it is difficult to reconcile that boast with a state of law which, practically, puts the brand of servitude and degradation upon a large class of our fellow citizens—our equals before the law. The thin disguise of "equal" accommodations for passengers in railroad coaches will not mislead any one, nor atone for the wrong this day done.

The present decision, it may well be apprehended, [predicted Harlan] will not only stimulate aggressions, more or less brutal and irritating, upon the admitted rights of colored citizens, but will encourage the belief that it is possible, by means of state enactments, to defeat the beneficent purposes which the people of the United States had in view when they adopted the recent amendments of the constitution.

If the state may so regulate the railroads, "why may it not so regulate the use of the streets of its cities and towns as to compel white citizens to keep on one side of a street, and black citizens to keep on the other," or, for that matter, apply the same regulations to street-cars and other vehicles, or to courtroom, the jury box, the legislative hall, or to any other place of public assembly? "In my opinion," concluded the Kentuckian, "the judgment this day rendered will, in time, prove to be quite as pernicious as the decision made by this tribunal in the Dred Scott Case."

The country received the news of this momentous decision in relative silence and apparent indifference. Thirteen years earlier the *Civil Rights Cases* had precipitated pages of news reports, hundreds of editorials, indignant rallies, Congressional bills, a Senate report, and much general debate. In striking contrast, the *Plessy* decision got only short, inconspicuous news reports and virtually no editorial comment outside the Negro press. A great change had taken place, and the Court evidently now gave voice to the dominant mood of the country. Justice Harlan spoke for the forgotten convictions of a bygone era.

The racial aggressions that the Justice foresaw came in a flood after the decision of 1896. Even Harlan indicated by his opinion of 1899 in *Cummings* v. *Board of Education* that he saw nothing unconstitutional in segregated public schools. Virginia was the last state in the South to adopt the separate-car law, and she resisted it until 1900. Up to that year this was the only law of the type adopted by a majority of the Southern states. But on January 12, 1900, the editor of the Richmond *Times* was in full accord with the new spirit when he asserted:

It is necessary that this principle be applied in every relation of Southern life. God Almighty drew the color line and it cannot be obliterated. The negro must stay on his side of the line and the white man must stay on his side, and the sooner both races recognize this fact and accept it, the better it will be for both.

With incredible thoroughness the color line *was* drawn and the Jim Crow principle applied—even to areas that Tourgée and Harlan had suggested a few years before as absurd extremes. In sustaining the constitutionality of the new Jim Crow laws, courts universally and confidently cited *Plessy* v. *Ferguson* as the leading authority. They continued to do so for more than half a century.

On April 4, 1950, Justice Robert H. Jackson wrote old friends in Jamestown, New York, of his surprise in running across the name of Albion W. Tourgée, once a resident of the nearby village of Mayville, in connection with segregation decisions then pending before the Supreme Court. "The Plessy case arose in Louisiana," he wrote,

and how Tourgée got into it I have not learned. In any event, I have gone to his old brief, filed here, and there is no argument made today that he would not make to the Court. He says, "Justice is pictured blind and her daughter, The Law, ought at least to be color-blind." Whether this was original with him, it has been gotten off a number of times since as original wit. Tourgée's brief was filed April 6, 1896 and now, just fifty-four years after, the question is again being argued whether his position will be adopted and what was a defeat for him in '96 be a post-mortem victory.

*Plessy* v. *Ferguson* remained the law of the land for exactly fifty-eight years, from May 18, 1896, to May 17, 1954. Then, at long last, came a vindication, "a post-mortem victory"—not only for the ex-carpetbagger Tourgée, but for the ex-slaveholder Harlan as well.

# The Case of the              XI
## Monopolistic Railroadmen

BY R. W. APPLE, JR.

(*Northern Securities Co.* et al. v. *U.S.*, 193 U.S. 197)

*The growth of business monopolies after the Civil War led Congress to pass the Sherman Anti-Trust Act of 1890, which declared illegal combinations "in restraint of trade or commerce among the several States, or with foreign nations." The constitutionality of the Sherman Act was never questioned; it clearly fell within the power of Congress under the "commerce clause," which John Marshall had defined so broadly in the Steamboat case. But the law was vague. What constituted "restraint" of trade and commerce?*

*During the 1890's, the Supreme Court limited the effect of the Sherman Act sharply, especially in the E. C. Knight case (1895), in which it held that the control over the manufacture of more than 90 per cent of the sugar refined in the United States was not* ipso facto *a violation of the law. Congress had not attempted "to deal with monopoly directly," Chief Justice Fuller declared in the Knight decision, and the government had offered no proof that the sugar refiners had intended to restrain trade. As a result of this and other court tests, by 1900 the Sherman Act had become practically a dead letter.*

*This was the situation when the events leading up to the case described below took place. R. W. Apple, Jr., a* New York Times *reporter, is the author of* Where There's Smoke, *a history of the smoking-health controversy.*

On January 7, 1901, for the first time in history, two million shares changed hands on the New York Stock Exchange, and brokers were pushed to the edge of exhaustion by the pace of trading. Less than two months later came the formation of the billion-dollar United States Steel Corporation, the climax of ten years of breath-taking industrial consolidation. McKinley was assured of another four years, the specter of Bryanism was banished, and the road to prosperity looked as smooth and as clear as the New York Central's best straightaway.

More than any other, the man who epitomized the era was the awesome figure in the glass-paneled office at 23 Wall Street. At sixty-three, J. Pierpont Morgan was a brusque and lordly man, with steel-gray hair, a big, straggling mustache, a bulbous red nose, and hazel eyes of an almost hypnotic intensity. Looking into his eyes, said the photographer Edward Steichen, was like staring at the headlight of an onrushing express train at night. During the preceding decade, he had reorganized four great railroads—the Southern, the Erie, the Reading, and the Norfolk & Western. The power of the House of Morgan grew with each reorganization, because Morgan saw to it that directors loyal to him were installed on the boards of each line.

Only one railroad man had both the bravado and the means to challenge the House of Morgan. His name was Edward H. Harriman, and he commanded, in addition to the considerable assets of the Union Pacific and the Southern Pacific, the support of William Rockefeller and Henry H. Rogers—the "Standard Oil boys." Small, frail, myopic, unkempt, he made a striking contrast to Morgan the Magnificent. When he assumed the leading role in the affairs of the Union Pacific in 1897, it had liabilities of $81 million, antiquated rolling stock, a poorly ballasted roadbed, and little traffic. It was scarcely more than a ribbon of rust. Three years later, the Union Pacific was free of debt, paying dividends regularly, and earning $20 million a year. "Bet-You-a-Million" Gates called it "the most magnificent railroad property in the world."

J. J. Hill's Great Northern and Morgan's Northern Pacific ran almost parallel from Minnesota to the coast; Ned Harriman's Union Pacific stretched across the plains from Omaha to Ogden, Utah. East of them lay the Chicago, Burlington & Quincy, reaching from the great marketplace on Lake Michigan northwest toward St. Paul and southwest across Iowa and Nebraska. The Burlington had a strategic position, and the man who controlled it would have a tremendous competitive advantage.

Harriman tried first. Early in 1900, he instructed Jacob Schiff of the investment banking house of Kuhn, Loeb & Company to acquire 200,000 shares of Burlington in the open market. Schiff's operatives went to work in May, but on July 25 Harriman gave up, having been able to buy only 80,300 shares.

The next year, it was Morgan's turn. He told his ally Hill, "Go ahead and see what you can do with the Burlington." A grim, craggy old man, Hill was the personification of the frontier myth. Perhaps his dress was a bit more elegant than it had been when he arrived in the raw village of Pig's Eye, Minnesota, as a young man. But then Pig's Eye was more elegant, too—it was now called St. Paul—and even fastidious clothes couldn't hide Hill's long, shaggy beard or his volcanic temper. Hill had no intention of trying to buy control of the Burlington on the Exchange. Instead, he went straight to the road's directors and offered them $200 a share, although the stock's market price was only $180. In March, 1901, the Burlington accepted, agreeing to sell one-half to the Great Northern, one-half to the Northern Pacific.

Harriman, frozen out, was furious. At a meeting with Hill in the home of New York financier George F. Baker a few weeks later, he demanded a one-third interest in the Burlington. Only in this way, he insisted, could peace be maintained in the country west of the Missouri. Hill refused. "Very well," said Harriman, "it is a hostile act and you will have to take the consequences." But Hill remained unconcerned. He had the Burlington, hadn't he? How could Harriman hurt him? Hill left for Seattle to look after the affairs of the Great Northern, and Morgan sailed for France to enjoy the sun at Aix-les-Bains.

The plan now concocted by Harriman was so audacious that even Morgan would never have believed it, had it not become a crushing reality. He would steal the Northern Pacific itself while Hill and Morgan congratulated themselves on their coup. It would be a gargantuan project—the Northern Pacific's stock was worth $155 million, so it would take $78 million to buy control—but that appealed to the little man's sense of grandeur.

Quietly, carefully, he put Schiff to work early in April. By April 15, the banker had 150,000 of the 800,000 shares of common and 100,000 of the 750,000 shares of preferred. The Hill-Morgan forces slumbered on. One of Hill's closest friends sold Kuhn, Loeb 35,000 shares, and a subsidiary of the Northern Pacific sold 13,000 shares from its treasury. On May 2, irony of ironies, the House of Morgan itself disposed of 10,000 shares.

Out in Seattle, Jim Hill finally became alarmed. He hurried to New York, stormed into the office of Jacob Schiff, and demanded an explanation. Schiff, for once, was not evasive; he told his agitated visitor he was buying for Harriman's account. "But you can't get control," Hill said. "The Great Northern, Morgan and my friends were recently holding thirty or forty million of Northern Pacific stock, and so far as I know, none of it has been sold." Answered Schiff, "That may be, but we've got a lot of it."

Schiff's confidence was well founded. By May 3, a Friday, the Union Pacific held 370,000 shares of common—a shade less than half—and 420,000 shares of preferred—more than half. Taking the two classes together (and both had voting rights), it held 790,000 of 1,550,000 shares—a clear majority and hence enough for control. But to Harriman, alert though too sick with excitement to leave his bed, it was not enough. He knew the preferred could be retired at the beginning of the next year by vote of the board of directors, and he was sure Morgan would try to do so. So he called Kuhn, Loeb on the morning of the fourth and placed an order for 40,000 more shares of common. Unfortunately for Harriman, the devout Schiff was at the synagogue. When the order was finally relayed to him, he ordered it held up, convinced that Harriman was wasting his money.

By Monday it was too late. Hill and Robert Bacon, partner-in-charge at 23 Wall Street while Morgan was in Europe, had at last decided that they were in danger. Led by James R. Keene, the most proficient market manipulator of his day, the Morgan forces were everywhere, snapping up N.P. for whatever price was asked. By Tuesday night, they had 410,000 shares of common, a clear majority.

And then the brokers began counting. If Harriman had 370,000 shares, and he did, and Morgan had 410,000, and *he* did, that left only 20,000 in other hands. Many more than that must be in strong-boxes and mattresses on both sides of the Atlantic. The answer lay with the "shorts"—that is, speculators who had sold N.P. shares they did not own, certain they could buy them back later, before they had to make delivery, at a lower price. If, for some reason, the price stayed up for several days, they could borrow shares from brokers for a nominal fee. All of this was—and is—

a normal part of the Wall Street routine. But these were not normal times, as the first clicks of the ticker on Wednesday morning made painfully evident.

It was a brutal day. Brokers fought, elbows flailing, to get at their posts. Prices melted away as the shorts unloaded their other holdings to get enough money to buy Northern Pacific. First Burlington, then Erie, then the whole list broke. Only Northern Pacific rose—to 160, to 170, finally to 180. After the din subsided, one desperate man paid $25,000 for the use of 500 shares overnight.

Old Jim Hill was still playing possum. "I have not bought a share of Northern Pacific in six months," he told a reporter. But the hundreds of men who filled the Waldorf-Astoria that night, milling from the café through the billiard room into the bar and back again, were not so sure. "It looks," said one of them, "as if the little boys have commenced something while the big boy was away."

Thursday, May 9, brought gray skies to New York and a slow, depressing drizzle. Huge crowds gathered in the financial district long before the opening. The suspense did not last long. Liquidation began with the opening bell, and soon the whole market was swept away—hundreds of millions of dollars in values were destroyed—as the hysterical shorts jettisoned every share they had. "In the [first] hour, the nearest to hell I ever saw in Wall Street," said one broker many years later, "the bottom seemed to drop out of everything." At first the declines were a point or so, then five, then ten, then twenty. The panic was on. Atchison, which had been at 90 the week before, touched 43; U.S. Steel fell from 54 to 24, Amalgamated Copper from 125 to 90. An elderly woman, arriving at the Exchange about eleven-thirty, asked a bystander where Steel preferred was selling. "Eighty-three," he said. "God help me," she gasped. "I'm ruined."

Above the whole list, like some loathesome star, hung the one stock that had caused it all, the one stock that was all but impossible to buy—Northern Pacific. The frenzied shorts bid it up to 300, to 650, to 800, and finally, just before noon, to $1000. A man from Schenectady sold his 100 shares at a profit of $55,000; a man from Connecticut sold his 100 at a profit of $60,000. Shortly after noon, the madness ebbed. The bankers made available several millions in short-term credit, and Bacon and Schiff, after unfor-

givable vacillation, announced that the shorts would be allowed
to settle for $150 a share.

The contest for control of the Northern Pacific remained substantially unchanged, with each side convinced it had effective
control. Morgan and Hill thought they could delay the stockholders'
meeting long enough to retire the preferred stock, and Harriman
had the word of five corporation lawyers that this was illegal.
Finally, Harriman decided, either on his own or at the suggestion
of his Standard Oil friends, to accept a compromise. He agreed
to a peace treaty, signed May 31 at the Metropolitan Club. On
July 17, Morgan—as provided in the agreement—named five new
Northern Pacific directors, including Harriman himself and two
others considered his allies.

But to Morgan and Hill, it was an uneasy truce. Each feared
that another raid might be launched from another direction.
Hill, moreover, had long cherished the idea of putting the Great
Northern stock that he and his friends owned into a holding
company so it would not be dispersed after his death. It was decided
to create a gigantic company to hold the stocks of the Great
Northern, the Northern Pacific, and the Burlington. Accordingly,
on November 12, under the particularly accommodating laws of
New Jersey, the Northern Securities Company was incorporated.
Its capital was a whopping $400 million—"large enough," said
Morgan, "so that nobody could ever buy it."

Just a few moments after the close of the stock market on
September 14, a pack of excited newspapermen had burst into the
sanctum at 23 Wall Street. Almost at the front door they came
upon the redoubtable Morgan, on his way to an East River pier
to board his yacht. "Mr. Morgan," the first one shouted, "President
McKinley is dead." For a moment there was silence; then one of
the bolder reporters asked the great man for a comment. "It is the
saddest news I ever heard," came the reply. "I can't talk about it."

For once, the reaction of Morgan was no different from that of
the average American. Men in all stations of life were shocked
and saddened by the terrible news from Buffalo. But if the death
of William McKinley affected the Indiana farmer and the Boston
shopkeeper like the death of a beloved uncle, it must have seemed
to J. P. Morgan like the loss of a general in the midst of battle.

Business had contributed more than $4 million to McKinley's campaign, and business leaders thought they had bought four years' worth of insurance against government "meddling." With his good friend Mark Hanna sitting at the President's elbow, Morgan had concluded, the government was as sound as any government made up of politicians could be.

Theodore Roosevelt, heir to the McKinley administration, had been Assistant Secretary of the Navy, Governor of New York, and, of course, Vice President. He had formulated nothing approaching an organic economic philosophy, but there were enough scattered indications of heterodoxy to give the business classes pause. Roosevelt had early conceived a dislike for mere wealth—especially wealth gained in speculation, an activity which offended his almost puritanical sense of morality. "The commercial classes," he had written at the age of twenty-eight, "are only too likely to regard everything from the standpoint of 'Does it pay?' " In 1894, he told Brander Matthews: "I know the banker, merchant, and railroad king well . . . and *they* also need education and sound chastisement." Such sentiments, a mild potion indeed compared to the heady brew of Bryanism, were nevertheless a distinct departure from those of McKinley.

Yet Roosevelt had opposed, in 1884, so primitive a measure of government control as a bill to limit the workday of streetcar conductors to twelve hours. And the bloody Pullman strike, which had moved Hanna to shout, "Any man who won't meet his men halfway is a God-damn fool," had elicited from Roosevelt a very different comment: "I like to see a mob handled by the regulars, or by good state guards, not overscrupulous about bloodshed."

Nowhere was the ambivalence of Roosevelt's attitudes more evident than on the question which meant most to Morgan—corporation control. "The quack who announces he has a cure-all," Roosevelt insisted, "is a dangerous person." Still, with his suspicion of great wealth, Roosevelt was unwilling to let corporations run roughshod over all other elements in society. "There *are* real abuses," he conceded. He announced his determination to "see that the rich man is held to the same accountability as the poor man."

Some time early in 1902, probably in January, Roosevelt asked his Attorney General, Philander Chase Knox, for an opinion on the legality of the Northern Securities Company. An old-line Republican from Pittsburgh who had once been Andrew Carnegie's lawyer, Knox had never shown the slightest inclination to interfere with business. But poring over the incorporation papers of the Securities Company, he came to the conclusion that it had the power to restrain trade in the Northwest, and that its capitalization would force it to exercise its power. More than 30 per cent of its $400 million of stock, Knox decided, was pure water, and only by gouging customers could it hope to earn a reasonable return on such a topheavy capital structure. On February 19, after the close of the stock market, he issued a terse memorandum to the newspapers. "Some time ago," it said, "the President requested an opinion as to the legality of this merger, and I have recently given him one to the effect that in my judgment it violates the Sherman Act of 1890." On March 10, a suit was filed in the Federal Court in St. Paul, just a few blocks from Jim Hill's office.

The attack on the Northern Securities Company was a symbolic act, not a grudge fight. "The men creating [the Securities Company] had done so in open and above-board fashion," Roosevelt wrote years later, "acting under what they, and most of the members of the bar, thought to be the law." As his later career made clear, Roosevelt considered regulation, not prosecution, the ultimate answer to the problems created by the New Industrialism. First, however, it was necessary to make sure that the forces of the left did not take matters into their own hands, that Debs and Bryan did not, like Marat and Robespierre, bring down the whole social structure. And it was necessary to make sure that Morgan and his friends did not, like Louis XIV and his courtiers, make revolution inevitable by their blindness. "When I became President," Roosevelt wrote later, "the question as to the *method* by which the United States Government was to control the corporations was not yet important. The absolutely vital question was whether the Government had the power to control them at all." The Northern Securities case was the test in which he sought to establish that power.

Governmental secrets were, as a rule, no better kept in the first decade of the twentieth century than they are in the sixth, but the Northern Securities suit was an exception. Even Secretary of War Elihu Root, usually Roosevelt's closest Cabinet confidant, was taken aback by Knox's announcement.

The surprise of Root was nothing, however, compared with the utter astonishment of Morgan. The financier was at home having dinner when he got the word. His face reflecting a kind of appalled dismay rather than the seething anger of which he was capable, Morgan spoke over and over of the unfairness of the President's action. The President, Morgan felt, had violated the rules of gentlemanly behavior. If a gentleman thought a friend was doing something out of bounds, he mentioned it to him discreetly. If the Securities Company had to be dissolved, Morgan told his friends, Roosevelt should have asked *him* to do it.

Morgan arrived in Wall Street an hour earlier than usual the next morning and spent the day in conference with Charles Steele and George W. Perkins, two of the firm's partners. Across the street, there was pandemonium. In the first twenty minutes of trading on the outdoor Curb Exchange—the ancestor of the American Stock Exchange—Northern Securities stock lost almost ten points before Morgan allies could shore it up. Speculators, of course, were furious at the President, because they were the ones who stood to lose the most in a short, violent swing of the market. The investors and underwriters, more concerned with the long term, were considerably less angry. "It is a good thing," said a prominent banker. "A decision by the highest authority is needed to let people know where they stand." Thomas Woodlock's editorial in the *Wall Street Journal* the next morning put the matter a little less delicately. "If securities combinations are legal," he wrote, "[the financiers] wish to be able to take full advantage of the fact. If they are not legal, the quicker the fact is established, the quicker some other method of accomplishing desired results can be sought."

On the twenty-second, Morgan, Hanna, William Rockefeller, and several other businessmen went to the White House to get the President's views firsthand. Apparently the meeting was not a success, for Morgan met privately later that afternoon with Roosevelt and Knox. Why, Morgan wanted to know, had he not been consulted in advance? "That," said the President, "is just what we did not want to do." Morgan was not easily put off. "If we have done anything wrong," he persisted, "send your man to my man and they can fix it up." "That can't be done," said Roosevelt, and Knox snapped, "We don't want to fix it up. We want to stop it."

This last must have impressed Morgan, because his next question was defensive. "Are you going to attack my other interests, the Steel Trust and the others?" "Certainly not," the President replied, "unless we find out that in any case they have done something that we regard as wrong." After Morgan had departed, obviously enraged, Roosevelt added a postscript. "That is a most illuminating illustration of the Wall Street point of view," he said to Knox. "Mr. Morgan could not help regarding me as a big rival operator who either intended to ruin all his interests or else could be induced to come to an agreement to ruin none."

Hill, who was in St. Paul, was too busy to go to Washington, but his irritation was evident. "If [this is] a grandstand play, of course, we shall hear little more about it," he said. "But if they do fight they will have their hands full, and they will wish they had never been born before they get through." In mid-March, a group of his friends paid a call on Senator Hanna at the Arlington Hotel in Washington. They asked Hanna to intercede with the President, but the Senator would have none of it. "I warned Hill that McKinley might have to act against his damn company last year," he grunted. "I'm sorry for Hill, but just what do you gentlemen think I can do?" When they pressed him further, Hanna put them off with another question: "The Senate passed the Sherman Anti-Trust Law; how can I take it off the books?"

All through the summer and fall of 1902, a special examiner heard testimony from Morgan, Hill, Harriman, Perkins, Schiff, and scores of lesser figures. There was a good deal of pulling and hauling as the government sought to establish its case and the high-priced battery of defense attorneys, headed by the suave Francis Lynde Stetson, Morgan's top lawyer, sought to keep it from doing so. The responses of the great capitalists were marked by an ingenuousness that is as unconvincing today as it was to the trial court. Schiff, for example, maintained that his firm had bought Northern Pacific for its own account, not for that of Harriman. And Morgan, he of the prodigious mathematical mind, found himself unable to recall any significant portion of the details of the transactions he had handled.

As to the pivotal questions involved, there was general disagreement. The government contended that the Great Northern and the Northern Pacific had been "engaged in active competition with one another"; the defense insisted that less than 2 percent of the total interstate business in the Northwest had been competitive. The government charged that the Burlington purchase had been part of a general scheme to put the Great Northern and Northern Pacific under common control; the defense ridiculed the allegation. The government argued that the Securities Company had been organized specifically to "restrain and prevent" railroad competition in the Northwest; the defense asserted that the company was designed solely to protect the Great Northern and the Northern Pacific from further raids like Harriman's. Finally, each side made a climactic extralegal appeal. If the Securities Company were not dissolved, the government brief contended, every railroad in the country could be "absorbed, merged and consolidated, thus placing the public at the absolute mercy of the holding corporation." The government was invoking that great rhetorical abstraction, The People; but Stetson had the perfect answer: he wrapped his clients in the Constitution. To dissolve the Securities Company, he said, echoing the phraseology of the Fourteenth Amendment, would be to deprive citizens of their property without due process of law "by taking away from them their right to sell it as their interest may suggest."

The circuit court decision was announced at St. Louis on April 9, 1903, by Judge Amos Thayer, speaking for a unanimous four-man court. It must have been clear to the defendants almost as soon as Judge Thayer began reading that their cause was lost, for the sixth sentence of his opinion began: "These railroads *are,* and in public estimation have ever been regarded, as parallel and competing lines." This was a key point. If the situation were otherwise, how could the court hold that trade was being restrained? Not much later, Thayer applied the *coup de grâce.* "The [Northern Securities] scheme," he said, "destroyed every motive for competition" between the two roads. "We must conclude that those who conceived and executed the plan" intended to do so. It did not matter whether competition had, in fact, been lessened; it was enough that there was a likelihood that it would be.

Eleven days later, the defendants filed notice of their intention to appeal the decree, and on May 11, 1903, the seventeen hundred closely printed pages comprising the record in the case now styled *Northern Securities Company et al.* v. *The United States* reached the Supreme Court.

Since 1895, the Supreme Court had been engaged in doing all it could to protect the rights of property. Few were the occasions when the court had seemed willing to admit that war and the industrial explosion which followed had wrought the slightest change in American life. As a result, the Sherman Act had remained, for nearly fifteen years after its enactment, an almost toothless tiger in a jungle of carnivores. Although robust enough to deal with price-fixing by railroads, or an occasional restraint-of-trade case, against the awesome industrial trusts—the targets of its authors—it was impotent.

Perhaps the Northern Securities case would change all this. Not since the Dred Scott decision in 1857 had the country been so fascinated by a lawsuit. Every captain of industry in the country, the *New York Times* said, awaited the court's decision "with the deepest anxiety." The *Times* forgot to mention it, but there were millions of other people anxious to know the outcome, too. Would the court decide for Hill and Morgan and Harriman? Or would it go along with Teddy Roosevelt?

On December 14, at the table reserved for the press, James Creelman, a reporter from the New York *World,* watched the justices file in. First came little Chief Justice Melville W. Fuller, looking like a dilettante poet; then John Marshall Harlan, with his shining bald head; Rufus W. Peckham, tall, silver-haired and pallid; Oliver Wendell Holmes, towering over the rest, ramrod-straight; David J. Brewer, who reminded Creelman of a medieval archbishop, except that he wore no beard; Edward D. White, square of jaw and resolute; Joseph McKenna, wearing glasses and a pointed little gray beard; William R. Day, small and emaciated. Only Henry B. Brown, ill with an eye infection, was missing.

Then John G. Johnson of Philadelphia was on his feet, addressing the Court in his almost conversational tone of voice. Nine years before, he had defended the Sugar Trust; now, massive and gray, he was speaking as the chief defense counsel of the Northern Securities Company. This Court, he began, had always held that it was the use of power, not the mere possession of it, that constituted the offense. But the circuit court had decided that the Securities Company was guilty because it had *the power to restrain trade.* Was that not in conflict with settled law? "Few of us have a desire to commit murder," he told the Court, "but many of us use a razor, which gives us the power to murder." Pacing about the courtroom, swinging his glasses on the end of their string, occasionally raising his hands above his head to drive home a point, Johnson asked the Court to put itself in the position of Hill and Morgan after the Harriman raid. "What was to be done?" he asked them. "Remain quiet and allow these people, who were waiting like the fox under the tree for something to drop, and let them have the prize, or to protect the alliance?" The second course was the only sensible one, he submitted, and the method chosen was entirely legal.

When C. W. Bunn of the Northern Pacific had finished his brief supplementary argument, Attorney General Knox, handsome and immaculate, rose from the chair where he had been sitting watchfully all afternoon. Slowly and calmly at first, then with rising passion, he laid out the government's case. Just before the adjournment, he went to the heart of the matter—the spot Justice Holmes liked to call the jugular. "The Securities Company," he said, "is guilty of the mischief the law is designed to prevent—namely, it brings transportation trade through a vast section of country under the controlling interest of a single body."

The next morning, Knox had but one point to make. "To deny that this is a combination challenges common intelligence," he said. "To deny that it is in restraint of trade challenges the authority of this court." He finished in only ninety minutes, less than half the time allotted to him. In rebuttal George B. Young of the Great Northern insisted that the holder of railroad stock was no more engaged in interstate commerce than the holder of stock in a baseball team was engaged in playing baseball, and asked that the lower court ruling be reversed. Then the lawyers gathered up their papers and departed, and the Court passed to a consideration of less dramatic matters. In New York, Jim Hill told a reporter:

"I am just as sure that the Northern Securities Company is lawful as I ever was."

Three months later the drama was re-enacted. Again the courtroom was packed with visitors, although the Court had tried to keep the decision date secret. The speculation was that the government would win, but no one could be sure, despite the rumor that Justice White had prepared a dissent weeks ago. When Justice Holmes opened the proceedings by reading the decision in an obscure probate case, the air of expectancy subsided. But then the Chief Justice nodded almost imperceptibly to Harlan, who began shuffling a great stack of papers in front of him. When he said "Case Number 277," a murmur went through the courtroom. As Harlan read on, a chain of messengers began feeding reports to newspapermen outside—noncommittal at first, because Harlan in his unhurried way was beginning with a recital of the whole Sherman Act and a long description of the facts of the case. Finally he came to the phrase "no scheme or device could more certainly come within the words of the act." The Associated Press sent out a bulletin: "NORTHERN SECURITIES DECISION AFFIRMED."

The opinion was vintage Harlan. It was blunt, interminably long, full of rhetorical questions. Most important, it bore on almost every page the marks of Harlan's impatience with legal formalism and his determination to look beyond the form of a transaction to its essence. "No scheme or device," the most telling passage began,

could more certainly come within the words of the [Sherman] act . . . or could more effectively and certainly suppress free competition between the constituent companies. This combination is, within the meaning of the act, a "trust"; but if it is not it is a *combination in restraint of interstate and international commerce*; and that is enough to bring it under the condemnation of the act. The mere existence of such a combination . . . constitute[s] a menace to, and a restraint upon, that freedom of commerce which Congress intended to recognize and protect. . . . If such a combination be not destroyed . . . the entire commerce of the immense part of the United States between the Great Lakes and the Pacific at Puget Sound will be at the mercy of a single holding corporation.

The decision simply pulverized the defendants' carefully wrought arguments. The suggestion that the federal government could not interfere with the Securities Company because it was acting pursuant to a state charter, Harlan wrote, "does not at all impress us." The contention that the Court was sanctioning the regulation of stock ownership rather than the regulation of commerce, he added, "is the setting up of mere men of straw to be easily stricken down." Justice Brown, Justice McKenna, and Justice Day voted with Harlan, and Justice Brewer agreed with their conclusion, although he arrived at it by slightly different reasoning. The other four members of the Court dissented.

Both Holmes and White wrote opinions taking Harlan to task. White's essay was one long wail of anguish over what he regarded as the nonlogic of the majority's stand. At least a half-dozen times he used the words "I fail to perceive . . ." and it was evident that the whole pattern of Harlan's thought had escaped him. In White's view, all the unknowns could be factored out of the case save one—whether "the ownership of stock in railroad corporations" was interstate commerce. Convinced that the answer was no, he argued that this meant Congress could not, under the Constitution, regulate such ownership.

If the central thesis of White's dissent was that Congress *could not* regulate the ownership of stock, the whole thrust of Holmes's was that it *had not*. He was happy, he said, that only four members of the Court had adopted the most extreme view—a view which, in his opinion, would

disintegrate society so far as it could into individual atoms. If that were its intent I should regard calling such a law a regulation of commerce as a mere pretense. It would be an attempt to reconstruct society. I am not concerned with the wisdom of such an attempt but I believe that Congress was not entrusted with the power to make it and I am deeply persuaded that it has not tried.

It was necessary, Holmes said, to consider dispassionately what the Sherman Act meant, to "read the words before us as if the question were whether two small exporting grocers shall go to jail."

The two key phrases in the statute are "contract in restraint of trade" and "combination in restraint of trade," Holmes wrote, and each has a settled meaning at English common law. In a *contract* in restraint of trade, A enters into an agreement with B under which the activities of A are restricted. Clearly this did not apply to the Securities Company. In a *combination* in restraint of trade, on the other hand, A and B join to exclude C from some field of endeavor. But, Holmes continued, the restraint does not begin until something is done to prevent the third party from competing with the combination. To be guilty of violating the Act's prohibition of combinations in restraint of trade, the Securities Company would have had to prevent another railroad from competing with the three it owned. Had this happened? Since the Sherman Act specifically had put corporations and individuals on equal footing, the best test was to inquire whether an individual who had done what the Securities Company had done would be guilty. "I do not expect to hear it maintained," he said, "that Mr. Morgan could be sent to prison for buying as many shares as he liked of the Great Northern and the Northern Pacific, even if he bought them both at the same time and got more than half of the stock of each road."

According to Holmes, the difficulty with the court's decision was that it had confounded the two terms. "If I am [wrong]," he concluded, "then a partnership between the two stage drivers who had been competitors in driving across a state line . . . is a crime. For . . . if the restraint on the freedom of the members of a combination"—rather than on outsiders—"caused by their entering into partnership is a restraint of trade, every such combination, as well the small as the great, is within the act."

"Great cases," said Justice Holmes in his dissent, "make bad law." There is no question that Harlan's opinion was marred by its refusal to consider the theses set forth so doggedly by White and so eloquently by Holmes. Nor did the decision succeed in fostering increased competition, either between the Great Northern and the Northern Pacific or among other corporations. Morgan and Hill continued to run the railroads in tandem, much as they had in 1900, and the merger trend continued. ("You cannot make men fight who have evolved the good sense to work together," said one journal.) There were, as Alexander Dana Noyes pointed out, some beneficial side effects—the minority holdings in the two roads were again in public hands, and the possibility that there would be other securities companies, each with dangerously watered stock, was averted. But these were, after all, relatively minor points.

Only a few people, apparently, understood at the time what

gave the decision its real importance and dulled the edge of all the criticism. It had nothing at all to do, in the deepest sense, with farmers in Minnesota, or even with railroads. It had to do with power; specifically, with the power of the government vis-à-vis business. Power is part substance and part symbol, and the Northern Securities decision was to become a symbol of the government's right to control the activities of business. It helped to give Roosevelt the leverage he needed to exercise stricter supervision and control over the corporations. And it is at least part of the reason we remember Roosevelt—and not Taft, who brought far more suits under the Sherman Act—as the "trust-buster." An anonymous writer for *The Outlook* saw this, as did few of his contemporaries, only two weeks after the decision. The important thing about the decision, he said,

is not that it prevents the consolidation of two competing railways, but that it paves the way to Governmental regulation of those railways after they shall have been consolidated; not that it cures a particular abuse of corporation powers, but that it establishes more firmly than ever the sound political and industrial doctrine that corporations deriving their existence from the hands of the people must submit to regulation by the people.

The significance of the legal issues in the Northern Securities case has been eroded by six decades of Supreme Court opinions in the anti-trust field, especially that of Justice Holmes in the Swift case and that of Justice White in the Standard Oil case. The economic philosophy of which it was an expression has been made obsolete by the realization, first during World War I and later during the railroad financial crisis of the fifties, that unlimited railway competition creates more problems than it solves. Its practical accomplishment may yet be wiped out, after sixty years, by the merger of the Great Northern, the Northern Pacific, and the Burlington. But by creating at a crucial moment in history a moral climate in which government could effectively control the power of business, the decision helped to work a permanent change in American life.

# The Case of the Overworked Laundress

XII

BY ALPHEUS THOMAS MASON

(*Muller* v. *Oregon*, 208 U.S. 412)

*By the beginning of the twentieth century an increasing number of laws regulating the conditions and hours of labor were being passed by state legislatures all over the country. Such acts were a natural "response to industrialism," being attempts to adjust to new conditions resulting from the growth of giant corporations, the increased mechanization of industry, and other factors. Inevitably, the Supreme Court was asked to answer the question "How did these laws square with the Constitution of the United States, drafted in a preindustrial age?" As Professor Alpheus T. Mason of Princeton University's Department of Politics explains, this was a difficult problem and it took the Court many decades to find a satisfactory solution. No one contributed more to the search than Louis D. Brandeis, first as a lawyer and then as a member of the Court. The story of his work and influence begins with the case described here. Professor Mason is the author, among other books, of* Brandeis: A Free Man's Life.

Nearly half a century separates *Muller* v. *Oregon* (1908), a judicial landmark unscarred by criticism, from the Supreme Court's unanimous decision of May 17, 1954, outlawing racial segregation in the public schools. The latter ruling, the most controversial judicial pronouncement since *Dred Scott*, has stirred mixed reactions. Certain Southern lawyers and lawmakers denounce the decision as based "solely on psychological and sociological conclusions," instead of on law and "factual truths." A few social scientists, noting Chief Justice Warren's sympathetic reference to the findings of modern sociological and psychological authorities, are ecstatic. The Warren Court had provided "the greatest opportunity ever accorded sociologists to influence high level decisions." Louis D. Brandeis' novel brief-making technique, introduced in the Muller case, had at long last, it was thought, paid off.

*Ex facto jus oritur*—out of facts springs the law—must prevail, Brandeis pleaded, if we are to have a living law. Justice David J. Brewer, speaking for a full bench in the Muller case, had apparently nodded his approval. The Warren Court, in language strikingly similar to Brewer's, had also yielded, it seemed, to the imperatives of authentic empirical data. Chief Justice Warren, like Justice Brewer, had responded favorably to Brandeis' blunt caveat: "A lawyer who has not studied economics and sociology is very apt to become a public enemy."

These assumptions, pleasant or shocking depending on one's point of view, may be illuminated by exploring the peculiar circumstances leading to Brandeis' participation in the Muller litigation. Prior to 1908 the constitutionality of statutes restricting working hours had been argued almost entirely on their legal merits. Briefs of counsel had been confined chiefly to the states' authority, under the police power, to enact such measures. Even on this narrow basis and despite interference with "freedom of contract" guaranteed by the Fourteenth Amendment, public health and welfare legislation was sometimes sustained. Increasingly, however, the justices looked askance at government encroachment on the right to purchase or sell labor, recognized as part of the "liberty" protected by the Constitution. No state, the Fourteenth Amendment enjoined, shall deprive "any person of life, liberty, or property without due process of law." With no precise criteria of contested legislation, no measure of validity save that most elastic yardstick "due process," the Court became final arbiter of economic and social policy. If predilection was not to have free rein, the justices would have to go beyond the customary bounds of constitutional exegesis. But the legal profession had developed no technique whereby the Court could be furnished with relevant social data and statistics. Briefs of counsel as well as judicial opinions were steeped in the convention that law, despite the tangles of sociology and economics, was to be mastered only by a series of syllogisms, informed (or misinformed) by "general knowledge" or "common understanding."

Forward-looking enactments did not suffer so long as the justices followed the self-imposed rule—to presume in favor of constitutionality until violation is proved beyond all reasonable doubt. But once the Court took the position that the states must show special justification for legislation restricting "liberty of contract," the need for a new method of brief-making became imperative.

The desperate urgency of a more realistic approach was highlighted in *Lochner* v. *New York* of 1905, known as the Bakeshop Case, a decision so far-reaching in its power-crippling implications as to evoke Justice Holmes's classic indictment—the Constitution "does not enact Mr. Herbert Spencer's Social Statics." In the Lochner case the Court was confronted with a New York statute limiting the working hours of bakers to ten a day or to a sixty-hour week. "Is this law," Justice Rufus W. Peckham asked, "a fair, reasonable, and appropriate exercise of the police power of the state. . . ?" Five justices answered "No." "There is," they said, "no reasonable ground for interfering with the liberty of persons or the right of free contract, by determining the hours of labor in the occupation of a baker." "This is not a question," Peckham added somewhat defensively, "of substituting the judgment of the Court for that of the legislature." To reconcile what seems to be obvious contradiction, one must understand the Justice's theory of the judicial process. His ruling against the New York law was not reached as an evaluative judgment, nor was it based on any factual investigation. The decision rested on "common knowledge" that "the trade of a baker, in and of itself, is not an unhealthy one to that degree which would authorize the legislature to interfere with the right to labor."

By 1907 events had taken place which were destined to undermine Justice Peckham's assumptions. In that year Curt Muller, an obscure laundryman of Portland, Oregon, was arrested for violating the state's ten-hour law for women. Muller tried unsuccessfully to build a defense on Justice Peckham's predilections in the Bakeshop Case. "Statutes of the nature of that under review," Peckham had observed, "are mere meddlesome interferences with the rights of the individual. . . . This interference seems to be on the increase. . . . We do not believe in the soundness of the views which uphold this law." Muller naturally appealed his conviction to the United States Supreme Court, where Brandeis, as counsel in defense of the Oregon statute, had a chance to demonstrate by recourse to facts that the Oregon legislators could reasonably have believed their ten-hour law to be an appropriate remedy for a probable evil. The dragon to be slain was judicial preference, the rugged dogma of *laissez-faire*.

As was his invariable practice, Brandeis did not volunteer his services. Through the good offices of the National Consumers' League, John Manning, the District Attorney in charge of the case in Oregon, invited the Boston lawyer to cooperate. Organized in 1899, the League had as its first general secretary Mrs. Florence Kelley, member of Hull House and a distinguished social worker. Among its first activities was the Consumers' League label, precursor of the now familiar union label. As preliminary to according its stamp of approval, reports were requested from local Boards of Health and state factory inspectors. The label stitched on a manufacturer's product meant that "the state factory law is obeyed; all the goods are made on the premises; overtime is not worked; children under sixteen years of age are not employed." The League also drafted legislation regulating hours, wages, and working conditions, and propagandized in support of its enactment. Not content merely to get laws on the statute books, it waged legal battles in the courts. *Muller* v. *Oregon* was the first effort of this type to gain national prominence.

On being alerted by the Oregon State Consumers' League that the Muller case was on its way to the U.S. Supreme Court, the national organization began to give serious consideration to the ammunition needed to meet the attack. More than the Oregon statute was at stake, for similar legislation had been passed in nineteen other jurisdictions. Massachusetts had earlier sustained an hours-of-work law for women, but the courts of Illinois had found its own legislation in conflict with both the state constitution and the Fourteenth Amendment. The record in the United States Supreme Court was not wholly encouraging. In 1896 Utah's eight-hour limit on hazardous employment in mines had been upheld, but within a decade a 5-to-4 decision set aside, as we have seen, the New York Bakeshop law. Even as the League received word of the Oregon case it was swallowing still another bitter pill in New York State. The attorney general had just decided to delay defense of a state labor law until after the election.

At this critical juncture, the League decided to tap the best legal talent in the country. In Mrs. Kelley's absence, the male members of the League's Policy Committee secured for her an appointment with Mr. Joseph H. Choate, then leader of the New York bar. Superficially, a retainer from a lawyer of Choate's standing seemed a grand stroke. The New Yorker, however, was not interested. Choate could not see, as he said, why "a big husky Irishwoman should not work more than ten hours if she so desired." The next day Mrs. Kelley was in Boston talking to the eminent corporation lawyer, Louis D. Brandeis.

.Turning to Brandeis was not accidental. Louis's parents, Adolph and Frederika Dembitz Brandeis, had come to America, along with other "forty-eighters," in search of the freedom Europe denied them. Trained as a lawyer, he emerged at the turn of the century as an uncommonly gifted reformer. The trait that distinguished him from the entire miscellany of liberals was his inductive, factual approach to evil conditions and immoral practices. "Seek for betterment," he advised, "within the broad lines of existing institutions. Do so by attacking evils *in situ*; and proceed from the individual to the general." The unsurpassed grasp thus gained of social and economic complexities developed in him a profound sense of urgency, an uncanny premonition that one generation's failure to resolve its own problems complicates tomorrow's issues.

The national spotlight first fell on Brandeis in 1897 when he spoke up for consumers before a Congressional committee amid the jeers of tariff-supporting legislators. He came into the public eye again five years later when Clarence Darrow consulted him while preparing the mineworkers' case for the Anthracite Coal Strike Commission created by President Theodore Roosevelt. Serving as counsel, without pay, in various public welfare contests in the Bay State had won for him the title "People's Attorney." The National Consumers' League sought his services, however, not as reformer but as lawyer. There was little or no expectation that he would resort to novelty. Direction of the League's court cases was in the hands of Miss Josephine Goldmark, Brandeis' sister-in-law. As chairman of the Committee on Legislation, Miss Goldmark had to keep informed and report to the Executive Committee all legislation concerning the objects in which the organization was interested. Recalling Brandeis' participation in the Muller Case, she observes:

What he would say, we had no idea. After all, he had had no hand in shaping the legal record nor in presenting the defense in the state courts. The verdict of the highest courts in Oregon was in our favor; but in the U.S. Supreme Court the adverse *Lochner* decision invalidating an hour law stood menacingly in our path. The time to prepare a brief was very short, probably not more than a month.

Brandeis went to work quickly. Realizing that the crux of the matter lay in human facts, in diverse medical and sociological data, he enlisted the services of nonlawyers, amassed the authoritative statements and testimony of medical and lay experts. He would need, Brandeis told Miss Goldmark, "*facts,* published by anyone with expert knowledge of industry in its relation to women's hours of labor, such as factory inspectors, physicians, trade unions, economists, social workers." Aided by ten readers, Miss Goldmark delved into the libraries of Columbia University, the Astor Library, and the Library of Congress. A young medical student devoted himself solely to research on the hygiene of occupations. Meanwhile, Brandeis constructed the legal argument.

The finished brief contained only two scant pages of "law" and over a hundred of extralegal sources. Besides the testimony of scholars and special observers, here and abroad, the brief included extracts from over ninety reports of committees, bureaus of statistics, commissioners of hygiene, and factory inspectors. A generation of experience in Europe and America had not only demonstrated widespread evil, but also the physical, moral, and economic benefits of shorter working hours. "Production not only increased but improved in quality. . . . Regulation of the working day acted as a stimulus to improvement in processes of manufacture. . . . Factory inspectors, physicians and working women were unanimous in advocating the ten-hour day. . . ." Some experts considered ten hours too long. "Long hours of labor are dangerous for women primarily because of their physical organization."

No one knew whether the Court would notice a brief so unconventional. In all previous cases in which social legislation had been invalidated, the judges, by recourse to abstract logic, had confidently denied any "reasonable" relation between the legislation and its stated objective of improved public health. In 1905, Justice Peckham had asserted categorically that "it is not possible, in fact, to discover the connection between the number of hours a baker may work in a bakery and the healthy quality of the bread made by the workman." One could not be sure that the Court would recognize the factual relation even if it were shown.

No lawyer, except Brandeis, had this faith either in the justices or in himself. Shrewdly playing down the revolutionary aspect of his brief, he tried to show that the Court had practically asked for a convincing demonstration of public health needs, not merely a logical array of precedents. The legal portion of his argument listed five rules established in the Bakeshop Case. He accepted them all, including Peckham's insistence that "No law limiting the liberty of contract ought to go beyond necessity." Brandeis diverged from Justice Peckham only in contending that in the determination of necessity, logic is not enough. "There is no logic that is properly applicable to these laws except the logic of facts," he said.

Brandeis appeared in oral argument January 15, 1908, before a Court dominated by superannuated legalists, including Chief Justice Melville W. Fuller, Justices Peckham, Brewer and William R. Day. Rattling the dry bones of legalism, William D. Fenton, counsel for Muller, argued that "Women equally with men, are endowed with the fundamental and inalienable rights of liberty and property, and these rights cannot be impaired or destroyed by legislative action under the pretense of exercising the police power of the state. Difference in sex alone does not justify the destruction or impairment of these rights."

But this time the Court could not be screened from knowledge of the living world. "Common knowledge" was reinforced by the testimony of experts. "The disinguishing mark of Mr. Brandeis' argument," Miss Goldmark recalls,

was his complete mastery of the details of his subject and the marshaling of evidence. Slowly, deliberately, without seeming to refer to a note, he built up his case from the particular to the general, describing conditions authoritatively reported, turning the pages of history, country by country, state by state, weaving with artistic skill the human facts—all to prove the evil of long hours and the benefit that accrued when these were abolished by law.

"We submit," Brandeis told the justices, "that in view of the facts of common knowledge of which the Court may take judicial notice and of legislative action extending over a period of more than sixty years in the leading countries of Europe, and in twenty of our states, it cannot be said that the Legislature of Oregon had no reasonable ground for believing that the public health, safety, or welfare did not require a legal limitation of women's work in manufacturing and mechanical establishments and laundries to ten hours in one day."

The justices listened with interest and admiration. In what Brandeis said they could discern no wholesale erosion of established principles, no "creeping socialism." Taking the Brandeis brief in stride, the Court's spokesman, Justice Brewer, mentioned the Boston lawyer by name and commented on his very "copious collection of material from other than legal sources." Continuing, the Justice struck a cautious note, observing that "Constitutional questions are not settled by even a consensus of present public opinion." Yet, he added, "when a question of fact is debated and debatable, and the extent to which a special constitutional limitation goes is affected by the truth in respect to that fact, a widespread and long-continued belief concerning it is worthy of consideration."

The Court's mention of Brandeis by name was unusual; the lawyer's factual approach was novel. As to the judgment reached, however, Brandeis' facts were corroborative, not decisive. What everybody knows, judges are presumed to know. It is general knowledge that women are mothers of the race. "Woman's physical structure," Justice Brewer declared, "and the performance of maternal functions place her at a disadvantage in the struggle for existence. . . . We take judicial cognizance of matters of general knowledge."

For the moment, the Court had at least recognized the usefulness of facts in establishing the "reasonableness" of social legislation. The mighty *laissez-faire* barrier had been penetrated. Requests for the Brandeis brief poured in from lawyers, economists, college professors, and publicists. The Russell Sage Foundation reprinted it in quantity, and the National Consumers' League aided in its distribution. Brandeis, the National Consumers' League, and the American people had taken an important step toward a living law. *The Outlook* of March 7, 1908, called the Muller decision "a victory for posterity," "unquestionably one of the momentous decisions of the Supreme Court," "immeasurable in its consequences, laden with vast potential benefit to the entire country for generations to come." More prophetic, however, was the magazine's observation, a month earlier, that the Supreme Court had not "always been strictly uniform" in passing on the constitutionality of social legislation.

The National Consumers' League, encouraged by this signal victory, pressed on, voting to set up a permanent committee in defense of labor laws. Brandeis appeared for oral argument in other states and sent briefs to fourteen different courts. Expanding its legislative campaign in Oregon, the League won in 1913 establishment of an Industrial Welfare Commission to regulate wages, hours, and prescribe safety, health, and welfare measures for industrial employees. The Commission immediately promulgated minimum wages for women in factories and stores. When the validity of this order was contested, December 17, 1914, before the United States Supreme Court, Brandeis was on hand for oral argument. With "facts," he fused compelling moral and humane considerations.

"Why should the proposition be doubted," he asked, "that wages insufficient to sustain the workers properly are uneconomical? Does anybody doubt that the only way you can get work out of a horse is to feed the horse properly? . . . Regarding cows we know now that even proper feeding is not enough; or proper material living conditions. . . . Experience has taught us that harsh language addressed to a cow impairs her usefulness. Are women less sensitive than beasts in these respects?" Brandeis' earthy and elemental argument was overpowering. An eyewitness, Judge William Hitz of the District of Columbia Supreme Court, reported:

I have just heard Mr. Brandeis make one of the greatest arguments I have ever listened to. . . . He spoke of the minimum wage cases in the Supreme Court, and the reception he wrested from that citadel of the past was very moving and impressive to one who knows the Court. . . . When Brandeis began to speak, the Court showed all the inertia and elemental hostility which courts cherish for a new thought, or a new right, or even a new remedy for an old wrong, but he visibly lifted all this burden, and without orationizing or chewing the rag he reached them all. . . . He not only *reached* the Court but *dwarfed* the Court because it was clear that here stood a man who knew infinitely more, and who cared infinitely more, for the vital daily rights of the people than the men who sat there sworn to protect them.

Before the Court could reach a decision, Brandeis was immortalized in a way that transcended his famous factual briefs. It was January 28, 1916. The nation's capital was relatively serene. Suddenly Washington and the country was stunned as if struck by a salvo from an unseen Zeppelin. That day President Wilson nominated Louis D. Brandeis Associate Justice of the United States Supreme Court.

Within a year after taking his seat on the bench the greatest gain derived from his brief-making technique was recognized and enforced. Having rejected—thanks in part to Brandeis' innovations —the freedom-of-contract fiction as to working women, the Court recognized an implied obligation to insist—certainly before setting legislation aside—upon a factual showing of the sort Brandeis introduced in 1908. The case was *Bunting* v. *Oregon,* involving an Oregon ten-hour factory law. Three additional hours might be worked at a time-and-one-half pay rate. Bunting employed a laborer for thirteen hours without complying with the overtime requirement. Indicted and found guilty, he appealed to the United States Supreme Court. A bulky sociological brief in behalf of the Oregon law was presented by Professor Felix Frankfurter. Later on an edition of four thousand copies was printed in book form and sent to 462 law schools, colleges, and libraries in forty-five states. In this particular case the effort seemed quite unnecessary. Presuming constitutionality, the Court, voting 5 to 3 (Brandeis not participating), cast the burden of proving the act's alleged invalidity on Bunting. "There is a contention made," the Court observed, "that the law, even regarded as regulating hours of service, is not either necessary or useful 'for the preservation of the health of employees in mills, factories or manufacturing establishments.' The record contains no facts to support the contention, and against it is the judgment of the legislature and the [State] Supreme Court." The record being barren of any factual demonstration tending to show unreasonableness, the act was sustained. This by-product of the Brandeis brief has been of incalculable importance. It set the pattern Brandeis himself followed as a Supreme Court Justice.

Though the Court in the Muller case may not have been decisively influenced by Brandeis' facts, the justices, nevertheless, approved his method. Even that was challenged in 1923, when the Supreme Court set aside a District of Columbia minimum wage law for women. Mr. Justice Sutherland, speaking for a majority of six, and reversing the stand taken in the Bunting case of 1914, presumed unconstitutionality. "Freedom of contract is the general rule and restraint the exception," he said. The Justice thereby called upon those who favored the restraint to justify the exception. Professor Frankfurter, again following Brandeis' example of 1908, had submitted a brief heavily freighted with facts. But Justice Sutherland considered these wholly irrelevant.

We have . . . been furnished with a large number of printed opinions [by special observers, students of the subjects, etc.] approving the policy of the minimum wage, and our own reading has disclosed a large number to the contrary. These are all proper enough for the consideration of lawmaking bodies, since their purpose is to establish the desirability or undesirability of the legislation; but they reflect no legitimate light upon the question of its validity, and that is what we are called upon to decide.

Nevertheless, the Brandeis way caught on. In recent years his type of brief has become the lawyer's stock in trade, particularly in cases involving racial discrimination. As part of the effort to induce the courts to create a new legal rule in the enforcement of restrictive covenants based on race, sociologists were called in as expert witnesses and queried about population patterns, availability and condition of housing, and the effect of racial ghettos on health, crime, and juvenile delinquency. The special sociological memorandum introduced in these cases was the precursor of the Social Science Statement appended to appellant's brief in the School Segregation Cases in which more than a score of psychologists and sociologists appeared as expert witnesses. In opposition Virginia called two psychologists and a psychiatrist. Prior to this dramatic development, government lawyers, using statistical and related data, were markedly successful in lawsuits against private corporations. Opposing lawyers soon began to file briefs of the same kind. The results, however, were not altogether satisfying for those promoting the factual brief as the champion of social advance. "There are ways of rigging your statistics," Charles Edward Sigety, teacher of statistical method, observes, "so that almost any conclusion can be reached from the same basic information."

The point was illustrated in the Supreme Court case of *Jay Burns*

*Baking Co.* v. *Bryan* (1927). In 1926 the Nebraska Legislature, in an effort to prevent fraud, prescribed the maximum and minimum limits for the weight of bread. When this act came before the High Court, counsel on both sides, employing the Brandeis method, flooded the justices with special reports of chemists and others dealing with the technical phases of bread making. Faced with conflicting expert testimony, the Court collected "facts" of its own. Seven justices, after exhaustive research, sustained the contentions of the plaintiff; two, presumably as well versed in the science of baking, were convinced that the state had proved its case. Justice Brandeis, dissenting, then set in clearer focus the role of social and economic statistics in the judicial process:

> Put at its highest, our function is to determine, in the light of all facts which may enrich our knowledge and enlarge our understanding, whether the measure, enacted in the exercise of the police power and of a character inherently unobjectionable, transcends the bounds of reason. That is, whether the provision as applied is so clearly arbitrary or capricious that legislators acting reasonably could not have believed it to be necessary or appropriate for the public welfare.
>
> To decide, as a fact, that the prohibition of excess weights "is not necessary for the protection of the purchasers against imposition and fraud by short weights"; that it "is not calculated to effectuate that purpose"; and that it "subjects bakery and sellers of bread" to heavy burdens, is, in my opinion, an exercise of the power of a super-legislature—not the performance of the constitutional function of judicial review.

For Brandeis the Court's function was equally circumscribed when confronted with a legislative policy he approved. In 1925 the Oklahoma Legislature provided that no one could engage in the manufacture of ice for sale without obtaining a license. If on investigation the State Commission found that the community was adequately served, it might turn down the bid of a would-be competitor, and in this way, perhaps, advance monopoly. On its face, this legislation encouraged precisely the trend Brandeis had tried to prevent. "The control here asserted," the Court ruled in a 6-to-2 opinion setting aside the act, "does not protect against monopoly, but tends to foster it." Yet Brandeis, in dissent, voted to uphold the regulation. "Our function," he wrote, "is only to determine the reasonableness of the legislature's belief in the existence of evils and in the effectiveness of the remedy provided."

The case was decided in 1932, the low point of economic depression. In an emergency "more serious than war," Brandeis observed,

There must be power in the States and the Nation to remold, through experimentation, our economic practices and institutions to meet changing social and economic needs. . . . This Court has the power to prevent an experiment. We may strike down the statute which embodies it on the ground that, in our opinion, the measure is arbitrary, capricious, or unreasonable. . . . But in the exercise of this high power, we must be ever on guard, lest we erect our prejudices into legal principles.

Brandeis' factual brief had been invented in response to a particular need. At the turn of the century, the evils of long hours, low wages, and improper working conditions were well known. Legislative attempts to provide correctives had been impressive. Required was a new weapon to neutralize the paralyzing effects of the *laissez-faire* dogma in judicial decisions. Among lawyers and judges particularly, effective support for an alternative gospel was crucial—*laissez-faire* for legislative reform. Brandeis' facts were prompted by Justice Peckham's disregard of the presumptive principle. For effective remedial action, facts had to be marshaled on a specific front and given moral voltage.

Failure to grasp Brandeis' purpose has led to the notion that he laid the groundwork for the Warren Court's alleged reliance on extralegal data in the desegregation decision of 1954. Those inclined thus to invoke Brandeis' authority make a twofold error: First, they exaggerate the effect of the Brandeis technique both in the Muller case and in the school decision. Second, they reverse the intent or aim of his method. As a lawyer and as a dissenting judge he amassed social facts to buttress presumption of legislative reasonableness; when writing for the Court, he relied solely on the presumption rule. In neither situation did he utilize facts in an attempt to prove that legislators had been unreasonable—indeed, in the Jay Burns case he protested against this practice.

Justice Brewer in 1908, like Chief Justice Warren in 1954, referred sympathetically to extralegal findings. In a footnote Brewer cited sources drawn from Brandeis' brief. Similarly, Chief Justice Warren, referring to the supporting data found in "modern authority," listed six sociological and psychological studies in the now famous footnote eleven. Like Brandeis' "authorities," these were merely indicative of "widespread belief" as to the psychological effects that had now become common knowledge. There was the further consideration, noted by Justice Frank Murphy in another context, that "racial discrimination is unattractive in any setting" and "utterly revolting among a free people who have embraced the principles set forth in the Constitution of the United States." The irony is that Chief Justice Warren's corroborative footnote eleven, tending to show the *unconstitutionality* of state action, should have ignited hot fires of protest, whereas Justice Brewer's footnote endorsement of Brandeis' findings, tending to support the *constitutionality* of state action, stirred not a ripple of discontent from any quarter. Tactically, footnote eleven has hurt more than it has helped.

Brandeis would have applauded use of the so-called task force as prerequisite to informed action in any area of the governing process —including constitutional interpretation. He would have concurred in Justice Harlan F. Stone's judgment of 1936 as to the need for "an economic service—a small group of men, trained as economists and statisticians, and thus qualified to assemble material for use of the Court." "Knowledge," Brandeis said, "is essential to understanding; and understanding should precede judging." In the role of dissenter, as in that of counsel, he would open the "priestly ears" to the call of extralegal voices. In the decision-making process, however, social science data are only one among the factors requiring consideration.

Without exception the opinions Justice Brandeis embellished with social facts and statistics are in dissent. His factual dissenting opinion, like the factual brief, was an imposing apparatus to support his conviction that "the most important thing the justices do is not doing." In man's eternal pursuit of the more exact, Brandeis recognized that there are facts and facts. Facts have to be interpreted. For him "economic and social sciences are largely uncharted seas." Social science experiments rarely exhibit convincing proof comparable to that achieved in a laboratory of physics or chemistry. One can never be sure all the facts are assembled; and even if this were possible, exploration and study of them would rarely point to only one conclusion. Policy decisions are too complex to be left to statisticians. Their findings need to be informed by opinions based on less specialized knowledge. As to whether the shoe pinches and where, we want the verdict of the wearer, not that of the skilled craftsman who made it.

"Government," Brandeis said, "is not an exact science." When the validity of its use as an instrument of social improvement is at issue, public opinion concerning the evils and the remedy "is among the important factors deserving consideration." He therefore attached great weight, as we have seen, to presumption of constitutionality, and objected vigorously when the Court in defiance of this principle, and on the basis of its own "facts," used its awesome power to strike down a novel and perhaps socially useful experiment. More than once, when his colleagues interposed the judicial veto because the measure seemed to them unwise or foolish, he admonished: "To stay experimentation in things social and economic is a grave responsibility. . . . If we would guide by the light of reason, we must let our minds be bold." Only in reviewing statutes affecting First Amendment freedoms and legislation directed against religious, national, or racial minorities need the Court subject legislation to "more exacting judicial scrutiny." Brandeis suggested that such encroachments run counter to "a fundamental principle of American government."

The primacy of facts, of informed action, is the hallmark of Brandeis' life and work. His brief in the Muller case is symbolic of his inflexible conviction that for wise action there must be "much and constant enquiry into facts." He relied on experts, utilized their findings, not their commands. Knowledge, along with promptings of the heart, alerted him to the perils of inaction, in the face of evils no one could deny. The solution of society's problems could not wait until every aspect was explored, every relevant fact presumably known. Overwhelming factual demonstrations alone do not account for the intensity of Brandeis' moral indignation and reformist zeal. "Mr. Brandeis," a friend once asked, "how can you be so sure of your course of action?" "When you are 51 percent sure," the Justice replied, "then go ahead."

# The Sick Chicken Case

# XIII

BY FRANK FREIDEL

(*Schechter v. U.S.*, 295 U.S. 495)

*The Great Depression of the 1930's, which everyone recognized as a major national crisis, led President Franklin D. Roosevelt and the New Deal Congress to experiment with a variety of new laws in an effort to restore good times. These laws obviously carried federal power to the outer limits of constitutionality. But did they go beyond these bounds? Many individuals and corporations, injured or restricted in some way by their operations, thought that they did, and went to court to prove the point.*

*Among hundreds of controversies, many came eventually to the Supreme Court. The Court was in a difficult position, for while the times called for experimentation and broad government power, much of the new legislation was hastily conceived and also path-breaking. Much hung on how the Court acted. None of the cases considered at this time was more significant than the one that Frank Freidel, Professor of History at Harvard University, describes. Professor Freidel, author of many books, is currently writing a major biography of Roosevelt, three volumes of which have so far appeared.*

It was no easy matter to earn one's living in the depression-haunted, racket-ridden wholesale poultry trade of the New York area in the thirties. Joseph, Alex, Martin, and Aaron Schechter could view with pride their achievement in building, despite these hazards, the largest such business in the Brooklyn area. The brothers owned two firms, the A. L. A. Schechter Company and the Schechter Live Poultry Market, Inc. In a trade so plagued by gangsters that within it had originated the term "racket," the Schechters managed to succeed. Once, at the beginning of the thirties, the stocky, shrewd boss of the business, Joe Schechter, tried to evade the outrageous rental that gangsters were charging for coops, and for his pains had two cups of emery powder poured into the crankcase of his truck. The government, trying to eradicate racketeering, forced Schechter to testify as one of its witnesses before a grand jury, and ultimately in 1934 won its case against the racketeers before the United States Supreme Court.

Meanwhile, in 1933 the Schechters themselves became subject to extensive federal regulation when they, together with fellow poultry dealers, joined the National Recovery Administration, displayed its emblem, the Blue Eagle, and promised to adhere to the numerous provisions of the Code of Fair Competition for the Live Poultry Industry of the New York Metropolitan Area. Like most businessmen, large and small, the Schechters hoped that the NRA would provide the magic formula for restoring prosperity through government intervention.

The optimism of the summer of 1933, when the NRA was announced, soon evaporated, and before long critics began to challenge the constitutionality of the program. The transcendent question was: "Under the Constitution can the government regulate business in an effort to restore prosperity?" The critics' answer was an emphatic "No," but there were various legal precedents which would indicate that the NRA might well be operating within the bounds of the Constitution.

Litigation over the NRA marked a significant phase in the struggle to shift interpretation of the Constitution from a late-nineteenth-century to a twentieth-century view. From the Federalist period through Reconstruction the Supreme Court had placed few impediments in the way of state or federal regulation of the economy. Then in the 1880's and 1890's the *laissez-faire* and social-Darwinist ideology so fashionable at the time became the doctrine of the Court. In a series of decisions it narrowly interpreted the power over the economy vested in either state governments or the national government. In later years, decisions in such controversies as the Northern Securities case and in *Muller* v. *Oregon* had indicated the Court's willingness to allow a wider degree of government control, but in the 1920's it had again veered toward a narrower interpretation.

However, at the time the New Deal legislation was drafted most observers thought the Court would again take a broad view of the question. Times had changed and with the times, presumably, the way in which the Supreme Court would view the Constitution. True enough, during the terrible depressions of the nineteenth century the federal government had done little to restore prosperity beyond bolstering public confidence through its efforts to maintain government solvency.

But when the nation plummeted into the severe depression of the thirties, few people expected the government to remain inactive. The aged Secretary of the Treasury, Andrew Mellon, recalling the depression of the 1870's, recommended to President Hoover that the government keep hands off, since he earnestly believed that the liquidation of a large part of the economy would be beneficial. Although himself a "rugged individualist," Hoover sharply disagreed:

I, of course, reminded the Secretary that back in the seventies an untold amount of suffering did take place which might have been prevented; that our economy had been far simpler sixty years ago, when we were 75 per cent an agricultural people contrasted with 30 per cent now; that unemployment during the earlier crisis had been mitigated by the return of large numbers of the unemployed to relatives on the farms; and that farm economy itself had been largely self-contained.

Mellon tried to answer by suggesting that however the economy had been altered, human nature never changed. This was true enough, but human expectations of the federal government had, in fact, sharply changed, especially as a result of the experience of the First World War when the government had established an array of agencies regimenting the economy. Through the War Industries Board it had regulated industry, through the Food Administration it had stimulated farm production, and through the War Finance Corporation it had made loans. No fear of unconstitutionality had inhibited Congress in establishing these regulatory bodies; the war emergency seemed to override whatever narrow interpretation the courts might in peacetime place on the Constitution. This assumption, however, had not been tested because, at the end of the war the new government agencies were quickly liquidated, and no test cases concerning them came before the Supreme Court. In any case, numerous people argued, could not the federal government reconstitute similar emergency agencies in time of depression in order to make war on the depression?

President Hoover, who had achieved a towering world reputation through his supervision of the relief of Europe's hungry millions during and after the war, had himself been head of the Food Administration. During the twenties he had added to his fame by promoting voluntary cooperation between business and government. Now, as the depression blackened, he enlisted the federal government in the struggle for recovery. He enormously increased public works spending, and persuaded Congress to establish the Reconstruction Finance Corporation, a loan agency somewhat analogous to the War Finance Corporation. Some businessmen, remembering the War Industries Board, urged him to create a similar government agency, which would put the force of federal law behind business efforts to stop price-cutting and overproduction. Hoover rejected these proposals indignantly. Earlier as Secretary of Commerce he had helped to promote voluntary trade associations, but had opposed giving them power to stabilize prices and control distribution. This power, he believed, would lead to the decay of American industry, the creation of monopolies, the destruction of human liberty, and ultimately, the imposition of Fascism or Socialism.

When Franklin D. Roosevelt became President in the spring of 1933, he expressed no such qualms. Like President Hoover, he was ready to enlist the full powers of the federal government to bring about recovery. Like Hoover, he was ready to call for voluntary cooperation on the part of business and agriculture. Unlike Hoover, he felt that these so-called voluntary recovery programs, if they were to be effective, must have behind them the force of federal law. His own personal experience led toward this conclusion, since in the 1920's he had been head of a voluntary trade association, the American Construction Council, which had proved powerless to bring order into the chaotic building industry.

Trade association agreements had been weak even in prosperous years; during the depression they were practically impotent. Many retailers in order to obtain business were shaving profit margins and advertising "loss leaders." They could remain solvent only if they forced their employees to work mercilessly long hours for pathetically low wages. Many wholesalers and small manufacturers were caught in the same relentless bind. In some industries like bituminous coal and petroleum, overproduction was glutting the market and wasting national resources. In the spring of 1933 a barrel of petroleum in some Texas fields sold for less than a bottle of the newly legal 3.2 percent beer.

The National Industrial Recovery Act of June, 1933, proposed the road to recovery that businessmen themselves had been advocating. Business obtained the right to draw up its own regulations in the form of codes of fair practices, which had behind them the force of federal law. In return, workers were granted certain objectives they had long been seeking: minimum wages, maximum working hours, and the right of collective bargaining. The law also protected consumer interests. By granting concessions to businessmen, employees, and consumers alike, the New Dealers hoped to aid business in breaking the disastrously deflationary spiral and in pushing prices up to a prosperity level. To raise buying power, employees should receive more money for working fewer hours. To further "prime the pump" of the economy, the Roosevelt administration was authorized to spend $3.3 billion on public works.

The National Recovery Administration began operations amid widespread fanfare and optimism. President Roosevelt described the enabling act as "the most important and far-reaching legislation ever enacted by the American Congress." He appointed as Administrator one of the most lively figures on the American scene, General Hugh S. Johnson, who had served with Bernard Baruch on the War Industries Board during the First World War. During the war, he had advanced from lieutenant to brigadier general in two years; afterward he had become vice president of the Moline Plow Company, which failed in the agricultural depression of the twenties.

Johnson had a flair for words. Early in his career he wrote two boys' books, both very popular, which combined the worst qualities of Rudyard Kipling and Horatio Alger. As head of the NRA, Johnson whipped up excitement for the recovery program, delighting the public with his vigorous, colorful language. Unfortunately, he had little except words with which to function. He had hoped to preside over both main recovery functions—simultaneously to draw up codes of fair practice for industries and to pour public works money into especially depressed spots in the economy. But Roosevelt allowed him to preside only over the code-making, entrusting the spending power to the cautious, slow-moving Secretary of the Interior, "Honest Harold" Ickes.

General Johnson, despite his enormous public acclaim, had little real authority. There was nothing to back up his energetic denunciation of "chiselers" impeding the recovery effort. From the outset, Johnson was aware of the difficulties he faced. "It will be red fire at first and dead cats afterwards," he remarked when he became administrator. "This is just like mounting the guillotine on the infinitesimal gamble that the ax won't work."

For a few weeks there was red fire aplenty as an inspired nation heeded Roosevelt's request to accept an interim blanket code, the President's Re-employment Agreement, to abolish child labor, and establish maximum hours of thirty-five or forty per week and minimum wages of thirty to forty cents per hour. In this one sweeping agreement the NRA achieved what reformers had sought since the dawn of the Progressive era. Parades and rallies helped persuade employers to sign the NRA agreement and display the Blue Eagle emblem and its slogan, "We Do Our Part." Consumers pledged themselves to buy only where they saw the Blue Eagle insignia.

Then began the drawn-out process of negotiating specific codes to cover each major industry. Manufacturers rushed to turn out goods before costs of material and labor went up under the codes, hiring quantities of workers for the few weeks they operated their plants at capacity. Wholesalers likewise bought in increased volume in anticipation of higher prices. The index of production (calculated at 100 for the boom year 1929) skyrocketed from 56 in March, 1933, to 101 in July. Payrolls also went up, but only from an index figure of 37.1 to 50.8. With prices rising more quickly than buying power, Secretary Ickes nevertheless followed President Roosevelt's wishes and only very slowly authorized public works expenditures. Before the end of the summer the NRA boomlet collapsed.

Meanwhile as the negotiation of codes for the major industries went on, minor industries also clamored for individual codes. The result by February, 1934 was, accordingly, not a handful of codes as had originally been planned, but 557 basic codes and 208 supplementary codes. Each of these had been negotiated by the representatives of a particular industry in association with representatives of labor and the consumers. The representatives of the industries so thoroughly dominated these negotiations that in effect the business leaders were allowed to draft their own codes of fair practices— in some instances copying them word for word from earlier trade association agreements. There were codes not only for the steel, automobile, textile, and bituminous coal industries, but also for the mop-stick, corn-cob pipe, and powder puff industries; for burlesque theaters, investment banking houses, and pecan shellers. The retail trade code covered nearly three and a half million employees; the animal soft-hair industry covered forty-five. Some sixty-two codes covered less than five hundred employees each, yet almost all of them contained intricate regulations.

In return for the government's prohibition of unfair practices, each industry had to guarantee its employees fair wages and hours and the right to bargain collectively. There were long enumerations of unfair practices: four-fifths of the codes tended to bolster minimum prices, three-fourths prohibited rebates, and a few major codes even set production quotas. It was of vital significance that the first code, regulating the textile industry with its 400,000 employees, set the minimum wage for forty hours of work at $12 in the South and $13 in the North. It also provided that no minor under sixteen should be employed, and that production machinery should not be operated for more than two shifts of forty hours each. But many codes contained numerous petty regulations. The macaroni code stipulated that noodles must contain not less than 5.5 percent of egg or egg yolk solids, must not be artificially colored, or packaged in yellow wrappers that would deceive the purchaser.

Altogether the businessmen's committees included within the different codes more than a thousand provisions regulating 130 different trade practices. Their aim was not so much the protection of the consumer as the elimination of unfair competition. Laudable though such regulations might be, they created an administrative problem for the NRA. Each code, when signed by President Roosevelt, had behind it the force of the National Industrial Recovery Act, and any violation of a code was a violation of the law.

When public enthusiasm over the Blue Eagle was running high, relatively mild threats were sufficient to bring successful enforcement. If a retailer did not comply with the President's Re-employment Agreement after receiving a warning, he received a telegram that sternly ordered him to return his Blue Eagle poster and other NRA paraphernalia to the nearest post office. Presumably, consumers would then boycott the offender's establishment. When public enthusiasm waned, removal of the insignia no longer sufficed. The NRA increasingly had to resort to litigation, but of 155,102 cases docketed by the NRA state offices, only 564 reached the courts.

Ironically, it was the regulation of trade practices so eagerly sought by businessmen rather than the enforcement of wages-and-hours and collective bargaining agreements that caused the most trouble. The public was sympathetic toward exploited employees, but had no enthusiasm for rules that might keep purchasers from obtaining "bargains." Consumer interest might coincide with that of the mayonnaise manufacturers in upholding the regulation that mayonnaise substitutes labeled "salad dressing" must meet minimum standards, but consumers could only feel that they were being deprived of bargains by regulations that forbade the sale of second-quality plumbing fixtures or the manufacture of bedding from secondhand materials. The drafters of the codes had argued that the sale of substandard merchandise depressed the prices of standard products, and they wished zealously to enforce these and similar trade provisions. It was difficult, they realized, to obtain evidence of evasion that would be acceptable in a court, yet if the evaders went unpunished, general compliance was likely to break down. Highly competitive businesses were especially faced with compliance problems; many a small businessman argued that evasion was the only alternative to bankruptcy.

For most Americans the NRA honeymoon was soon over. After the upturn in the summer of 1933, prices steadied and General Johnson emphasized that they must not go up further until buying power had risen. Yet Clarence Darrow, the iconoclastic lawyer who headed a National Recovery Review Board, was widely supported when he charged in the spring of 1934 that the NRA was under the domination of big business, and that big business was forcing living costs upward. There were other complaints. Those who feared union labor were alarmed over the great organizing drives launched by John L. Lewis and others, and were outraged by the numerous strikes that accompanied the new militancy on the part of the unions. Workingmen, on the other hand, feeling that they had gained but little from the NRA codes or the collective bargaining guarantees, wisecracked that the initials NRA stood for "National Run Around."

Even as General Johnson had predicted, in the fall of 1934 he became the victim of the guillotine. President Roosevelt replaced him with a five-man board, which tried to make the NRA more acceptable by remodeling and simplifying its activities along more enforceable lines. But it was by no means certain that Congress would renew the Act as its date of termination approached in the spring of 1935. Also, by that time, the issue of constitutionality was becoming increasingly troublesome.

In the exciting spring of 1933 the question of constitutionality had not seemed very important. Public opinion was overwhelmingly behind President Roosevelt's call for drastic powers with which to combat the depression, and there was considerable feeling that the crisis made it possible to act in ways that in ordinary times might not be legal. Whether emergency New Deal legislation would be sanctioned by the Supreme Court remained to be seen. In any event, the drafters of the National Industrial Recovery Act argued that it was within the power of Congress to regulate commerce among the states. Since the 1895 sugar decision (the Knight case), the Supreme Court had broadened its interpretation of the commerce clause, so there seemed to be adequate precedent. However, the New Dealers could not be entirely sure. While handing down strong decisions in protection of civil liberties, the Court was split into two wings on questions that involved government regulation of the economy.

Because of the unpredictability of the Supreme Court, the Roosevelt administration was not dismayed that a test of the NRA was delayed into 1935. In addition to the certain opposition of the conservative wing of the Court, there was the possibility that the NRA might run afoul of the moderate Chief Justice Charles Evans Hughes's dislike for the practice of delegating broad regulatory powers to administrative agencies. In 1931, addressing the American Bar Association, Hughes had warned that this tendency threatened to overwhelm American institutions. Moreover, there was the possibility that Justice Brandeis, long a foe of industrial giantism, might object to the way the NRA had in effect suspended the antitrust laws.

Nevertheless, by the spring of 1935, with criticism of the NRA mounting and defiance of the codes spreading, a Supreme Court decision had become essential. While there was a danger that the Court might act unfavorably, in two cases which it had decided early in 1934 it had seemed to regard the depression emergency as justifying drastic economic regulation by the states. These were a Minnesota case involving a mortgage moratorium and a New York case fixing the price of milk. In the mortgage decision Chief Justice Hughes pointed out that "While emergency does not create power, emergency may furnish the occasion for the exercise of power."

But these two cases involved state, not federal, legislation. Early in 1935, when cases involving the federal prohibition against making payment on contracts in gold (the gold-clause cases) were decided, the government won by an uncomfortably close 5-to-4 margin, made more unpleasant because the majority through Chief Justice Hughes castigated the administration for its immorality. It was on this occasion that Justice James C. McReynolds in dissenting added extemporaneously, "As for the Constitution, it does not seem too much to say that it is gone."

The "hot-oil" decision, involving a provision of the National Industrial Recovery Act that authorized the President to prohibit or not, as he saw fit, the transportation in interstate and foreign commerce of petroleum produced in excess of legal quotas, was still more ominous. With only Justice Benjamin N. Cardozo dissenting, the Court held that Congress had unconstitutionally delegated too much discretionary power to the President. This setback to the New Deal led the Solicitor General on April 1, 1935, to drop a Southern lumber case (*United States* v. *Belcher*) which it had been generally assumed would serve as the test of the NRA. The lumber case was too close to the "hot-oil" cases for the government attorneys to feel comfortable.

Since opposition newspapers were thundering editorially that the New Dealers were welching, it was necessary to find another test case in a hurry. At this point the government won in the Circuit Court of Appeals a case that involved the New York live poultry code. The defeated defendants petitioned for a Supreme Court review, and there was not much the Department of Justice could do except to use this not entirely satisfactory case for its test of the NRA. Thus the fate of the NRA, and to a considerable degree the power of the government to aid business in fighting the depression, came to depend upon how the Supreme Court would look upon the right of the federal government to punish Brooklyn poultry dealers who, among their other offenses, had sold a sick chicken. The dealers were the Schechter brothers.

The Code of Fair Competition for the Live Poultry Industry of the Metropolitan Area in and about the City of New York was one of the multitude of lesser codes that contained lists of especially applicable unfair practices, the enforcement of which had made the course of the NRA so difficult. It was not one of the dozen or more major industries indisputably lying athwart interstate commerce, the sort that the framers of the NRA had contemplated regulating. On the other hand, most counts in the case had been decided unanimously in favor of the government by the three distinguished justices of the Circuit Court of Appeals, of whom one was Learned Hand. Further, the Supreme Court justices themselves had given some indication that they regarded the racket-ridden New York live poultry industry as falling within the scope of interstate commerce. Only a year before, when the racketeers had appealed against a federal injunction on the grounds that their acts did not interfere with interstate commerce, the Court had sustained the injunction.

Racketeering and cutthroat competition had lead the operators of Kosher wholesale poultry slaughterhouses in the New York area to seek the protection of a code. The code established a minimum wage of fifty cents an hour, a maximum work week of forty-eight hours, and prohibited the sale of poultry that was either uninspected or unfit for human consumption. It also required "straight killing" (customers purchasing less than a full coop must take "run of the coop" rather than pick out the best birds).

The four Schechter brothers, earlier in federal court as witnesses for the government against racketeers, now found themselves back in court as defendants. They were charged with having violated the wages-and-hours and several of the trade-practice provisions of the code in order to beat their prices below those of their rivals. For example, they had allowed customers to select the best chickens out of a coop. But above all, witnesses testified at a jury trial before Judge Marcus B. Campbell of the United States District Court in Brooklyn, they had sold thousands of pounds of diseased chickens at four to eight cents per pound below the market price.

This would seem of little consequence if, as one NRA inspector reported, they had merely sold chickens that were "egg-bound"—that is, unable to lay eggs. What made their offense a menace was that many of the chickens suffered from tuberculosis, which was communicable to human beings. One witness testified to thirty-seven instances in which persons had contracted tuberculosis from sick chickens. Before passage of the NRA code, New York had served as a national dumping ground for diseased poultry. Rejects from Western packing stations—"anything with a head on it," said one witness—had been shipped east. Others estimated that although only 2 percent of the poultry sold in New York prior to the code was unfit for human consumption, these birds had so disgusted unwary purchasers that thereafter many refused to eat any chicken. As a result, poultry consumption fell about 20 percent. The bargain prices also depressed the market price for good poultry. After a three-week trial the Schechters had been found guilty on seventeen counts, given brief jail sentences, and fined $7,425. The Circuit Court had reversed the conviction on the wages-and-hours counts, but upheld the conviction on the unfair-trade-practices counts.

In preparing their brief for the Supreme Court the government attorneys made the most possible use of the fact that the Court had earlier considered the New York poultry business as affecting interstate commerce. But in the criminal conviction of the Schechter brothers the government attorneys had a liability, since the Supreme Court might well balk at sending anyone to jail because of a code violation.

The government's brief pointed out that over 96 percent of the live poultry marketed in the New York area came from other states; that some thirty-five states, chiefly in the Middle West and the South, shipped to New York; and that 175 to 200 freight carloads a week arrived at the New York markets, more than the combined shipments made to all other large cities. Detailed evidence was presented to prove that the market price of live poultry in New York set the price of poultry throughout the United States. It was argued that unfair trade and labor practices in the live poultry business in New York City tended to lower poultry prices throughout the country, and that these practices therefore contributed to the obstruction of interstate commerce. The brief also cited numerous earlier Supreme Court decisions as precedents: "Under the decisions of this Court, the Code provisions which the petitioners violated are within the commerce power of the Congress," the government lawyers asserted.

The Schechter case was argued before the Supreme Court on May 2 and 3, 1935, in the small, red-plush courtroom in the Capitol which had once been the Senate chamber. Solicitor General Stanley Reed (who was himself later to sit on the Court) used one of the government's allotted two hours to expound the constitutional arguments. A distinguished New York lawyer, Frederick H. Wood, who had become associated with the defense, countered learnedly that when the chickens were delivered to the commission merchants in New York they "came to rest," and were no longer involved in interstate traffic.

At the close of the first session, Justice McReynolds ominously quizzed Solicitor General Reed on two points:

*McReynolds: "Were these defendants among those who agreed to the live poultry code?"*

*Reed: "They were not, but I may add that they were present at all the conferences which preceded the adoption of the code."*

*McReynolds: "What does unfair competition mean? Is it anything industry says is unfair?"*

*Reed: "The only standard is what industry considers unfair, plus the judgment of the President as to whether they are fair trade provisions."*

The second session, the next day, was more lively. The Schechters' original lawyer, Joseph Heller, stole the limelight from his constitutionalist associate Wood, as in uninhibited and colloquial language he strove to convince the Court of the local nature of the Schechter poultry business. Heller described the problems of the Schechters in doing business under the code in a fashion that convulsed the justices with laughter and did serious damage to the government's case. He parried the charge that the Schechters had been selling diseased poultry, pointing out that the one sick chicken purchased by the NRA agent had only been "egg-bound" and earlier had been passed by a government inspector.

When he was asked what straight killing meant, he explained, "Straight killing means you have got to put your hand in the coop and take out whichever chicken comes to you. You hand the chicken over to the rabbi, who slaughters it."

"And it was for that your client was convicted?" Justice McReynolds inquired.

"Yes, and fined $5,000 and given three months in jail."

In summation for the government, Chairman Richberg of the National Industrial Recovery Board was less entertaining but more eloquent. He emphasized that the NRA was a vital response to the calamitous effects of the depression upon interstate commerce. "The NRA law was enacted for the purpose of checking the progressive destruction of industry, to make possible an orderly advance by industry rather than a disorderly retreat," he asserted. "Congress alone could deal effectively with the causes contributing to this breakdown of interstate commerce." If Congress could not stop the "vicious cycle of wage-cutting, then it is impotent indeed," he declared. Trying to lift the case above the "run-of-the coop" and "egg-bound" level, Richberg declared: "For the court to pass on this case only as if it fitted into the Schechter poultry case would be like trying to diagnose a case of scarlet fever by examining one small spot on the skin."

Decision day came on Monday, May 27. Solicitor General Reed and Chairman Richberg, both in fine spirits, took their places at the counsel table. "I feel," smiled Richberg, "as though I were waiting for a jury to come in—guilty or not guilty." When the nine justices filed in, they also seemed cheerful, but almost immediately events took an ominous turn. Justices George Sutherland and Louis D. Brandeis each read a lesser decision; both were unanimous and unfavorable to the New Deal. Then Chief Justice Hughes announced that he would read the Schechter decision. Richberg stiffened and paled as Hughes launched into a detailed discourse on the background of the case. The crowd of Congressmen and lawyers who filled the small chamber fidgeted expectantly. The Chief Justice went on and on. Finally, looking Olympian as he stroked his white beard, he read the crucial sections, slowly and vehemently. They were devastating.

"Extraordinary conditions do not create or enlarge constitutional power," Hughes declared. "Congress cannot delegate legislative power to the President to exercise an unfettered discretion to make whatever laws he thinks may be needed or advisable for the rehabilitation and expansion of trade or industry." Against the government's assertion that the Schechters' transactions were in interstate commerce, he stated, "So far as the poultry here in question is concerned, the flow in interstate commerce had ceased. The poultry had come to a permanent rest within the State."

The Chief Justice provided precedents for all these points from earlier Supreme Court decisions (even as the government lawyers had backed their pleas with a different set of precedents). What of the decision only a year earlier, restraining New York poultry racketeers from interfering with the flow of poultry in interstate commerce? This earlier case (*Local 167* v. *United States*) was different, Hughes said.

The proved interference by the conspirators "with the unloading, the transportation, the sales by marketmen to retailers, the prices charged and the amount of profits exacted" operated "substantially and directly to restrain and burden the untrammeled shipment and movement of the poultry" while unquestionably it was in interstate commerce. The intrastate acts of the conspirators were included in the injunction because that was found to be necessary for the protection of interstate commerce against the attempted and illegal restraint.

As Hughes read off the crucial sentences Richberg slumped in his chair and cupped his chin in his hands. A newspaperman scribbled a note and passed it to him: "Can there be a new Recovery law?" Richberg inscribed a large question mark. Reed and Richberg left the courtroom unable to conceal their gloom.

In the Department of Justice office, Attorney General Homer S. Cummings put down a ham sandwich he had been munching and entered into a hurried conference with them. Late in the afternoon the three men went to the White House, there to spend two hours studying the Court's decision with President Roosevelt. When Richberg came out of the President's office he announced: "This decision of the Supreme Court makes all codes of fair competition unenforceable as a matter of law." From his headquarters Chairman Richberg wired orders to suspend immediately all enforcement of NRA codes. Businessmen were now liberated from the machinery they had themselves created. They could again engage in whatever trade practices they pleased and treat their employees as they saw fit. They were freed from government interference. But they were also left without protection against unscrupulous competitors.

Throughout the nation there was an excited, though mixed,

reaction. The National Association of Manufacturers was jubilant. "As a result of the court's notable decision the opportunity is again afforded to industry to go forward on a basis of voluntary self-government," its spokesman proclaimed. Anti-New Deal Senators exulted. "The Constitution is re-established," William E. Borah announced. Carter Glass, who as early as August of 1933 had dubbed the Blue Eagle a "black buzzard," commented: "I have always been opposed to any such exercise of tyranny." The stock market shot upward, then swiftly dropped, as investors on second thought demonstrated their fear of deflation. The commodity market was shaken. Retail stores quickly revived trade wars that the NRA had held in abeyance. Gimbel's cut the price of Modern Library books from fifty-six cents to twenty-nine cents. Some stores reduced the price of a carton of cigarettes to little more than the tax on them.

Many retailers found it necessary to recoup such price cuts by lengthening the working hours of their employees. Only days later the head of the Food and Grocery Distributors' Code Authority declared that already 90 percent of all grocery employees were being obliged to work sixty-five to seventy-two hours per week rather than the forty-eight-hour NRA week. Of some seven hundred telegrams that arrived at the White House the day after the Court's decision, eight out of nine urged some sort of new NRA. The Washington *News* editorialized that critics of the NRA had "prayed for rain and got a cloudburst."

At his first press conference after the decision, on May 29, President Roosevelt had relatively little to say. Was the President going to accept the decision calmly? During the next two days excitement increased, and letters and telegrams continued to arrive at the White House.

Roosevelt did intend to reply to the Supreme Court, but in his own time and fashion. The time was eleven o'clock on the morning of Friday, May 31, and the form was not a message to Congress or a radio "fireside chat" to the American public. It was an unbroken discourse of an hour and twenty-five minutes before two hundred assembled reporters at his press conference. The newsmen were allowed to take notes, but could report the President only in indirect discourse. Through them Roosevelt would put his case to the American people.

When the reporters jammed into the President's office, he had the stage set for them. Leaning back in his swivel chair as they crowded forward, he regarded them with a laconic smile. Behind him sat Mrs. Roosevelt, knitting a blue sock. Another chair was being held for Senate Majority Leader Joseph Robinson, who arrived ten minutes late. On one side of Roosevelt's desk lay a pile of telegrams; on the other, an open copy of the Supreme Court decision.

Lighting a cigarette, he opened the conference by inquiring facetiously of the reporters: "What is the news?" Then, when the inevitable question came concerning the NRA, he launched into his disquisition. Taking the sheaf of telegrams from his desk, he remarked, "I have been a good deal impressed by . . . the rather pathetic appeals that I have had from all around the country to do something. They are very sincere as showing faith in government . . . so sincere that you feel the country is beginning to realize that something in the long run has to be done." And he read a number of excerpts from the telegrams, all of them from businessmen, most of whom complained that their businesses were already suffering from the decision. Several urged that something be done about the Supreme Court.

"The implications of this decision," Roosevelt told the reporters, "are much more important than any decision probably since the Dred Scott case." What Roosevelt felt made it significant was not the stricture against undue Congressional delegation of power. That could easily be remedied through more specific instructions. Rather it was the way in which the Supreme Court had reverted to the earlier view of the power of Congress to regulate commerce, limiting it apparently to what was actually in interstate transit. "The big issue is this," Roosevelt emphasized: "Does this decision mean that the United States Government has no control over any national economic problem?" Did it mean that the government had no right to try to better national social conditions?

Roosevelt pointed out in detail the difficulties of trying to solve economic problems through forty-eight sets of state regulations. The Supreme Court decision implied that the federal government could neither legislate concerning fair trade practices and wages-and-hours regulation nor control agricultural production, stock market activities, and other areas, he said. As for self-regulation, he remarked sarcastically: "Can we go ahead as a nation with the beautiful theory, let us say, of the Hearst press, 'At last the rule of Christ is restored. Business can do anything it wants and business is going to live up to the golden rule so marvelously that all of our troubles are ended'? . . . It is a school of thought that is so delightful in its naïveté."

In sum, Roosevelt declared, these implications made the decision one of the most important ever rendered, since it raised the question as to how the nation was to proceed in the area of economic regulation. "We are the only nation in the world that has not solved that problem," he concluded. "We thought we were solving it, and now it has been thrown right straight in our faces and we have been relegated to the horse-and-buggy definition of interstate commerce."

"Horse-and-Buggy" echoed in headlines all over America, and the lines were drawn for the bitter struggle between the New Dealers and the Supreme Court. The New Dealers found it easy enough to replace the useful parts of the NRA through various separate laws: the Wagner Act (National Labor Relations Act) to protect labor in its collective bargaining; the Guffey Act, in effect re-enacting the bituminous coal industry code; other legislation to protect retailers from some of the unfair trade practices. The difficulty was that these measures in turn were likely to be invalidated by the Supreme Court —and so indeed the Guffey Act soon was. Several other New Deal measures, most notably the processing tax program established by the Agricultural Adjustment Act, fell afoul of the Supreme Court. At about the same time the Court in another decision denied to states the power to regulate the economy. Such was the background of President Roosevelt's ill-fated attempt in the spring of 1937 to "pack" the Supreme Court.

Then, remarkably, in the midst of the great national furor, the Supreme Court began to take a different view of both state and federal control over the economy. Chief Justice Hughes and Justice Owen J. Roberts abandoned the conservative wing of the Court to join the liberal trio, Holmes, Brandeis, and Cardozo, who by this time were ready to take an even more liberal view of federal authority. In a test case involving the Wagner Act, the Court's 5-to-4 decision held that labor relations in the steel industry did come within the Congress' power to regulate commerce among the states. A host of similar decisions followed. A "sick chicken" might have downed the Blue Eagle of the NRA, but only two years later the

Supreme Court was demonstrating that it was taking a modern rather than a "horse-and-buggy" view of the power of Congress to regulate the economy.

As for the Schechters, at first they had enjoyed emerging from the obscurity of their Brooklyn business into the national limelight. When Joe Schechter was stopped by a guard as he entered the Supreme Court chamber, he asked, "Me? You don't know who I am?" If he and his brothers thought it strange that one of the most distinguished New York law firms, Cravath, de Gersdorff, Swaine and Wood, had entered the case, associating themselves with the Schechter lawyer, Joseph Heller, they kept their opinions to themselves. Nor did they reveal who paid this high-priced firm its fee. When the favorable decision came, they and Heller celebrated with champagne. But a year later Drew Pearson found them in distress. They had lost their business and were being forced to sell their home. "The Liberty Leaguers sent us a lot of swell letters saying they appreciated what we had done," Aaron Schechter lamented, "but they didn't put any money in the letters." And Joe Schechter added: "I honestly think the NRA could have been a good thing if there had been safeguards against racketeering. That was what wrecked us."

# The Case of the Smuggled Bombers

## XIV

BY ROBERT A. DIVINE

(*U.S.* v. *Curtiss-Wright Export Corp.* et al., 299 U.S. 304)

*Few of the great constitutional decisions of the Supreme Court have risen out of more sordid circumstances than the one described by historian Robert A. Divine of the University of Texas. Yet none has been wiser and not many have had such widespread and beneficial results. Professor Divine, a specialist in diplomatic history, is the author of* The Illusion of Neutrality.

   One June morning in 1932, a detachment of three hundred Bolivian troops stormed and overwhelmed the garrison of a Paraguayan fort in the Gran Chaco. A wild, primitive wasteland, stretching from northern Argentina to eastern Bolivia, and populated by savage Guarani Indians, carnivorous piranha fish, and fierce ihenni flies, the Chaco had been in dispute between Bolivia and Paraguay since 1879. The jungle swamps and lagoons of the south and the desert plains of the north, where water holes were often fifty miles apart, offered little attraction for economic development, but land-locked Bolivia was determined to seize control of the northern Chaco to gain access to the Atlantic via the navigable Paraguay River. With a heavier population and great wealth from the world's largest tin mines, Bolivia looked forward to an easy conquest.

But Paraguay, with only 800,000 people and few natural resources, resisted fiercely. In the steamy Chaco jungles, Paraguayan bush fighters, armed only with machetes and antiquated rifles, quickly proved themselves capable of waging full-scale war. For three years the two countries fought for control of this desolate frontier in one of the least-known and most senseless wars of the twentieth century. The Chaco War wasted over 100,000 lives and endangered the peace of all Latin America. It also created a vital constitutional issue affecting the foreign policy of the United States.

Bolivia won the first few skirmishes, but by the fall of 1932 Paraguay had gained the initiative. The brilliant French-trained Paraguayan general, José Estigarribia, outflanked the Bolivian forces and regained control of the central Chaco. Bolivian hopes revived in December, when General Hans Kundt, a German officer who had trained the Bolivian Army, arrived to take command of the troops. Using flame-throwers and tanks purchased in Europe, Kundt pushed the Paraguayans steadily southward. But then Estigarribia, bolstered by modern arms bought from Germany, England, and Italy, counterattacked. By early 1933 his troops were driving across the Chaco toward the Bolivian frontier. In desperation, the Bolivian Government turned to American aircraft manufacturers for help.

These overtures came at a crucial time for the American aviation industry. After Lindbergh's transatlantic flight in 1927 convinced many people that flying was ready to leave the barnstorming stage and take its place as the new mode of transportation, the aircraft industry had boomed. Wall Street bankers took a sudden interest in aviation; in early 1929 the United Aircraft and Transport Company purchased the Pratt and Whitney Company, makers of the Wasp engines, to complete the United Aircraft combine, which also included Boeing Airplane and Chance Vought. Later in the year, to compete with this corporation, Richard Hoyt, a Harvard graduate who had married into a powerful New York investment house and gained control of the Wright Aeronautical Corporation, merged his interests with Clement M. Keys, Greek scholar, hockey player, and former Wall Street reporter, who ran the Curtiss Aeroplane and Motor Company. The new firm, christened the Curtiss-Wright Corporation, was composed of twelve operating companies with holdings in aircraft factories, engine plants, airfields, flying schools, and passenger lines. Three months after the corporation's formation, however, the stock market crashed. Soon the depression was threatening to wipe out this ambitious enterprise. In 1930 Curtiss-Wright lost $9 million; the next year, after Hoyt and Keys liquidated their more flamboyant investments, it still dropped $4 million. The bulk of the firm's business was with the United States Government, but the big profits necessary to prevent bankruptcy could only come from export sales. In selling planes to the armed forces, the company set prices high enough to pay off the enormous research and development costs required for new models; then they modified the designs and sold the planes to foreign governments at the same prices. Since the engineering costs had been covered by sales to the U.S. Army and Navy, they doubled and sometimes even tripled their profit margins on these foreign transactions.

This lucrative trade was controlled by the Curtiss-Wright Export Corporation. Clarence K. Webster, known as "Web" to his associates, was its president. When the Chaco War broke out, Webster entered into negotiations with the Bolivian authorities, and in early 1933 he sold them two Curtis-Wright Hawks. These were single-engine pursuit planes which carried two machine guns and a bomb rack on each wing and had a top speed of 205 miles per hour. They sold for $26,000 apiece. The Bolivian pilots were delighted with the Hawks, which became the nucleus of their air force. To instruct them in the use of the planes, Webster sent Captain Clifton Travis, a retired Army pilot, to La Paz. Travis quickly won the confidence of the Bolivians, and negotiated orders for more Hawks. When Webster suggested that Travis move on from Bolivia to find other customers for Curtiss-Wright products in Latin America, the veteran pilot replied: "We cannot neglect Bolivia; they are our best customers at the present time. A small country but they have come across with nearly half a million dollars in the past year and are good for quite a bit more if the war lasts."

Webster had no intention of neglecting Bolivia, but he also wanted to explore the possibility of selling planes to Paraguay! In February, 1933, he wrote Lawrence Leon, the Curtiss-Wright agent in Buenos Aires, suggesting that he take the "rotten trip" up to Asunción to sound out the Paraguayan authorities. "If we are able to sell them anything," Webster cautioned Leon, "we will have to work very carefully and quietly, and possibly through you, as an individual, as the Bolivian Government would naturally raise 'merry hell' if they believed that we were dealing with their enemies." Though Leon was unable to sell any planes to Paraguay, Webster remained bullish about the Chaco War. "National pride and stubbornness will not permit these countries to quit until they blow up through absolute bankruptcy," he wrote to Captain Travis, "and while the show is going on, it is our job as distributors of munitions to get our share. If we don't, someone else will."

In the spring of 1933, Webster took another step toward insuring a full share of the Bolivian business. On the advice of Travis, he made the La Paz firm of Webster and Ashton his agents in Bolivia. The Bolivian Comptroller General, Castro Lopez, who passed on all contracts signed by the government, was a silent partner in Webster and Ashton, which received a 5 percent commission on all Curtiss-Wright sales to Bolivia. With Lopez' help, Webster was able to maintain an absolute monopoly over the export of military aircraft to Bolivia. In May, the Bolivian Government ordered nine more planes, and Webster sent Harry Berger, a mechanic, to La Paz to aid Travis in servicing aircraft. On at least one occasion, Berger traveled down to the front lines in the Chaco to repair Bolivian planes.

Though Webster continually worried about rumors of peace in the Chaco, the war continued, with Paraguay maintaining its offensive. The Bolivians were pleased with the performance of the Curtiss Hawks, but the pilots were disappointed because they only carried 460 pounds of bombs in their wing racks. In May, Travis reported that the Bolivians had gone "bomb-minded" and were interested in purchasing several large bombers. The possible profits of such a deal were so large that Webster resigned as president of the Curtiss-Wright Export Corporation in June and formed his own export firm, which became the sole South American distributor for Curtiss-Wright. In October, he joined Travis in La Paz to negotiate a deal with Bolivian authorities for the sale of some Condor bombers, two-engine planes capable of carrying two thousand pounds of bombs in wing and fuselage racks, and selling for $70,000 apiece. Comptroller General Lopez arranged for Webster to meet with the Ministers of War and Finance, while Travis flew down to the Chaco with the Chief of Staff for a conference with General Kundt and aviation officials at the front. After prolonged negotiations, Webster signed the final contract at La Paz in February, 1934. Bolivia agreed to buy nine airplanes—five fighters and four Condors—together with a large quantity of spare parts, for $629,000.

Webster was jubilant. He had now sold the Bolivians a total of thirty-four airplanes (their entire air force) and had closed a deal which represented nearly two-thirds of the total exports of the

Curtiss-Wright company for the previous year. The Chaco War might yet enable the company to weather the depression.

Webster's jubilation proved to be short-lived. In the first few months of 1934, a series of books and magazine articles appeared attacking the munitions-makers as "merchants of death" and accusing them of fomenting and prolonging wars in the conduct of their business. In *Iron, Blood and Profits*, George Seldes described the arms-makers as "organized into the greatest and most profitable secret international of our time—the international of bloodshed and profits." Leaders of the peace movement, who had been unsuccessfully advocating a curb on the munitions trade for many years, seized on the public outcry against the arms manufacturers to demand a Congressional investigation of the industry. In April, Senator Gerald Nye of North Dakota, a former newspaper editor with a sharp eye for popular causes, succeeded in gaining Senate approval for an intensive inquiry into the arms trade.

Meanwhile, the League of Nations, concerned over the war between Bolivia and Paraguay, had sent an investigating committee to the Chaco. This committee recommended an arms embargo on the belligerents. But several leading members of the League doubted that such a move would be successful without the cooperation of the United States. In early May, 1934, British officials sounded out the State Department on the possibility of separate but parallel action. President Franklin D. Roosevelt and his Secretary of State, Cordell Hull, quickly agreed to seek Congressional authorization for an embargo. Legislation was introduced in Congress on May 18. The public outcry against munitions-makers forestalled opposition from developing, and on May 24 both houses passed a joint resolution empowering the President to forbid the sale of arms to the Chaco belligerents if, in his opinion, such an embargo would contribute to the re-establishment of peace. On May 28, 1934, the President issued a proclamation banning the sale of arms to Bolivia and Paraguay.

The Chaco embargo ended the possibility of future profits for Curtiss-Wright and other American companies selling weapons to Bolivia and Paraguay. However, the fate of materials contracted for and manufactured before May 28 remained in doubt. On June 14, the Justice Department seized $600,000 worth of arms and weapons at a pier in New York Harbor which were destined for Bolivia. Included were the five Curtiss-Wright fighters Bolivia had ordered in February. After vigorous protests by the Bolivian Minister, the State Department announced that weapons completed before May 28 could be exported, but that any products finished after that date could not be shipped. As a result, Curtiss-Wright was able to export the five fighter planes, but the four Condor bombers, valued at $290,000, and the spare parts came under the embargo. Thus Clarence Webster lost half of his last contract with Bolivia.

Richard Hoyt, now serving as chairman of the board of Curtiss-Wright, refused to acknowledge defeat. Calling in Webster and John Allard, the new president of the Curtiss-Wright Export Corporation, Hoyt worked out a plan to get around the Chaco embargo. In the fall of 1934, at the Curtiss-Wright factory in St. Louis, workmen removed the bomb racks and the gun turrets from the four Condors and installed eighteen seats in each fuselage. Miraculously, the Condors were converted from deadly bombers into innocent passenger planes. Curtiss-Wright sold these planes to the Tampa, New Orleans, and Tampico Airlines Company, a New York corporation formed to develop air service between New York and Buenos Aires. The new company was a one-man operation headed by Hugh Wells, a World War I flier who had piloted the first airmail flight from Key West to Havana. On March 15, 1935, Wells applied to the Department of Commerce for permission to fly the four Condors to Arica, Chile, to survey the possibilities for establishing air service to Latin America. The request was sent to the State Department. The Department, perhaps alerted by newspaper reports from Argentina, feared that the planes, which could easily be refitted as bombers, were destined for Bolivia. But when Wells promised not to violate the embargo, he received clearance for the flight.

On the morning of March 28, Wells, three other American pilots, and a complement of co-pilots and mechanics, took off from a small airfield in Patterson, Louisiana, in the four Condors. Flying only by day and spending the nights at Pan American Airways facilities, the planes moved leisurely to Brownsville, Texas, south across Mexico and Central America, with a stop in Panama, and arrived in Lima, Peru, on April 2. They were preparing to leave the next day when a Department of Commerce official arrived from Washington with orders to stop the flight. Charging that Wells had deviated from his flight plan by stopping in Peru, the Commerce Department canceled the authorization for the flight, suspended the pilots' licenses, and asked the Peruvian Government to ground the planes indefinitely. The local authorities complied with this request, and the four Condors were placed under military guard at Las Palmas airport outside Lima.

Wells immediately protested and threatened to sue the United States Government for damages. He told reporters that he had stopped in Lima to make arrangements for establishing air service from there to Beunos Aires. It was rumored, however, that he had planned to meet a Bolivian agent in Lima to receive the final payment for the Condors. The State Department then disclosed that it had been responsible for the seizure of the planes, and announced that the Justice Department had been requested to conduct an investigation to determine if the planes were destined for Bolivia in violation of the Chaco embargo. On May 15, Martin Conboy, the United States Attorney for the Southern District of New York, resigned that post to accept an appointment as special assistant to the Attorney General and announced that he would go to Lima to carry out the investigation. When Conboy sailed from New York on May 18, he was accompanied by Ira A. Schiller, a lawyer hired by Wells to defend his interests.

By the time Conboy and Schiller arrived in Peru on June 1, Wells and his party had been stranded in Lima for nearly two months. They waited idly in hotel rooms for official permission to leave Peru; their only excitement came when one pilot was rushed to a hospital for an emergency appendectomy. The planes remained under close guard at Las Palmas airport. Peruvian officials even refused to allow them to be serviced, though they did permit Wells to equip them with eight extra gas tanks. The planes flew only once, when Wells and the Peruvians allowed a Cal Tech scientist working on a study of cosmic rays in the Andes to use them to gather data for his experiments at high altitudes.

The waiting ended on June 2, when Conboy began questioning the pilots and mechanics at the American Embassy. On the advice of Schiller, Wells instructed his men to answer questions freely. Ten days later, Conboy completed his interrogations and left for the United States without giving any indication that he had secured incriminating information about the flight. Nevertheless, he continued his examination of the affairs of Curtiss-Wright and Wells' airline through the summer and fall of 1935. Finally, he found the evidence that he needed. When Curtiss-Wright had been building the four Condors for the Bolivian Government, it had ordered twenty machine guns from the Colt firearms company, five for each bomber. Five of the machine guns had been shipped to Bolivia before the embargo went into effect, but fifteen were still in the United States on May 28, and since they were designed as part of the equipment for the Condors, the government refused to allow their export. During the summer of 1934, Webster, Allard, and a clerk for the Curtiss-Wright Corporation had placed the fifteen machine guns in the crates containing the five fighter planes which the government had permitted to be exported. The clerk had then filed an export declaration in which he failed to include the guns in the manifesto describing the contents of the crates. The guns thus left New York on September 28, 1934, and arrived in Bolivia in violation of the Chaco arms embargo.

Conboy was now ready to go to court. The machine-gun evidence confirmed his suspicions about the Condors. He still could not prove that the Curtiss-Wright officials had entered a conspiracy to deliver the planes to Bolivia, but the illegal shipment of the machine guns gave him a clear-cut case to prosecute. In October a federal grand jury began hearing the evidence and on January 27, 1936, it indicted the Curtiss-Wright Export Corporation, Clarence Webster, and John Allard on charges of conspiring to violate the Chaco arms embargo.

When the case came before Judge Mortimer J. Byers in the Federal District Court in New York City, lawyers for the defendants, without referring to the details of the case, asked that the charges be dismissed. They contended that the Chaco arms embargo resolution was unconstitutional because Congress had unlawfully delegated legislative power to the President. Citing the recent Supreme Court decision in the Schechter case, which had invalidated the NRA on similar grounds, Judge Byers found for the defense and dismissed the charges. The joint Congressional resolution had authorized the President to decide whether an embargo would serve to re-establish peace in the Chaco before putting the ban into effect. Byers ruled that such a grant of discretionary power constituted "an attempted abdication of legislative responsibility." Congress alone could decide whether a given law would work, he concluded.

This decision had a profound impact on the Roosevelt administration. The fate of the Curtiss-Wright executives was of minor importance—the fighting had stopped in the Chaco in 1935 and the President had revoked the arms embargo. However, in that same year, the exposures of the Nye Committee, revealing the heavy American munitions trade with the Allies from 1914 to 1917, had led Congress to pass a temporary neutrality law built around an arms embargo against all belligerents in future wars. Though the State Department had advocated a discretionary embargo which could be applied exclusively against an aggressor nation, President Roosevelt accepted the Congressional view and invoked an arms embargo when Italy invaded Ethiopia in September, 1935. In the spring of 1936, this legislation was extended for another year, and Congress made it clear that it considered an impartial arms embargo essential to prevent American involvement in another world war. Government spokesmen pointed out that if Judge Byers' decision were allowed to stand, the foundation of the nation's new neutrality legislation would be undermined.

With the major tenet of American foreign policy under constitutional challenge, the Roosevelt administration appealed to the Supreme Court to reverse Judge Byers' ruling in the Curtiss-Wright case. There was little reason for optimism. In a steady series of decisions on New Deal legislation, the Court had consistently denied excessive power to the executive. In addition to its decree in the Schechter case, in early 1936 the Court had invalidated the Agricultural Adjustment Act on the ground that Congress had exceeded the limits of its powers in authorizing benefit payments to farmers to induce them to restrict their acreage. Refusing to heed the argument that the emergency conditions of the depression demanded more flexible legislation, the Court seemed determined to restrict both President and Congress to traditional channels. The Curtiss-Wright case would reveal whether or not the justices would use the same standard in regard to foreign policy.

For two days in mid-November, 1936, the Court heard the arguments presented by Martin Conboy, pleading the government's case, and George Z. Medalie, attorney for the Curtiss-Wright company. Both men had once served as United States Attorney for the Southern District of New York, and both kept close to the constitutional issue: did Congress have the right to delegate broad discretionary power to the President in foreign affairs? Three justices, George

Sutherland, James C. McReynolds, and Charles Evans Hughes, gave the case unusual attention, breaking into the oral presentations with probing questions. All three had a special interest in foreign policy; Sutherland and McReynolds had been members of the Senate Foreign Relations Committee, while Chief Justice Hughes had served as Secretary of State under Harding and Coolidge. When Medalie echoed Judge Byers' opinion by asserting that the Chaco embargo resolution amounted to "almost an abdication of the essential functions of Congress," Hughes questioned him at length about arms embargoes enacted by Congress in 1912 and again in 1922.

Since Congress was preparing to enact permanent neutrality legislation at its next session, the Court acted swiftly. On December 18, 1936, it handed down its decision. Justice Sutherland, a staunch conservative who believed in restricting to the absolute minimum the federal government's role in domestic affairs, delivered the majority decision. Only six months before, Sutherland had voided the Guffey Coal Act, designed to bring order to a chaotic industry, by denying that the Constitution gave Congress the power to legislate for the general welfare. But now he revealed a radically different view in the field of foreign affairs. Reversing the judgment of the lower court, Sutherland stated that since the United States had existed as a sovereign nation before the adoption of the Constitution, its power in the international sphere was without constitutional limit. Then he went on to assert the supremacy of the President in conducting relations with other nations. "In this vast external realm," Sutherland maintained, "with its important, complicated, delicate and manifold problems, the President alone has the power to speak or listen as a representative of the nation." Moreover, Sutherland argued that Congress was acting within its constitutional authority in granting the President broad discretionary powers in the Chaco arms embargo. "Congressional legislation which is to be made effective through negotiation and inquiry within the international field," he concluded, "must often accord to the President a degree of discretion and freedom from statutory restriction which would not be admissible were domestic affairs alone involved." Six justices agreed with Sutherland, and only one, Justice McReynolds, dissented, though he did not file a separate opinion.

The Chaco arms embargo had been upheld, and the neutrality legislation was secure. However, for Clarence Webster, John Allard, and the Curtiss-Wright Export Corporation, the ordeal was not yet over. The Supreme Court directed that the case be continued in district court. In late 1937, another federal grand jury indicted the defendants again, and once more Martin Conboy sought a conviction. The trial proved to be a long and frustrating experience for the prosecuting attorney. After two weeks of proceedings, a member of the jury conversed with one of the defendants on the street outside the courthouse, and the Judge declared a mistrial. A second jury heard the case anew and after three days of deliberation reached an ambiguous verdict—it acquitted the defendants on one count and failed to reach a decision on three others, despite a blistering lecture from the bench.

By this time, Curtiss-Wright had been caught up in the great aircraft boom brought about by the approach of World War II. In 1938 the company sold over $150 million worth of aircraft and engines to the armed forces and foreign governments, and its executives wished to avoid the adverse publicity of a third trial. Consequently, in February, 1940, Webster, Allard, and the Curtiss-Wright Export Corporation pleaded guilty. The Court fined the company $260,000 and the two executives $11,000 apiece. Martin Conboy did not request prison sentences for Webster and Allard, explaining to the court that they had been acting under orders from Richard Hoyt, who had since died. Thus the search for profits in the lean years of the depression had cost Webster, Allard, and the Curtiss-Wright company years of litigation, large legal fees, and, ultimately, a fine nearly equal to the value of the planes they had tried to smuggle out of the country.

Yet by the time the case was finally settled in 1940, its importance was clear. The arms embargo section of the neutrality act had been repealed two months after the outbreak of World War II in 1939, and the illusion that the nation could ride out the European war had been shattered. But as Roosevelt transformed himself from Dr. New Deal to Dr. Win-the-War, he did not have to face another battle with the Supreme Court. Justice Sutherland's historic decision had given the Chief Executive wide latitude in the conduct of diplomacy at a time of great national peril. When Congress passed the Lend-Lease Act in 1941, it granted the President enormous discretion in disbursing vast sums of money to nations fighting against the Axis powers. After the invasion of Russia, Roosevelt was able to include the Soviet Union among the recipients of Lend-Lease aid without consulting Congress, and thus he was able to send vital war material to the Russian front without delay at a time when Hitler's forces were threatening to destroy Soviet resistance. This significant policy, as well as the destroyers-for-bases deal, the Declaration of the United Nations, and the multitude of executive agreements which characterized American diplomacy during the Second World War, rested securely on the far-reaching opinion of the Court that the President was the sole agent of the nation in the conduct of foreign affairs. From the perspective of the Cold War, the Curtiss-Wright decision stands as a landmark for a nation whose destiny and survival today depend on issues that far transcend our continental frontiers.

# The Flag-Salute Cases                    XV

BY IRVING DILLIARD

*(Minersville School District* v. *Gobitis,* 310 U.S. 586;
*West Virginia State Board of Education* v. *Barnette,* 319 U.S. 624)

*Throughout its history, the Supreme Court has had frequently to deal with controversies involving civil liberties, and not merely with those of Negroes. Generally speaking, the Court has stood firmly for freedom of speech, religion, and the press and for guaranteeing that procedural rights such as trial by jury are properly protected. There are, however, necessary limits to individual freedoms when they conflict with the interests of society. The right of free speech, as Justice Oliver Wendell Holmes pointed out in an important 1919 decision, "would not protect a man in falsely shouting fire in a theater and causing a panic."*

*Unfortunately, the boundaries between the rights of individuals and those of the public at large are often difficult to define. Men of goodwill sincerely devoted to individual liberties frequently disagree when the interests of one man or a small minority clash with those of society in a specific instance. In the following chapter Irving Dilliard, a member of the faculty of Princeton's Woodrow Wilson School of Public and International Affairs and author of* One Man's Stand for Freedom: Mr. Justice Black and the Bill of Rights, *describes how the liberal members of the Court struggled with this problem in a series of cases involving freedom of religion.*

Look closely at the map of Pennsylvania for Minersville and you will find it in semi-fine print in Schuylkill County, near Pottsville, about four-fifths of the way from the Ohio boundary across the keystone toward New Jersey, on an east-west line running just a little below the middle.

Geographically, Minersville is a kind of hub for central-eastern

Pennsylvania although not even the businessmen on Minersville's main street probably have ever thought of it that way. Wilkes-Barre and Scranton are north-by-northeast. Allentown and Bethlehem lie east. Philadelphia, its museums, historic shrines and Main Line are to the southeast. Lancaster and the steady Amish folk are due south, and Harrisburg and the state capitol with its shining dome southwesterly. The crow that flies straight west from Minersville soon passes over the Susquehanna River.

As towns shaped up in the mid-1930's, Minersville was pretty much an average American community. It was older than many and not so old as others. Its first settlers built their cabins and began wresting a livelihood out of the forests about 1793. Their sons drew up a plat in 1830, the year that Chicago was laid out. But the founding fathers of Minersville moved faster than their counterparts in the village on Lake Michigan. Minersville was incorporated in 1831, Chicago not until 1833.

A hundred years later the census takers of 1930 counted 9,392 souls in Minersville. This population was enough to move Minersville up the municipal scale a bit, but not enough to make it very large. It relied perhaps too much on the anthracite coal industry and also went in for producing clothes.

Minersville had the run of community organizations, institutions and activities for a place its size. It had men and women and children of a variety of interests and tastes and affiliations and beliefs. Among its God-fearing citizens was the family of Walter Gobitis, pronounced "Go-bite-us."

One afternoon in 1936 Lillian Gobitis, aged twelve, and her brother William, aged ten, came home from public school with news that distressed their parents. The principal had told Lillian and William that they could not attend school any more unless they would agree to salute the national flag as their classmates did at the opening patriotic exercises each morning.

Other children, along with their teachers, repeated the oath of allegiance every day. Other children saluted the flag without objection. The Gobitis children must do likewise or stop coming to public school in Minersville.

The reason Lillian and William were not saluting the flag was simple enough. They meant no disrespect to Old Glory. They admired the Stars and Stripes when they saw it fluttering in the breeze above the schoolhouse. It was just that they had been taught in their church and in their home that saluting the flag was a violation of their religion.

For the family of Walter Gobitis belonged to the Jehovah's Witnesses faith and they took seriously as well as literally the Bible's Ten Commandments. In the Old Testament they found clear instructions on what to do about saluting the flag. There it was written out for all to see in the Book of Exodus, Chapter XX, verses 3 through 5:

3. Thou shalt have no other gods before me.

4. Thou shalt not make unto thee any graven image, or any likeness of any thing that is in heaven above, or that is in the earth beneath, or that is in the water under the earth:

5. Thou shalt not bow down thyself to them, nor serve them. . . .

How could it be plainer than that? When you saluted the flag you were bowing down before a graven image and that was prohibited by the Word of God, as expressed in the Holy Writ, as long ago as the delivery of the Ten Commandments to Moses on Mount Sinai. And so the mother and father of Lillian and William Gobitis told their children not to join the teachers and the other children in the morning patriotic exercises at school.

Here was head-on conflict between the individual citizen and his government—at the level nearest the citizen, his local school board.

The Minersville Board of Education consisted of a broad range of the community's leaders, including business and professional men, from the offices and stores and industries. Dr. T. J. McGurl and Dr. E. A. Valibus took precious time and went to monthly meetings. So did David I. Jones, Claude L. Price, Thomas B. Evans, and William Zapf. The Superintendent of Public Schools was Charles E. Roudabush and he too was a solid and respected citizen.

These men had acted in good faith when they placed the pledge of allegiance and the flag salute in the daily public school program. They believed that the ceremony of the salute would promote patriotism and good citizenship. But the family of Walter Gobitis was acting in equally good faith. The family also was patriotic for it believed that patriotic citizens were first of all religious citizens who obeyed the commands of God. It asked not that the ceremony be abolished for all, but that conscientious objectors be excused from participating in a rite offensive to their cherished beliefs.

The members of the Minersville Board of Education talked the question over, up one side and down the other. In the end they just could not see how it would hurt any American child to salute the national flag. So they declined to make an exception for the Gobitis children. The board members directed Superintendent of Schools Roudabush to expel the children, which he did.

When you really believe that an act is a deadly sin, forbidden by the Ten Commandments, you do not give in easily. Walter Gobitis did not yield an inch. He and his wife took Lillian and William out of public school. But the family circumstances were modest and the costs of a private school became a matter of economic concern.

Gobitis discussed the situation with fellow members of his church. He got some legal advice and some help. He discovered that beyond Minersville, in Philadelphia, in New York, and elsewhere, there were people and organizations interested in questions like the one he had raised. Since the early 1920's the American Civil Liberties Union had as its major purpose the provision of legal help in such situations.

The head of the house of Gobitis thought about it a lot before he did anything, for he wanted to do only what was right. Then, regretfully but resolutely, he filed a suit in court on behalf of his children, and on his own behalf, to be relieved of the financial burden of the additional educational costs. He also sued to prevent the Board of Education from continuing to require the flag salute as a condition to his children's attendance at the Minersville school. He pointed to the fact that the laws of Pennsylvania made attendance at school compulsory and yet his children were not allowed to attend free public school because of the regulation of the Minersville Board of Education.

The case was heard in Federal District Court in Philadelphia by Judge Albert B. Maris, who had been appointed to the federal bench in 1936 by President Franklin D. Roosevelt. Judge Maris granted "relief" to the Gobitis father and children. He did so, the United States Supreme Court said later, "on the basis of a thoughtful opinion, at a preliminary stage." The Minersville Board of Education appealed to the United States Circuit Court of Appeals for the Third Circuit at Philadelphia. After further proceedings, the Court of Appeals upheld the decree of Judge Maris.

Legally, what happened was that the courts had denied a motion of the Minersville Board of Education to dismiss the bill of complaint which sought to enjoin the school authorities from continuing to require the flag salute as a condition to attending school.

Walter Gobitis had now carried the day at the first and second levels of the federal judiciary. There remained the third and highest level in Washington, and to the Supreme Court of the United States the Minersville School Board took its appeal of the case against Lillian and William Gobitis and their father. The year was 1940.

Three times before the question of a compulsory flag salute had been appealed to the Supreme Court. Three times the Supreme Court had disposed of it briefly in an unsigned *per curiam* opinion, declaring that no substantial federal question was involved. It was a local or at most a state matter. The first flag-salute regulation appeared in Kansas in 1907, and three decades later it had been taken up in only eighteen states. One hundred and twenty children were known to have refused for religious reasons to comply. As recently as April, 1939, the Supreme Court had unanimously denied an appeal from the Supreme Court of California which had upheld the requirement of a flag salute.

This time, however, the appeal situation was different. Instead of upholding the flag-salute requirement, the lower courts had granted relief to a father and his children who opposed the rite as part of a school program. Furthermore, Europe had gone to war. People all over the United States were wondering how long this country could stay out of the bitter conflict. As the danger increased, there was more and more in the way of patriotic ceremony and exercise, not less.

And so the Supreme Court of the United States put its precedent rulings to one side and agreed to listen to arguments in the case of *Minersville School District* v. *Gobitis*. It did so, the Supreme Court said, "to give the matter full consideration."

Things were going from bad to worse in Europe when Case No. 690 of the October, 1939, term was argued on April 25, 1940. Sitting on the highest tribunal that uneasy spring day were a Wilson appointee, Justice James Clark McReynolds of Tennessee, a Coolidge appointee, Justice Harlan F. Stone of New York, two Hoover appointees, Chief Justice Charles Evans Hughes of New

York and Justice Owen J. Roberts of Pennsylvania, and five who held their commissions from President Roosevelt. The New Deal quintet were Justices Hugo L. Black of Alabama, Stanley F. Reed of Kentucky, Felix Frankfurter of Massachusetts, William O. Douglas of Connecticut, and Frank Murphy of Michigan. It was a Supreme Court with a lot of fresh blood and the newcomers had markedly lowered the average age.

Word went around Washington that the arguments would be something to hear. The case had not drawn as counsel a Daniel Webster or a Joseph H. Choate or a John W. Davis, but even so it would be worth anybody's time. Joseph W. Henderson of the Philadelphia bar spoke up for the Minersville Board of Education. He presented three major contentions:

1. The expulsion of the Gobitis children did not violate their rights under the Constitution of the United States.

2. The expulsion did not violate their rights under the Constitution of the Commonwealth of Pennsylvania.

3. The refusal of the Gobitis children to salute the flag at school exercises because they believed to do so would violate the law of Almighty God, as contained in the Bible, was not founded on a religious belief.

George K. Gardner of Boston, a professor at the Harvard Law School, carried the burden of the argument for the Gobitis children and their father, who appeared in the title of the case as "their next friend." He and his associates made two main points. The first was that "The creature man shall be free to exercise his conscientious belief in God and his obedience to the law of Almighty God, the Creator, and may not be compelled to obey the law or the rule of the state, which law, as he conscientiously believes, is in direct conflict with the law of Almighty God." The second was that "the rule made and enforced by [the Minersville Board of Education] compelling children and teachers to indulge in a ceremony of saluting the flag is violative of the Fourteenth Amendment of the Constitution of the United States of America."

The Gobitis family could not have been other than surprised at the array of legal talent from over the country that came to sit, figuratively at least, on its side of the counsel table. For in addition to the professor from the Harvard Law School, there were the others who joined in the friends-of-the-court brief of the

American Civil Liberties Union—Arthur Garfield Hays, Osmond K. Fraenkel, William G. Fennell, and Jerome M. Britchey of New York and Alexander H. Frey of Philadelphia. Among these distinguished members of the bar were veteran fighters for freedom in the United States for more than a quarter-century.

Between the expulsion of the Gobitis children and the appeal of their case to the Supreme Court, a remarkable thing had happened. Alarmed by the rash of so-called loyalty statutes of the early 1930's, teachers' oath laws and other infringements on individual freedom, one of the bar's most eminent members, Grenville Clark of New York, had persuaded the American Bar Association to set up a Committee on the Bill of Rights to investigate "seeming substantial violations of constitutional liberties" in the country. The committee was created in 1938 and its authority to enter into litigation defined in January, 1940. Almost at once the chairman, Grenville Clark, and one of the committee members, Zechariah Chafee, Jr., professor of law at Harvard and an authority on civil liberty, went to work on a brief supporting the stand taken by the Gobitis family. When their brief was submitted to the Supreme Court, it bore the names of some of the most eminent members of the legal profession over the country. They included Charles P. Taft of Ohio, Lloyd K. Garrison of Wisconsin, Douglas Arant of Alabama, George I. Haight of Illinois, Monte M. Lemann of Louisiana, and Ross L. Malone of New Mexico.

Their brief was bold and challenging. "So far as the respondent children are concerned, the salute must be regarded as a religious ritual," it declared. "We suggest that no American court should presume to tell any person that he is wrong in his opinion as to how he may best serve the God in which he believes." Its second major point was that "There is no such public need for the compulsory flag salute as to justify the overriding of the religious scruples of the children." Here the committee struck doubly hard. It contended not only that the "alleged public need [was] not sufficiently urgent," but that "even if the challenged legislation be deemed to serve a public need, there are other reasonable ways of accomplishing the purpose without infringing the religious convictions of children."

The American Bar Association's committee saw still other objections to the demand of the Minersville Board of Education.

"Even if the salute be considered incapable of any religious meaning, compulsory salute legislation is void as an unjustifiable infringement of the liberty of the individual." Furthermore, "the compulsory flag salute cannot be sustained on the ground that public school education is granted as a matter of grace so that the requirement, even though arbitrary and capricious, can be enforced by expulsion from public school."

A brief so courageous deserved a courageous conclusion. Here was the high note struck on its final page:

> The philosophy of free institutions is now being subjected to the most severe test it has ever undergone. Advocates of totalitarian government point to the speed and efficiency with which such systems are administered, and assert that democracy can offer nothing to outweigh these advantages. The answer is to be found in the value of certain basic individual rights and the assurance afforded by free institutions that these shall not be required to yield to majority pressure no matter how overwhelming.
>
> The worth of our system must ultimately be judged in terms of the importance of those values and the care with which they are safeguarded. We consider them immeasurably important. We believe that the letter and spirit of our Constitution demand vindication of the individual liberties which are abridged by the challenged regulation.

Now the case of Lillian and William Gobitis and their father had gone all the way. Starting in their home town in 1936 it had completed the three levels of the courts of the United States in four years. It had been finally argued with dignity and earnestness and conviction on both sides at the apex of the judiciary and then taken for decision.

Alas, the impressive arguments, oral and written, and the briefs of the American Civil Liberties Union and the American Bar Association committee were almost completely unavailing so far as the *Gobitis* decision went. By a vote of 8 to 1, the Justices reversed the lower court decision.

Chief Justice Hughes assigned the writing of the majority opinion to Justice Felix Frankfurter, who had arrived on the bench barely a year earlier. Frankfurter was a 1906 graduate of the Harvard Law School, a classmate of Grenville Clark and Monte M. Lemann of the American Bar Association's committee. Latterly, Justice Frankfurter had been a colleague of Professor Zechariah Chafee and George K. Gardner on the Harvard Law faculty. But these old associations counted for little if anything. Something that might have mattered, although of course nothing was said about it, was the fact that Justice Frankfurter was the only member of the Supreme Court who was not native born. It is more than possible that Hughes had this in mind when he placed the Court's opinion in Frankfurter's talented hands. The Chief Justice knew that an opinion by Frankfurter on the side of the Minersville School District would not only be eloquent, but would also appeal to the nation's spirit of patriotism in an increasingly trying time of international danger.

And so Felix Frankfurter, emigrant from Austria at the age of eleven, went to work on an opinion concerning the Stars and Stripes that he expected would be supported by all of his black-robed brothers. But Justice Stone had met the Jehovah's Witnesses in earlier Supreme Court tests. "All human experience teaches us that a moral issue cannot be suppressed or settled by making its supporters martyrs," he had written. Even while the Gobitis case was under deliberation, Justice Stone addressed to the famous international lawyer, John Bassett Moore, words that recalled Justice Oliver Wendell Holmes's historic dissent in the Rosika Schwimmer citizenship case. "I suppose there are limits," wrote Stone, "beyond which personally offensive free speech cannot be pressed, but there would not be much necessity for free-speech protection if it extended only to those things we would like to hear."

Without saying much about it, Justice Stone had made up his mind to dissent in behalf of the rights of the Gobitis family. This impending stand by a senior member of the Court disturbed Justice Frankfurter to such an extent that just a week before the decision was to be handed down, he wrote his older colleague a five-page letter in an attempt to convince him that the *Gobitis* opinion was really only an application of principles which Justice Stone himself had asserted in other important cases.

The compulsory-flag-salute question was, Justice Frankfurter wrote, a "tragic issue," and all the more sensitive for him because it presented a "clash of rights, not the clash of wrongs" and "for resolving such a clash we have no calculus." Stone's feelings had made him re-examine his own views, Frankfurter went on, for he had always opposed "foolish and harsh manifestations of coercion" and favored "the amplest expression of dissident views, however absurd or offensive." But the school authorities certainly could establish "flag-saluting exercises." Since they felt that exempting the Gobitis children would disrupt the ceremony, "it seems to me that we do not trench upon an undebatable territory of libertarian immunity" by allowing them to make the children conform.

After recalling "many talks with Holmes about his espionage opinions,"[1] which he regarded as providing a guideline for the flag-salute case, Justice Frankfurter explained his opinion would be "a vehicle for preaching the true democratic faith of not relying on the Court for the impossible task of assuring a vigorous, mature, self-protecting and tolerant democracy." This task was the responsibility of "the people and their representatives."

Bear in mind how very little this case authorizes and how wholly free it leaves us for the future [he continued]. . . . It is not a case where conformity is exacted for something that you and I regard as foolish—namely a gesture of respect for the symbol of our national being—even though we deem it foolish to exact it from Jehovah's Witnesses. . . . It is not a case where the slightest restriction is involved against the fullest opportunity to disavow—either on the part of the children or their parents—the meaning that ordinary people attach to the gesture of respect. . . . We ought to let the legislative judgment stand and put the responsibility where it belongs.[2]

Justice Stone replied in an undated, pencil-written note. He distinguished between a "vulgar intrusion of law" in the domain of

---

[1] *Schenck* v. *United States* (1919) and *Abrams* v. *United States* (1919). In the Schenck case, the Supreme Court upheld the conviction for conspiracy under the Espionage Act of the general secretary of the Socialist party who had sent out 15,000 leaflets urging conscripted men to oppose the World War I draft law. In the unanimous opinion, Justice Holmes asserted his famous doctrine that what must be determined is whether the words are used in circumstances that would "create a clear and present danger" such as Congress has a right to prevent. In the Abrams case, five Russians were found guilty of violating the Espionage Act by publishing two leaflets that denounced "capitalist nations" for "interfering" with the Russian Revolution. The leaflets urged workers in munitions factories in the United States not to "betray" their "Russian comrades." The Supreme Court upheld the convictions, 7 to 2, Justices Holmes and Brandeis dissenting.

[2] This intimate and revealing letter from Justice Frankfurter to his senior colleague is little known. The only place where it appears in full in print, so far as the author knows, is as an appendix to A. T. Mason, *Security Through Freedom: American Political Thought and Practice* (Cornell, 1955). It is extensively quoted in Mason's monumental biography, *Harlan Fiske Stone: Pillar of the Law* (Viking Press, 1953, 1956).

conscience and in legislation dealing with the control of property. The Court's responsibility is the larger, he wrote, in the domain of conscience. Then he said: "I am truly sorry not to go along with you. The case is peculiarly one of the relative weight of imponderables and I cannot overcome the feeling that the Constitution tips the scales in favor of religion."

The much awaited decision came down on June 3, 1940, almost as if an observance by the Supreme Court of Flag Day that year. By then Hitler's armored might had run through the Netherlands, Belgium, and Luxembourg. The heroic withdrawal from Dunkirk had been written imperishably in the annals of free men. It was a time for heroic thinking as well. Partly under the prodding of his law clerk, Allison Dunham, who very strongly opposed the compulsory flag salute, Justice Stone drafted his dissent. But he waited so long that by the time it could be circulated to the other Justices, support for the Frankfurter opinion was general. Justices Black, Douglas, and Murphy were not very happy about it and devoted their efforts to bringing about certain modifications in the Frankfurter opinion on the side of freedom of conscience. Had Justice Stone prepared his dissent earlier he might well have had company in his disagreement.

Justice Frankfurter's opinion faced the dilemma of the liberals squarely in the first paragraph. "A grave responsibility confronts this Court whenever in the course of litigation it must reconcile the conflicting claims of liberty and authority." The pursuit of one's convictions "about the ultimate mystery of the universe and man's relation to it" was clearly beyond the reach of law, but at the same time, the community as a whole had rights that must also be respected. "The mere possession of religious convictions which contradict the relevant concerns of a political society does not relieve the citizen from the discharge of political responsibilities."

"The ultimate foundation of a free society is the binding tie of cohesive sentiment," Frankfurter declared. The flag is "the symbol of our national unity . . . the emblem of freedom in its truest, best sense." To argue that a law requiring schoolchildren to salute the flag violated the constitutional guarantees of freedom of conscience would be to exceed the limits of judicial "competence." He continued:

The influences which help toward a common feeling for the common country are manifold. Some may seem harsh and others no doubt are foolish. Surely, however, the end is legitimate. And the effective means for its attainment are still so uncertain and so unauthenticated by science as to preclude us from putting the widely prevalent belief in flag-saluting beyond the pale of legislative power. It mocks reason and denies our whole history to find in the allowance of a requirement to salute our flag on fitting occasions the seeds of sanction for obeisance to a leader.

Why might the school board members insist on the authority to expel Lillian and William Gobitis rather than to allow them to be excused from the morning flag ceremony? Justice Frankfurter answered this way:

What the school authorities are really asserting is the right to awaken in the child's mind considerations as to the significance of the flag contrary to those implanted by the parent. In such an attempt the state is normally at a disadvantage in competing with the parent's authority, so long—and this is the vital aspect of religious toleration—as parents are unmolested in their right to counteract by their own persuasiveness the wisdom and rightness of those loyalties which the state's educational system is seeking to promote. . . . That the flag-salute is an allowable portion of a school program for those who do not invoke conscientious scruples is surely not debatable. But for us to insist that, though the ceremony may be required, exceptional immunity must be given to dissidents, is to maintain that there is no basis for a legislative judgment that such an exemption might introduce elements of discipline, might cast doubts in the minds of the other children which would themselves weaken the effect of the exercise.

Although Frankfurter had been expected to read his opinion before the assembled Court, he merely announced the result, allowing interested persons to follow his reasoning in the printed record. Justice Stone, however, was so stirred by the case that he read his dissent in full. Moving forward in his chair, he spoke with deep emotion in a raised voice.

After paying tribute to the good citizenship of the Gobitis children and their father, he hit hard at the regulation of the Minersville Board of Education, which, he said, "does more than suppress freedom of speech and more than prohibit the free exercise of religion. . . . For by this law the state seeks to coerce these children to express a sentiment which, as they interpret it, they do not entertain, and which violates their deepest religious convictions."

Justice Stone conceded that the government may "make war and raise armies" and that to do so it may subject citizens to military training despite their religious objections. "But it is a long step and one I am unable to take to the position that government may, as a supposed educational measure and as a means of disciplining the young, compel public affirmations which violate their religious conscience." There were better ways of inculcating patriotism in a child, he insisted, than forcing him "to affirm that which he does not believe." It is one thing to "elicit" expressions of loyalty, another to "command" them.

The Constitution expresses more than the conviction of the people that democratic processes must be preserved at all costs [Justice Stone concluded]. It is also an expression of faith and a command that freedom of mind and spirit must be preserved, which *government* must obey, if it is to adhere to that justice and moderation without which no free government can exist. . . . I cannot say that the inconveniences which may attend some sensible adjustment of school discipline in order that these children may be spared, presents a problem so momentous or pressing as to outweigh the freedom from compulsory violation of religious faith which has been thought worthy of constitutional protection.

There it was: 8 to 1. The lower courts had been reversed, the Minersville School District upheld. Walter Gobitis and his children, Lillian and William, had lost. Yet the country remained to be heard from, and a large part of the reaction, which came quickly, was on the dissenting side. More than 170 leading newspapers condemned the decision while only a few supported it. "We think this decision of the United States Supreme Court is dead wrong," the St. Louis *Post-Dispatch* said.

We think its decision is a violation of American principle. We think it is a surrender to popular hysteria. If patriotism depends upon such things as this—upon violation of a fundamental right of religious freedom, then it becomes not a noble emotion of love for country, but something to be rammed down our throats by the law.

Some of Justice Frankfurter's closest friends were dismayed. The British political scientist Harold J. Laski wrote from London to Justice Stone: "I want to tell you how right I think you are in that educational case from Pennsylvania and, to my deep regret, how wrong I think Felix is." The New Deal lawyer Benjamin V. Cohen said: "When a liberal judge holds out alone against his liberal brethren, I think he ought to know when he has spoken not for himself alone, but has superbly articulated the thoughts of his contemporaries who believe with him in an effective but tolerant democracy." John Bassett Moore made this comment: "I am sorry to see Frankfurter acting as the mouthpiece of such measures which are likely to create disloyalty more than to promote loyalty."

On the heels of the decision came a wave of fanatical patriotism, with violence heaped on the Jehovah's Witnesses in many places. A meeting hall was burned in Kennebunkport, Maine. A Bible meeting was attacked in Rockville, Maryland. A lawyer who attempted to represent embattled Jehovah's Witnesses at Connersville, Indiana, was beaten and driven from the town. Veterans organizations participated in the bitter reaction in many communities. In Jackson, Mississippi, the Witnesses were banned. Arkansas, California, Texas, and Wyoming were among the other states which saw instances of violent reaction attributable at least in part to the flag-salute decision. In several states children in Jehovah's Witnesses families who continued to refuse to salute the flag in school exercises were declared delinquents by the courts and committed to reformatories.

After a caravan of Witnesses' automobiles was overturned in Litchfield, Illinois, the St. Louis *Post-Dispatch* took an over-all look at the lamentable situation:

It would be a mistake to attribute these outbreaks of violence against religious minorities solely to the United States Supreme Court's opinion upholding the compulsory flag salute in public schools. . . . Yet there can be little doubt that that most unfortunate decision will be an encouragement for self-appointed guardians of patriotism and the national moralists to take the law into their own hands.

Two facts about the decision reassured Justice Frankfurter. One was the overwhelming vote of eight to one. The other was the presence of Chief Justice Hughes among the eight, for Hughes, more than any other member of the Court, had spoken up in the past for the liberties protected by the Bill of Rights. In cases involving freedom of the press, freedom of speech, and freedom of association the elderly, bewhiskered Chief Justice had written some of the strongest decisions in Supreme Court history.

But change was overtaking the Supreme Bench, and with it would come a new point of view. In less than a year the ultra-conservative Justice McReynolds stepped down and Senator James F. Byrnes of South Carolina was appointed to his seat. Shortly thereafter, Chief Justice Hughes retired. The following October, President Roosevelt elevated Justice Stone to the chief justiceship and nominated Attorney General Robert H. Jackson of New York to the vacancy created by the advancement of Stone.

Meantime, a new Jehovah's Witnesses case—or rather set of cases—was on the way to the Supreme Court. All grew out of tests of the constitutionality of municipal ordinances under which members of that faith were convicted for not paying license taxes on the religious publications which they sold on street corners and from door to door. Roscoe Jones ran afoul of such an ordinance in Opelika, Alabama, Lois Bowden and Zada Sanders in Fort Smith, Arkansas, and Charles Jobin in Casa Grande, Arizona. Meantime also, Justices Black, Douglas, and Murphy were growing increasingly concerned about their support of the *Gobitis* decision. For added to the editorial reaction and the violence which came in the wake of the decision was the almost uniformly adverse judgment of the law reviews and journals.

And so Justices Black, Douglas, and Murphy resolved to get themselves separated from the *Gobitis* decision at their earliest opportunity. They found it in *Jones* v. *Opelika,* as the new cases were called. They left the Frankfurter standard en masse and joined Stone. In addition to supporting the dissent of the Chief Justice, the three added a separate statement of their own, doubtless unique in Supreme Court history:

The opinion of the Court sanctions a device which in our opinion suppresses or tends to suppress the free exercise of a religion practiced by a minority group. This is but another step in the direction which *Minersville School District* v. *Gobitis* took against the same religious minority and is a logical extension of the principles upon which that decision rested. Since we joined in the opinion in the *Gobitis Case,* we think this is an appropriate occasion to state that we now believe that it was also wrongly decided. Certainly our democratic form of government functioning under the historic Bill of Rights has a high responsibility to accommodate itself to the religious views of minorities however unpopular and unorthodox those views may be. The First Amendment does not put the right freely to exercise religion in a subordinate position. We fear, however, that the opinions in these and the *Gobitis Case* do exactly that.

The disavowal of *Gobitis* by three of its adherents made the decision in *Jones* v. *Opelika* 5 to 4. Supporting Justice Reed's majority opinion upholding the license tax ordinances were Justices Roberts and Frankfurter from *Gobitis*, and the new Justices, Byrnes and Jackson. But this was only a transitional step, although a most significant one. Outright reversal of *Gobitis* was on the way. Justice Byrnes resigned from the Court in a year to become War Mobilization Director. To his place President Roosevelt appointed Court of Appeals Judge Wiley B. Rutledge of Iowa. Justice Rutledge, a former law school dean, was a staunch libertarian and his views on freedom of religion were well established.

The compulsory flag-salute issue quickly came up again in several states. In West Virginia the legal basis of the salute requirement was much broader than the authority of the Minersville school district. Now it was an order of the West Virginia State Board of Education, based on an act of the West Virginia Legislature, duly signed by the Governor. That the *Gobitis* decision prompted this action cannot be doubted. For West Virginia amended its laws in 1941 so as to require all schools, public, parochial, and private, to prescribe courses "for the purpose of teaching, fostering and perpetuating the ideals, principles and spirit of Americanism, and increasing the knowledge of the organization and machinery of the government."

Implementing this statute, the State Board of Education, on January 9, 1942, approved a resolution that drew heavily on Justice Frankfurter's *Gobitis* opinion. It ordered school authorities in each community to make the flag salute "a regular part of the program of activities." This directive commanded that all teachers and pupils "shall be required to participate in the salute honoring the Nation represented by the flag." It also provided that "refusal to salute the flag be regarded as an act of insubordination, and shall be dealt with accordingly." The penalty was expulsion with readmission denied until compliance was agreed to. Moreover, an expelled child, not in school, was "unlawfully absent" and subject to proceedings as a "delinquent." Parents or guardians were liable to fine and jail term.

As a result of the decree a number of the children of Jehovah's Witnesses were expelled from West Virginia schools and threatened with incarceration in reformatories for criminally inclined juveniles. Fathers and mothers were prosecuted. A group of these parents challenged the law and the implementing regulations as an invasion of individual rights. Walter Barnette, Paul Stull, and Lucy McClure sued in Federal District Court in Charleston, for an injunction to stop enforcement of the compulsory aspects against Jehovah's Witnesses.

The positions taken by the contending sides amounted to a rematching of the adversaries in the Gobitis case. The parents, speaking for their children, objected to "an unconstitutional denial of religious freedom and free speech." The State Board of Education asserted its authority, cited *Gobitis,* and asked that the complaint be dismissed as without merit. Because of the importance of the controversy the Federal District Court set up a special bench of three judges to hear the case and called in a jurist from the Federal Court of Appeals at Richmond, Virginia, Judge John J. Parker of North Carolina, as one of the three. The spin of the wheel of fate that brought Judge Parker into the case was curious, since the scholarly North Carolinian had reason to believe that adherence to precedents had been a leading factor in preventing his confirmation by the Senate when he was appointed to the Supreme Court in 1930 by President Herbert Hoover.

Be that as it may, Judge Parker and his colleagues on the special bench did not follow the *Gobitis* precedent. Pointing out that at least four justices were now opposed to *Gobitis* and that the majority in *Jones* v. *Opelika* distinguished *Gobitis* instead of relying upon it, the three judges issued a decree against enforcement of the compulsory flag salute in schools. Speaking through Judge Parker, they said:

Under such circumstances, and believing as we do that the flag salute here required is violative of religious liberty when required of persons holding the religious views of plaintiffs, we feel that we would be recreant to our duty as judges if through a blind following of a decision which the Supreme Court itself has thus impaired as authority, we should deny pro-

tection to rights which we regard as among the most sacred of those protected by constitutional guaranties.

Thereupon the West Virginia State Board of Education appealed
directly to the Supreme Court, as the law provided it might do.
The case was heard in Washington, on March 11, 1943. The West
Virginia State Board of Education was represented before the
highest tribunal by W. Holt Wooddell, State Assistant Attorney
General, and from Indianapolis came a friend-of-the-court brief
on behalf of the American Legion, which was beating the drums
for the compulsory flag salute. The protesting West Virginians
relied on counsel Hayden C. Covington of Philadelphia, who had
assisted the Gobitis family three years earlier. The American Civil
Liberties Union again presented a strong brief for individual liberty
and so did the Committee on the Bill of Rights of the American
Bar Association. Changes in the bar committee's personnel brought
the names of Basil O'Connor and Abe Fortas, among others, to
the side of the Jehovah's Witnesses.

When the Supreme Court handed down its second flag-salute
decision in 1943, it truly was a Flag Day observance for the date
actually was June 14. The *Gobitis* precedent was not ignored or
by-passed. It was squarely and completely overruled, with direct
reference to its wrongness. Chief Justice Stone, who had been
joined by Justices Black, Douglas, and Murphy in the *Opelika* tax
case, now had the further support of Justices Jackson and Rutledge.
The 8 to 1 in *Gobitis* had become 6 to 3 the opposite way. In
*West Virginia State Board of Education* v. *Barnette* only Justices
Roberts and Reed were on the side of the Frankfurter dissent and
they did not join in that opinion, but merely noted that they
adhered to the views expressed in *Gobitis* and so believed that the
judgment in the West Virginia case should be reversed.

The majority opinion of Justice Jackson and the dissent of
Justice Frankfurter were two of the strongest opinions in Supreme
Court history. Each was clear, direct, eloquent, and fraught with
a sense of urgency, making the most convincing argument its
author could marshal. A few sentences from the pros and cons
will suggest what awaits the reader who goes to the full opinions.
Justice Jackson stated:

A person gets from a symbol the meaning he puts into it, and what is one man's comfort and inspiration is another man's jest and scorn. . . .

To sustain the compulsory flag salute we are required to say that a Bill of Rights which guards the individual's right to speak his mind, left it open to public authorities to compel him to utter what is not in his mind. . . .

Those who begin coercive elimination of dissent soon find themselves exterminating dissenters. Compulsory unification of opinion achieves only the unanimity of the graveyard. . . . It seems trite but necessary to say that the First Amendment was designed to avoid these ends by avoiding these beginnings.

In conclusion Jackson struck off one of the golden paragraphs in the literature of the Supreme Court:

If there is any fixed star in our constitutional constellation, it is that no official, high or petty, can prescribe what shall be orthodox in politics, nationalism, religion, or other matters of opinion or force citizens to confess by word or act their faith therein. If there are any circumstances which permit an exception, they do not now occur to us.

On that high note, the new majority declared the action compelling the flag salute and pledge to be an unconstitutional invasion of "the sphere of intellect and spirit."

Justice Frankfurter began his dissent with what must be the most personal and poignant sentence ever written in a Supreme Court opinion. "One who belongs to the most vilified and persecuted minority in history," he said, "is not likely to be insensible to the freedoms guaranteed by our Constitution." After this arresting reference to himself, he continued:

Were my purely personal attitude relevant I should wholeheartedly associate myself with the general libertarian views in the Court's opinion, representing as they do the thought and action of a lifetime. But as judges we are neither Jew nor Gentile, neither Catholic nor agnostic. We owe equal attachment to the Constitution and are equally bound by our judicial obligations whether we derive our citizenship from the earliest or the latest immigrants to these shores. As a member of this Court I am not justified in writing my private notions of policy into the Constitution, no matter how deeply I may cherish them or how mischievous I may deem their disregard.

Justice Frankfurter then proceeded to reply to the majority with his own epigrammatic thrusts:

In the light of all the circumstances . . . it would require more daring than I possess to deny that reasonable legislators could have taken the action which is before us for review.

The constitutional protection of religious freedom terminated disabilities, it did not create new privileges. It gave religious equality, not civil immunity.

Law is concerned with external behavior and not with the inner life of man. . . . One may have the right to practice one's religion and at the same time owe the duty of formal obedience to laws that run counter to one's beliefs.

And so, three years almost to the day after the delivery of the *Gobitis* decision, that ruling was most impressively reversed. Seldom has the Court experienced so complete a change of heart in so short a time. As Justices Black and Douglas wrote in their concurring opinion in the *Barnette* case, the principle of *Gobitis* (that state legislatures must be allowed much freedom of action in dealing with local problems) was sound, but "its application in the particular case was wrong." And they added: "Words uttered under coercion are proof of loyalty to nothing but self-interest. Love of country must spring from willing hearts and free minds."

Chief Justice Stone, the lone dissenter in 1940, expressed his personal appreciation to Justice Black in a letter: "The sincerity and the good sense of what you have said will, I believe, make a very deep impression on the public conscience. It also states in simple and perfectly understandable form good constitutional law as I understand it." A venerated friend wrote him a congratulatory note, and the head of the Court replied: "All's well that ends well, but I should like to have seen the case end well in the first place without following such a devious route to the desired end."

In the next two decades many cases involving the constitutional separation of church and state would reach the same august bench. These tests would concern transportation of parochial school pupils, "released time" and "dismissed time" programs of sectarian devotions in public schools, the use of the mails for highly dubious appeals in the name of religion, conscientious objection to arms-bearing as a bar to the practice of law and admission to citizenship. Still other legal controversies would swirl around censorship of motion pictures on grounds of immorality and sacrilege, Bible reading and recitation of officially approved prayers in public school rooms, and the requirement of a declaration of belief in the existence of God as a condition to holding public office.

Popular views about these and other issues concerning man's religion—or lack of it—would differ widely. But the Compulsory Flag-Salute Cases were in a class by themselves. For they wrote a unique chapter in the history of the Supreme Court and its changing personnel in the midst of the worst war of all time. They would remain the most fascinating of all these cases for they dealt with little children and their parents, with intensely held faith in the Ten Commandments and with the red, white and blue symbol of the American nation under which some citizens would serve by withholding obeisance while others offered their lives.

# The School Desegregation Case XVI

BY ALFRED H. KELLY

(*Brown* v. *Board of Education of the City of Topeka,* 347 U.S. 483)

*No more fitting conclusion to this series of essays could be found than the following account of the best-known and most important case in the modern history of the Supreme Court. The contrast it presents with the Court's early days, when John Marshall decided the fate of William Marbury, is startling. Then the nation was small, the Court's authority uncertain, the general concept of the power of the federal government (indeed of all government) limited. The effectiveness of the Constitution was untested. In 1954 the United States was the most powerful nation on earth, the Court a tribunal of acknowledged might, the government's right to act with immense force in order to advance the general welfare unquestioned. The Constitution had proved itself the most stable and respected frame of government in the world.*

*The meaning of the Constitution, however, still remained subject to debate, and as individuals quarreled over its cryptic phraseology, the Supreme Court continued to interpret it, thus maintaining its vitality and securing the stability of the American political system.*

*As Alfred H. Kelly, Professor of History at Wayne State University, makes clear in this last chapter, the meaning of the Constitution has more and more come to depend upon the general wisdom of the justices. But as his discussion also makes clear, the power of the Court still depends upon the actions of citizens intent upon their own ends who have brought their quarrels before it for settlement. Their strengths and weaknesses, their prejudices, canniness, determination, and intelligence inevitably influence the decisions of the Court. And these shape the future of all the people.*

*Professor Kelly, an authority on constitutional history, played an important behind-the-scenes role in the drama he describes. He is co-author of* The American Constitution.

On a certain warm and humid day in May, 1896, when the Supreme Court of the United States delivered its opinion in the Louisiana "Jim Crow" car case, entitled *Plessy* v. *Ferguson*,[1] the American Negro stood at a kind of new nadir in his long struggle for decency and humanity. An overwhelming number of white Americans both North and South, the idealism of the Radical Republicans of a generation earlier now conveniently forgotten, rested secure in the comfortable assumption of the biological, cultural, and social superiority of the white race.

The "separate but equal doctrine" which incorporated this racial myth into law and upon which Justice Brown rested his decision, was almost a half-century old in 1896, having first been formulated in 1850 by a distinguished Massachusetts Supreme Court jurist, Lemuel Shaw, in a now famous school segregation case, *Roberts* v. *the City of Boston*. As of 1868, when the Fourteenth Amendment with its "equal protection clause" went onto the books, virtually all the states outside New England had possessed some form of legalized racial segregation, most frequently in their public school laws.

Adoption of the Fourteenth Amendment had made no practical difference whatever in the status of such legislation, for one state supreme court after another had ruled that laws of this kind did not come within the purview of the new constitutional guarantee of "equal protection." Even as Brown spoke in 1896, nearly thirty states of the Union, including the entire South, the border states, New York, Indiana, Kansas, and most of the West including California, had "separate but equal" school laws on their books. At law there was a close parallel between Jim Crow car acts and Jim Crow school statutes, and Justice Brown brought them all together with a stroke of the judicial pen.

Constitutional purists frequently observe that Brown's remarks on segregated schools were technically mere obiter dicta, that is, mere side remarks not essential to the settlement of the case at hand, and under the rule of *stare decisis* therefore not legally binding on the Court in subsequent school cases. They observe, also, that the Court for some thirty years after the Plessy decision managed to

[1] See Chapter X.

avoid, seemingly with almost meticulous care, any specific decision that the Plessy rule applied to segregated state public schools and that state laws providing for such were compatible with the "equal protection" clause.

Not until *Gong Lum* v. *Lee,* in 1927, did the Supreme Court at last face the segregated school question squarely. Then Chief Justice William Howard Taft declared that the matter of the constitutionality of segregated state public schools was one "which has many times been decided [by the Supreme Court] to be within the power of the state legislatures to settle without the intervention of the federal courts under the federal constitution." Technically, Taft was wrong and the constitutional purists are right—it had not been formally "so decided" at all, let alone many times. But practically Taft was right; there had been no serious disposition on the part of the courts of the previous generation to challenge the "separate but equal" rule, embodiment as it was of the overwhelmingly prevalent myth of the Negro's inferiority.

It was to be a long road from *Plessy* and *Gong Lum* to that day in May, 1954, when Chief Justice Earl Warren, speaking for a unanimous Supreme Court, tossed the "separate but equal" rule into the rubbish heap of outworn constitutional doctrine. But just as in 1896, when Brown had spoken for a segregated America, the Supreme Court in 1954 was still adhering to its own larger rule: it was again "following the election returns." For in between *Plessy* and *Brown* v. *the Board of Education of the City of Topeka* there ensued a vast sociopolitical revolution in the status of the American Negro.

Seen in historical perspective, it is now apparent that this twentieth-century "revolution" in Negro status was to be no less far-reaching in its social and political consequences than that earlier revolution in Negro status precipitated by the Civil War and Radical Republican Reconstruction. The "first Revolution," 1861-68, freed the Negro and endowed him with nominal citizenship and legal equality. Once the revolutionary tide had subsided, however, it left the ex-slave stranded in what amounted, throughout most of the Republic, to an inferior status reminiscent of that of the Helots of ancient Sparta or the Untouchables of modern India. The "second Revolution" in Negro status, which even today is far from complete, was to inaugurate the progressive destruction of the racial caste system in the United States and to commence at the same time the genuine integration of the Negro into the social, economic, and political fabric of American life.

The rise and progress of this vast new twentieth-century revolution in Negro status makes up too complex a story to be told in great detail here, but there can be no real grasp of the meaning of *Brown* v. *Board* without some understanding of it. Perhaps it is no great oversimplification to assert that it had its beginnings in the rise of numerically important and hence politically significant Negro communities in the many large and middle-sized cities of the American North, resulting in turn from successive waves of colored migration from the states of the Old Confederacy. Between 1910 and 1940, the Negro population of New York City, for example, rose from 60,000 to 450,000. That of Detroit increased from 4,000 to about 100,000 in these years, while Philadelphia's Negro population grew from 60,000 to 250,000 and that of Chicago from 30,000 to 277,000. Lesser cities, such as Akron, Canton, Gary, and Rockford, experienced a like Negro growth. By 1940 twenty-six Northern cities had Negro populations of 10,000 or more.

The small Negro elite in these cities, composed of lawyers, doctors, schoolteachers, social workers, ministers, and the like, exercised a political influence all out of proportion to their numbers. They represented a community which even in the North was frightfully ghettoized and discriminated against economically, but which nonetheless had one all-important instrument of political power denied them in the South—the vote. Negro leaders used the votes they controlled to make alliances with local urban political machines, and so to win concessions for the Negro community. In Chicago, for example, Negroes were an important element in the political machine put together in the 1920's by William Hale Thompson and his henchmen. Negroes traded votes with Thompson for jobs on the city police force and the city hall bureaucracy, assurances of fair play for Negroes in the courts, access to a "fair share" of the city's bathing beaches, a lax attitude toward rent evictions, and so on. Similar alliances in the 1920's came into existence between the Negro community and the Vare machine in Philadelphia and the Tammany Hall organization in New York.

Negro political power of this kind in the 1920's was still essentially localized and without much influence on national political parties or national policy. However, the Great Depression and the New Deal nationalized the Negro's political significance in the great cities of the North by incorporating the colored voter as an essential ingredient in the new political machine which Franklin Roosevelt put together after 1933. The Negro suffered severely in the depression, and he came into the Roosevelt political combine with a new awareness of the significance of his political allegiance and a powerful determination to make the most of it. For the first time since Reconstruction, the Negro had a recognized position in a winning political combination of national scope.

The Negro's new political power revived almost immediately in the colored community an old, old dream—that of "first-class citizenship" in an integrated America. For two reasons, however, this dream found no very important political expression in the immediate postdepression period. First, the early New Deal had an overwhelming preoccupation with problems concerned with economic rehabilitation, a preoccupation which the Negro fully shared. In some cities of the North, for example, both direct relief and such agencies as WPA and PWA amounted almost to Negro rescue operations.

Equally important in inhibiting any powerful New Deal drive for desegregation was the fact that Roosevelt's political combination rested upon a delicate balance between two exceedingly disparate parts: Northern urban political machines, including their politically powerful Negro component, and Southern white Democratic conservatives of the type represented by Senators Joe Robinson of Arkansas, Tom Connally of Texas, and Pat Harrison of Mississippi. To these men any desegregation drive would have been anathema, and thus would have threatened party unity.

However, the World War II crisis worked another substantial acceleration in the growth of the Negro's national political power and influence. First, it created an unprecedentedly large demand for Negro labor in the great cities of the North. This not only produced a new wave of migration from the South which increased the voting power of the Northern urban community; it also forced the Negro into jobs, pay ratings, union memberships, and the like never open to him before. The wartime Detroit story of the Negro laborer who upon drawing his first defense-job paycheck cried out in jubilation, "Thank God for Hitler," is not without its point. The war, in short, brought an enlarged Negro community a substantial increase in economic power.

Second, the equalitarian ideology of American war propaganda, which presented the United States as a champion of democracy engaged in a death struggle with the German racists, created in the minds and hearts of most white persons a new and intense awareness of the shocking contrast between the country's too comfortable image of itself and the cold realities of American racial segregation. Both pragmatic propaganda interests and the new idealism demanded certain steps for the Negro's further integration, both in society and in the war effort.

Some of this crisis-imposed, wartime integration took place on an official level: in a series of executive orders, the Roosevelt administration expanded the employment of Negroes in the federal bureaucracy, wrote "no discrimination" clauses into war contracts, established in 1941 a Fair Employment Practices Commission, and even took a few hesitant steps toward racial integration in the armed forces. Meantime, in 1939, Attorney General Frank Murphy, already something of a radical idealist on the integration and Negro civil rights questions, had established a Civil Rights Division in the Department of Justice, which in turn undertook what was to prove to be a generation-long legal quest for new federal guarantees against lynching and new safeguards for Negro voting rights. Congress, also, bestirred itself. The Soldiers Vote Act of 1942 abolished the poll tax as a prerequisite for voting by members of the armed services, while the so-called La Follette Civil Liberties Committee began its own investigation into the lynching problem.

It was inevitable that the Negro's new nationalized political power, his enhanced economic position, and the vast improvement in ideological climate in the country presently would spill over into the courts, to produce a new series of decisions reflecting the altered position of the Negro in America. The dynamics of this process are hardly very mysterious. Several of the Roosevelt appointees to the Court after 1937 were practical politicians whom the exigencies of the New Deal had made intensely aware of the "political power shift" implicit in the Negro's new party role. Hugo Black, Robert Jackson, Frank Murphy, and Wiley Rutledge all fell into this category. Or, like Felix Frankfurter and William O. Douglas, the new appointees were legal academicians who reflected the equalitarian idealism of the liberal university communities of the North.

James Byrnes, to be sure, was a thoroughgoing conservative on the race question who later would mobilize his state in an all-out defense of the Southern segregation citadel, but he did not remain on the Court very long. And over against him one could balance Harlan Fiske Stone, whom Roosevelt rewarded for his imaginative treatment of New Deal legislation with promotion to Chief Justice in 1941 upon the retirement of Charles Evans Hughes.

It needs only to be added here that the succession of justices appointed to the Court after the war—Fred M. Vinson, Harold Burton, Sherman Minton, and Tom Clark—while they tended generally to be more conservative than New Deal era justices, nonetheless had been trained in the hard practical school of politics and shared to the full an awareness of the altered position of the Negro in American society. Earl Warren, the mild-mannered middle-of-the-road Republican who came to the chief justiceship in 1953, epitomized as no one else could have this new politico-judicial understanding. The Negro's altered role was no mere matter of New Deal radical idealism. It was a point of view which had been thoroughly absorbed by the working politicians of both parties.

It is hardly open to question, then, that this flow of Democratic and Republican appointees to the High Court after 1937 would in no great length of time have produced something of a constitutional revolution in the Negro's status. But this process, inevitable as it may well have been, was vastly accelerated by the legal assault on segregation first launched in the late 1930's by a powerful and dedicated Negro interest group, the National Association for the Advancement of Colored People. The desegregation campaign commenced about 1935 by the NAACP got under way very slowly, but it continued without interruption and with growing success for the next generation. It was a campaign which would make the NAACP the "cutting edge" of all the complex social and political forces that were at work to produce a desegregated America.

The NAACP, organized back in 1909 as an offshoot of the so-called Niagara Movement after a series of infamous Illinois race riots, had speedily become one of the two or three most influential Negro pressure groups in the country. Under the leadership of board chairman Joel R. Spingarn, a Columbia University English professor, the Association by 1922 had attained to a membership of some 100,000, and had about four hundred active chapters scattered across the country.

During the 1920's, however, the NAACP was as yet not devoted very clearly to any broad integrationist program, although on occasion its leaders gave expression to the old Negro dream of first-class citizenship. Walter White, the exceedingly competent executive secretary who took over principal direction of the organization in the mid-twenties, devoted most of his energies to activities that promised more immediate returns: campaigns against lynching, interventions to secure fair trials for Negroes in criminal cases which had racist overtones (as in the notorious 1922 Sweet murder trial in Detroit, where the Association enlisted the services of Clarence Darrow in a successful defense of a Negro who had fired into a crowd attacking his home), and so on. In 1930 the Association succeeded in blocking the nomination of Alton B. Parker as a Supreme Court justice. So far from any clear desegregationist objective was the NAACP in this era that W. E. B. Du Bois, the distinguished Negro historian who edited the Association's principal journal, *The Crisis*, consistently preached a kind of extreme militant Negro segregationism, then in harmony with the professed objectives of the Communist party.

However, the nationalization of Negro political power in the New Deal era produced a radical new shift in NAACP objectives. It was now possible for Negroes once more to take up seriously the old dream, all but completely abandoned after Reconstruction, of total integration in the American social order. Walter White, who now envisioned the Association as the principal instrument for accomplishing this objective, soon came to a complete break with Du Bois, who in 1934 severed his connection with the organization. White's call for a desegregation campaign soon justified itself completely, however, for it brought a great leap forward in Association membership, which by 1945 was to total more than 300,000 in some sixteen hundred active chapters. Significantly, much of this new activity centered in the South, where White's militancy awoke the Negro from his old lethargy and evoked startling expressions of new Negro spirit.

Along with new objectives came a fresh crop of Negro leaders.

White, who realized very early that one of the most promising "fronts" in the campaign was destined to be the courts, deliberately attracted into the Association a number of brilliant young Negro lawyers, who were to become the Association's principal reservoir of brains and legal skill in its generation-long campaign for legal desegregation in America.

The Association's early desegregation cases were under the general direction of Charles Houston, an Amherst Phi Beta Kappa, Harvard Law School graduate, and dean of the Howard University Law School, whom William Hastie was later to describe as "the Moses" who "led us through the wilderness of second-class citizenship toward the dimly perceived promised land of legal equality." Houston's ability and dedication in turn attracted numerous young Negro lawyers to the Association cause. Among them were Hastie himself, one day to become a judge of the United States Court of Appeals; James Nabrit, who presently succeeded Houston as dean of the Howard Law School; Ralph Bunche, who after 1945 would acquire world fame as a delegate to the United Nations; and William R. Ming, successively a professor of law at Howard and the University of Chicago and a highly successful practicing attorney in Chicago. Others included Loren Moore, a Chicago lawyer and officer of the National Bar Association; Spottswood Robinson III, a Richmond lawyer who would one day assume a prominent role in the Brown case; Loren Miller of Los Angeles, and George Vaughn of St. Louis.

Destined to become by far the greatest legal asset of the Association however, was Thurgood Marshall, a native of Baltimore, graduate of Lincoln University in Pennsylvania, and a product of Houston's training at the Howard Law School. Marshall, who joined the NAACP legal staff in the mid-thirties, brought to the Association a wonderfully keen and incisive mind, a sharp sense of legal strategy and political realities, and an ebullient spirit tempered both by a mordant sense of humor and a deep dedication to the Negro cause. In 1939, he became general counsel of the newly created NAACP Legal Defense and Education Fund, a unit technically divorced from the Association's propaganda and legislative activities. By 1950, Marshall, through the Legal Defense Fund, was directing the expenditure of some $150,000 annually in the prosecution of various desegregation cases throughout the country. So great was his success that the Negro community had come to know him as "Mr. Civil Rights."

There were a number of "fronts" in the Association's early legal campaign against segregation of which the attack on Jim Crow schools was only one. Others included suits against so-called "white primaries," against restrictive covenants in housing, and against Jim Crow transportation. The attack on white primaries, after some reverses, met success in 1944 when the Supreme Court ruled that such elections violated the Fourteenth Amendment. Prosecution directed against segregation in transportation also was very successful. Milestones came in *Mitchell* v. *United States* (1941), where the Supreme Court in effect ordered the desegregation of Pullman facilities; in *Morgan* v. *Virginia* (1945), in which the Court struck down state laws imposing racial segregation in interstate transportation facilities; and in *Henderson* v. *United States* (1950), in which the Court knocked out dining car segregation. This series of decisions was to be capped in 1955 by an Interstate Commerce Commission order directing the complete desegregation of all interstate transportation facilities in the country.

Of more ultimate significance for the Brown case was the Association's campaign to destroy restrictive racial covenants, in the course of which the NAACP developed a series of techniques which were to prove of great value in the campaign against school segregation. Of great importance was the resort to a series of regional and national lawyers' planning conferences, in which Marshall's New York office became a kind of "general staff headquarters," coordinating policy and strategy with the local attorneys handling such cases. The Association also engaged in extensive consultation with academic experts in economics, sociology, housing, and public administration, another technique which would prove to be of great value in fighting school segregation. It was also able to bring about publication of numerous sympathetic articles in legal journals propounding the Association's point of view toward restrictive convenants. Finally, Marshall and his colleagues expended much time and money on careful staff planning, both in New York and in "the field." The climax of this carefully staged and well-coordinated campaign came in 1948, when the Supreme Court, in *Shelley* v. *Kraemer*, ruled that neighborhood racial covenants, while not in themselves unlawful, nonetheless could not be enforced in state courts, since such enforcement constituted state action in support of discrimination and hence violated the Fourteenth Amendment.

The Association's attack on segregated schools began in the middle thirties, but for some years it yielded decidedly meager results. For a time, Houston and White toyed with the notion of flooding the Southern states with a massive series of taxpayers' suits against elementary and secondary school segregation, which they hoped, somewhat optimistically, would force the Southern states to abandon dual school systems as impossibly expensive.

However, Houston sooned junked this idea as impracticable. Instead, he and his lieutenants hit upon the stratagem of an "indirect attack" on the "segregation fortress"—a series of suits to force the admission of Negroes to Southern graduate professional schools, above all state university law schools. Several major considerations led NAACP officials to adopt this scheme. First, most Southern states did not even attempt to maintain a façade of equality in professional educational facilities for Negroes, so that their classic "separate but equal" defense, the Association hoped, would prove to be inapplicable. Second, NAACP lawyers believed that if the Southern states countered this strategy by trying to provide genuinely equal facilities for Negroes in graduate education, the effort would prove to be both awesomely expensive and impossible of actual achievement. In any event, since the education of only a few graduate students would be at issue, the Association hoped that the Southern states, confronted with a long and difficult legal battle, might "break down" and admit qualified Negroes to "white" professional schools.

The NAACP lawyers were also deliberately exploiting a peculiarity of Southern racial sentiment. The South, Houston and his colleagues knew, somehow regarded racial mixing in graduate and professional education as far less invidious than in primary and secondary schools or even in collegiate education. As a consequence, they hoped, Southern officials might be expected to resist graduate school integration with less emotional conviction than would be the case for lower-level schools. As Marshall, with characteristic humor, later put the matter:

Those racial supremacy boys somehow think that little kids of six or seven are going to get funny ideas about sex and marriage just from going to school together, but for some equally funny reason youngsters in law school aren't supposed to feel that way. We didn't get it but we decided that if that was what the South believed, then the best thing for the moment was to go along.

This "beachhead" strategy in the attack on school segregation started slowly enough, although it eventually yielded spectacular results. The first important victory came in 1938, when the Supreme Court ruled, in *Missouri ex rel Gaines* v. *Canada*, that refusal of a state university to admit a Negro to its law school, there being no comparable "separate but equal" institution available for Negroes, constituted a violation of the "equal protection" clause. Missouri, following a custom then common among Southern states, had offered to pay the prospective student's expenses to an unsegregated school in the North. But the Court refused to accept this device any longer. By Missouri's laws, Chief Justice Hughes's opinion pointed out, "a privilege has been created for white law students which is denied to Negroes." Sending the student to school in another state could not "remove the discrimination," which violated the Fourteenth Amendment.

The Gaines decision constituted, after all, only a very small breach in the wall of Southern segregation, and for some time no further advances occurred. War conditions and—as Marshall admitted later—a general lack of interest on the part of potential Negro graduate and professional students prevented the Association from following up its victory for the next several years. Ironically, even Gaines failed to take advantage of the educational opportunity won for him and instead mysteriously disappeared.

Then at length, in 1948, in *Sipuel* v. *Board of Regents*, the Association's lawyers scored again, as the Supreme Court unanimously struck down an Oklahoma attempt to deny a Negro admission to the state university law school. Superficially, the decision resembled that in the Gaines case, but its significance became apparent when the Oklahoma Board of Regents soon thereafter voted, seven to one, to admit Negroes to any course of study not provided by the State College for Negroes. In short, Oklahoma now recognized that duplication for Negroes of white facilities for professional education was impossible. "You can't build a cyclotron for one student,"

Oklahoma University President George L. Cross was said to have remarked at the time.

Two years later, in 1950, came Marshall's far more dramatic victory in *Sweatt* v. *Painter*, in which the Supreme Court spoiled a spectacular Texas attempt to turn the equal-protection question aside by setting up overnight a separate Negro law school. The plaintiff, a Houston mail carrier, had pressed an Association-backed suit in the state courts for admission to the law school of the University of Texas. But the State Supreme Court, instead of granting the request, had merely ordered the university to furnish Sweatt with "substantially equal" facilities for a legal education. Thereupon the university, in an atmosphere of intense controversy highlighted by faculty and student mass meetings on both sides of the question, "fitted out" a Negro law school and invited Sweatt to attend.

Sweatt, backed by Marshall and his colleagues, of course refused to oblige, and instead sued once more in the state courts for admission. Marshall now deliberately drew very heavily upon the techniques which the Association had matured in the covenant cases. A parade of legal and academic experts came to the stand, all of them carefully calculated to furnish testimony which would overwhelm the state's argument that the fly-by-night law school in question could in any real sense constitute substantial equality. Professor Malcolm Sharp of the University of Chicago Law School, and Dean Charles Thompson of the Howard University Law School both testified to the hopeless inadequacy of the Negro law school when measured against its white counterpart.

Marshall's *pièce de résistance* was the testimony of Robert Redfield, distinguished University of Chicago anthropologist. Very carefully Marshall led Redfield through testimony calculated to show that contemporary anthropology had virtually discarded the notion that there were any inherent differences between whites and Negroes. Thus, quite deliberately and without fanfare, Marshall opened his attack upon the social theory lying behind the "separate but equal" dictum, even though this strategy was not immediately relevant to settlement of the Sweatt case itself. The Texas Supreme Court, setting testimony of this sort to one side, again ruled against Sweatt.

However, the Supreme Court of the United States on appeal ordered Sweatt's admission to the university's "white" law school. Chief Justice Vinson's opinion ridiculed the Texan claim that the state had managed to establish facilities for legal education that had any substantial equality, in faculty, library, or prestige. "It is difficult to believe," Vinson said, "that one who had a free choice between these law schools would consider the question close."

Once admitted, Sweatt promptly flunked out. But this unhappy denouement hardly damaged the case's legal significance: the attempt to provide overnight "separate but equal" facilities could not stand up in court.

*McLaurin* v. *Oklahoma Regents,* another Supreme Court decision handed down the same day as the Sweatt case, constituted an almost equally significant Association victory. Here the University of Oklahoma, compelled by suit to admit a Negro to its School of Education, had attempted to maintain segregation within the university itself by compelling the student to sit in a roped-off class section marked "reserved for colored," to use like reserved sections in the library and dining room, and so on. Unhesitatingly, the Court struck this practice down. Restrictions of this sort, Vinson's opinion said sternly, inevitably "handicapped" the student in his pursuit of "effective graduate instruction" and so violated the Fourteenth Amendment.

It was obvious to Marshall and his lieutenants that the Sweatt and McLaurin cases were of great significance, for they could be used to destroy racial segregation in graduate education virtually everywhere in the South. On the other hand, technically the Court had done nothing whatever to undermine the old *Plessy* "separate but equal rule." On the contrary, in one sense, at least, it had strengthened it, since in both cases it had held that the facilities in question were inadequate solely because they failed to meet the standard that the "separate but equal" rule required. Although equality in segregated facilities might well be impossible to achieve at the graduate level, there seemed to be no reason why the South at large, given a little time and the willingness to spend a goodly amount of money, might not achieve such equality for its Negro primary and secondary schools. Indeed, all over the South, white boards of education, reading this implication into the Sweatt and McLaurin decisions, began crash programs of Negro school building, calculated, as Governor Byrnes of South Carolina presently frankly confessed, "to remedy a hundred years of neglect" of Negro education, lest the Supreme Court "take matters out of the state's hands."

Marshall later admitted that the NAACP was at this point at a kind of crossroads. The legal gap between the Sweatt and McLaurin cases on the one hand and an outright destruction of the Plessy precedent appeared to be appallingly wide, and he and his colleagues were not at all sure they could cross it. Might it not be well to "go along" with the Southern procedure, at least in part? At this stage of the game, Marshall later told the author, if the school boards in key Southern states had shown a general disposition to accept any kind of gradualist program combining more adequate schools with some primary and secondary desegregation, the Association might well have agreed to cooperate, at least for a time.

Instead, school boards in South Carolina and in Virginia's Prince Edward County, both critical areas in the Association's planning, rejected outright all overtures for a gradualist program. "Sometimes history takes things into its own hands," Marshall said later, indicating that in his opinion Southern intransigence literally drove the NAACP to wage all-out war in the courts on segregated schools at every level.

Following a national conference on strategy in New York in September, 1950, Marshall and his staff commenced the prosecution of five segregation suits, at carefully selected points around the country. In Topeka, Kansas; in Clarendon County, South Carolina; and in Prince Edward County, Virginia, the Association filed suits in equity in federal district courts, in the name of local Negro schoolchildren, demanding their admission to "white" schools. These suits charged not only that local Negro schools were inferior to their white counterparts, but also that the "separate but equal" rule itself violated the equal-protection clause of the Fourteenth Amendment. Another suit commenced in the Chancery Court of the State of Delaware made substantially the same demands. A fifth action, begun in the District of Columbia, charged that segregation in the nation's capital violated the due-process clause of the Fifth Amendment, the same constitutional provision which Chief Justice Taney, nearly a hundred years earlier, had drawn on in the Dred Scott case to rule that Negro slavery could not be barred from any federal territory.

As Marshall had calculated in advance, these cases at the outset encountered substantial failure. In the Topeka case, which presently would lend its name to the celebrated 1954 decision, the three-man

federal court ruled not only that *Plessy* v. *Ferguson* was still the
law of the land, but also that local Negro and white schools were
substantially comparable in quality. The three-man federal court
in South Carolina conceded that local Negro school facilities were
indeed unequal, but it merely ordered the Clarendon school board
to initiate measures calculated to raise Negro schools to a level of
excellence comparable to that of the white schools. And like the
court in Kansas, it also ruled that *Plessy* was still good law, although
one member of the court dissented at length, arguing that school
segregation violated the Fourteenth Amendment on its face.

In the Virginia suit, Spottswood Robinson and his associate
Oliver Hill used the now familiar technique, borrowed originally
from the covenant cases, of introducing extensive testimony from
social scientists, including the distinguished Negro psychologist
Kenneth Clark of New York University. These experts testified
at length both as to the marked inferiority of local Negro schools
and the damaging effects of segregation generally upon both Negro
and white children. But the court, sweeping all this testimony
aside, refused to grant plaintiffs any relief whatever. Conceding
that local Negro schools were indeed "substantially inferior," the
court held that the school board was now moving rapidly to
construct new Negro schools, so that "an injunction could ac-
complish nothing more." Meanwhile, in the District of Columbia
case, Marshall's carefully drawn brief encountered a similar fate,
the court refusing to overturn adverse precedents of earlier years.

Only in Delaware, where Marshall's assistant Jack Greenberg
and the quiet, Harvard-trained Louis Redding argued the Association's cause, did an initial suit score even a partial victory.
Here the Chancery Court granted an injunction ordering the
Negro children in question forthwith admitted to white schools
on the ground that the Negro and white schools involved were
indeed "substantially unequal." On appeal, the Delaware Supreme
Court upheld this finding. Even here, however, the court refused
to overturn the *Plessy* rule itself, implying instead that a more
adequate Negro school program might sometime in the future
make racial segregation lawful.

All this, of course, amounted to little more than preliminary
legal sparring. During the course of 1952, the Supreme Court
granted reviews in all five of the foregoing cases, and in December

the Court heard arguments from both sides. Marshall, Nabrit, Redding, Greenberg, and the other NAACP lawyers involved contended that *Plessy* v. *Ferguson* had been erroneously decided and was in any event obsolete, while Edward T. McGranahan, President Truman's Attorney General, also filed a brief as *amicus curiae* asking the Court to declare school segregation invalid under the equal-protection clause. In addition, in an appendix to the Association's brief, thirty social scientists of national reputation, among them R. M. McIver, Floyd Allport, Robert Redfield, Alfred McClung Lee, and Kenneth Clark, not only attacked school segregation as possible in fact "only insofar as it is combined with discrimination" against the Negro child, but also argued at length that segregation did vast psychic damage both to Negro and white children. In turn, John W. Davis, distinguished constitutional lawyer and former Democratic Presidential candidate of 1924, presented a "powerful and effective" argument in defense of segregation for the school boards.

In June, 1953, after a six-month silence, the Supreme Court spoke. Instead of handing down a simple "yes" or "no" decision, however, the justices set the case for reargument, and asked counsel to prepare answers to a series of historical questions the justices now propounded, most of them having to do with the original intent of the framers of the Fourteenth Amendment with respect to school segregation.

"What evidence is there," the Court now asked, "that the Congress which submitted and the state legislatures that ratified the Fourteenth Amendment . . . understood that it would abolish segregation in the public schools?" Assuming that Congress and the states had made no such assumption, the Court continued, was there nevertheless any evidence that the framers of the amendment had understood that Congress might legislate in pursuance of it to abolish school segregation or that the federal courts might properly construe the amendment as "abolishing such segregation of its own force"? And was it, in any event, within the Court's judicial power to order the abolition of segregated schools, even if the framers' original intent remained unclear? Finally, and very significantly, the Court asked counsel whether, if the justices were to declare school segregation unconstitutional, it would thereby necessarily follow that it must forthwith admit Negro children to the "white schools of their choice," or whether it might, in the exercise of its equity powers "permit an effective gradual adjustment" from existing segregated school systems "to a system not based on color distinctions."

The very nature of these queries made it evident that the NAACP already had scored a significant victory. In a sense, the Court already had "taken sides," in that it had at long last consented to re-examine the question of the Fourteenth Amendment's "original" meaning. The implication in the very raising of such a question was obvious enough. The Court intended to destroy the "separate but equal" rule if it could discover a plausible rationale for doing so. The justices, in fact, seemed virtually to be saying something like the following to the NAACP lawyers: "Provide us, if you can, with some plausible historical argument which will relieve us of undue embarrassment and we will only too gladly set the 'separate but equal' rule aside."

Here was opportunity—magnificent opportunity, as Marshall and his fellows recognized—but it was opportunity hedged about with evident danger. The Association lawyers were not historians, and they had no idea of what a careful examination of the evidence might reveal. The debates in the *Congressional Globe* for 1866 might not reveal the framers' intent with respect to school segregation. Worse yet, investigation of the historical record might even provide the proponents of segregation with historical arguments so decisive that the Court would feel itself obliged to confirm the *Plessy* rule. As Marshall put it later, what looked like a "golden gate" might "turn out to be a booby trap with a bomb in it."

Confronted with this touchy problem, Marshall decided to turn once more to the academic world for assistance—a step he would later characterize as "the smartest move I ever made in my life." He called an NAACP conference to meet in New York in late September, and issued invitations to some 130 social scientists, most of them American historians and constitutional experts. At the same time, he sought out and commissioned several historians to prepare research papers on various aspects of the questions the Court had posed. Howard J. Graham of Los Angeles and the present author, both constitutional historians, prepared monographs on the passage and ratification of the Fourteenth Amendment by

Congress and the states, while C. Vann Woodward of Johns Hopkins[2] and John Hope Franklin of Brooklyn College prepared monographs on the role of segregation in Southern Reconstruction. And Horace Bond, then president of Lincoln University in Pennsylvania, prepared a monograph on state public schools in the Reconstruction Era.

All this activity promised to be exceedingly expensive, and in late June Marshall announced that the Association had raised a special fund of $32,700 for legal research, conferences, and other expenses in connection with the forthcoming presentation to the Supreme Court. The CIO presently donated $2,500 to the Legal Defense Fund for this purpose, while the Pittsburgh *Courier,* a leading Negro newspaper, also raised several thousand dollars to help pay the expenses of the September conference. Other gifts, both large and small, poured in over the next few months from a variety of sources. One morning in November, for example, Marshall found fifteen shares of a valuable oil stock in his mail, together with a simple penciled notation—"Use for school cases." All this was dramatic evidence of the Negro's new position in American society. No longer was he a helpless pawn whose fate rested in the hands of contending white factions. Instead, Negro economic power and political prestige enabled the Association's lawyers to raise the funds necessary to fight this last critical school segregation battle.

The strategy conference convened on September 23, with headquarters at the Press Club and the Algonquin Hotel. Some forty historians and constitutional experts had answered the Association's call. Present were all the authors of the various monographs Marshall had commissioned, with the exception of Howard Graham, while Marshall had also recruited constitutional experts Robert K. Carr, then of Dartmouth and now president of Oberlin, Robert Cushman, Jr., and Milton Konvitz of Cornell, Walter Gellhorn of the Columbia Law School, and John Frank of the Yale Law School. In addition, the various NAACP staff lawyers were in attendance; these included, beside Marshall himself, Robert Carter (who had argued the Kansas case in the lower courts), Jack Greenberg, and Constance Motley. Present, also, were the various lawyers from "the field" who had worked on one or another phase of the

[2] Professor Woodward, author of our account of the Plessy case, is now at Yale.

several cases, among them Robinson, Redding, Ming, and Nabrit.

The conference, which organized itself into a series of small seminars broken by periodic general sessions, concerned itself mainly with the evidence which the historians had turned up in their various research papers and the way this material ought to be incorporated in the forthcoming brief. The evidence involved was both good and bad. The most serious difficulty which emerged was clear enough: the Civil Rights Act of 1866, quite generally regarded by historians as the immediate progenitor of the Fourteenth Amendment, had been amended in the House specifically to eliminate any prohibition of state racial segregation laws. This had been done at the insistence of John A. Bingham of Ohio, who shortly became one of the authors of the amendment itself. At first blush, this looked very bad for the Association's cause.

Fortunately, however, there was a good deal more to the historical record. Bingham himself, in arguing for the critical amendment to the Civil Rights Bill, had asserted that his objections rested solely upon a want of Congressional power, and that the proper way to achieve the desegregation objective was by constitutional amendment. This was conceivably a reference to the Fourteenth Amendment itself, presently reported to the floor of Congress by the Committee of Fifteen, of which Bingham was a member.

An examination of the debates on the Amendment itself added strength to this supposition. In the Senate, Jacob Howard of Michigan had asserted categorically in presenting the amendment that the proposal "abolishes all class legislation in the states" and "would do away with the injustice of subjecting one class of persons to a code not applicable to another."

In both Houses, proponents of the amendment had talked grandly of equalitarian purposes far broader than the relatively narrow guarantees of the recent Civil Rights Act. Senator Poland of Vermont, for example, described the amendment as one which would "uproot and destroy" all discriminatory legislation which "violates the spirit of the Declaration of Independence," and he went on to point out that such an amendment was deemed necessary because "persons entitled to high consideration" (i.e., Bingham) had raised objections to doing so by legislation alone. In short, it appeared that the amendment, when carefully considered, could be conceived as having purposes broad enough to encompass the destruction of segregation either by statute or Court decision.

The historians, in short, had succeeded in demonstrating that the NAACP had something of a case with respect to Congressional intent to destroy state segregation laws generally. But it was by no means an open-and-shut case. It rested upon the demonstration of a certain "general atmosphere" of broad purpose in the Thirty-ninth Congress rather than upon any specific showing of formally announced purpose.

The problem of strategy for the Association's lawyers therefore remained very serious. At the conference, William Ming argued forcibly that the evidence from the actual Congressional debates was too scanty to build a convincing case on specific intent and that the Association's lawyers therefore ought to fall back upon a demonstration of the very broad equalitarian purposes of the anti-slavery crusaders and Republican Radicals before and during the Civil War. The historians present contended, on the contrary, that there appeared to be enough specific evidence to provide the Court with at least a plausible series of favorable answers to the questions it had asked. The September conference ended with this question of fundamental strategy unresolved.

In mid-October, Marshall called Ming and the present author back to New York. He asked the former to essay the drafting of a brief, with the constitutional historian sitting at his shoulder to advise him upon what he could or could not legitimately say without exceeding the bounds of historical accuracy. Three or four days of sharp interchange and argument produced a draft which Ming thought satisfactory.

However, after a series of conferences with the various staff and field lawyers, Marshall decided that this draft, while very valuable, needed drastic revision. For the Ming brief failed to come to grips directly with the questions which the Court had posed, resorting instead to a very generalized exposition. Marshall feared that the justices, particularly Frankfurter and Douglas, the academicians on the Court, would resent this tactic as sophistic, devious, and even dishonest. "I gotta argue these cases," Marshall presently explained, "and if I try this approach those fellows will shoot me down in flames."

Accordingly, in early November, Marshall staged a new series of small conferences at the Legal Defense Fund offices in New York. Over a period of several days, Marshall, John Frank of the Yale Law School, and the present author reworked the Ming draft very carefully, this time coming to grips directly with the historical queries the Court had posed. The new line of argument emphasized the distinction between the narrow scope of the Civil Rights Act of 1866 and the much broader purposes of the Fourteenth Amendment itself. It came down hard on Senator Howard's sweeping language in presenting the amendment to the floor of the Senate, and it dwelt at some length on the broad equalitarian objectives which Bingham, Poland, Thaddeus Stevens, and other members of Congress had expounded in the course of the subsequent debate. So modified and rewritten, the brief was then polished and perfected in numerous long and exhausting sessions participated in both by interested social scientists and by the various lawyers involved. By mid-November, the brief was ready.

The brief's argument was, of course, not history in any professional sense; rather it was legal advocacy. That is, it sought to place the most favorable gloss upon the critical historical evidence that the Association's staff and advisers could develop without going beyond the facts. This process has since been attacked severely by Southern segregationists, who have argued that the NAACP, with the unscrupulous help of social scientists, somehow succeeded in deceiving the Court into making a wholly unjustified decision.

Such criticism, however, ignores the whole Anglo-American system of advocacy, which demanded that Marshall and his colleagues —and the other side as well—present the Court with the best case they could muster. Inherent in this system is the assumption that the court will itself be able to reach a balanced and intelligent conclusion after weighing the arguments presented by both sides. That the Court, in any event, was deceived either by Marshall's brief or the equally biased and lopsided prosegregationist brief of John W. Davis is unlikely in the extreme. The Court unquestionably was looking for a way out. Repeatedly, during the planning of the NAACP case, Marshall had told his advisers that they did not need to *win* the historical argument. All that was required was a face-saving draw. "A nothin'-to-nothin' score," he said with typical directness, "means we win the ball game." Actually, in *Brown* v. *Board* the justices put aside the historical evidence and based their decision upon "sociological" grounds. In short, no deceit was intended, and none occurred.

On November 15, the Association filed with the Court its formal brief in *Brown* v. *Board of Education of the City of Topeka.* "The evidence makes clear," this document proclaimed, "that it was the intent of the proponents of the Fourteenth Amendment that it could, of its own force, prohibit all state action based upon race or color" and "all segregation in public education." The "separate but equal" rule of *Plessy* v. *Ferguson,* the brief added, had been "conceived in error" and should be reversed forthwith. Moreover, any delay in executing the judgment of the Court would involve "insurmountable difficulties" so that the plaintiff children in question should be admitted at once, "without distinctions of race or color," to the schools of their choice.

A few days later, Attorney General Herbert Brownell, acting technically as "a friend of the Court," filed the long-awaited brief of the Department of Justice. The stand the Eisenhower administration would take on school segregation had been the subject of considerable political speculation, for it involved a critical matter of Republican party strategy: whether the administration should continue its courtship of Southern Democrats or recognize frankly the political importance of the powerful Northern Negro vote. This dilemma, which was further sharpened by the decisive stand in favor of desegregation which the Truman administration had assumed a year earlier, had lately been the subject of repeated conferences between Brownell and the President.

Brownell's brief cut through the Republicans' dilemma very nicely by declaring in favor of desegregation but expressing the hope that the Court would order a transition period before desegregation became fully effective. The brief conceded that the historical evidence as to the intent of the amendment's authors was "not conclusive," but emphasized nonetheless the amendment's broad equalitarian purpose—"to secure for Negroes full and complete equality before the law and to abolish all legal distinctions based upon race." Hence, the brief concluded, the Court now could properly construe the amendment to prohibit segregated schools, but it would do well to order a one-year transition period in the South, because of the complex social and educational problems involved.

This analysis produced an outburst of anger and disappointment in the South. Representative E. C. Gathings of Arkansas accused the Attorney General of "trying to subvert the will of the people," while Governor Tallmadge of Georgia attacked the brief as "wholly political." "Radical elements are vying with each other to see who can plunge the dagger deepest into the heart of the South," Tallmadge proclaimed.

The briefs for the various "respondent" school boards, filed over a period of several days in late November, contained hardly any surprises. The Delaware brief, for example, emphasized the significance of the fact that Reconstruction Congresses had repeatedly voted funds for segregated schools in the District of Columbia, clear evidence, it contended, that the authors of the Fourteenth Amendment had not intended to strike at segregated schools. South Carolina's brief, while reinforcing this historical argument, also argued that the fundamental issue was one of states' rights— "whether the people of South Carolina may, on the exercise of their judgment, based on a first-hand knowledge of local conditions, decide that the state objective of free public education is best served by a system consisting of separate schools for white and colored children." Virginia asserted on her part that a reversal of the "separate but equal" rule would "overthrow the established meaning of the Fourteenth Amendment." The City of Topeka already had notified the Court that it was voluntarily desegregating its school system, but Kansas nonetheless filed a brief arguing that "federal interference" in the state's schools "is neither necessary nor justified." The District of Columbia's brief, evading higher argument, merely pointed out that the Fourteenth Amendment did "not apply" to it.

On December 8, a Supreme Court chamber filled to overflowing heard Marshall and Spottswood Robinson argue that the framers of the Fourteenth Amendment had intended to ban segregation "as a last vestige of slavery." John W. Davis, presenting oral arguments for the respondents, asserted in reply with equal confidence and force that "it is not within the judicial power" for the Court to set aside, merely "on a sociological basis," a school system that "has stood for three-quarters of a century."

The justices themselves interrupted from time to time to ask an occasional searching question. Frankfurter rather pointedly inquired of Marshall whether, if the Southern states now were to agree to spend money for "more and better schools for Negroes," he would still insist that segregation was unconstitutional. Needless to say, the Justice got a strongly affirmative answer. And Douglas asked Solicitor General J. Lee Rankin, who presented the government's brief, whether the Court properly could decide the present cases "either way." No, Rankin insisted, the Court "properly could find only one answer."

The Court's decision, handed down on May 17, 1954, after another long silence, could hardly have occasioned any great surprise either to the proponents or enemies of segregated schools. Chief Justice Warren's opinion for a unanimous Court was remarkable both for its simplicity and for the extraordinary fashion in which it avoided all legal and historical complexities. The historical question of intent which had occasioned both sides so much anxiety he pushed aside almost impatiently as impossible of resolution. But in the light of conditions in the twentieth century, he said, it was obvious that enforced segregation generated "a feeling of inferiority" in Negro children which might well inflict such grave damage to their minds and hearts that it could never be undone. Public school segregation by state law, therefore, violated the equal-protection clause of the Fourteenth Amendment; the old *Plessy* "separate but equal" rule, he added, was herewith formally overruled.

Thus the NAACP came to its greatest triumph—a landmark decision destroying completely the constitutional foundations upon which legalized segregation in the South rested.

It was the end of a long road, yet in another sense only a beginning. For the justices did not order immediate desegregation of Southern schools in the 1954 opinion; instead, in a subsidiary decision a year later, the Court invoked a principle from equity law to order desegregation carried out under local federal court direction "with all deliberate speed."

Thus the justices carefully separated the delineation of the principle of integration from the actual implementation thereof. At the same time they avoided very nicely the crisis they would have produced had they ordered *immediate* desegregation. And one can speculate that this very careful separation of principle from implementation was one reason why the Court was able to present a united front to the world in its 1954 decision.

Yet for all its cautious self-limitation, the Court's decision in *Brown* v. *Board* remains one of the great landmarks in the history of American liberty. In a sense, the Court was "legislating," for, sweeping aside state decisions and decisions based on mere law and precedent, it vested its opinion on broad considerations of national welfare. Thus the decision was indeed "political" in the deepest sense of the word, as the Court's enemies charged. Yet the fact is that the Court's greatest decisions have always been political, for unless we subscribe to the notion of a completely static Constitution and a "slot machine" theory of constitutional law, the Court must perforce decide questions of the kind it faced in *Brown* in a "political" fashion.

In this connection it is interesting to compare the Court's decision in *Brown* v. *Board* with another piece of judicial "legislation" on the Negro question—that involved in the Court's decision in *Dred Scott* v. *Sandford,* almost a hundred years earlier. In both cases, the Court used its extraordinary powers to "legislate," in bold and powerful strokes, upon the role and future of the Negro in American society. But in the Dred Scott case, the Court not only spoke for slavery and against the development of liberty in the American social order; it also flouted in flagrant fashion the wishes and aspirations of a large majority of the American people. In so doing it helped plunge the American Republic into a terrible Civil War.

But in *Brown* v. *Board* the Court not only spoke for liberty, thereby giving expression to the deepest and most profound ethical aspirations of a great majority of Americans; it also reflected quite accurately certain new power realities in the evolving political structure and in the social order. For these reasons, despite the fact that *Brown* v. *Board* precipitated a protracted political and social conflict in the South over desegregation, the court's decision will in all probability endure for many years as one of the great foundations of a stable and ordered constitutional system, and one possessing epoch-making significance in the evolution of constitutional democracy.

# Index

*The Nose*

# The Nose

A Profile of

Sex, Beauty, and Survival

## Gabrielle Glaser

 NEW YORK LONDON TORONTO SINGAPORE SYDNEY

The ideas, procedures and suggestions in this book are intended to supple-
ment, not replace, the medical advice of trained professionals. All matters
regarding your health require medical supervision. Consult your physician
before adopting the medical suggestions in this book as well as about any
condition that may require diagnosis or medical attention.

The authors and publisher disclaim any liability arising directly or indirectly from the use of this book.

 ATRIA BOOKS
1230 Avenue of the Americas
New York, NY 10020

ISBN: 0-671-03863-X

First Atria Books hardcover printing August 2002

10   9   8   7   6   5   4   3   2   1

ATRIA BOOKS is a trademark of Simon & Schuster, Inc.

Printed in the U.S.A.

For information regarding special discounts for bulk purchases, please
contact Simon & Schuster Special Sales at 1-800-456-6798 or
business@simonandschuster.com

To Ilana, Moriah, and Dalia,
who have exquisite noses

# contents

# Contents

## *M e m o i r   o f   a   N o s e*

When I was growing up, I learned very early that I had—or was it that I developed?—an unusually acute sense of smell. This was often a blessing—I was able to sniff out hot wires before they caught fire, predict weather changes, and detect food on the verge of going bad. But my fifth sense also predisposed me to worry. Even before normal cues told me things had gone astray, my nose sensed danger, or fear. When I was a child, my father once severed a finger with a circular saw. I could smell his blood as soon as he rushed into the house, long before I saw the scarlet pools staining the wooden floor, or the tight panic of my mother's face. My sensitive nose could also make me sick: heavy perfume, diesel fuel, even the halitosis of someone nearby—had the ability to make me nauseous, or give me a migraine.

My parents had four children, and we lived on a beautiful but isolated farm overlooking Oregon's Cascade Mountains. In the countryside, smells mark seasons—of labor, of rest, even of grief—as neatly as the calendar organizes months. One wet April, the air was weighted with the sweet, cloying scent of hyacinths. They bloomed in a nearby pasture, unmindful that just steps away the man who had planted them was dying. As he lay motionless, my father, his only son, picked handfuls of the short stocky stems and brought them to the old man's railed bedside in jam jars. His ashen face sank into the pillow, and he labored to breathe. Silently my father pushed get well cards and pill bottles to one side of the nightstand, and gently set down the purple blossoms. My grandfather's nostrils fluttered to life like eyelids flying open after a startling dream. With his bruised yellow hand he reached to grasp my father's outstretched palm, and his head turned slowly toward the flowers. "Bring them closer, son," he rasped. I stood in the corner, too scared to go near.

That fall, we dropped some of those bulbs into the ground near his grave. Symbols of spring, they summon instead a blur of stale dark hospital air, chiseled granite, and my father's red-rimmed eyes.

It was my father, after all, who taught me to smell. He is an articulate man, but words are not his language. And so I became fluent in the same way all children learn to communicate, by mimicking. On mornings when he'd take us to school, he would pause a moment before opening the creaky door to his pickup, coffee mug in hand, and inhale the air around us as if he were breathing in life itself. "Smell that," he'd command,

and we would dutifully sniff, both trying to please and grasp the importance of what was unseen and unheard.

My father, a farmer like his father before him, had a devotion to the land so fierce you'd think God had given it to us and us alone, granting the deed at Mount Sinai. He fortified his ties to the farm with rituals, as if to convince him that what was ours would remain so forever.

Over time I learned just what he meant as he drew his great breaths, trying, fleetingly, to catch smells that the breeze would throw first one way and then the other. For odors told you when crops, from wheat to rye grass, were ripe; one whiff of morning air could convey that it was still too damp to run the combines, or too dry to fertilize.

On days when conditions were just right, growers ignited their harvested fields to kill pests and burn chaff. Naturally, those unattached to farming complained about the stink—and danger. Smoke from those fires could, and did, easily traverse a highway with a slight change in wind, obscuring drivers' vision and causing fatal pileups. Yet whenever the newspaper carried stories of peoples' concerns, my mother, angry at any hint of disrespect toward farmers, would throw it down in disgust. Even when great black plumes swirled into the bright August sun and bits of scorched straw floated onto our clothesline, she would be righteous in her indignation. "Smells like money to me," she'd mutter, to no one in particular.

For with my mother, too, scents had totemic value. But they didn't represent our livelihood, or tell us when to harvest crops. They symbolized something much more esoteric: her state of mind.

In the winter, I could tell upon waking when the creek separating our house from humanity was about to overflow. When it rose in the rainy months, no one could come in, and we could only get out—to school, to the grocery store—in a rusted old four-wheel drive. With the swollen water came a sense of dread. To smell the wet, murky air and the muddy, mossy creek was always to know that my mother's mood would soon deflate.

Food smells, though, were the biggest portent of all. My mother, a product of the 1950s, was raised to be a lady, to wear nylons in airports and never raise her voice. She told us frequently we were her career; she didn't need another. Trained as a teacher, she was intellectually curious. But there was little time for reading if we were her job. And, of course, there was also the matter of helping to run a 4,000-acre farm. During harvest, she fed a hungry crew—a responsibility that wasn't so bad on good days. Slender neck bent over steaming pots, strong hands kneading bread dough, she would disappear the way a person gets swept away in an engrossing novel, unmindful that hours have passed.

But sometimes the pressure of keeping house, rearing four kids, and worrying about the weather (on farms, it's always an obsession) caught up with her. The kitchen, my mother's sacrosanct refuge, with its marble slab and gleaming stainless steel sink, could also be a prison, both hers and ours. Whether it was hormones, a tiff with my father, or one child too many with the flu, something would tip the scale between happy and not, and the only way out for her would be to bake: sour cream chocolate cakes, cinnamon rolls, Nestlé's Toll House cookies she stacked onto metal racks. On the way home from school, I'd get a sweet whiff of melting chocolate or an earthy waft of sourdough bread through an open window. My palms would sweat and my jaw would clench. For me, those warm, loving smells, which were intended to please us all, spelled peril.

Once, I opened the door to find my adolescent logic put to a very adult test. My brother, a childhood asthmatic, was alone and prostrate on the couch, struggling to breathe. Acrid clouds of sugar-turned-carbon billowed from the oven, and my mother sat slumped over the counter, fingers splayed in her dark hair (overindulging in chocolate had triggered a migraine). She seemed unaware of everything, except her very real need for Darvon. I still don't remember what I did first: thwart a fire, attend to my brother's breathing, or track down, by two-way radio, someone who could get my mother to the hospital for painkillers.

In the summertime and on rainy weekends—especially on rainy weekends—my mother would take my sisters and me to my grandmother's beauty shop, a squat white building near the county airport. We all had long blonde hair, but mine was the most "difficult." It hung down my back in thick straw-colored bumps. "Can't make up its mind to be curly or straight!" Nana exclaimed, as if it were a character flaw. So she tried to help it decide, and squeezed me in between her other appointments. She would iron it so that it hung in curtains around my face, the faint burn of dried ends settling, deadened, into my nostrils. Or she'd spiral it into pin curls with her fingers, dipping her pointy comb into a jar of green setting lotion that smelled like the fake evergreen of tree-shaped air fresheners.

Once, she insisted on giving us all permanents. She wrapped our necks with scratchy white paper and secured plastic capes around our shoulders, then led us, one by one, through the row of dangling pink plastic beads that separated one room from the next. They swayed, clicking gently, for as long as it took to get our hair washed. Afterward, my hair reeking of permanent solution, I sat in exile under a hot plastic dryer, air blasting from its tiny holes. Women talked and laughed so hard they slapped their thighs, but you could never hear what they were saying over the drone of the dryer. So I thumbed through forbidden old copies of *Cosmopolitan,* and watched the planes take off and land like so many rickety insects.

The air of that shop was a swift departure from the gentle smells on the farm. There was nothing natural inside—no fresh blackberries, no wood stoves crackling, no delicate roses in bud vases. Nana loved smells as far from the outdoors as you could get. She misted herself with White Shoulders each morning, and slathered peach-scented lotion on her reddened hands as her customers were "drying" in their pink Naugahyde recliners. On her break, she'd sit down, put her feet up, and pass around her pack of Virginia Slims. The women would flick cinders off their magazines into the tiny steel ashtrays embedded in the arms of their seats.

Smoke, nail polish, neutralizer, hair dye, bright blue barbicide. The smells were harsh and raw, but they were also freedom. If the farm felt like a bed-and-breakfast, Nana's shop was like a speakeasy. Women came to smoke and change their hair with permanents and peroxide. They'd come on payday (the fifteenth and thirtieth were always booked), after their shifts at the paper mill. Often, they had bad husbands, bad kids, or both, and my grandmother dispensed advice as freely as she fogged fresh curls with hairspray.

Some days, rank sulfur from the mill blew our way, overtaking even the chemicals inside the shop. But the worst was on muggy afternoons in summer, after a rain. A taxidermist worked in a converted garage down the road, and the stench of decomposing elks seemed to seep even through the walls of the shop. On such afternoons Nana lit incense she got from the Import Plaza and waved it around with the fervor of a preacher before the damned. But nothing was a match for the stink of rotting flesh, especially not cheap jasmine.

Smells, and the memories they inspire, have come back to me in inexplicable ways. On several occasions I've been taken aback by how powerful their effect can be. One hot, miserable morning in Manhattan nearly twenty years after I left my little hometown for good, I was on my way to give a speech to a group of bankers and psychologists. I hadn't prepared what I was going to say, and I began to feel very anxious as I plodded along the sticky streets. I passed a subway station and got a pungent whiff of urine mixed with roasting hot dogs and the sickening sweetness of sugar-roasted peanuts. A woman yammering into her cell phone walked by, leaving gusts of Eternity in her wake. I was really starting to panic when a Dominican woman opened the door to her crowded beauty salon. A waft of familiar odors—dye, acetone, and neutralizer, came my way; inexplicably, I felt better. I forgot about my speech, and wandered back, to those long afternoons in Nana's shop where lunch was a raspberry Pop-Tart and a can of Fresca, as my hair, tethered to curlers, dried.

One spring day when my older daughters were little, I had them both with me in the supermarket. As we rolled past the cheap floral display—it was decked out for Easter—my eldest daughter stopped to sniff some purple blooms that were nose-high to a three-year-old. "Pretty," she said, and thrust a plastic pot in my face. No sooner had I taken a whiff than tears sprang to my eyes. For more than twenty years I had avoided hyacinths as a painful souvenir of my grandfather's death.

And a few winters ago I was walking up the hill to my house in New York on a cold Saturday. The kitchen window was cracked open, and a warm baking smell was drifting onto my suburban street. It was far from the winding gravel driveway of my youth, but the smell was the same, and my jaws tensed immediately. Before I knew it, my gait had quickened to a jog despite the bags I was carrying. I burst through the door, expecting disaster, only to find my husband and daughters giggling as they stole bites of slice-and-bake cookie dough. Only then did I realize why I, who love to cook, never bothered to bake. I had always blamed my indifference on the tedium of having to measure precisely. But the smell of that warm chocolate suddenly made clear why I had always avoided making cookies and cakes.

While smells, for me, were paramount to navigation, my nose was also influential in other matters. As the product of several diverse gene pools, it set me apart. In my sparsely populated universe, most people were descendants of Scandinavian and German immigrants, with swimming pool–blue eyes and unas-

suming noses. My forebears, however, were slightly more exotic: my paternal great-grandparents, Polish Jews, had obscured
their heritage so that their children might better fit in with their
neighbors, and an American Indian grandmother on my
mother's side passed herself off as a "gypsy." All this helped explain an obsession with the size of our noses, a vanity that
seemed out of place amongst the abstemious Yankee and
French Canadian ancestors we were purported to have. In any
case, those disparate strands of DNA seemed to have a hand in
shaping my nose into a remarkably unique appendage. By the
time I was twelve, it was long enough so that, like a roll of film
taken with a finger hovering over the camera lens, it was always
in sight. But its shape didn't really vex me so much—I look a lot
like my father, and I admired *his* nose. I did begin to take notice, however, once others let me know they had. In seventh
grade I entered a teacherless classroom to see a small blond boy
writing my name on the chalkboard. "Ask Gabrielle," he had
scribbled. I stared at the writer's back, my heart fluttering as I
waited to see what else he would say. When he turned away, the
boy grinned at the class, his mouth glinting all silver braces.
"She Nose It All," the words read. Students burst into laughter,
and I slunk to my desk, trying hard not to let anyone think I
cared.

Throughout my adolescence, I consoled myself with tales of
famous oversized noses. Jimmy Durante was so taunted by
schoolmates that he vowed never to make fun of anyone with
crossed eyes or big ears. Judy Collins, as a child, hated her nose
so much she slept with a clothespin pinched to the tip of it, like
Jo in *Little Women*. I had never heard her sing, but I adored

Maria Callas after I saw a picture of her glorious profile in *Time* magazine. And my heart nearly leapt out of my throat when I read that Diana Vreeland said that people only liked small noses because they reminded them of "piglets and kittens." A strong face, she declared, had a nose with a real bone in it.

But celebrities were far away. I might have shrugged off indignities like the one in Mrs. Durfee's class if my nose had actually functioned well, but it didn't (and doesn't today). My genes also left me prone to all kinds of respiratory infections, especially sinusitis. My sick nose affected my breathing, my sleeping, and my time—cumulatively, I've easily spent a year in doctors' offices—and eventually deteriorated to the point of total dysfunction. I am one of millions of Americans who have had repeated sinus surgery (four). I've been hospitalized for serious sinus infections, and have spent weeks wandering around with lines stuck in my veins for intravenous antibiotics. I'm quite healthy otherwise (I've been checked for every possible frightening disease), but I shy away from people with the sniffles as if they had drug-resistant TB. For me, an ordinary cold can turn into an ordeal.

The most troubling aspect of my dysfunctional nose was the abrupt disappearance of my sense of smell. My sinuses were so scarred and swollen after one operation that for two years, no odor molecules could get where they needed to go. I was depressed and lost—"smell-blind," as the ancients called it; for me, the period seemed a particularly cruel curse. I couldn't smell my children, my husband, my favorite lilies, or the food I loved to cook. Words, somehow, failed to describe my loss.

I was lucky. My ability to smell eventually returned, but

only after several rounds of powerful steroids. One day the aroma of the garlic I was sautéing slowly, surely lifted into my nostrils. I was overjoyed—I could *smell* again—but my reaction was so primal that language didn't accompany the realization. What was it about the nose, this feature that doubled as a sense and an organ, that was so central to my life—and to most of humanity? As I thought about the nose's interplay in my life, I began to see its prominence everywhere. Consumers could buy incense, candles, and room sprays even while shopping for jeans. From Gogol to *Tristram Shandy,* the nose loomed large in literature. It was an obvious feature in pop culture and politics. Bill Clinton's proboscis was the butt—and focus—of thousands of caricatures. Jennifer Grey told TV viewers and magazine readers that her nose jobs had left her a stranger to herself.

Suddenly, science was investigating the nose as if it were a hidden body part that had only recently been discovered. New drugs administered through it could stop migraines and the flu in their tracks. Women whose noses picked up the sweat of other women began menstruating in sync. Neurologists looked to the nose's olfactory neurons—the brain's only contact with the outside world—for larger clues about our gray matter.

The more I learned, the more I began to realize that the understanding of the nose, unlike that of the heart or the lungs or the skin, was in its infancy. Its reign over our memories, its rule over beauty, and its role in our health, were only beginning to be decoded.

My quest to understand the nose led me on a three-year odyssey that went from perfumers on Madison Avenue to dusty medical archives, and from tony plastic surgeons' offices to re-search labs across the United States. As I retraced the steps of the researchers who have struggled to understand the workings of the nose, I came to see how little we truly know about this essential organ.

Some of what I ran across seemed banal, at least on the surface. For example, one-third of American adults picks their noses at least once an hour. Despite its inclination for third-grade yuks, nose-picking has grave implications. The touch of a contaminated finger to the eye or nostril is a primary culprit in spreading bacteria and viruses—ever more serious as germs become deadlier.

And some of what I found was shocking. As recently as the 1940s, doctors at Cornell Hospital in New York City treated their sick sinus patients with a variety of unusual approaches. In one they thrust electric prods up their subjects' noses to see how much "discomfort" they could tolerate. (The data later went into an oft-cited study on headaches.) One man, disabled by severe allergies, sought help from the doctors for his chronic sneezing. Rather than treat him with antihistamines, which were available at the time, they stuffed his nose with ragweed pollen, to "see" if he was indeed allergic. (He was; it took hours for his respiratory system to recover.)

My research also took me to the Mayo Clinic, where I met doctors who believe that the cause of chronic sinusitis—from which one in seven Americans suffers—may well be tiny, easily vanquished fungi. And on Manhattan's Upper East Side, where the rich and famous flock for nips, tucks, and facial overhauls, I met a plastic surgeon who was obsessed with the nose. He had

grappled with his own large one for thirty-nine years before finally "fixing" it. His experience—and anguish—of traversing
the role of doctor to patient gave me a special glimpse into the
history, culture, and implications of changing our faces.

Researchers devoted to the study of olfaction, or smell, now
know more about what happens when you take a whiff of coffee,
or drive past a fish cannery, than ever before. New knowledge
shows how important smell is—or at least was, evolutionarily
speaking—to our very existence. Progress may have obscured the
necessity of smell in surviving—now chirping phones, vibrating
beepers, and red e-mail flags seem far more pressing than any
odor—but eons ago, it was our species' lifeline. Science has now
identified the initial path of synapses when we sniff, and how
messages are transmitted to the olfactory bulb and olfactory cortex. But it is still pondering the larger question: exactly how tiny
odor molecules prompt us to act, think, and remember.

In order to put it all in perspective, I had to turn to the distant past. I started with a gentleman whose training was both
historic and cosmic: my rabbi, Lawrence Perlman. Rabbi
Perlman is a tall, imposing man with elegant suits and a complex set of passions; Judaism, good food, good wine, and hockey
(he played professionally). When I mentioned my research, he
said the nose was threaded throughout Jewish texts, and invited
me to come for a discussion. Our appointment was on a cold
day in March, just as spring was beginning to flirt. Given our
subject, I thought I'd bring something thematic along, so I
sliced a couple of branches of daphne off the plant outside my
window—its scent, a cross between lemon and cinnamon, is
my favorite—and put them into a small vase.

When I got to the office, I set the glass near the window and sat down opposite the rabbi's giant antique desk. I could hardly keep up with his thoughts as he reached for first one and then another book marked with Post-its. We traversed texts from Genesis to Maimonides, and topics from respiration to odors, nasal shapes and nose rings. God created man by blowing into Adam's nostrils "the soul of life" (Genesis 2:7). The Hebrew word for breath, *neshima,* shares a root with *neshama,* soul. A Hebrew expression used to describe wrath, *haron-af,* evokes the nose: *haron* means rage, and *af* is the word for nose; together, they paint an image of someone so furious their nostrils are flaring. Only men with prominent noses could be chosen as priests. Even God, the rabbi said, had favorite smells.

As the weak afternoon light waned, the heat clicked on and the spicy scent of the daphne, perched above the radiator, infused the office. It seemed a fitting backdrop, as the rabbi began to sneeze. Between Kleenexes, he found a reference in the Talmud even to the meaning of sneezes.[1]

"The nose," said Rabbi Perlman, "is never just a nose."

And he is right. It moves through art, science, and popular culture from the sacred to the profane, and back again. From hieroglyphics to modern medical journals, the nose has been both an enduring mystery and an obsession, as fascinating to Pliny as it was to Picasso.

Part One

# History of the Nose

## The First Two Millennia

*t w o*

# Centuries of Stench

In the beginning, the world stank. That, of course, is not surprising. The human animal is a powerfully industrious machine for producing odors—breathing, running, breeding, eating, defecating. Ancient man's first goal was to get in from the elements and learn how to use fire. Not much longer afterward—recorded history doesn't tell us exactly when—people turned to the problem of conquering smells, specifically their own. But odor was an enemy that, it turns out, was not easily vanquished. Unlike saber-toothed tigers and woolly mammoths, which could be stabbed with sharpened spears, the stench of man was a more complex problem.

In our modern, deodorized world, it's hard to imagine exactly how foul life could have been. Consider the ancient world, where almost everything people did created smells. Animals were roasted in entirety, skins, greasy entrails, and all, so cooking smells were a far cry from the cleaned-up, hairless barbecues we know today. Tents were made of bark, reeds, or wool, not some quick-drying microfiber. Just try soaking a woolen blanket with a garden hose and leave it outside for a month or two to get an idea of what would have been a mere minor assault to your olfactory system.

But smells did not only exist to menace. While the stench of life before sewers was a constant reminder of man's mundane needs, fragrance, on the other hand, was a powerful conduit to the esoteric. Smell could seduce lovers, cure the sick, and most importantly, link man to the divine.

## Placating the Gods

The ancient Egyptians believed all pleasant odors derived from the tears and sweat of their many deities, and they reasoned that fragrance helped to underscore the importance of their prayers. And so the first perfumers used crushed seeds, roots, petals, wood, and fruit of the many aromatic plants found in the fertile Nile Valley, and mixed them with animal fat or oil. They were used as incense or unguents, sticky creams in an oily base. As early as the twelfth century BCE, formulas for these primitive perfumes list dozens of ingredients—lilies, dill, marjoram, and iris, all native to Egypt—as well as complex techniques for making them. Fragrance was so important that it was among the first items traded: by 3000 BCE, foreign roots, barks, and resins, which were all easily transported, appeared in the recipes as well. They included frankincense and myrrh, resins from small shrub-like trees in Somalia and Arabia; cinnamon bark from East Africa, juniper from Syria, camel grass, a rose-scented plant from Lebanon, and mastic, a fresh-smelling bush from Greece.

The name of the most popular Egyptian fragrance, *kyphi*, means "welcome to the gods." It had a variety of uses, from decongesting stuffy noses to coaxing sleep. Priests slathered themselves with it before visiting temples. There, they used it to "awaken" the gods by wafting it under the statues' noses.[1]

Everyone from noblemen to slaves bathed daily, and used aromatic oils and ointments liberally. Perhaps the fixation with fragrance was born of good reason: there was no soap. (The first soap, a crude mixture of ash and animal fats, was produced in ancient Babylon in 2500 BCE.) Though it is unlikely that any amount of fragrance could offset the body odor generated by the intense heat, the Egyptians made various attempts at the first deodorants. One method called for wadded up balls of pine resin that were then placed in the armpits.[2] Of all the remarkable techniques the Egyptians used to scent themselves, perhaps the most peculiar was what Egyptologists call "unguent cones." On special occasions, people wore an oily, waxy mass of semisolid perfume on top of their heads; they eventually melted, of course, and streamed down the face and neck in slick trails (apparently, they were thought to be cooling).

Scent was thought to carry the dead along on their journey to the afterlife, too. Bodies were embalmed with herbs and oils; even perfume trays were buried along with mummies for the trip to the next world. When Howard Carter finally cleared King Tutankhamen's tomb in the Valley of the Kings

1922, he and fellow archeologists found a bowl of frankincense inside. They burned a sample, and found that even after 3,500 years underground, it gave off a "pleasant, aromatic odor."

## Smells of the Book

In ancient Israel, riverbeds were so paltry that rainfall was stored and collected for irrigating crops, not people. Waterproof cisterns weren't developed until 1550 BCE; until then, people settled near springs or wells. Without water to drink or to bathe in, human smells took on powerful meaning. Bad breath was so common—and offensive—that by Talmudic times (third century BCE–700 CE) the rabbis listed remedies for it—chewing the bark and resin of the mastic tree.

Bodies themselves fared little better. Much of Israel is humid, so perspiration clung to garments and left a film on skin. Imagine, for a moment, ancient style: clothes—washed about as often as the people who wore them—consisted of linen or cotton tunics. They were covered by loose-fitting cloaks made of animal skins, with an extra long flap in front that could be folded up and belted for carrying everything from diaperless babies to small animals—the first pockets. It wasn't as if they ever got aired out, either—the coats often doubled as a sleeping bag, and were likely caked with sweat, dirt, and manure. Everyone wore their hair long; sweaty heads were swathed by veils and headdresses, which protected against the sand and sun. They weren't changed with any regularity, so the olfactory picture is clear: people reeked.[3]

The distinctive smells people emitted due to their diets, work, and lack of bathing are at the crux of one of the Bible's greatest deceptions, the story of Jacob and Esau. Esau was a skillful, if hirsute, hunter, a man of the fields; his twin brother was a quiet, smooth-skinned man who "lived in tents." (Genesis 25:27) Esau was his father's favorite son; Jacob was his mother's. First, Jacob extorts Esau's inheritance—his birthright as the eldest son—from his brother. But Jacob also wants his dying father's blessing. Jacob ponders how to dupe the blind Isaac, and, with Rebecca's help, covers his hairless arms and neck with goatskins. Rebecca realized this would not be enough to fool Isaac in an era when everyone's smell was as instantly identifiable as hairstyles and clothing are today, so Jacob wore Esau's clothing as an olfactory disguise. In the story, Isaac is confused—he recognizes Jacob's voice, but touches the hairy hand of Esau. Jacob, silent, plays his trump card, drawing close enough to receive his father's kiss and, he hopes, his blessing. Isaac "smelled the smell of his garments, and blessed him, and said, 'Ah, the smell of my son is like the smell of a field that the Lord has blessed. May God give you the dew of heaven, and the fatness of the earth, and plenty of grain and wine.' " (Genesis 27: 27–28)

The Bible notes that God himself had olfactory preferences, and the ancient Israelites took great pains to produce them. To an ancient society both anxious to please God and fearful of his dismay, creating and dispensing smells was a physical assurance to the participants that their worship was acceptable.

The Lord commands Moses to slay a ram, "and turn the whole ram into smoke on the altar; it is a burnt offering to the Lord; it is a pleasing odor, an offering by fire to the Lord." (Exodus 29: 18) God also dictates a recipe containing myrrh, cinnamon, and olive oil, to be used for consecrating Aaron and his sons into the priesthood. He instructs Moses to anoint everything inside the meeting tent, from the sanctuary to an altar, for burnt offerings. The sanctity of the perfume was enormous: it was to be used by the priests for the consecration of objects and new priests only, and it rendered holy whatever it touched. Anyone who dared copy the oil, or use it in any other manner, risked estrangement from God and the other Israelites.

Though perfume was an extravagance only the wealthy could afford, fragrant people—likely because they were so uncommon—were the romantic ideal. In the Song of Songs, the scents described by the young couple are metaphorical for their unconsummated love. The boy compares his bride to an aromatic garden—one he longs to enter: "Your lips distill nectar, my bride; honey and milk are under your tongue; the scent of your garments is like the scent of Lebanon. A garden locked is my sister, my bride, a garden locked, a fountain sealed. Your channel is an orchard of pomegranates with all choicest fruits, henna with nard, nard and saffron, calamus and cinnamon, with all trees of frankincense, myrrh and aloes, with all chief spices—a garden fountain, a well of living water, and flowing streams from Lebanon." (Song of Songs 4: 11–15)[4]

## Decadence and Decay

Fragrance also infused three pillars of ancient Greece: trade, mythology, and art. One Greek word *aromata,* describes a world of scent: perfume, spices, incense, even aromatic medicine— the first aromatherapy. The Greeks learned of perfumes from the Egyptians and Babylonians and began their own perfume industry; by the seventh century BCE, Corinth was renowned for its intricate terra cotta perfume jars. As in Egypt and Israel, incense accompanied prayer. The gods themselves were said to emit perfume: Homer said that Zeus is "wreathed in a fragrant cloud." Euripides wrote that in heaven, "streams flow with ambrosia."

Sanitation on earth was another matter. People used lidded chamberpots for wastes, and spread them in the fields for fertilizer. They were dumped directly into the streets, so the great cities of Athens, Rhodes, and Thessaloniki (and indeed, cities everywhere) stank of excrement. The poor conditions fostered diseases such as cholera and typhus, and the mortality rate was high. While the link between illness and waste would not be made for millennia, Hippocrates believed that one way to preserve good health was to avoid bad odors. He advanced the Aristotelian notion that air, when combined with the wrong qualities (variations in temperature, humidity, or consistency), was responsible for disease. Noxious air, or *miasma,* had the potential to influence the physical and mental health of all living things.

The cities may have stunk, but people didn't. Homer describes baths among deities and citizens alike; in the cities, there were many public baths. Treatments ranged from dunks in hot water to hot air "baths," or *laconica,* from which the word "laconic" is derived.[5] In Athens, scents were so popular that perfume shops evolved as a counterpart to taverns: people gathered there to buy fragrance, hear news, and trade gossip.

When Alexander the Great conquered Egypt and Persia, he was taken by the vast array of fragrant plants, and sent seeds and saplings back to his teacher Theophrastus in Athens. Theophrastus, in turn, created a botanical garden and wrote the first Western book on smell, *Concerning Odors.* Alexander died in 323 BCE, probably of typhus, and was cremated on a pyre of frankincense and myrrh. His empire crumbled at his death, and Cleopatra, the last of the Ptolemaic rulers, dreamt of uniting Egypt with an ascendant Rome. When her lover Mark Antony entered the port of Alexandria, she is said to have greeted him on a barge with sails that were drenched with fragrance.

The Romans, of course, were notorious for their prodigious appetites, and their indulgence with scent was no exception. In the early days of the empire, in the second century BCE, bathhouses, or *balnere,* dotted neighborhoods throughout the city. The city of Rome itself had eleven public baths and more than 850 private ones. Some were able to serve up to 2,000 people. Inside, fragrant oils and creams were stored in vats, and incense burned continuously. Indeed, the word perfume comes from the Latin *per fumus,* "through smoke," to describe the pleasant smells that drifted through the air when incense was burned.

The Romans were so dedicated to their ablutions that the bathhouse became a central focus of Roman life: people gathered, ate, and even held political discussions there. There were hot water baths, cold water baths, and sweat rooms—even the first public toilets. Seats carved into semicircular blocks of marble were constructed over flowing channels of water that flushed waste to nearby rivers. People wiped themselves with sponges affixed to sticks, left in the latrines for common use.

Since soap was only used for cleaning clothes, hygiene was merely a by-product of the bathhouse "culture."[6] People visited the baths to socialize and relax—even prisoners were taken to the baths regularly. The Romans used fragrance both in and outside the bathhouses. Galen and Dioscorides, two of the era's greatest physicians, investigated the curative powers of aroma; Pliny discussed them in *Natural History.*

The Romans, like the Greeks, thought that stench, or foul air—*malaria*—was responsible for spreading disease. When epidemics struck, they looked to the lethal gases they believed stemmed from the fires and miasmas that lay deep in the earth's core. The philosopher Seneca faulted the sulfuric air released in an earthquake for the deaths of 600 sheep.[7] The poet Lucretius blamed a "deadly breeze" for the plague that swept through Athens from lower Egypt. In the book-length poem *On the Nature of Things,* written in 50 BCE, he described a tree so putrid it could "kill a man outright/by fetid odor of its very flower."

Not only foul air was harmful. Body odors were also offensive, and revealed the social cleavage inherent in Roman society. The fixation with smelling good, of course, excluded those who could afford neither perfume nor hours at the baths— slaves. Their physically demanding chores, from toiling in hot wheat fields to lugging impossibly large temple cornerstones, was no doubt manifest in their body odor. Smelling good, in other words, was a clear sign of status in ancient society.

It was also linked to intelligence. Indeed, knowledge and

wisdom were often described by sensory terms.[8] The Latin word *sapidus,* meaning both "pleasant to the taste," and "prudent" evolved to the French *savoir,* and *saveur;* the Spanish *saber* and *sabor* and the Italian *sapere* and *sapore*—"to know" and "to taste," respectively.

Consider a scene from *Pseudolus,* a play by Plautus:

> *Pseudolus: But about that slave who's just come from
>   Carytus, is he pretty sharp?*
> *Charinus (holding his nose with a meaning wink): Well,
>   he's pretty sharp under the armpits.*
> *Pseudolus: The fellow ought to wear long sleeves. How's his
>   wit: pretty pungent?*
> *Charinus: Oh, yes, sharp as vinegar.[9]*

## Smell and the Church

Yet for those who *chose* not to surround themselves with fragrance, there were worse outcomes than ridicule: early Christians who refused to light incense before images of the emperor were put to death. Once Christianity began to take hold in the fourth century, Church leaders called incense "food for demons" and urged the new converts to differentiate themselves from their hedonistic forebears.

Just as the Egyptians, Greeks, and Romans used incense to please their gods, the new religious followers believed that man, in his unwashed state, layered with perspiration, dust, grime, smoke, food, blood, was symbolic of devotion. Denial of earthly pleasures only improved one's status within the Church. In his letters, St. Jerome, the third-century ascetic, wrote admiringly of the martyrs Paula and Melanium:

> Was I ever attracted by silk dresses, flashing jewels, painted faces, display of gold? No other matron in Rome could dominate my mind but one who mourned and fasted, who was squalid with dirt, almost blinded by weeping. . . . Had they frequented the baths, or chosen to use perfumes, or taken advantage of their wealth and position as widows for extravagance and self-indulgence, they would have been called "Madam" and "Saint." As it is they wish to appear beautiful in sackcloth and ashes, and to go down to the fires of hell with fastings and filth![10]

But Church officials fought a losing battle. Early missionaries soon discovered it was far simpler to adapt pagan customs than it was to prohibit them. And while many had abandoned bathing, people clung to rituals—now millennia old—joining fragrance and prayer. By the sixth century, incense and flowers reappeared in church ceremony, serving as symbols of sanctity and grace. Roses, so adored by the emperor Nero (petals were tossed about Rome like confetti during his reign), came to embody Mary; lilies, symbolizing the goddess Juno, came to represent the resurrection. Some scholars say that the origins of the Christmas tree trace in part to Saturnalia, the Roman celebration honoring Saturn, the god of agriculture. For a five-day period beginning on December 17, revelers exchanged gifts, paraded the streets with candles, and decorated their homes with laurel, cedar, and cypress boughs. The festival was so raucous that the elite usually fled the city for the country-side, and the Church outlawed it in 375. But many continued the practice despite the ban. Eventually, Christmas sup-planted Saturnalia and winter solstice festivals elsewhere in Europe. But the cutting of evergreens, whether in thanks to Saturn or in homage to Christ, remained a pungent symbol of immortality.

## Fragrance Blooms

As the practice of toilette fell into disrepute in the West, it flourished in the East. After Rome fell, Arab scholars carried on many of the scientific achievements of classical Rome, particu-larly in pharmacy, chemistry, and distillery—crucial, of course, for perfumes as we would recognize them today. The prophet Mohammed (570–632) named "women, children, and per-fume" as his top three earthly loves. By the seventh century, the religion that emerged from his beliefs helped also to spawn a quest for more sources of fragrance. The cities that cropped up along the spice route established special inns, caravansaries, for those who carried the precious cargoes of clove, cinnamon, pepper, and rose water. Incense was burned continuously, in tents, in homes, at weddings, and at funerals. Even prayer beads, fashioned of rose petals and resins, released scent when touched.

Ibn-Sina (980–1037), the Arab alchemist, astronomer,

philosopher, and physician, is often credited with discovering distillation (in fact, Avicenna, as he is known in the West, was simply improving on methods that traced to ancient Mesopotamia). He used oils distilled from herbs to treat diseases from cancer to obesity. One of his one hundred books was devoted entirely to the use of roses, which included curing headaches and "fortifying the senses."

In contrast to the early Christians, cleanliness and fragrance were crucial to Islamic worship. (The Koran calls for followers to wash their hands, feet, and faces before the five calls to prayer. It also recommends showering at least weekly, particularly before the Muslim Sabbath, clipping fingernails, shaving pubic hair, plucking armpit hair, and keeping one's mouth "fresh.") Mortar for early Arab mosques was often mixed with musk, so that worship could be infused with scent during the hottest part of the day.

Malodors were especially inauspicious in Muslim society, and linked to evil. In Morocco, for example, flatulence was so much feared because it was thought to blind—or even kill—the angels who resided inside mosques. (No doubt the concern was linked to a diet heavy in beans and grains, but such beliefs abounded even until modern times. So did acts of contrition.) If a person passed wind *outside* a mosque, the action was so connected with demons that people marked spots where it occurred with small piles of stones, as if to entrap the evil. And among the Berber tribes of Morocco, the notion of breaking wind was so shameful and offensive that suicide, in consequence, was not uncommon.[11]

By the ninth century, Muslim traders had reached China, and soon its favorite scents—orange, camphor, and musk (an aromatic substance taken from the gland of an Asian male musk deer)—were incorporated into Islam as well. The Chinese had their own beliefs about fragrance, and classified it into six basic categories, depending on the moods they were thought to inspire—the first aromatherapy. During the invasion of India in the 1500s, one Mughal emperor, Jahangir, built a special garden for his favorite wife, filling it with cedar, roses, and carnations. He called it "Shalimar," or "abode of love," a name Guerlain would use for its great perfume some four centuries later.

But it was the Japanese who advanced perfumery to a fine art. Though incense didn't arrive there until the fifth century, the Japanese soon developed ways to beautify it. Mixing aromatic herbal pastes with seaweed, charcoal, and salt, they pressed them into little cones and figures that were burned on a bed of ashes. Soon, it was used throughout society: Buddhists burned incense in temples, and artisans created boxes inlaid with gold and mother-of-pearl for carrying and storing it. The appreciation of incense even evolved into a game in which participants sniffed unlabeled incense samples to match by scent. The aromatic gums and resins used to make Japanese incense sticks were of such high quality that soon enough, the rate at which it burned became a way to measure time, and by the eighteenth century, geishas were able to tally their charges according to the number of incense cones they used per client.

## The Stench of Death

From the Middle Ages to the nineteenth century, the stench of Europe was unimaginably wretched. Foul odors emanated from London to Budapest, worsening as cities grew. The streets were sewers, full of rotting garbage, manure, and diseased and dying horses, donkeys, dogs, and cats. Human waste was dumped into communal cesspits that were cleaned out at quarterly intervals, or from chamberpots directly onto the street. (Scholars believe that the British term "loo" is a corruption of the French *"Gardez l'eau,"* "Look out for the water!") Some cities had privies, separate toilet facilities where users squatted on rotten floorboards—often at risk of falling through them. (Decrepit planks were said to have given way on the Holy Roman Emperor Frederick I in the year 1184.) When the Italian explorer Marco Polo visited the Chinese city of Hangzhou in the thirteenth century, he was shocked to find the sewer system emptying waste into the ocean. He reported that it made the city's air "very wholesome."

Europe's filth, of course, set the stage for the most disastrous epidemic in history: the Black Plague. From 1347 to 1351, the disease, named for the bulging black welts that appeared on the bodies of the afflicted, killed more than 20 million people. Almost certainly the disease was the bubonic plague, transmitted to humans from fleas via black rats that fed on rotting detritus scattered through the streets. Fleas infected with the bacillus, *Yersinia pestis,* fed on the blood of warm rats. When the fleas sucked blood from rat skin, the proboscis would inject the bacillus back into the rat's bloodstream. Once the germ reached the animal's brain, it would convulse and die, and the fleas, highly sensitive to temperature changes, would jump off the dead rat's cold body. Because rats and people lived within such close proximity, the next closest host was a warm human. Within days of a bite from an infected flea, victims suffered fierce headaches, weakness, high fevers, delirium, and uncontrollable coughing. Their tongues turned white, and purple pustules, a sign of internal bleeding, appeared where the flea had bit.

The disease, medical historians say, most likely originated in China and then traveled west to Tashkent. In the port town of Caffa, on the Black Sea, Genovese traders warring with the local Tatars withdrew behind citadels. In what scientists believe was the first instance of biological warfare, the Tatars tossed rotting bodies of plague victims over the fortress walls. The newly infected sailors fled to Sicily, where the disease spread instantly through crowded cities. Authorities tried to cordon off cities as word of the epidemic spread, but it was too late: the sick began to stumble, delirious, about the streets, emitting a terrible stench—everything about them reeked. "Their sweat, excrement, spittle, breath (was) so fetid as to be overpowering. Urine (was) turbid, thick, black or red. . . ."[12]

Theories on the cause of the disease abounded. Some thought it was triggered by the alignment of the planets; others argued that it was the fumes released during earthquakes. Some blamed Jews and lepers, who were flogged and burned alive. Most, though, were convinced that the afflicted had earned God's wrath as a punishment for their sins. The rank odor of the diseased could represent one thing only: the devil, who in medieval minds reigned over a "bog of stench." Simple reasoning gave man but one armament: resisting the disease by avoiding all smells, or with odors fiercer than even the stink of the plague itself.

Officials in the town of Orvieto decreed that men must avoid "fleshly lust and putrefaction with stinking women." Elsewhere, authorities advised against opening windows, so that bad odors would remain outdoors; indoors, people were to stoke cooking fires indefinitely. Pope Clement, in fact, was said to have sat for weeks in Avignon between two bonfires. Other measures were even more desperate. Some people lingered in latrines, breathing in the stench, and smeared themselves with the excrement and urine of healthy people. Others swallowed pus from the boils of plague victims.

Doctors took to covering themselves for protection from head to toe: they wore long leather or woolen gowns, gloves that reached to their elbows, and beak-like masks filled with herbs thought to ward off the disease. They recommended that people sniff nosegays and pomanders made with aromatic plants believed to have antiseptic qualities: lavender, myrrh, and rosemary, among others. Indeed, so many bodies were stacked up in parish courtyards and on the outskirts of cities and towns that they presented nearly as big a challenge as the disease.

As the disease ravaged city after city, it provoked wives to abandon husbands, and parents to flee their children at the first hint of symptoms. Marchione di Coppo Stefani, a Florentine chronicler who survived the outbreak, wrote that the afflicted languished and died alone. "They remained in their beds until they stank. And the neighbors, if there were any, having smelled

## *The Doctor's Protective Suit*

**The doctor's robe.** *The long woolen robes and strange-looking beak of the doctor's costume were thought to protect as an olfactory shield for doctors battling the plague. The beak was filled with herbs such as lavender and rosemary. Ironically, doctors complained of the fleas, which nested in its folds, helping to spread the disease even further. Illustration from* Historiarum anatomicarum medicarum *(1661), by Thomas Bartholin.*

the stench, placed them in a shroud and sent them for burial." In the nearby town of Pistoia, authorities decreed that families must bury their dead in wooden caskets, nailed shut, two-and-a-half arms deep "in order to avoid the foul stench which the bodies of the dead give off."[13]

## Discovery—and Olfactory Shields

The plague continued to erupt across the continent until the early seventeenth century. The Church took extraordinary measures to protect the public as well, consecrating new saints as protectors (such as St. Roch of Montpellier), shrines, and orders of monks as interceptors of the plague. Slowly, public health measures gained currency—Milan, for example, suffered only a 15 percent death rate after it locked up the homes of any diseased person, leaving all family members to die. Indeed, Church authorities began to redouble civic efforts to halt the spread of disease, ordering churches shut down, processions banned, and shrines closed.

People avoided bathing on the theory that exposing one's skin to the air would make one vulnerable: Queen Isabella of Castile noted with pride that she had had only two baths in her life—at her birth and before she got married. But while she herself stank, she cared enough about Spain's edge in the spice trade to dispatch Christopher Columbus to "India." While the *Niña, Pinta,* and *Santa Maria* never reached Asia, the trips to the New World did yield exotic foods and riches. The voyage to deliver them to Spain, however, was an olfactory abomination: no amount of cocoa, peppers, and vanilla beans could mask the stench of the ships, which reeked of vomit, excrement, maggots; mold that had ravaged food supplies, and sopping woolens that never quite dried.

And yet the introduction of these "new" goods, as well as those from the Middle East, ushered in new smells, tastes, and habits. Islamic officials in Constantinople and Cairo tried to ban coffee once it arrived from Ethiopia in the 1510s; they believed its aroma and consumption would distract worshippers from prayer. Still, coffeehouses stayed open, and travelers to the Orient found the drink so tantalizing that they brought it to Western Europe. A French explorer, meanwhile, introduced tobacco seeds to his native land from Brazil. By the 1570s, it was prescribed as "medicine," and smoke enveloped the French and British courts. The Dutch distilled juniper berries into gin in 1650; it quickly gained ground as a popular drink.

Through it all, though, the specter of the plague hovered in the minds—and noses—of an entire continent. Tobacco, coffee, and gin were all touted as prophylactics. People scattered rushes of rosemary and lavender on their floors, and brides carried chives in their wedding bouquets. Meanwhile, though, the reeking of the piled-up dead and the shallow grave pits endured. Stench *was* disease.

In 1721, once again, the plague spread west across Europe, decimating Provence. The Dutch imposed a strict quarantine on all shipping from the East. The port of Rotterdam was choked with smoke and the stink of scorched wood, grain, and fabric. The English government imposed an embargo on all goods from the Mediterranean, infuriating merchants eager to trade in the exotic new commodities.

It was during this time that the writer Daniel Defoe published a semifictional account of the year 1665, when the epidemic struck London. Memories of the year had grown dim, but Defoe drew on medical accounts and diaries to write *A Journal of the Plague Year*. Throughout the book, the protagonist, a saddler, evokes the reek of London and its inhabitants. The calamity, Defoe wrote, was spread by "the breath, or by the sweat, or by the stench of the sores of the sick persons, or some other way, perhaps, beyond even the reach of the physicians themselves . . . (the effluvia) affected the sound who came within certain distances of the sick, immediately penetrating the vital parts of the said sound persons, putting their blood into an immediate ferment, and agitating their spirits to that degree which it was found they were agitated; and so those newly infected persons communicated it in the same manner to others."[14]

Those who somehow escaped the plague were both feared and admired. A gravedigger and his wife, a nurse, had been surrounded by the dying and the dead for more than twenty years, with never so much as a "day of distemper." Their immunity was olfactory: "He never used any preservative against the infection, other than holding garlick and rue in his mouth, and smoaking tobacco. . . . And his wife's remedy was washing her head in vinegar and sprinkling her head-clothes so with vinegar as to keep them always moist, and if the smell of any of those she waited on was more than ordinary offensive, she snuffed vinegar up her nose and sprinkled vinegar upon her head-clothes, and held a handkerchief wetted with vinegar to her mouth."[15]

There was no telling who among the healthy might be sick tomorrow, and whose stink, whether caused by perspiration, filth, or clothes that absorbed the hazy smog of medieval and Renaissance cities, might be contaminating others. The plague generated such immense anxiety about the odors of others that it prompted people to undertake smelly rituals designed to shield themselves from the noxious, uncertain air around them. From the gravedigger's garlic talisman to smoking the tobacco brought from the New World, people enclosed themselves in what some anthropologists now call "private olfactory bubbles."[16]

## A Cleaned Up Continent

In Italy, knowledge about contagion spurred public health measures such as quarantine (the word derives from the Latin *quadraginta,* forty days), placed on people and goods coming in and out of cities. This allowed the trading ports of Venice and Genoa to resume trade gradually with the East. Florence, meanwhile, flourished as a center of thought, art, and science. Gradually, these trends popularized cleanliness and fragrance, which had retained its predominance outside of Europe. People began to use imported sandalwood and rose soaps to wash themselves, and bathing returned to vogue. Venice developed a perfume industry of its own, producing scented gloves, stockings, and shoes—even aromatic coins. Cinnamon, nutmeg, cloves, pepper, and ginger added new flavors to drinks and food (and helped conceal decay). Consider the odor of hands alone: cutlery wasn't commonplace before the seventeenth century, so people ate fatty meat, sticky rice, and greasy chicken with their hands (this is one reason why glassware had coarse knobs—it gave diners "traction"). In Italy, noblemen and women resolved this problem by rinsing their hands with bowls of rose water that were set by each plate.

While Italians gradually cleaned up, elsewhere, people tried to cover their lack of hygiene with fragrance. Caterina de' Medici, who married Henry II in 1533, brought the sophistica-

tion of her native Florence with her to Paris. Her court included her personal perfumer and alchemist, and together they
helped transform a society choking in medieval stink. Caterina
chose Grasse, the Provence village, as the perfect site for the
herbs and flowers that would go into making her personal perfumes. Yet for all its pleasant scents—it became (and remains)
a center for growing lavender, verbena, and bergamot—it was
also central to the leather industry. So the sweet wafting of
flowers in bloom was juxtaposed with the acrid, foul odor of
sixteenth-century tanneries. Soon, perfume was used for, and
on, everything in all of France, from hair to gloves to shoes.
Even a guild to protect perfumery workers was established in
1656.

By the time Louis XV was crowned in the eighteenth century,
perfume use in France was at an apex. Louis himself demanded
a different fragrance for his chambers daily. His mistress,
Madame de Pompadour, ordered new scents created on whims.
She helped to propagate even more uses for fragrance by dous-
ing it on the elaborate wigs she helped make famous, as well as
on handheld fans and even furniture. *Potpourri,* a dried blend of
rose petals, salt, and spices, became fashionable in parlors and
boudoirs alike (before the concoction is fully dry, it is so cloying
and strong it earned the mix its name—literally, "rotten pot").
Fragrance also doubled as jewelry: pomanders, scented balls
made of ambergris, spices, wine, and honey that dangled from
belts or around necks (*pome d'ambre,* literally, "apple of amber"
in Middle French).

And while Versailles was known as *"la cour parfumée," "*the
perfumed court," beneath those scents, eighteenth-century

France smelled awful. As writer Patrick Suskind describes pre-Revolution Paris,

> The rivers stank, the marketplaces stank, the churches stank, it stank beneath the bridges and in the palaces. The peasant stank as did the priest, the apprentice as did his master's wife, the whole of the aristocracy stank, even the king himself stank, stank like a rank lion, and the queen like an old goat, summer and winter. For in the eighteenth century there was nothing to hinder bacteria busy at decomposition, and so there was no human activity, either constructive or destructive, no manifestation of germinating or decaying life that was not accompanied by stench.[17]

Indeed, the French historian Alain Corbin writes that in the eighteenth century, smells were so ferocious that much of the nation could "hardly breathe." From the reek of the streets to the iris-scented breath of the bourgeoisie, smells overpowered—and obsessed—France. Scrupulous attention was paid to body odors as portents of disease and keys to seduction. The French army, ravaged by a "fever" outside of Nice in 1799, emitted an "odor similar to phosporous gas in combustion."[18] But other body odors were alluring. A menstruating woman was "conveying the vitality of nature . . . making an appeal for fertilization, and dispersing seductive effluvia."[19] In a famous letter, Napoleon appealed to Josephine "not to wash" for the two weeks prior to his return to Paris. During their tempestuous union, the couple indulged their passion for perfume, ordering gallons of it monthly. Napoleon liked violets; Josephine was partial to the strong, lingering scent of musk. When Napoleon was granted an annulment, Josephine doused the chambers of his new bride, Maria Louisa, with vats of musk, knowing the scent would endure even though her marriage hadn't.


## From Chaos to the Cult of Clean: The Smell of America

From the first writings of Columbus to the dispatches of de Tocqueville, the people of America projected a rugged image. While American Indians had frequent baths and herb-infused steam tents, the settlers who arrived were far less fastidious. The Puritans outlawed bathing upon their arrival; they issued jail terms for those caught soaking. Indeed, by the 1850s, a quarter of all New Englanders didn't bathe even once a year.[20] Bodies and clothes were filthy; animal waste littered the countryside, and rats infested sewage-strewn cities. Men spat their chewing tobacco on the floors of taverns, pubs, even the sitting rooms of their own homes. Standards weren't altered until epidemics of cholera, combined with the religious revival of the nineteenth century, swept much of the nation. Like the Methodists in England, who had heard from their founder John Wesley that "cleanliness was . . . indeed, next to godliness," Americans, both rural and urban, began bathing on Saturdays in preparation for church the next day. But preparations for the bath—boiling gallons of water and pouring it into a tin tub—were as dangerous as they were cumbersome.[21]

During the Civil War, the diarrhea, cholera, and typhus spawned by filth killed more soldiers than battle. Because cleaning was seen as "women's work," most young men, away from their mothers, sisters, or wives for the first time, had no idea how to save themselves—or their surroundings—from squalor. ". . . They behaved as boys, whooping it up in the streets with their bugles and drums, getting drunk . . . neglecting to wash and 'change their underwear for weeks at a time.' "[22] Latrines were next to cooking areas, bedding was infested with lice and rodents, and clothing and hair were filthy. Conditions were so wretched that President Lincoln appointed a "Sanitation Commission" for the Union Army, headed by Frederick Law Olmsted, the creator of Manhattan's Central Park. Nurses, influenced by the experiences of Florence Nightingale during the Crimean War, were enlisted to help "scrub soldiers." The writer Louisa May Alcott was among the volunteers. Overwhelmed by the magnitude of filth, Alcott took to guarding herself—and her nostrils—with a bottle of lavender water, which she sniffed as an antidote to "the vilest odors that ever assaulted the human nose."[23]

For years to follow, disease hovered over America's growing cities. As the Industrial Revolution transformed the country from a hardscrabble colonial outpost to an economic powerhouse, the urban population grew from 1.8 million in 1840 to 54 million in 1920. Sewer systems and refuse removal, such as they were, were overwhelmed by factory wastes and mounds of horse manure.

By the turn of the century, New York had emerged as the country's dominant financial and cultural power, but was frequently crippled by outbreaks of typhoid, hookworm, and cholera, all traceable to filth. With its economic viability and physical health under constant siege, the city embarked on a widespread plan to reform public health and improve sanitation. In 1895, it appointed Colonel George E. Waring, Jr., a sanitary engineer, as the city's street-cleaning commissioner. Waring believed that community participation was essential in his goal to clean New York, where litter and sewage from the city's rising pool of newcomers sometimes obstructed whole blocks.

He enlisted the help of "juvenile street cleaning leagues," comprised largely of immigrant children, to help bring the public in line with modern notions of sanitation. Each participant took a civic pledge and compiled weekly progress reports of their respective streets; based on their activity, the children were assigned ranks ranging from helpers and foremen to superintendents. In sections of the city where English was a foreign language, the street-cleaning leagues became an important link to a new, Americanized life—and provided whole families with new ideas of health and hygiene. "Cleanliness," Waring said again and again, "is catching."

In time, cleanliness did catch hold in the national psyche,

shifting from a method of preventing disease to a way of be-coming—and being—truly American. By the mid-twentieth century, the nation could boast near-universal plumbing, vac-uum cleaners, as well as a plethora of washing powders, sham-poos, and toothpaste. With disease now beaten back by vaccines, antibiotics, and cleaner cities and homes, Americans had a new reason to scrub: status. As in ancient Rome, a dirty, smelly body in America now carried serious social implica-tions. Odors—or the lack of them—became a way of defining class.

But just as it became possible to live in cleaner cities and homes, and to wear cleaner clothes on cleaner bodies, the new standards, paradoxically, created a new set of circumstances. Because it was easier to clean and be clean, Americans began doing so obsessively. As Americans strove to conform in the immediate postwar years, advertisers played upon social fears of rejection and spinsterhood by hawking products designed to wipe out embarrassing odors. Newfangled contraptions such as the garbage disposal, a "must-have" item for the new class of suburban homeowners in the 1950s, wiped out kitchen smells, along with flies and rodents. Dial soap could help a person stay clean "hour after hour." The "right" appearance, writes histo-rian Suellen Hoy, "became everything, more important than personality or character in shaping one's fate." Statistics pub-lished in *Newsweek* in 1958 reveal this as well as anything: by that year, Americans spent $200 million on products that made them smell better, taking more than 500 million baths a week.[24]

By 2000, Americans spent nearly $10 billion on products to both subtract their odors and add allure, and they took an average of 260 million showers a day. In a mere half-century, America had traversed a terrain of stench and disease to earn a dubious honor that endures today: the most odor-free place on earth.

# The History of Science (As Told Through the Nose)

The quest to understand the external nose proceeded even more slowly than the attempt to diminish stink. Throughout history, scientists trying to figure out the human body were drawn to the nose, which they believed held clues to the secrets of the brain, the lungs, and even the soul. But until the mid-twentieth century, scholars were ignorant of how the body worked in general, let alone the intricate specifics of the nose. An examination of the nose in science turns up, by today's standards, one absurd notion after the next. Its appearance and host of functions lent it a predominant role in medical fads from physiognomy to reflex irritation theory, and helped to bolster biases about women, looks, and ethnic groups. Each era, in fact, seemed to get the nose it sought: Eighteenth-century phrenologists focused on the size and shape of the nose as a key to personality and intelligence; Freud and Victorian doctors linked the nose to everything from painful cramps to masturbation. As recently as the 1950s, American physicians used ordinary allergies and congestion as proof of psychological maladjustment.

To be fair, the nose held many mysteries. Its dark passageways ferried aromas and breath, as well as a strange, viscous liquid that came and went, often inauspiciously. Galen, the second-century Greek physician, believed the fluid signaled a "purging of the brain" that "percolated" through the base of the skull to the nose. (The notion would endure for 1,500 years.) By the Middle Ages, postnasal drip, hay fever, allergies, and sinus infections were all lumped together as "catarrh," from the Greek word *katarrhous,* "to stream down," and were symptoms of more sinister problems. The sinuses themselves were believed to harbor drawn-in odors that could "taint" the brain, a well for tears, or even evil spirits.

Observers long made connections between the nose and male genitalia: "The truth of a man lies in his nose," Ovid wrote. Virgil wrote of an adulterer who had been "spoil'd of his nose." In the hand-to-hand combat of ancient wars, the nose was a common target for attack. (Perhaps warriors saw it as a way of symbolically castrating their foes.) In one treatise, Renaissance scholar Giovanni Battista della Porta wrote that "the nose is like the rod."

For millennia, doctors struggled to find cures for nasal problems. Papyrus scrolls from ancient Egypt prescribed iris oil for polyps. For colds and stuffy noses, the Chinese gave ephedra (today's Sudafed is a synthetic twin), and the Turks had steam rooms. The efficacy of some remedies remains, even if beliefs about what caused the ailments does not. Deviated septums, for example, were thought to be the result of chronic nose-picking. Polyps were believed to be outgrowths of the brain, bulging through the sinus wall (doctors in Renaissance Italy sliced them off with hot wire "snares"). Elsewhere, others turned to more mundane substances as preventatives for the common cold: in Central Europe, people irrigated their noses with urine; Indians used boric acid; Malians in the Sahara stuffed their nostrils with camel dung.

The sinuses were particularly bewildering. Doctors knew they were connected to the nose, but couldn't find a way to examine them. In order to get a look, doctors sat their patients next to windows, or had them hold their breath while they placed a candle near—or in—the mouth, trying not to singe the flesh. The understanding of the sinuses got an unexpected boost when a patient of seventeenth-century British doctor Nathaniel Highmore stuck a silver hairpin into the gaping hole left by an extracted tooth: "(She) was exceedingly frightened to find it pass, as it did, almost to her eyes. And upon further trial with a small feather stripped of its plume, was so terrified as to consult the Doctor and others about it, imagining nothing less than that it had gone to her brain." Highmore used the opportunity to probe the space, and published a book about his findings, *Corporis Humani Disquisitio Anatomica.*[1]

## Physiognomy: You Are Your Nose

The nose was central to the eighteenth-century revival of physiognomy, the pseudoscience of judging a person's character based on the notion that physical beauty displayed moral goodness; coarse features, on the other hand, revealed dishonesty, laziness, and stupidity. The practice dates to Aristotle, but returned to prominence with the 1775 publication of *Essays on Physiognomy Designed to Promote the Knowledge and the Love of Mankind,* by the Swiss theologian Johann Caspar Lavater. The book featured drawings of scholars and artists from Shakespeare to Dürer. Lavater analyzed the nose, forehead, eyes, and chin of his subjects, and gave guidelines for his readers to do the same. A quick glance at anyone, he argued, was all that was needed to understand a person's morality, intelligence, even religiosity. "Physiognomy is the very soul of wisdom, since it elevates the pleasure of intercourse, and whispers to the heart when it is necessary to speak and to be silent, when to forewarn, when to excite; when to reprehend," Lavater wrote in his preface.[2] First published in German, *Essays* appeared in translation throughout the continent well into the nineteenth century.

Its influence was soon felt in art, literature, and social life, both in Europe and the United States. Portraitists rendered George Washington in profile so as to capitalize on his "large, well-shap'd nose," admired by new Americans as evidence of his strength and hawk-like foresight. Napoleon wrote that when he needed a good strategist, "I always choose a man, if possible, with a long nose." And Robert Fitzroy, captain of the HMS *Beagle,* nearly turned Darwin away from its great voyage in 1831 because of his bulbous nose. ". . . On becoming very intimate with Fitzroy, I heard that I had run a very narrow risk of being rejected [as the *Beagle's* naturalist], on account of the shape of my nose! He was an ardent desciple (sic) of Lavater, and was convinced that he could judge a man's character by the outline of his features; and he doubted wheather (sic) anyone with my nose could possess sufficient energy and determination for the voyage. But I think he was afterwards well-satisfied that my nose had spoken falsely."[3]

Public fascination with physiognomy, and noses in particular, spawned a book devoted entirely to the subject, *Notes on Noses,* in London in 1854. George Jabet, the pen name of Eden Warwick, felt it necessary to justify his subject at the outset: ". . . It might appear prudent, if not altogether necessary, to commence by vindicating the Nose from the charge of being too ridiculous an organ to be seriously discoursed upon. But this ridiculousness is mere prejudice; intrinsically one part of the face is as worthy as another, and we may feel assured that He who gave the *os sublime* to man, did not place, as its foremost and most prominent feature, a ridiculous appendage. . . . We believe that, besides being an ornament to the face, a breathing apparatus, or a convenient handle by which to grasp an impudent fellow, it is an important index to its owner's character. . . ."[4]

The mind, in fact, shaped the nose, Jabet wrote. This theory led to five simple nasal classifications:

    I.  The Roman, or Aquiline nose, indicated "great decision, considerable Energy, Firmness, and Absence of Refinement."

II. The Greek, or Straight nose, revealed "refinement of character, Love for the fine arts and belles-lettres. . . . It is the highest and most beautiful form the organ can assume."

III. The Cogitative nose, which "gradually widens from below the bridge" indicates "strong powers of thought, given to close and serious Meditation." (In a footnote, Jabet cautioned: "A Nose should never be judged . . . in profile only; but should be examined in front to see whether it partakes of Class III.)

IV. The Jewish or Hawk Nose, very convex, thin, and sharp, denoted "considerable Shrewdness in worldly matters; a deep insight into character, and facility of turning that insight into profitable account."

V and VI. The Snub, or "Celestial Nose" were similar enough to combine in one category. Both revealed "natural weakness, mean, disagreeable disposition, with petty insolence, and diverse other characteristics of conscious weakness. . . . The general poverty of their distinctive character makes it almost impossible to distinguish them. Nevertheless, the Celestial, by virtue of its greater length, (is) decidedly preferable to the Snub . . . and is not without some share of small shrewdness and fox-like common sense."[5]

Jabet discussed feminine noses, which apparently did not fall under such strict divisions, in a separate chapter. On a woman, a Roman nose "mars beauty," and "imparts a masculine energy to the face which is unpleasing (and) opposed to our ideas of woman's softness and gentle temperament." A Greek nose, on the other hand, was highly attractive. The home would surely profit by having such a refined soul at its helm. "It will exhibit itself in her needlework by an artistic arrangement of colours and a poetic choice of subjects; in a neat and elegant attire, in the decoration of her drawing-room, or in the paraphernalia of her boudoir."

Cogitative noses did not much appear on the female sex, as "women rather *feel* than think." Nor did the Jewish nose. "Neither are its indications material to the perfection of the female character. It is the duty of men to relieve women from the cares of commercial life, and to stand between those who would impose upon their credulity."

While Celestial and Snub noses were abhorrent on men, they were, in fact, agreeable on the female face. "We confess a lurking *penchant,* a sort of sneaking affection which we cannot resist, for the latter of these in a woman. It does not command our admiration and respect like the Greek, to which we could bow down as to a goddess, but it makes sad work with our affections." While on a man such a nose represented frailty, a woman, after all, embodied just that: "Weakness in a woman . . . is excusable and rather loveable; while in a man it is detestable. It is a woman's place to be supported, not to support." Jabet acknowledged that in writing about the female nose—"a difficult and nervous subject"—he tread on delicate ground. "We have endeavored, however, to say nothing but the plain truth."

In a final chapter, Jabet discussed "national noses." His thoughts reflected the racist theories advanced by scholars, who along with physiognomy had embraced phrenology, a "science" popular in mid-nineteenth-century Britain that drew conclusions about intelligence and character based on the structure of the skull, jaw formation, and facial angles. "Every nation has a characteristic Nose; and the less advanced the nation is in the civilization, the more general and perceptible is the characteristic form. ". . . the most highly organized and intellectual races possess the highest forms of Noses, and those which are more barbarous and uncivilized possess Noses proportionately Snub and depressed, approaching the form of the snouts of lower animals, which seldom or ever project beyond the jaws."

Jabet's contempt for the noses of non-Anglo-Saxons was unrelenting, but no national nose received more vitriol than that of the new Americans. In stark contrast to their conscientious Puritan forebears, young Americans lacked honesty, integrity, and diligence, Jabet wrote. Its nose, therefore, was "the most unthinking of any Gothic stock." But he did hold out hope. Perhaps one day, he wrote, ". . . It will yet furnish its quota of thinkers to the history of the human mind."[6]


## Freud and the Victorians: The Nose as a Sexual Organ

Medicine's view of the nose was a similar mix of surmise and superstition. By the nineteenth century, doctors had begun to fasten on the theory of "reflex action," which held that nervous connections running along the spine joined all the organs of the body together, including the brain. The blood and the nervous system worked in tandem so that a change in one organ could effect sympathetic consequences elsewhere. Conditions in one part of the body easily spread to distant ones: an upset stomach could lead to a troubled mind, and so on.[7]

By the turn of the century, many in mainstream science began to focus on the nose as the culprit in many illnesses, even "slowness." In Great Britain, children who suffered from chronic ear, sinus, and throat infections were thought to be "dull." Like anyone with a bad cold, they breathed through their mouths instead of their noses (this is because adenoids, lymphoid tissue at the top of the palate, become so swollen that they block air coming from the nose to the lungs). Such a habit made a child look dim-witted, doctors thought. One surgeon, William Watson, found that if he removed the adenoids, the children resumed breathing through their noses, and "looked" cleverer almost immediately. As a result, the operation became popular among Victorian doctors and parents alike, who believed the procedure could boost a child's I.Q.

And J.R. Mackenzie, a Baltimore physician, addressed the Baltimore Academy of Medicine regarding the reciprocal relationship between the nose and the genitals. While ancient observers from India to Greece had reported the "evil effects of undue excitation" on sight and hearing, Mackenzie set out to convince his fellow doctors of similar results on the nose. Women were not immune from this most uncomfortable plight. Indeed, they were especially susceptible to such misery on account of menstrual irregularities, which forced blood up to the nose, engorging the tissue. Mackenzie also noted the tendency for young ladies to have "vicarious nasal menstruation"—nosebleeds.

Mackenzie interpreted chronically swollen, runny noses as the body's own punishment for a lack of sexual self-restraint. "Amorous contact" between husband and wife was likely to result in temporarily stuffy nasal passages for both sexes, but more troubling were the chronically swollen noses of those who made a habit of "overstimulating" their genitals. "Repeated and prolonged abuse of the organs may (cause) a constant irritative influence on the turbinate tissue," he warned. (Three pairs of turbinates, membrane-covered cartilage, line the walls of the nose. They are essential for humidifying the sinuses and for protecting them against bacterial and viral infections.) But worst of all were the poor noses of masturbators. "Victims of this vice . . . are constantly subjected to discharge from the nostrils and perversion of the sense, which is simply the outward expression of chronic nasal inflammation."[8]

Mackenzie concluded "that the natural stimulation of the reproductive apparatus . . . when carried beyond its normal physiological bounds, as in coitus or menstruation . . . (is) often the exacting cause of nasal congestion and inflammation." (Embedded among Mackenzie's bizarre theories, this actually had a germ of truth. Decades later, scientists would discover that the nose actually did swell during sexual excitement, but only temporarily. Indeed, the nasal septum is made of erectile tissue like that of the genitals and the nipples. In women, monthly changes in estrogen and progesterone can result in swelling of all extremities, including the nasal tissues, but hormones would not be discovered until the 1930s.)

While Victorian mores and "reflex action theory" made this believable to some—the speech was later published in a prominent medical journal—other scholars found his musings preposterous. Dorothy Reed Mendenhall and Margaret Long, two of the first female medical students at Johns Hopkins School of Medicine, were among those who heard Mackenzie hold forth on his pet topic. "From the start he dragged in the dirtiest stories I have ever heard, read, or imagined," Mendenhall wrote. Though nearly fifty years had passed since that night,

> much of what he said is branded in my mind and still comes up like a decomposing body from the bottom of a pool that is disturbed. . . . Dr. Mackenzie spent most of his hour discussing the cavernous tissue present in the nasal passages and comparing it with corpus spongiosa of the penis. We sat just opposite the speaker and the chairman, so that the flushed, bestial face of Dr. Mackenzie, his sly pleasure in making his nasty points, and I imagine the added fillip of doing his dirt before two young women, was evident. . . . Roars of laughter filled the room behind us at every dragged-in joke. . . . I cried all the way home— hysterically—and Margaret swore. The next few days I stayed at home . . . debating with myself whether I should leave medical school.[9]

But conventional wisdom at the turn of the century was dominated by the belief that sex and sexuality formed the basic core of a person's identity. While the Victorian bourgeois were modest enough to wear stockings even with their bathing suits, their focus on sex and its effects on health was a hallmark of the period.

Masturbation, the "solitary vice" was deeply sinister. Doctors warned that it could permanently maim a child, and urged parents and teachers to keep a watchful eye out for anything suspicious. Some physicians even designed devices aimed at saving boys from temptation: one delivered electric shocks to a sleeping boy's penis should it become erect; another was equipped with bells that enabled alert fathers to rush in if self-control had failed.

Meanwhile, doctors believed that a woman's health centered on her reproductive organs. The uterus and ovaries controlled all parts of the body, they asserted, and were responsible for illnesses from tuberculosis to hysteria. As a "cure" for any range of disorders, doctors in the United States and Britain advocated "leeching" of the vulva (which invariably resulted in "losing" some of the creatures) and injecting liquids such as "linseed tea" and milk directly into the uterus.[10]

Female reproductive organs were inevitably tied to the nose as well. Wilhelm Fliess, a Berlin otolaryngologist, was fascinated by the nose, and claimed that it contained "genital spots." The spots, Fliess believed, grew swollen with "sexual substances" which circulated in twenty-three-day periods for men and twenty-eight-day periods for women; each sex had some of each substance. They coursed through the body in excess if sexual pleasure was not properly achieved—that is to say, if a person masturbated, used condoms, or engaged in coitus interruptus. Fliess gained notoriety for his premise, and published a book on the subject in 1897, *The Relationship Between the Nose and a Woman's Genitalia.*

Fliess had a powerful friend, Sigmund Freud, with whom he corresponded regularly. During the early years of their friendship, Freud became obsessive about his own nose, and filled his letters to Fliess with details of its discharge and inflammation. Fliess also complained of a runny nose, and both men turned to cocaine for treatment; Freud called it a "magical drug," for its mental and physical effects. Apparently, Freud applied his directly to the mucous membrane.[11] Initially, cocaine can reduce inflammation in the sinuses because it dilates blood vessels. But chronic use can irritate, even ulcerate, the nasal passages; cause "rebound" congestion; and perforate the septum.

Fliess treated patients first by applying cocaine locally, then cauterizing tissue inside the nostrils. But only surgery would guarantee permanent relief from "hysteria." Fliess's solution was to remove a portion of bone from the left middle turbinate. This, he said, would permanently cure all female sexual disorders. In a letter to Freud, Fliess wrote: "Women who masturbate are generally dysmenorrheal. They can only be finally cured through an operation on the nose if they truly give up this bad practice."[12]

Fliess's sway over Freud grew paramount in the treatment of one of his early analytical patients, Emma Eckstein, the daughter of prominent Viennese socialists. Like many of Freud's patients, Eckstein suffered from stomach pains and menstrual problems, which Freud traced to excessive masturbation. He summoned Fliess to Vienna in 1895 to perform his signature operation. (Jeffrey Moussaieff Masson describes the ordeal in his book, *The Assault on Truth*.)

Fliess returned to Berlin shortly after the February twenty-fifth surgery. Not only did Eckstein fail to recover, she grew sicker—and even began to stink—as the days passed. On March 4, Freud wrote a panicked letter to Fliess describing her worsening condition:

> . . . the day before yesterday she had a massive hemor-rhage, probably as a result of expelling a bone chip the size of a [small coin]; there were two bowlfuls of pus. Today we encountered resistance to irrigation; and since the pain and the visible edema had increased, I let myself be persuaded to call in Gersuny [another doctor]. . . . He ex-plained that the access was considerably narrowed and in-sufficient for drainage, inserted a drainage tube, and threatened to break it open if that did not stay in. To judge by the smell, all this is most likely correct. Please send me your authoritative advice. I am not looking forward to new surgery on this girl.

Four days later, he sent another dispatch:

> I wrote to you that the swelling and the hemorrhages would not stop, and that suddenly a fetid odor set in, and that there was an obstacle upon irrigation. . . . [Two days later] there still was moderate bleeding from the nose and mouth; the fetid odor was very bad. Rosanes [a third doc-tor] cleaned the area surrounding the opening, removed

some sticking blood clots, and suddenly he pulled at something like a thread, kept on pulling and before either of us had time to think, at least half a meter of gauze had been removed from the cavity.

Freud seemed more disturbed by his own reaction to the fiasco than he was by Fliess's obvious ineptitude. "At the moment the foreign body came out and everything became clear to me, immediately after which I was confronted by the sight of the patient, I felt sick. After she had been packed, I fled to the next room, drank a bottle of water, and felt miserable. The brave Frau Doktor then brought me a small glass of cognac and I became myself again."

Gersuny performed a second operation, and Freud arranged for Eckstein to recover in a sanitarium. When it appeared as though she was out of danger, Freud acknowledged the "injustice" of the procedure—but not for long. "That this mishap should have happened to you; how will you react to it when you hear about it; what others could make of it; how wrong I was to urge you to operate in a foreign city where you could not follow through on the case; how my intention to do the best for this poor girl was insidiously thwarted and resulted in endangering her life—all this came over me simultaneously. I have worked it through by now. . . . Of course, no one is blaming you, nor would I know anyone who should.[13]

Eckstein nearly bled to death between the second and, implausibly, yet a third operation. They so severely gouged the delicate bones of Eckstein's nose and cheek that they began to cave in, disfiguring a once-pretty face. At first, Freud felt responsible for the disaster, but later blamed it on Eckstein's hemorrhages, which "were hysterical in nature, the result of sexual longing."

Undeterred by Fliess's incompetence, at some point in 1895 he submitted to Fliess's procedures himself. In order to "treat" Freud's sinusitis—likely worsened by cocaine—Fliess cauterized Freud's turbinates to help relieve pain and drain the infected mucus. The surgery appears to have been unsuccessful, but Freud couldn't bring himself to admit it. Instead, he simply applied more cocaine, which he claimed augmented the surgery's "positive" effects. Indeed, he praised Fliess: "in your hands [you hold] the reins of sexuality, which governs all mankind: you can do anything and prevent anything."

In the early half of the twentieth century, Freud's disciples popularized psychoanalysis in the United States. From the 1920s to the 1950s, the nose emerged as a central figure in medical thinking among psychoanalysts and physicians alike. Between the years of 1914 and 1948, dozens of papers on the nose were published in scientific journals ranging from *Laryngyscope* and *Endocrinology* to the *Psychoanalytic Quarterly*.

Early on, doctors readily embraced Fliess's prescriptions for menstrual irregularities. Emil Mayer, the chief of the Ear and Throat Department at Mt. Sinai Hospital in Manhattan, treated women who suffered from cramps by applying cocaine to their nasal passages. He delighted in reporting that invariably within a few minutes of the treatment, a patient's "color came back, her breathing was fine and she went upon her duties instead of to bed as usual."[14]

Intervention on the nose for sexual problems was endorsed by many, but in psychoanalysis, where a man's nose is a powerful "penis substitute" in both dreams and reality, it was interpreted as symbolic castration. In 1929, C.P. Oberdorf, a New York psychoanalyst, wrote of a deeply religious twenty-four-year-old Irish Catholic bachelor who felt so guilty about his sexual desires that he had attempted suicide. The patient, called "Tim O'Brien," longed to have sex in spite of his religious teachings. Yet whenever he was about to have intercourse, he began sniffling so incessantly that he quickly lost his erection. Eventually, he sought treatment for his troubles—the surgical removal of his turbinates. The procedure didn't relieve O'Brien's problem, and it also "flattened" his nose, giving his entire countenance a "tough, coarse appearance" he was convinced would dampen his chances at snagging a suitable bride. Such a nose was sure only to attract "common, low-born girls" such as waitresses and servants.

O'Brien's sexual development revolved around his nose, and Oberdorfer soon determined why. From the time he was a small boy until he was nineteen, he "cuddled" with his mother, his head at her breast, and was devastated at the age of twelve to learn of the reality of procreation. For years he refused to accept a sullied image of his mother, insisting that her purity exceeded that of the nuns themselves. He loved all of her odors, from sweat to gas; they regularly figured in his dreams. And he was both excited and tormented by a recurring fantasy. He longed to shrink enough so that he could enter a woman (especially a nun; the fatter, the better) with his nose by way of her rectum. "Once I was within her body, I could expand to normal size, my legs in her legs, my arms in her arms, moving as she moved—that was the acme of satisfaction."

Oberdorfer called on the established theory of the nose as an "erotogenic zone" in early childhood. "The nose, which in early infancy had assumed the function of the penis, was in turn replaced by the whole face, the head and finally the entire body became the organ for re-entry into, reunion with, the mother-substitute," he wrote. Rather than use the usual sex apparatus, O'Brien instead relied on a penis substitute, the nose, to enter a woman—a mother-substitute. So guilt-ridden was he that he sought "punishment" for the offending organ—surgery, or mutilation of his nose, being the only "logical way out." Oberdorfer concluded: "The nose being the penis, this [surgery] was nothing more or less than a castration. When accomplished, it resulted in all the helplessness of the castrated male body—namely, a female. But even the symbolic castration did not completely remove the need for punishment, nor, for that matter, did it diminish in the least his sexual urge."[15]

The nose was also at the forefront of psychosomatic medicine, which became especially popular in the 1940s after the arrival of the émigré psychoanalyst Franz Alexander. Centers of psychosomatic medicine were founded at hospitals from Massachusetts General in Boston to Columbia Presbyterian in New York, and soon internists and other physicians adhered to the belief that personality type combined with difficult situations to create bodily symptoms. Asthma, for example, was thought to be a conflict between the need for dependency—wheezing was a symbolic cry for mother—and the fear of dependency. Patients with peptic ulcers were believed to equate the need for love with the need for food, much like infants.

Though germ theory was introduced by Pasteur in the mid-nineteenth century, many were unwilling to accept it as medical fact. Leon Saul, a Manhattan psychoanalyst, broached the topic of communicable disease in a paper: "That an infectious agent, a filterable virus, may play an etiological role is apparently established. . . . [But] in certain instances emotional disturbances may play a role." This emotional factor, he wrote, was likely the "most prominent feature in precipitating the symptoms of the 'common cold' and sore throat."

### America at Mid-Century: Your Problems Are Your Own Damn Fault

Those twin themes—emotional problems and sexual activity as the culprit in nasal illness—were elaborated on in a series of studies at Cornell University Medical College in Manhattan in the 1940s. The medical treatment of what was delicately termed "women's troubles" had advanced little from the days of Emma Eckstein. If women were treated for their symptoms at all, doctors often approached them radically, with tranquilizers, hysterectomies, or complete mastectomies. Menstruation was referred to as a period of "unwellness," and many of women's physical complaints were dismissed as emotional nattering. Not far behind women on the ladder of medical scorn were immigrants, namely Jews, Irish, and Italians, with African-Americans on the lowest rung.

In the 1940s, three Cornell professors, Thomas Holmes, Stewart Wolf, Harold G. Wolff, and an assistant, Helen Goodell, conducted research to determine the extent to which patients' nasal symptoms—stuffiness, postnasal drip ("vasomotor rhinitis"), sneezing—were related to anxiety, depression, or "hysteria." The experiments were published in a 1950 book, *The Nose: An Experimental Study of Reactions Within the Nose in Human Subjects During Varying Life Experiences.*

The description of the case studies—and what the doctors saw as the "real" problem—leaves little to the imagination: "Vasomotor Rhinitis and Sneezing in Dissatisfied, Frustrated, Resentful, Weepy Woman." "Chronic Disease of the Sinuses and Vasomotor Rhinitis in an Anxious, Dissatisfied, Resentful Woman who Based her Security on her 'Good Looks' and 'Sexual' Assets, and Who Feared She Was Losing Both." "Chronic Rhinitis, Polyposis (35 Operations) and Ultimately Asthma in a Frustrated, Resentful and Defeated Woman."[16] Others were similarly described: "a rejected, insecure Jewess who experienced strong feelings of resentment and nasal obstruction." "Nasal Obstruction in an Insecure, Dependent, Ambitious, Lachrymose Man." Charts and graphs accompany the patient summaries, complete with traumatic histories corresponding to their nasal symptoms: the death of a parent, the loss of a job.

| Year | Age | Event | Symptoms |
|---|---|---|---|
| 1916 | BORN | PARENTS ILL TBC | |
| 1919 | AGE 3 | PARENTS DIED | |
| | AGE 1-5 | UNWANTED NEGLECTED | |
| 1921 | AGE 5 | ADOPTED DYNAMIC FAMILY | MANY HEAD COLDS |
| | | 1 FOSTER SISTER | |
| 1934 | AGE 18 | COLLEGE | |
| 1936 | AGE 20 | DEATH OF DEVOTED FRIEND | |
| | | GRIEF | VASOMOTOR RHINITIS |
| | | FEAR OF BEING DESERTED | |
| | | WEEPING | |
| 1937 | AGE 21 | FAMILY ARGUMENTS | |
| | | INSECURE | VASOMOTOR RHINITIS |
| | | FEAR OF LOSING FAMILY | |
| | | WEEPING | SUBMUCOUS RESECTION |
| 1938 | AGE 22 | ENGAGED AND MARRIED | |
| 1940 | AGE 24 | FIRST PREGNANCY | V. RHINITIS ABSENT |
| 1943 | AGE 27 | SECOND PREGNANCY | |
| | | HUSBAND ENLISTS | |
| | | WEAK HEART | |
| | | FEAR TERROR WEEPING | VASOMOTOR RHINITIS |
| JAN. 1944 | | SON BORN | |
| | AGE 28 | DIFFICULT LABOR | |
| | | HUSBAND LEAVES FOR NAVY | |
| FEB. 1944 | | CONFLICT WHERE TO LIVE | |
| | | LONELINESS | V. RHINITIS SEVERE |
| | | FEAR AND WEEPING | |
| MARCH 1944 | | FOUND ALLERGIC TO | |
| | | COFFEE AND CHOCOLATE | |
| | | BREAKING UP HOME | V. RHINITIS UNCHANGED |
| MAY 1944 | | HOUSE NEAR HUSBAND | |
| | | COLD FOGGY WEATHER | V. RHINITIS IMPROVED |
| SUMMER 1944 | | LIVING WITH HUSBAND AND | |
| | | CHILDREN | |
| | | CHOCOLATE AND COFFEE | (NO V. RHINITIS) |
| JAN. 1945 | | HUSBAND ORDERED TO SEA | |
| | AGE 29 | PANIC AND FEAR | V. RHINITIS 12 HOURS |
| | | WEEPING | |
| SUMMER 1945 | | BACK IN HOME | WELL |

*Lift chart illustrating coincidence of situational threats and nasal disturbances in an insecure, anxious woman. The black bars at the right indicate the occurrence, duration, and intensity of troublesome symptoms.*

In a foreword to the book, the authors wrote that their aim was to "study the man and his nose at once as a unit, thus integrating these points of view for the better understanding of the human organism." But the methodology of studying that integration seems about as rational as the theory of "genital spots." The authors—who insisted that they avoided the subjects' "discomfort" or "inconvenience," although some were examined daily for as long as a year—seated their patients next to a lamp, and, using a nasal speculum, peered up their noses to chart the level of swelling, amount of secretions, and color of the mucous membrane. The subjects were asked about their "dreams,

prevailing attitudes, preoccupations and moods" in order to determine the relationship between their nasal symptoms and
"life situations." Before interviews, many were given Amytal, a
sedative hypnotic occasionally used in psychotherapy with
trauma patients to "access" repressed or unconscious feelings
and memories. (Even though Amytal has been referred to as a
"truth serum," psychiatrists today say that it does not guarantee
honest recall of events any more than any other interview technique.)

The authors said there were clear links between humiliation,
rejection, anxiety, and dejection to everything from runny noses
to sinus disease. In one case, a forty-year-old itinerant salesman
had recurrent stuffiness ever since his wedding fourteen years
earlier. The son of an abusive Russian Jewish immigrant father
and a "tearful, unhappy mother," the man quit school to help
support his ten younger siblings. His adult home life was
scarcely happier than the one he had dreamed of abandoning as
a child. The couples' sex life was miserable, and the man's wife
was a bitter, resentful woman who had been "rendered sterile"
by a botched surgery.

"I've been robbed of a compatible marriage," the patient is
quoted as saying. "Robbed of a family. Robbed of the opportunity to do the things I wanted to do. . . . My wife held me back . . .
She made a damn fool out of me. A jackass. . . . Yesterday I accused her of being 75 percent the cause of my sickness."

Wolf blamed the man's wife, too. He wrote that whenever his
hapless patient was reminded of his wife's "lack of devotion,"
his nose began to swell and run.[17]

The book devotes a separate chapter to the nose and sexual

function, and the doctors cite Dr. Mackenzie liberally. One "observation" involved a twenty-nine-year-old doctor who complained of a persistent runny nose and stuffiness, from which he was freed only by having intercourse with his wife, "a willing partner to the sex act." However, months later, the doctor "tenderly insisted" on lovemaking with his wife only four weeks after she had given birth to their first child. Despite the wife's hesitation—she was afraid of "sustaining injury," the authors wrote—the couple nevertheless proceeded. The husband, aware of his wife's reluctance, "reacted to the situation with feelings of guilt and humiliation." During fondling, he noticed a "moderate increase in obstruction to breathing." During "copulation," obstruction became "complete." The authors, as they do throughout the book, draw large conclusions from minor events. "After ejaculation, the subject was aware of a small amount of secretion in both nasal cavities."[18]

One seventeen-year-old woman had her nose examined several times during her twenty-hour labor and seven-day postpartum hospital stay. The patient had a difficult labor, during which she struggled to breathe; further, she was grappling with the dueling visits of parents and new in-laws, who openly disapproved of the shotgun marriage. The authors, unlike Mackenzie, attributed this woman's nasal problems, as well as those of other female patients, to personal circumstances. They wrote that those who "accepted pregnancy as desirable" sailed through pregnancy without nasal symptoms. Those "to whom pregnancy posed a threat to the maintenance of their precarious security props," whatever those may have been, developed or experienced increased symptoms during gestation.[19]

In a chapter that focused on "physical threats" to the nose, the doctors examined a fifty-eight-year-old man who suffered from a severe ragweed allergy in March, when he was symptom-free. Doctors stuffed ragweed pollen up his nostrils to see if he would "react." (Antihistamines, meanwhile, were synthesized for medical use in the early 1940s by the Swiss researcher Daniel Bovet, who would later win a Nobel prize in medicine.) The patient suffered an acute allergic attack, lasting for more than ninety minutes.[20]

Finally, the doctors attempted to explore the "sinus headache" using eighteen patients and themselves as healthy controls. The experiment consisted of inserting an electronic probe into the nostrils and sinuses and sliding a catheterized balloon into the sinuses and "blowing air through it." Not surprisingly, the doctors discovered that these implements provoked considerable pain, especially in those already suffering from disease.[21] This research, which went on to earn Dr. Wolff renown as a pioneer in the study of headaches, found that the turbinates and ducts of the sinuses were much more pain-sensitive than the lining of the sinuses themselves.

The authors concluded their book with some sweeping thoughts. "Nasal obstruction," they wrote, "though effective in keeping out dust and irritant gases, is less effective against blows or unrequited love. . . . Closing the air passages and increasing the mucous membrane secretions [minimize] the damaging effects of a gas or irritant, but . . . do not protect against a thorn in the foot or make less destructive the hostility of a parent or marital partner. Indeed, they often lead to additional distress."

The procedures the Cornell doctors performed were hardly the only unscientific studies conducted in the name of medicine in the 1940s. Nazi doctors, of course, were convicted of the atrocities they committed on concentration camp prisoners—submerging them in freezing water to determine how long the body could withstand cold; deliberately infecting them with smallpox and malaria; operating on them without anesthesia. And, throughout the Cold War, the U.S. government enrolled unsuspecting patients in "research" designed to test the body's absorption of radiation. But perhaps most notorious was the Tuskegee syphilis study from 1932 to 1972, in Macon County, Alabama. Over those four decades, U.S. government doctors examined and withheld treatment from 399 African-American men infected with the disease. Though penicillin was found to kill the syphilis bacterium in the early 1940s, it was still denied the men, who were given aspirin for their discomfort and told they were being treated for "bad blood."

While the medical establishment had embraced informed consent after the Nuremberg Trials in 1945, the disclosure of the Tuskegee study in 1972 finally made it an unquestioned requirement for experiments involving human subjects.[22] As bizarre as it might seem today, the Cornell research would hardly have raised an eyebrow in its time.

The doctors' theories about the underlying causes of sinus

disease—emotional stress and sexual frustration—reveal more about their own preconceptions and biases. Studies of the nose were particularly open to this sort of misconception, since the technical tools that would allow a true test of the hypothesis had not yet been invented. Because their functions were neither visible nor measurable, the limited data could be manipulated to say whatever was needed.

In recent years, experts in nasal disease have identified the environment and, increasingly, genetics, as the root cause of allergies and sinus problems. And there is some evidence that the Cornell doctors were right about some aspects of their work, albeit for the wrong reasons. Recent studies suggest there is some relationship between psychological health and the immune system. And it is now understood why a woman's nasal passages can swell in pregnancy and at certain points in the menstrual cycle.

Still, the Cornell interlude is one medical science seems determined to forget. Dr. Harold G. Wolff's research and reputation in the cause and treatment of headaches continues to be held in high regard; a postgraduate fellowship at the American Headache Society is named for him. His data on headaches continue to be cited without reference to how they were obtained.[24]

To be sure, medical science made some astounding breakthroughs in the mid-twentieth century: penicillin was isolated for antibiotic use in 1940; the Pap smear was introduced as a routine cancer screen in 1943; DNA was discovered in 1944; smallpox was virtually eliminated worldwide by 1951; and Jonas Salk introduced the polio vaccine in 1952. But the science of the nose involved little more than guesswork, and had as much relation to a cure as throwing spilled salt over your left shoulder does to ensuring good luck. A biomedical revolution was beginning to take place, but the nose was stuck in the Dark Ages, a mysterious, feared, and little-understood organ.

# four

# Nagasaki Up the Nose

## Monel Metal Nasopharyngeal Applicator

*50 Milligrams of radium element in a 21.5 mm. × 2.3 mm. × 0.3 mm. capsule on a 6" handle.*

While doctors at Cornell labored to prove the relationship between the nose and psychological problems, physicians in Baltimore knew its very real links to bona fide ailments such as deafness and sinus disease. They were intent on finding a treatment for upper respiratory problems, and came up with what they were sure was a stroke of brilliance. But little did they imagine that their revolutionary cure—radium administered up the nose to shrink adenoids and tonsils—would mar the lives of millions of patients.

In the early half of the century, hearing loss, especially for children, was a real and present threat; such a disability could marginalize a person for life. And by 1948, chronic upper respiratory infections had left an estimated 4 million Americans under eighteen deaf.[1] Prior to antibiotics and vaccinations for rubella (which, if contracted by a woman in the first trimester of pregnancy, can lead to the blindness and deafness of her child), hearing loss was an entrenched and perplexing problem. Samuel Crowe, the director of the Department of Otolaryngology at Johns Hopkins University in Baltimore, was particularly troubled by the plight of young patients who could hear one month, and barely make out their mother's voice the next.

To prepare for his post at Johns Hopkins, Crowe had trained in Germany, which in the early part of the century was home to some of the most pioneering ear, nose, and throat researchers. In Germany, physicians experimented widely with radium in the shrinkage of animal tumors. By the late 1920s, radium was used to treat polyps in the United States. (Pierre and Marie Curie discovered radium in 1898, and found that it killed human cells. They reasoned that if it destroyed healthy organisms, it could do the same for unwanted tissue as well.)

In treating young patients at a Maryland clinic for the deaf, Crowe wondered if radium might be suitable for their problems. The culprit was swollen adenoids, lymphoid tissue located behind the nose and soft palate, which blocked the Eustachian tube and resulted in hearing loss. While it was possible to remove adenoids surgically, the procedure was risky, painful, and was not always permanent; the tissue sometimes grew back. Radium, Crowe believed, would not only destroy adenoids, it could be administered simply, without anesthesia.

In the early 1940s, Crowe also sought out army and navy doctors to discuss the use of his radium on servicemen. Airmen and submariners were routinely suffering hearing loss and severe ear pain due to the lack of pressurized cabins in aircraft and submarines, and military doctors had been hard pressed to come up with a solution as they lost personnel. (Approximately one-third of all U.S. Air Force aviators were grounded during the war because of their hearing loss, called "aerotitis media.") The navy enthusiastically agreed, and before long Crowe and his protégé, Donald F. Proctor, set to work on designing a device that could deliver the radiation.

In 1943, with the help of the New York–based Radium Chemical Company (which later gained notoriety as one of America's most polluted Superfund sites), Proctor came up with suitable tools: long, wire-thin rods with radium tips, to be inserted up into the nostrils until they reached the swollen tissue. The rods, left in place for eight to twelve minutes, hit the adenoids with at least 2,000 rads of radiation, although some estimates are much higher. Nearby organs such as the brain, thyroid, and pituitary glands also received substantial doses of radiation; estimates range from a few rads to 150. By comparison, cancer patients undergoing radiation to shrink their tumors get some 6,000 rads; an average chest X-ray delivers about .01 rad. Scientists today generally agree that the government limit for occupational radiation exposure—five rads per year to the whole body—is safe.

The standard protocol was to repeat the procedure two

times, at two-week intervals, for a total radiation dosage up to 2 million times that of a typical dental X-ray. The army first called the rod the "Army Irradiator," but later used a less martial moniker, dubbing it the "Aerotitis Media Control Program."

The treatments were hailed as a miracle cure for the servicemen. One study found that 90 percent of those who received them—and more than 8,000 did—were permanently relieved of their ear problems. Before long, their use caught on among civilians, too: by current Centers for Disease Control and Prevention estimates, between 500 thousand and 2.6 million children were treated with the devices between 1948 and 1961. The rods were lauded by the *Saturday Evening Post* in 1948 in an article titled "Will Your Child Be Deaf?" The treatments, known as nasal radium irradiation, or NRI, were a "spectacular" and "remarkable" way to prevent deafness and upper respiratory problems, the article said. The therapeutic "limit" for NRI was ostensibly two courses, but some children received eight or twelve doses, often separated by a week or less. The treatments hurt. Children screamed in pain, and parents were routinely enlisted to hold their charges down. Proctor noted that if very young children could not be kept still, they should be strapped into special chairs that immobilized their heads during treatment. Many complained of a burning sensation that lasted for weeks. The article didn't mention such unpleasantness, however. Rather, it noted that children who had done poorly in school went on to blossom after the radium, both academically and socially.

Radium, in fact, was in use everywhere, and for the most

part, the attitude toward it was relaxed. Nuclear bombs were detonated in the open desert; shoe store customers could slip their feet into X-ray machines to examine their bones, and special X-ray photo labs offered lovers the opportunity to immortalize the intertwined bones of their fingers on film. Surely, a dab of radiation up the nose could hardly be harmful. On the contrary, radiation appeared to be a cure-all: doctors used it not only in X-rays and killing cancer cells but also for treating acne and removing birthmarks.

Nasal radium had not been subjected to rigorous scientific evaluation either. Long after he had been using the procedure widely, between 1948 and 1953, Crowe undertook a study of Baltimore schoolchildren. Its aims were to determine "the feasibility of irradiation of the nasopharynx as a method for controlling hearing impairment in large groups of children . . . (and) to draw conclusions concerning the per capita cost of such an undertaking as a public health measure," he wrote. Further, Crowe added that while the procedure itself was not new, "this is the first adequately controlled experiment of sufficient size for accurate statistical analysis."[2] (Not surprisingly, the study found that the treatments were highly successful.)

Warnings about the overuse of radium in medical treatment first surfaced when Marie Curie, who was awarded two Nobel prizes for her research with the metal, died in 1934 of radium poisoning, which experts traced to her constant exposure. (Pierre was killed in an accident shortly before the couple received their first Nobel, in physics.) By the 1950s, unusual head and neck irradiation was being linked to thyroid cancer. But the medical profession was slow to cut back on radiation use.

Throughout the 1950s, the treatment was as accepted in some circles for a child's nasal allergies and ear infections as Tylenol is for fevers today.

Not everyone was enthusiastic. Two Boston doctors, Laurence Robbins and Milford Schulz, presented a paper at a 1949 meeting of otolaryngologists, stating: "That radiation of any sort should become a routine is unwise; certainly if this does occur, the results should be checked and rechecked at intervals in order to anticipate an untoward effect. Lack of an immediate reaction should not lull to rest the fears for possible latent reaction." The decision to treat a benign condition with such a potent agent as radium should be weighed carefully, they warned, as "unknown dangers may not appear for as long a time as 10, 20, or more years."

Dr. Kenneth Day, a Pittsburgh ENT, also had growing concerns about the overuse of nasal radium, and the same year presented a paper at a different annual meeting of otolaryngologists. "There is no question it has become big business. . . . the use of radium applicators in the nasopharynx has definitely reached the racket level," he said. Some doctors were even using the device "for such alien conditions and symptoms as head colds, tinnitus [ringing in the ears], and chronic cough." Day warned that the use of the radium rods—which could be used successively on an "officeful of patients"—could become a lucrative source of income for the user. "We are rapidly reaching the point where the cure is worse than the disease," he continued.[3]

Still, the radium rods became a routine. Proctor assured parents in a 1960 book that "These treatments have now been given . . . to hundreds of thousands of patients and no instance of damage from irradiation has yet been reported. Nevertheless, both because two series of well planned treatments should suffice, and to eliminate any danger from excess irradiation, the limit should be set at two."[4]

By 1970, nasal radiation was supplanted by antibiotics and, in chronic pediatric cases, drainage tubes were surgically inserted directly into the eardrum. The treatment became less popular as the public realized the dangers of radiation, and eventually faded from sight.

About ten years later, Stewart Farber, a public health researcher, was having coffee with a childhood friend. Michael Krabach, a recreational diver, mentioned that in the late 1960s a colleague had recommended that he see Henry Haines, a doctor from Connecticut, who had a unique treatment—nasal radium—to help divers adjust to water pressure changes while underwater. Krabach (who had so far suffered no ill effects from the treatments) thought little of it until his meeting with Farber. "I was absolutely floored," Farber says. "I thought he was putting me on." Krabach insisted that Haines said the treatment was safe, and had been used on thousands of people for decades.

Farber, fifty-five, a chemist with a degree in public health who had been involved for about a decade in conducting radiation monitoring programs around nuclear plants, saw the "whole sorry episode," as he calls it, through a unique prism: his own training in the body's tolerance for radiation. "I'm the opposite of no-nukes activists," he says. "I've worked to promote the safety of nuclear radiation my whole life." A power-fully built man with brown hair and a trim graying beard, Farber's long résumé includes posts as a senior radiological en-gineer with the New York Power Authority, and, four months after the Three Mile Island accident, as the assistant manager for nuclear information with the New England Electric System.

Farber began the task of researching Haines's treatments and their repurcussion. Haines, it turned out, had been trained by Crowe, and began work in the mid-1940s at the navy's submarine school in Groton, Connecticut. It didn't take long for Farber to conclude that the whole experience was "to-tally botched." He began to scour records for studies, which were scarce. One was a doctoral thesis published in 1980 by a Johns Hopkins researcher, Dale Sandler, which found twice the rate of both benign and malignant tumors among those treated with the rods as among a control group. Treated sub-jects had a higher rate of brain cancer and a nearly ninefold increase in the rate of thyroid disorders such as Graves's dis-ease. Strangely, the women Sandler studied had a lower-than-average rate of breast cancer, but the figures were not statistically significant.

A Dutch paper offered a conflicting view. In 1989, Dr. Peter Verduijn found that the nasal radium had not been linked to a single death. Moreover, there was no incidence of breast cancer among the women who had been treated as children. (There are some possible explanations for the differences. Farber was not persuaded. Dutch children who received the treatments had a 3.5 times lower rate of radium delivered to their adenoids than did the American youngsters. At the time, the two reports were the only significant nasal radium studies.

Farber was appalled at what he was learning. "It wasn't clear that anyone was tracking these people, spread all across the country, and notifying them of what their risks were. You've got people saying, 'Oh, cell phones! Cell phones cause cancer!' And here millions of people had these treatments, using massive doses of radiation. By comparison with any other head and neck cancer risk, it was a Nagasaki up the nose! And who cared? Nobody!"

Outraged, Farber made it his mission to raise public consciousness about the issue. He found a window of opportunity in 1993 when the *Albuquerque Tribune* published a series of articles on government-sponsored experiments in the 1940s in which civilian hospital patients were injected with plutonium. The series won national attention (and earned a Pulitzer prize for the paper). Other stories of radiation experiments emerged, including one in which the testicles of prisoners in Oregon and Washington were irradiated; another involved scientists from Massachusetts Institute of Technology who fed mentally retarded children at a Boston-area school breakfast cereal and milk with radioactive tracers to study the absorption of iron and calcium.

Soon afterward, President Clinton appointed a fourteen-member panel, the Advisory Committee on Human Radiation Experiments (ACHRE), to investigate the Cold War treatments that took place under the auspices of national security. It calculated that children who had received the nasal radium faced a 62 percent higher risk than the normal population of getting brain cancer. These statistics put nasal radium in a special category: its high risk exceeded the committee's stated threshold of one case per thousand for mandatory notification and follow-up.

But the committee decided not to notify patients. After all, those at risk for long-term complications had probably already found them—or were dead. The report said that the brain, head, and neck were most at risk, but that there was no "accepted" screening procedure. If new screening measures were developed, or new information about the risk was discovered, the nasal radium experiments should be reevaluated. Still, Dr. Eli Glatstein, a committee member and the former Chief of Staff of Radiation Oncology at the National Institutes of Health, recommended monitoring military personnel.[5]

Dan Guttman, who served as executive director of the committee, says that finding people where the criteria are met would be a logistical ordeal. Many of the records are missing and incomplete. Logs noting the treatments exist in small hospitals throughout the country, but many lack patients' names. How do you notify such people—and toward what end? Guttman asks. "We had to worry about creating a national panic."

Meanwhile, a Veterans Administration study compared deaths among 1,214 submariners treated with the nasal radium against deaths in a control group of 3,176 randomly selected veterans who were not treated. The report found that those who had had the NRI had a 47 percent higher rate of death from head and neck cancers and a 29 percent higher overall mortality rate than veterans who weren't treated.

Not everyone read the data the same way, and many have clung to the early Dutch data that had shown no serious side effects. In fact, the government has provided no definitive statement for those who received the treatment. On the contrary, the government's actions have been inconsistent at best. The CDC and the Veteran's Administration concluded that further testing was unnecessary among healthy adults. Citing the Verduijn and Sandler studies, they said: "Current studies do not indicate substantial increases in risks . . . among those who received NP (nasopharyngeal) radium treatments."[6]

The CDC has, however, suggested that doctors consider head and neck examinations for patients with a history of nasal radium, and that they ask patients over thirty-five with head and neck complaints about past irradiation, presumably to spot any problems that might be developing.

The CDC has devoted an extensive Web site to nasal radium treatments, in which it urges patients who had nasal radium to notify their doctors. What of those who were toddlers when they received the treatments, or simply don't remember? Dr. Paul Garvey of the CDC shrugs this off, saying that most would recall such an uncomfortable treatment. "We don't feel that this presents a significant problem."

Unfortunately, the CDC may be relying on out-of-date data. Even Verduijn, the Dutch researcher, produced new research showing that the treatments may not have been as benign as his initial findings indicated. In a follow-up study in 1996, he found that those treated with nasal radium had a doubling of overall cancer incidence, with most of the excess due to head and neck cancers.

As Farber puts it, "These people are in a Catch-22." On one hand, the government says the existing studies aren't comprehensive enough to attribute various disorders to the treatments; on the other, it is not willing to pay for a larger, more exhaustive study. "Either way, there are hundreds of thousands—millions—of people out there who may not even know about their risks," Farber says. "What about them? It's severely impeachable science," he says. "The children who received these treatments got zapped at a much higher rate than did the adults, simply by merit of the size of their bodies."

The government eventually took a different view toward veterans. In 1998, Congress required the U.S. Department of Veterans Affairs to provide health care to the estimated 8,000–20,000 veterans with head or neck cancer who had the treatments.

Meanwhile, Farber became the center of the loose network developed by those who had had the treatments, and formed a group, the Radium Experiment Assessment Project, which he runs from his home in Warren, Vermont. More than a thousand people have contacted him in search of information about NRI and its potential risks. Further, in logs he has kept from those who had received the treatment, odd repetitions began to appear, as those patients, now in their forties, fifties, and sixties, complained of tumors, thyroid and immune disorders, brittle teeth, and reproductive problems.

The effects of the radiation appear to be complex. Studies show a lower-than-average incidence of breast cancer among those treated with NRI. Researchers theorize that the radium dispersed by the rods somehow disrupted the function of the pituitary gland to produce its growth, reproductive, and labor-inducing homones. Oncologists, meanwhile, have linked reproductive homones to breast cancer.

Many of the women treated with NRI report an array of similar, strange symptoms. Jan Nelson, a California woman in her mid-fifties, had several treatments for chronic ear infections as a child in Los Angeles. She has had several precancerous nodules removed from her thyroid and suffers from Sjögren's syndrome, an autoimmune disorder that targets the body's moisture-producing glands and causes dryness in the eyes and mouth. Sjögren's is largely hereditary, but Nelson has no family history of the disease. In addition, she suffered bizarre menstrual irregularities that few doctors could puzzle out. Her cycles sometimes lasted for months on end, and while she did have two full-term pregnancies, she went three weeks overdue with both children, and her labor was finally induced. Her doctors told her that her body simply didn't produce a labor-triggering hormone. Rosemary Noel, a Kansas schoolteacher who was treated with radium in Mississippi as a child, suffered from excessive monthly periods until she was thirty-four, when she underwent a hysterectomy. Arlene Lavin, a California woman who also received the treatments, suffered similar problems, leading to two procedures while in her thirties to stop the bleeding.

Most of those who reach Farber seek information on head-and-neck tumors and thyroid irregularities. John Rushton, a computer systems engineer in Pennsylvania who was treated with NRI at a clinic in Elkton, MD, in the mid-1960s is typical of those who have contacted him. Doctors said tissue that had returned after a tonsillectomy and adenoidectomy was exacerbating his asthma, so they recommended nasal radium. He thought nothing of the treatments until Johns Hopkins University Hospital notified him in 1976 as part of a study on increased risk for thyroid cancer among people who had received radiation to the head, neck, or chest. As a Johns Hopkins patient for endocrine problems, his records were already on file. A thyroid scan showed some irregularities, and surgery revealed a disease called Hashimoto's thyroiditis, an autoimmune disorder of the thyroid gland, which doctors said could well be traced to NRI.

In 1995, Rushton found a malignant lump on his neck, later diagnosed as non-Hodgkin's lymphoma. He had six months of chemotherapy and remains cancer-free, but he worries constantly about the disease returning. His oncologist at the University of Pennsylvania thought the disease was likely traceable to the childhood radiation. "I'm not a fearful man, but health problems have dogged me my whole life. I'm not saying they're all tied to NRI, but when even your doctors wonder, you sure do, too," Rushton says. He also suffers from a glandular problem in his leg that doctors link to his lymphoma.

Rushton has read a great deal about the treatments, and follows each developmental blip carefully. He is puzzled by authorities now telling him not to worry about longitudinal studies about NRI, when in 1976 officials at Johns Hopkins had the wherewithal to contact him about his risk for thyroid cancer. "I was just shy of 18 and I've thought about it every day since."

While they cope with dire diagnoses—Graves's disease

here, cancerous thyroid cells there—those in Farber's network also battle rage. On a message board Farber established for those who had the treatments, notes are often darkly despondent. "Still angry after 40 years," reads one. "I hated that dr. . . . [when he died] I felt no sympathy for this miserable piece of trash of a man. I still have nightmares." Another man, just learning of his risks from press reports, writes: "Even as a child I wondered why the doctor who gave me the treatments had to leave the room due to excess radium exposure, when I was the one lying there with the rods up my nose."[7] Many on the board lionize Farber, and there is a floating suggestion that he receive a grant or award—some kind of national recognition—for his efforts. None of it gives Farber any comfort. "I'm totally burnt out," he says. Frustrated, feeling abandoned by the scientific community, and bankrupt—the energy and time he had devoted to the subject left him more than $100,000 in debt—Farber persists, but is resigned to small victories.

Massachusetts alone took firm public action: in 1997, it became the first state in the nation to alert doctors to the risks associated with nasal radiation. The state Department of Public Health's advisory instructs doctors to perform "thorough head and neck examinations" on patients who say they've had the treatment and to report any apparent health effects to the state. It is the strongest step yet taken in response to nasal radiation concerns.

Radiation facts and figures flow from Farber like batting averages from a baseball junkie. Former radiation workers at nuclear weapons facilities whose cancers are proven to be related to excess radiation exposure—in some cases, less than the standard safe limit presented by the CDC, five rads per year—are eligible for $150,000 lump-sum payments approved by Congress in 2001. "Compared to the 2,000 rads or more per nasal radium treatment, that's nothing!" he exclaims.

In 1996, Farber began gathering research for attorneys who were interested in filing suits on behalf of NRI patients, but soon, the case looked hopeless. The Radium Chemical Company, plagued by its own environmental and legal troubles, was defunct. Johns Hopkins, another possible defendant, was seemingly bulletproof: Since nasal radium was accepted treatment at the time, proving private negligence would be nearly impossible. And because the CDC had dismissed the issue, attorneys had little confidence that they could prove long-term damage. Farber throws up his hands. "They all said it was a legal morass," he says.

He had high hopes for a doctoral thesis published by a Johns Hopkins researcher in 1997. In it, Jessica H.C. Yeh surveyed patients treated with NRI by Johns Hopkins physicians at a Maryland clinic between 1940 and 1960. Her findings linked cancer and NRI even more dramatically than the Sandler study.

The study was reported in the *American Journal of Epidemiology* in 2001. But the abstract highlights the low rate of reproductive cancers rather than its central discovery: the significant increased risk of other cancers as well as benign tumors. Yeh found that the risk of developing brain tumors, both malignant and benign, was thirty times greater for those exposed to nasal radiation. The risk of salivary gland tumors was fourteen times greater. Irradiated women had a lower, but not statistically significant, incidence of breast and female genital cancers, suggesting damage to the pituitary gland resulting in a reduced level of hormones and a delayed menarche. In addition, thyroid cancer was also four times more common among those who had had the treatments than those who had not, but according to Yeh, that figure is not statistically significant. The dissertation studied 2,925 patients; 904 had received the nasal radium; the remaining 2,021 had not. "This study alone cannot provide conclusive evidence of the causal relationship between [nasal] radiation and cancers," wrote Yeh. "Nevertheless, along with similar observations from other studies, such a conclusion is reasonable."

To Farber, the paper was a smoking gun. Extrapolated to the entire treated population, he says, over 10,000 excess brain cancers or brain tumors are likely among 1 million treated children.

Yeh does not agree. Because the treatments were variable, and were given at different intervals and at different lengths of time, she says, one can't assess the risk for those who got the treatment outside the clinic she surveyed. "But I agree that these studies suggest that something is probably going on with the treatment," she adds.

How widespread is the problem? That remains to be determined. Most distressing is the failure to be more careful regarding exposure of young children to the ill-understood effects of radiation. As Dan Guttman, the former executive director of ACHRE, asks, "Were these researchers sufficiently cautious as they began their work with children? It's a tough call."

By today's standards of informed medical consent, nasal radium irradiation would be regarded as a flagrant abuse of trust.

Not surprisingly, the CDC has preferred to sweep doubts about the procedure away, confining its warnings and assistance to the squeaky wheel of veterans' groups. And the government hasn't seemed to help matters with its unusual steps—acknowledging risks of the treatment for veterans, underrating them for civilians.

But much remains the same. It took the Food and Drug Administration until 1998 to require drug manufacturers to provide information about how their drugs can safely and effectively be used on children. Testing drugs on children is more complicated than on adults; they often metabolize or absorb drugs at a different rate, and suitable doses are therefore difficult to estimate. Still, they are prescribed medications for a host of illnesses—including nasal disease. Children over four are routinely prescribed antihistamines and nasal steroids.

Farber, of course, is deeply cynical about this chapter of dubious medicine, as well as the climate in which it took place—and now continues. If the medical establishment could successfully "spin" past treatments, he wonders, what prevents them from doing the same with those being offered now? "Today's research institutions are no different from the government during the Cold War," he says ominously. Surely, the back-and-forth about treatments for conditions from back pain (surgery is the answer; surgery is not the answer) to cancer (early mammograms save lives; early mammograms are a waste of time) do give one reason to lack confidence, even in an era of increased accountability and openness. "Nothing has changed," he says.

But from the nose's perch, at least, something did change. By the end of the twentieth century, the idea of the nose as a problem to be solved was joined by the notion of exploiting it—as a resource, as a key to understanding the brain, and as a commercial tool.

*Part Two*

# *The Nose and Modern Science*

*f i v e*

# What Smells?

". . . the nose acts always as a sentinel and cries,
'Who goes there?' "

—Brillat-Savarin

By the late twentieth century, researchers had begun to have some clearer idea of how the nose worked, and how everything from viruses to vicious odors could attack it. The mechanism was one that could scarcely have been appreciated by early pioneers in the field. In order to understand how we smell, scientists first had to understand the molecular workings of the brain itself.

A cramped lab at Columbia University's medical school is home to many of the most crucial findings. In an office high above Manhattan's Washington Heights, tiny white mice—tomorrow's experiments—squeal in cages, and young doctoral students rush past each other in the halls with frenetic urgency.

It is a muggy day in late summer, and from the sliver of the window, you can see the steel magnificence of the George Washington Bridge. Dr. Richard Axel, a tall, terse molecular biologist and biophysicist who directs the lab, chain-chews Nicorette as he glides purposefully through the corridor.

A decade ago, Axel and his colleague Linda Buck discovered that as much as 3 percent of the human genome—an extraordinary figure—is devoted to identifying odors. Humans can detect up to 10,000 different odors, which we achieve by having 1,000 different protein receptors—each of which requires a gene to encode it. (There are an estimated 30,000–100,000 genes in the human genome.) Recent estimates show that humans have roughly 5 million olfactory receptor cells, about as many as a mouse. A rat has some 10 million, a rabbit 20 million, and a bloodhound, which can track scents for longer distances than most mammals, has as many as 220 million.

Many human olfactory genes are more than 10 million years old. Some scientists suggest that not all of them function today (one estimate is 400). Our prehistoric ancestors relied on odors to live, but as the intense need for smelling faded over time, some of the genes mutated. Today many of them contain major defects, but are still recognized as olfactory genes.

Axel wanders throughout the lab with a menacing scowl, checking his breast pocket for his blister pack of gum. After a brief meeting—he makes clear he has little patience for writers—he asks his graduate students to show me something "little" and "pretty." Joseph Gogos, a thirty-eight-year-old geneticist and neurologist from Athens, looks up from his lens, and motions me to approach him. He has thick dark hair that is threaded with gray. "Do not pay attention to him," he says with a shy smile. "No one is smart enough for him." (Such a declaration is hardly reassuring: Gogos earned his M.D. from one of the world's oldest medical schools, at the National University of Greece in Athens, and got his Ph.D. from Harvard.)

When he talks about the olfactory bulb of mice, Gogos speaks so quickly he drops Greek words into his sentences. "Look!" he shouts, instructing me to peer into the scope. "Isn't it just beautiful?" Before me, on a slide smeared with formaldehyde, is a slice of a mouse's olfactory bulb—a dirty white triangle spattered with jagged blue lines. Dozens of the turquoise scrawls end in a single point, resembling lightning that has been captured on film.

The lines are neurons leading from the animal's nose to its olfactory bulb—a "map" discovered by Axel and Buck that highlights the first step of the olfactory process. By tracing the path of these neurons, they discovered that those responsible for a single type of odor molecule reached a single point in the olfactory bulb. "Isn't it amazing?" Gogos asks quietly.

On a yellow legal pad, Gogos depicts what happens when an odor molecule hurtles through the air, the nose, and finally the brain. He draws concentric circles: the nose, the olfactory cortex, the brain, and the human head. Beneath them, he sketches a square Chanel bottle.

When we smell perfume, odor molecules from the liquid bind to receptors on a dime-sized patch of tissue at the very top of the nose called the olfactory epithelium. The receptors are part of neurons that extend three to four centimeters from the epithelium to the brain. Unlike other neurons, which are encased in the skull, those in the olfactory epithelium are exposed

Gabrielle Glaser

to the air we inhale. While there is significant scientific debate about whether or not brain cells regenerate, researchers agree that olfactory neurons replace themselves every two months or so. A layer of stem cells beneath them creates new olfactory neurons, maintaining a healthy supply.

Each olfactory neuron in the nose has a long fiber, or axon, that pushes through a tiny space in the bone above it, the cribriform plate. There, it makes a connection with other neurons in the olfactory bulbs, two cylinders about the width of a pencil that rest behind the gap in the eyebrows. Like a telephone switching point, the olfactory bulbs are the site of key connections; from there, impulses are relayed to the brain's limbic system, which governs emotions, sexuality, and drive, and the hippocampus, which is thought to encode the information into memory. Connections between the olfactory bulb and the neocortex, the part of the brain responsible for thoughts, language, and behaviors, are thought to be more circuitous.

The neurons are placed randomly throughout the epithelium. Yet when the axons reach the olfactory bulbs, those that picked up a signal from the same receptor converge on the same place in the olfactory bulb—the tiny blue point I saw in the slide.

Most odors consist of mixtures of different molecules, meaning that the brain "reads" different odors by the receptors it sets off. "The neurons tell the brain, 'I see something at point A, point G, point X,'" Gogos says. "Then the brain does the calculation—'if it's A, G, and X, it must be garlic.' This means that the chaos we have in everyday life—all the smells around us— are actually regimented and organized in the brain." We know the pattern of the taste buds lining the tongue—salty and sweet in front, sour on the sides, bitter in the back. Odors reach the brain with a similar structure.

A few months later, we trudged through dirty piles of snow to an overheated café. When the door opened onto the cold street, a rush of odors hit us: ginger, cinnamon, tea, coffee—a perfect mix for Gogos to discuss. "We always use this imagery to describe it, but it seems to work: olfaction is like a lock and a key. The receptor is the lock, and it can be activated by a specific key whose shape fits into the lock's. That lock is a protein with a specific shape and distribution of charged molecules. So different protein receptors can only be matched to different odors. When an odor fits into the right receptor, that protein in turn processes the cell—and that sends messages to the brain that it has 'smelled.'

"A single scent is made up of more than one type of molecule—sometimes even dozens. You might imagine that for every odor molecule, there may be a different receptor, determined by specific genes. But this would be impossible—the brain would do nothing but detect odors! The brain only remembers ones it needed in order to survive, to evolve. That means we keep track of things like ripening food, poisons, mates we respond to."

Each olfactory receptor has the ability within it to bind with several odor molecules. Conversely, each odor molecule has the ability to bind with a range of potential receptors. The intensity of the binding, Gogos says, varies, depending on the quality of the fit. (In fact, each of your nostrils also detects odors differently. This may in part answer why we have two nostrils in the first place—to add to the brain's stereo perception of scent.)

Outside, a mutt sniffs the steel pole of a parking meter, and

Gogos waves toward it. "Most animals are more sensitive to smells than humans, but the brains of all mammals work exactly the same way," he says. Like the blue-tinted signals that fired to the mouse's brain, the dog's brain is being "unlocked" by odor molecules left behind by another dog. "We may think that animals are more in tune to odors, but humans are pretty sensitive to them too. We just stand on two feet, away from most odors. Odor molecules are heavy, and the farther up you go, the fewer there are. The most interesting odors float just above ground. You can see this with dogs and cats—they sniff the ground when they're trying to catch a scent. Our ancestors probably did that, too. Smell itself is a very elegant and orderly process, but somehow the ideas and images that surround it are exactly the opposite."

Darwin, in fact, theorized that the relatively large visual cortex in primates had superseded the olfactory cortex, which had withered over time. He and other scholars believed that our upright posture, which allowed for better visualization of our surroundings, diminished the necessity of detecting odors. Likewise, Freud suggested that our bipedalism was the triumph of sight over smell. And as recently as 1981, the Norwegian neuroscientist Alf Brodal wrote ". . . the sense of smell is of relatively minor importance in the normal life of civilized man."[1] The concept that smell is important, even integral, to our knowledge of the brain—of life—is a new development.

Until the 1980s, scientists say, research involving smell was viewed by many as marginal, even frivolous. "You cannot imagine the reactions you'd get twenty years ago when you'd tell people you were a grown man who studied the sense of smell," says William Cain, an environmental psychologist who specializes in olfaction at the University of California at San Diego School of Medicine. "People just looked at you in disbelief," he says. "You'd have to explain it, spell it out. 'Olfaction. It's the science of smelling.'" Yet today, the number of olfactory scientists who work in academic research, the fragrance industry, or both (often, large companies such as Proctor and Gamble or Nabisco fund research) has risen dramatically from the ranks of just a decade ago.

For example, Monell Chemical Senses Center, founded at the University of Pennsylvania in Philadelphia in 1968 as an institute for multidisciplinary research on taste, smell, and chemosensory irritation, has trained more than 370 scientists. The researchers work in government, industry, and academia in areas as diverse as waste management and fragrance development.

Since 1980, the National Institutes of Health has more than quadrupled its funding for research in olfaction, which went from $4.3 million in 1980 to $25.7 million in 1999.[2] Meanwhile, membership in the Association for Chemoreception Sciences, an organization of researchers from neurologists to zoologists who are involved with taste and smell, has risen from some three hundred a decade ago, to 650 in 2001.[3]

The progression of how the brain turns odor molecules into smells seems straightforward, but research efforts aside, Gogos and other scientists caution that the picture is—as yet, anyway—incomplete. "We don't know all the answers," Gogos shrugs. "It's not like Greek runners dashing through the brain with an odor molecule as their baton," he says.

The brain's pathways are still only partially deciphered; no one is sure how one part communicates with others. But by studying how olfactory neurons make connections with other neurons in the brain, researchers hope they can identify how nerve fibers connect elsewhere, and may point to ways of making neurons regrow in other parts of the nervous system. Researchers are also studying how receptors respond to different odors, which may lead to treatments for people in whom age, disease, or other factors have destroyed or damaged the sense of smell.

While researchers understand some stages of how the brain perceives odors, others remain mysteries. For example, what happens to information about smells after it has made its way from the olfactory bulb to the olfactory cortex? How does the brain process that information? And how does it reach the higher brain centers, in which information about smells is linked to behavior? Researchers in Miami found that adults who sniffed lavender before and after tackling simple math problems worked faster, felt more relaxed, and made fewer mistakes than those exposed to other odors. And in one small British study, elderly insomniacs who sniffed lavender before going to bed fell asleep sooner—and stayed asleep longer—than those using sedatives.

But because the human brain is so complex, many researchers look to animals for answers. John Kauer, a neuroscientist at Tufts Medical School and New England Medical Center in Boston uses the salamander's nasal cavity—a flattened sac beneath the skull—to analyze the entire olfactory system, from the first olfactory neurons to how odors affect behavior. The sac can be opened easily, providing access to olfactory neurons. Kauer devised an optical recording system in order to make observations with dyes and video cameras instead of probes. With it, Kauer says, you can actually watch the brain as olfactory perception takes place.

Research on smell is, of course, far from simply research on smell. As it turns out, the receptors used to detect odors are closely related to the protein receptors in our brains that recognize neurotransmitters such as serotonin and dopamine—those responsible for our emotional well-being. Genes much like those for odor receptors may, it is thought, control other types of chemical sensing, such as the ability of sperm to locate an egg. Similar receptors also may function in a special structure in the nose called the vomeronasal organ. They help to detect special chemical signals called pheromones, which regulate hormone release, mating, and social functions in animals—and possibly in humans. "Learning about how odors affect us isn't simply learning about how odors affect us," says William Cain. "It's learning about how we live."

Scientists say that one of the most complicated and challenging aspects of research on smell is assessing how, in humans, the sense interacts with reasoning and emotion—and how those, in turn, affect smell.

Our ability to detect scent is the most ancient sense. Even the most primitive organisms had an olfactory system that detected food, poison, and predators. Imagine the brain as an archeological site, with three layers. The oldest part, the brain stem, is sometimes called the "reptilian" layer, the remains of our days as amphibians. It controls basic functions like heart rate, digestion, and breathing, and it is also the main channel for sensory and motor signals. Built like a thick stalk, the brain stem originates in the spinal cord and reaches up to the next layer, the limbic system, which encases the amygdala, two almond-sized organs largely responsible for feelings and temperament. In a bow to its close connection to smell, the limbic system was originally called the "rhinencephalon," literally, the "nose-brain." The neocortex, the newest part of the brain, is the outer two-thirds of the organ; language and reasoning are processed here. The early brain's ability to decode smell, in fact, helped spawn our ability to feel and rationalize. As the poet Diane Ackerman wrote, "We think because we smelled."

But smelling something, or thinking about it, doesn't mean we can describe it. In fact, most people can scarcely even characterize what they smell. When sniffing, say, a jar of peanut butter, sweaters stored in a mothball-filled trunk, or a charcoal grill on a hot July afternoon, people are apt to turn the noun they're smelling into an adjective. Peanut butter smells . . . nutty. The sweaters? Stuffy—mothbally. The grill, for my husband, summoned the following depiction: "Acrid? Sweet? Hot?" Ask a person to describe his or her worst blind date, or even fish they saw while scuba diving, and get an animated recall: a stubbly goatee, neon green scales. With smells, however, even the most articulate among us become tongue-tied.

For years, scientists attributed this to the lack of "wiring" between the part of the brain that recognizes odor and that which processes language. Another common belief was that smell had a greater influence on emotions than other senses because of the olfactory cortex's proximity to the limbic system. New technologies that allow scientists to glimpse the brain at work have challenged those views, which date to the 1930s and 1940s. Using equipment such as functional magnetic resonance imaging (fMRI), which provides a continuous picture of brain activity, and evoked potentials, a test which charts the electrical activity of the brain with electrodes, researchers have documented interactions between the olfactory cortex and other parts of the brain.

Tyler Lorig, a psychologist at Washington and Lee University in Lexington, Virginia, has been searching for the external manifestations of those connections for twenty years. A soft-spoken man with a salt-and-pepper beard and a gentle Georgia drawl, Lorig spends his days in his lab, "thinking about smelling." He believes that one reason we are at such a loss to describe smells is because the brain's mechanisms for odor compete, quite literally, for brain power—especially that used for language. "They actually interfere with each other when they are simultaneously processed," Lorig says.

"Picture the brain like an orchestra, with a trumpet section, violins, clarinets—the works. When you tell the brain to both simultaneously smell and describe that smell, it's like telling the violins to play two different melodies at once," he says. "You can get by, but the performance is degraded."

Lorig believes the phenomenon is rooted in part in industrialized Western society simply not "developing" its sense of smell. Even the English verb "to smell" is imprecise. It is both transitive and intransitive; a person can simultaneously smell bad and smell something bad. Other cultures, and thus their languages, treat scent differently. Some traditional societies, such as the Kapsiki of Nigeria and Cameroon, have specific vocabularies to describe odors, from "old grain" to "white millet beer." Likewise, the Desana of Colombia have odor hierarchies for "bland" and "strong" smells.[4]

Yet many Westerners struggle to describe the nuances of odor. The notion that culture holds our olfactory capabilities back is clear in the case of Stephen D., a young medical student the neurologist Oliver Sacks describes in *The Man Who Mistook His Wife for a Hat*. One night, Stephen dreamt he was a dog. The dream was so redolent with aromas that upon waking Stephen actually smelled with a perception he had never experienced. He found himself sniffing perfumes in fragrance shops, and recognizing friends and patients by their scents. Even days afterward, he was finding his way around Manhattan by odors, like a German shepherd.

Sacks attributes the heightened awareness—disinhibition, he calls it—to the drugs Stephen regularly took, likely amphetamines. And indeed, three weeks after his unusual ability to smell appeared, it waned just as startlingly. "That smell-world, that world of redolence," Stephen exclaims. "So vivid, so real! It was . . . a world of pure perception, rich, alive, self-sufficient, and full. If only I could go back sometimes and be a dog again!"[5]

In a society dedicated to the suppression and eradication of odors, it is little wonder that we lack a rich lexicon for what we try to abolish. Experts in the fragrance industry—known straightforwardly as noses—can distinguish minute changes in thousands of odors in devising new perfumes. Yet such sensibilities are far from the norm. While most humans are capable of identifying and labeling odors—the perfume industry alone channels $6 billion through the U.S. economy—they are rarely encouraged to exercise their sense of smell.

Lorig points to himself as a perfect example. "For twenty years I've been around smell labs and ideas and theories about odors. I've tested my sense of smell dozens of times, and the truth is, I'm average.[6] But because I'm accustomed to smells, and identifying them, I've gotten pretty good at being able to label them. It's all part of a larger question about smell. There are people who can perceive odors with more precision than others, sure. But the truth is, noses at perfume houses and vineyards are simply above average—they're not off-the-charts in terms of their abilities. What's different about them is that they *use* their abilities better. Was Michael Jordan always destined to be the greatest basketball player? Well, that depends. He had the raw talent, but he also put it to use. It's the same thing with people in this line of work—if you're going to come up with new scents, you have to have a good nose. You can't have an anosmic putting together perfumes. But it's also what you do with what nature gives you, how you develop it."

A glance at our "olfactory education"—this is what researchers like Cain and Lorig call it—shows that the chances of developing that are slim. Toddlers don't sit in front of games that waft odors—they learn to distinguish triangles from squares, moos from barks. Kindergartners don't differentiate between rose petals and lily of the valley; they learn the alphabet and musical notes. "When a kid goes around sniffing something, the parent doesn't say, 'Oh, good boy, Johnny, you're picking up on odors!' " Lorig says. "The parent says things like, 'That's not polite.' Somehow, we get the message early on that our sense of smell is primal—too primal for polite society." The result, Lorig says, is a fundamental portion of the brain that science—and possibly even learning—have overlooked.

Lorig's research underscores how humans repress their awareness of odors. In one recent study, he and his colleagues told ninety-three subjects that the experiment in which they were about to participate was designed to "evaluate the effects of sensory conditions on their judgments about art." Yet only three subjects noticed that odor was involved in the experiment—despite the strong smell of lavender or vanilla emanating from behind the slide projector. One participant in the vanilla room said she thought lighting levels were being manipulated—then told researchers she felt like going back to her dorm "to bake some cookies."

"When I heard her say that, a big old smile just crossed my face," Lorig recalls. "I just knew she had to be in the vanilla room. But the real question is this: why does the brain play down this information? What's going on?" One possible explanation could be the space and time at which the brain "received" the message. Perhaps the student was concentrating on the colors on the screen, and the odor molecules from the vanilla reached her just as she was trying to decide what to say about the artwork. "It could be simply that the brain experiences a temporal overlap—it's trying to do two things at once, and can't."

In another experiment, Lorig and his researchers compared the brain's electrical responses to odors and tones. All stimuli, whether delivered through sight, smell, taste, hearing, or touch, evoke minute electrical signals, which travel along nerves and through the spinal cord to specific regions of the brain; electrodes attached to the scalp register the data.

The researchers asked the subjects' ability to judge the size of objects, words, and numbers that flashed on a screen as odors and then tones were piped into the lab. Electrical impulses were collected as the subjects calculated whether the item on-screen was larger than its predecessor.

The researchers found that when the tone was played, the brain's electrical activity was similar, whether the image was displaying a thing, a word, or a number. But when odor was introduced, pictures had a different effect than words or numbers. "We don't know why, but the brain would then go about making the decision in a different way—activity would shift. It didn't disrupt the ability to finish the task, but it did alter the impulse that went together to complete it."

Does this study explain how some people can "block" out foul odors? On the commuter train that takes people from my suburb to Manhattan, I am always amazed that anyone can sit in the same car as the grungy bathroom, let alone right outside it. Yet people plunk right down without seeming to notice. Once I had a dermatologist's appointment in a building a few floors up from a Chinese restaurant. I walked in, sat down, picked up a magazine, and was so repulsed by the odor of old fried shrimp that I just couldn't bear to be there (although arguably I was not eager to have a wart burned off my foot). The doctor was forty-five minutes late, so eventually I feigned indignation about the fact that civilians have schedules, too, and left. But the truth is that I was too embarrassed to say that the place reeked—it seemed unduly insulting to the poor receptionist. Yet the waiting room was full.

Studies indicate that, depending on a person's view of a particular odor, he or she may become temporarily desensitized to it. In other words, if you are a hog farmer who makes a living selling pork meat, or work for a nice dermatologist who pays you generously but who happens to be upstairs from a smelly take-out place, chances are that, in time, you will become habituated to offending odors. "Your 'baggage' about a certain scent will influence how your brain reacts to it," says Charles Wysocki, an anatomist and psychobiologist at the Monell Chemical Senses Center in Philadelphia. If you're a trash collector, over time the brain may well "learn" that the scent of rotting garbage is not harmful. (The same effect holds true for perfume counter employees.) Since one of olfaction's biggest functions is to sniff out danger, the brain may simply set up "filters," Wysocki says, that let that malodorous information pass right through, unnoticed. If, on the other hand, you live downwind of the hog farm, and are convinced that it's the cause of your headaches, you may find it impossible to ignore.

But how does this explain the people who sit next to the bathroom? Is it poor acuity? Or a good ability to block out negative sensory information?

"That's one of the great unanswered questions about smell," Lorig says. "We just don't know how odors—good or bad—affect concentration." When odors are introduced while subjects are reading, they are barely noticed. It is as if their channel to the cortex is blocked by attention to reading. This is one of the reasons why I think constant exposure to a smell doesn't interrupt cognitive processes. In our experiments, we irregularly presented very short bursts of odors. We didn't give people a chance to get used to the odor so each time the odor came in, they had to deal with it. That's why I think we saw a change in the way the brain processed the nouns. If we had done the experiment with constant odors, I don't think we'd see a difference."

Lorig acknowledges that scientists' understanding of these issues is in its infancy, but is confident the brain will someday yield its secrets. When it does, he says, the current state of understanding will be seen as cartoonish. "We'll look at this and think 'Man, we were using leeches,'" Lorig says. "But that's the only way to get from here to there."

There is almost certainly a connection between how mankind evolved and the effect smells have on brain functioning, but it remains unclear what was cause, and what was effect. "Since so much of human behavior, and arguably all cognition, is filtered through language, our limited language for odors may be a cause of our disregard of this sense rather than an effect of our getting our noses off the ground," Lorig says. "Maybe it even worked the other way: standing on two feet reduced the olfactory information load and allowed language to flourish. Either way, odor and language don't seem to work together."

One clue to the centrality of brain activity and olfaction is that aging and many neurodegenerative disorders have a measurable impact on the sense of smell. "We're not sure why smell deteriorates with age, but pictures of the brains of older people show atrophy of the olfactory bulb and some reduction of the receptors," says William Cain.

As researchers study smell and aging, several truths have emerged, Cain says. Age takes a much greater toll on smell than on taste. Women at all ages are generally more accurate than men in identifying odors. Smoking can adversely affect the ability of both men and women to identify odors. Although certain medications can cause smell and taste problems, others—notably antihistamines—seem to improve the senses of smell and taste, he says.

Viral infections, sinusitis, and certain medications can impair your sense of smell, as well as tobacco smoke and other irritants. Workers exposed to harsh chemicals, such as those in paper mills and chemical manufacturing industries, often have compromised olfactory ability. Hunting dog pens are warned not to clean the close quarters of dog pens with harsh cleaning products, for fear of damaging the dog's ability to pick up scent. Dairy and livestock farmers also risk numbing their sense of smell: constant exposure to the urine and gases from manure can diminish sensitivity.

People with certain neurological disorders, such as Parkinson's and Alzheimer's, also suffer smell loss. Of all the indignities of Alzheimer's—and they are legion—perhaps most striking is the frightened confusion of those stricken with the disease. Words become impossible to summon. Sounds are threatening. Faces of friends and relatives, some beloved for a half-century, are as indistinct as blurry crowd photographs. Odors, too, are lost.

In a study at Columbia University, researchers administered a standard smell identification test to seventy-seven people with mild cognitive impairment (MCI) whose symptoms also included moderate memory loss. Studies have shown that people with MCI develop Alzheimer's at a higher-than-average rate, and researchers hoped that the test might be a valuable early detection test. Test subjects were given cards scented with familiar odors such as menthol and peanuts, and were scored on how well they could identify those odors. Two years after taking the test, those who had scored lowest were much more likely to develop symptoms of the disease than those who scored higher.

Proust wrote that when nothing else exists from the past, after people are dead and objects are broken or lost, "the smell and taste of things remain poised a long time, like souls bearing resiliently, on tiny and almost impalpable drops of their essence, the immense edifice of memory." Now, too, it turns out, Alzheimer's strips us even of the core human perception of smell.


## The Nose and Sex

Because modern science of the nose is so new, there is, as one might expect, a great deal of controversy among researchers. While the work of Axel and Buck is universally acknowledged as fact, many who work to decipher the inner workings of the nose have received far less recognition for their labors. Some, for instance, work to solve mysteries such as anosmia, the inability to smell, but are seen as downright quacks. Yet no few millimeters of nasal tissue stirs controversy quite like the vomeronasal organ, or VNO, which some say detects pheromones.

David Berliner, an anatomist, tends to be controversial. As a young professor at the University of Utah in the 1960s, Berliner worked with substances he had found in human skin. In those days, skin cells were plentiful in Salt Lake City, surrounded as it is by ski resorts—and grounded skiers with broken limbs. Dead skin accumulated in plaster casts in such abundance that, at least to Berliner, it seemed a natural thing to study. So he leached some of the cells and put them in solvents. To his surprise, when he left some of the extracts in open vials around the lab, he noticed a sudden—and puzzling—rise in camaraderie among a group of coworkers. Normally, they snapped at each other, and ate their sandwiches hunched over papers in their cubicles. Yet when the liquid skin extracts were left out in the open, Berliner's colleagues suddenly laughed, joked, ate lunch together, and even played bridge. Strange, Berliner thought, as he observed the group. Some months later, he put the containers away, and the group became churlish again.

Researchers had just begun to identify pheromones (the word is derived from the Greek *pherein*, "to transfer" and *horman*, "excitement") in creatures ranging from ants to elephants. Berliner theorized that the extracts contained pheromones, chemicals given off by insects and mammals that affect only others of the same species. In many species they reach the brain by way of the VNO, which transmits signals to the brain.

Berliner became convinced of the importance of pheromones in human behavior. Other research on the topic was proving intriguing. In the 1970s a Wellesley undergraduate named Martha McClintock observed that many women in her college dormitory had synchronized menstrual periods, and documented the phenomenon in her senior thesis. At the same time, Winnifred Cutler, a biologist and behavioral endocrinologist, was finding that women with active sex lives have more regular menstrual cycles than those with only sporadic sexual encounters. Both researchers believed pheromones played a role in their findings.

The VNO and pheromones had been discussed in scientific literature since the early eighteenth century, when a Dutch doctor named Frederick Ruysch identified the human VNO, a bilateral pea-sized cavity lodged in the nasal septum. In modern times, though, scientists assumed that it had become useless, like the appendix, with no apparent function. Chemical communication in the animal world is complex and varied; many mammals can detect pheromones and other signals through their glands, urine, and saliva, as well as the VNO, which is connected to parts of the brain involved in reactions rather than cognition. But in humans, the links from the VNO to the brain, and behavior, are much less clear.

For decades after her groundbreaking thesis, McClintock, now a psychologist at the University of Chicago, devoted her research to identifying the mechanism behind the timing of the menstrual cycles. She and others believed that pheromones were the cause, but evidence was elusive. Berliner, who shortly after his stint in Utah left research behind for commerce, had put his curiosity about the substances on hold. As a Silicon Valley venture capitalist in the early 1990s, Berliner still dreamed of bridging the gap between business and academe, and the possible role of (and market for) human pheromones. By then, the human nose was attracting attention both in science and the marketplace. Fragrance, and its emphasis on sexuality, was ubiquitous. So was talk of animal pheromones. In the mid-1980s, researchers using an electron microscope discovered the existence of the human VNO in more than two hundred adult subjects. New findings on animal pheromones were being published all the time. One study showed that a male pig breathes a chemical called androstenol into a sow's face; she then spreads her legs so the male can mount her. Queen bees use pheromones to thwart the sexual maturity of female worker bees, and animals from crabs to marmosets release pheromones to mark their territory.

Finally, Berliner thought, the time was right for a look into the extracts he had saved and frozen from the Utah lab—the memory of experience had left a lasting impression. "The change in attitudes and emotions of my colleagues was extraordinary, it was impossible to forget. I kept coming back to it," he says in his Spanish-accented English. The son of Eastern European Jews who emigrated to Mexico, Berliner had a unique childhood. He was surrounded by independent thinkers, writers, and artists; Diego Rivera and Frida Kahlo were often guests in his parents' home. A signed Rivera print— "To David"—hangs prominently in the entranceway of Berliner's Menlo Park office. Huge pink oleander blossoms wave outside his window.

The more scientific papers he read, the more Berliner was convinced that humans responded to pheromones as well. Was it possible that the skin of certain people emitted a substance that could alter the moods of others, he wondered? Berliner reasoned that the centimeter-long VNO acted as a sensor for airborne human pheromones. As in animals, he thought, the VNO provided the pheromone molecules a direct line to the hypothalamus. Though tiny, the size of an unshelled peanut, the hypothalamus has many functions: it regulates body temperature, blood pressure, heartbeat, appetite, thirst, the metabolism of fats and carbohydrates, and sugar levels in the blood. As part of the limbic system, the hypothalamus is also thought to be the principal site for emotions such as fear, joy, and anger, as well as sexual behaviors. Structurally, it is joined to the thalamus; the two work together to monitor the sleep-wake cycle.

But while the VNO is clearly present in the human fetus, it has significantly atrophied in size even by the time a baby reaches full term. Many scholars questioned its function. Humans still have wisdom teeth, but that doesn't mean they need them. Still, Berliner was determined, and enlisted colleagues back in Utah to investigate his skin extracts, among them Luis Monti-Bloch, a Uruguayan neuroscientist at the university.

Monti-Bloch, an elegant, soft-spoken man in his early fifties, measured electrical activity in VNO tissue in response to chemical stimulation. While fragrant compounds produced no electrical effect from the VNO, Berliner's skin extract, on the other hand, made it activate. Berliner and Monti-Bloch isolated a substance from the skin of males they called androstadienone. When they applied the substance to the VNOs of women, the women showed signs of being more relaxed: they experienced a decrease in their heart and breathing rates, and their body temperatures rose. The team was thrilled. This, Berliner says, likely explained the experience in the Utah lab. (A similar substance, estratetraenol, extracted from the skin of women, was also identified.)

I visited Monti-Bloch at a Utah lab on a cold February day in 2000. The lab, sequestered in a Salt Lake City office park at the foot of the Wasatch Mountains, seems an unlikely place for unlocking the mysteries of sex and desire. The conservative center

of the Mormon universe is better known for its choir and caf-
feine-free living than for its exploration of human appetites.

"The VNO is truly the body's sixth sense," Monti-Bloch says,
pointing to an enlarged picture of the organ on his desk. "It's
right here," he says excitedly, "right here, in almost everyone."
The organ can be inadvertently removed during nasal operations. I mention that I've had four sinus surgeries. "I hope its
still there," he says. "Let's take a look." He gestures to an examining table, and I hop up onto it. A graduate student from
Mexico looks on, and Monti-Bloch peers into my nose with a
tiny scope. "It's there!" he exclaims. "You have it!"

What a relief. But I knew I hadn't lost my sixth sense. Once,
on a near-empty train from Baltimore to New York, I moved
away from a man, who, an hour later, raped a woman in the
bathroom. Another time, I stood on the landing of my apart-
ment, which looked absolutely normal. But I somehow knew
that I had been burgled. Something told me to put down my
keys and find a neighbor before going in. I tell Monti-Bloch of
these episodes. He informs me that my VNO was picking up on
pheromones, and that I reacted. Pheromone researchers are
deluged with tales like mine. One Pennsylvania woman, who
had tried for years in vain to have a child, experienced pregnancy symptoms—and even tested positive on pregnancy
tests—when she had traveled, and roomed with, pregnant colleagues. Both times, she says, the women were so early in their
pregnancies they didn't yet know of their condition. Her doctors
were at a loss to explain it. Monti-Bloch, on the other hand,
thinks her VNO was picking up on pregnancy pheromones released through the other women's skin. "I cannot explain more,"

he says. "Just that it happened—and that there is so much more to learn."

Berliner believes that one reason mainstream scientists are skeptical of his work is because he became a millionaire in business, seeking profit from commerce rather than government grantsmanship. But now, he stands poised to get his due. Proof of human pheromones received a big boost when McClintock, the Chicago psychologist, published a 1998 paper showing definitively that women respond to the pheromones of other women. She took sweat samples from underarm pads worn by young women who had not yet ovulated that month, and wiped them on the upper lips of study subjects. The pads accelerated the surge of LH, or luteinizing hormone, which triggers ovulation, cutting the subjects' cycles by as much as two weeks. McClintock also found that subjects who were exposed to women who had already ovulated had their cycles delayed by as many as twelve days. (In men, LH stimulates testosterone. Researchers say that pheromones may explain why men find women who are mid-cycle—and most fertile—more attractive than during other times of the month.)

In 2000, neurogeneticists at Yale and Rockefeller University announced that they had found the first human gene associated with the function of pheromones. Researchers isolated a human gene, labeled V1RL1, they believe makes a pheromone receptor. Pheromones, they say, attach to this receptor when they are inhaled into the mucous lining in the nose.[7]

While many researchers say the report promises to settle the pheromone existence question once and for all, others still wonder. Catherine Dulac, a professor of molecular and cellular biology at Harvard, is also dubious. The brain might be subtly informed about the presence of pheromones, she says, but humans are so influenced by other stimuli—and experience—that the leap is just too big.

Meanwhile, Berliner continues to mine possible uses for synthetic pheromones, which he calls vomeropherins. He believes that the studies about pheromones and menstrual cycles suggest that vomeropherins might one day be used as fertility treatments for couples who want to conceive, or as contraceptives for those who don't. Couples who are having sexual problems might be able to use pheromones combined with traditional therapy to enhance desire. The Utah team, which also pours its efforts into developing these drugs for a company Berliner owns called Pherin Pharmaceuticals, are further convinced that vomeropherins can enhance mood, alleviating depression and anxiety. Berliner even thinks that the drugs could one day be used as a preventative for prostate cancer.

Large pharmaceutical companies are encouraged enough by the Utah lab's findings to support development of vomeropherins. Johnson & Johnson recently agreed to fund trials for two antianxiety agents—one for women, one for men. Berliner says the antianxiety agent works as a simple prophylactic. "If you have to give a speech, and are terrified of facing crowds, you sniff the drug and immediately feel better," he says. "The panic dissipates immediately." The synthetic pheromone is delivered in a nasal spray, sending signals to the hypothalamus to relax. Dosages are minute—mere picograms (one-billionth of a milligram)—and, because they are not ingested, have no toxic effects, Berliner says.

Another pheromone-based drug is aimed at helping women with PMS. That drug, funded by Organon, a Dutch pharmaceutical company that specializes in reproductive and psychiatric medications, is in Phase II trials. (The FDA has three categories for human drug trials, each used on wider numbers of people.) Once a drug succeeds in entering the marketplace, there's no telling how it will do financially. But the antidepressant Paxil, which is used by people who suffer from the same social phobias Berliner hopes vomeropherins can treat, had revenues of $1.9 billion in 2000.

A study performed by Martha McClintock and Suma Jacob added more weight—at least for women—to findings on androstadienone and estratetraenol, the substances produced by men and women, respectively. (In the paper, the researchers referred to the substances as steroids.)[8] The researchers used a series of psychological tests to assess both physical and mood changes in subjects after their exposure to each steroid. Both elicited an immediate, short-term positive mood in women, but a negative mood in men. Despite the clear sex differences in responses to steroids, the authors concluded that steroids are not able to trigger specific behaviors in humans. "It is premature to call these steroids human pheromones," the authors wrote, adding that they were nonetheless "psychologically potent"— and mandating future research into their actual function. Indeed, Jacob and McClintock went on to show that these compounds have widespread effects on the brain, even when they can't be detected as odors. "Clearly unconscious odors, if not pheromones, play a much bigger role than we thought."

But others see assurance in studies showing that we may

glean clues about the immune systems of potential mates through their odors—or perhaps odors packed with pheromones. (Some researchers believe that human armpits produce both in large quantities. Pheromones mix with sweat, evaporate, and float into the air if they aren't washed away.)

In the late 1990s, Carol Ober, a geneticist and gynecologist at the University of Chicago, concluded that women choose mates with genetic backgrounds different from their own. She theorized that the behavior tended to give their offspring a strong immune system.

Ober conducted a study of South Dakota Hutterites, a small, tight-knit religious community in the American Midwest and Canada who trace their ancestry to a handful of the faith's early followers in sixteenth-century Moravia. She wanted to examine their MHC, or major histocompatibility complex. Each person has a unique combination of MHC genes that encode various components of their immune system. The Hutterites are ideal for MHC study, since they marry only within their small community (the entire group, dispersed throughout the two countries, numbers only 35,000; Ober's research into their genome is ongoing). When they are of marriageable age, single men and women visit nearby Hutterite colonies, and meet potential spouses during holiday celebrations or farmwork. And since they don't use perfumes or deodorants, their odors—and pheromones—are in abundance.

Ober wondered if the Hutterites naturally chose partners with dissimilar MHC, and examined 411 couples drawn from thirty-one Hutterite colonies. While the genetic variation among the group was obviously limited, only forty-four couples, roughly 11 percent, matched for certain types of MHC. The chances of this happening randomly are only about 5 percent. Ober believes that the study's results show that MHC genes may actually influence mate choice.

Ober also found that those who had similar MHC tended to have longer periods between pregnancies and higher rates of miscarriage. Fetuses who receive the same MHC genes from each parent, Ober believes, may be more likely to abort, perhaps because of some unknown immunologic mechanism. The more varied a person's MHC, the more robust its immunity.

In similar research, in the mid-1990s Swiss zoologist Claus Wedekind sought to see if clues to genetic dissimilarity lay in body odor among forty-nine female subjects at the midpoint of their menstrual cycles, when olfaction is at its keenest. Then they were asked to sniff six sweaty T-shirts from male subjects. The women, who had given DNA samples, were asked to "rate" the T-shirts for intensity, sexiness, and pleasantness. Three T-shirts were from men whose MHC were similar to their own, and three from men who were less similar. Women found the odors of men who were genetically dissimilar more pleasant than those who were similar—unless the women were on birth control pills. When the women were on oral contraceptives, which can mimic the first trimester of pregnancy, they preferred the scent of men who were genetically linked to them. Wedekind says the results may indicate a throwback to ancient women, who relied on next-of-kin for protection during pregnancy. Pregnant women—and women whose bodies are tricked into thinking they're pregnant—might have the same tendency, Wedekind says.

Of course, humans make decisions about their mates based on a vast number of cues, from looks to financial security. Do the effects of the Pill really scramble normal signals of mate selection? "It's a reasonable question," says Monti-Bloch. "Whether it is sabotage to the reproductive system, is impossible to say."

But what is it that is actually attractive about odor—or pheromones—and what do they have to do with love and sex? Sweat glands in the armpit area are only active during the times in which the human being is capable of reproduction. They first kick in during puberty, and slow down during menopause. Researchers say it's no accident that during intercourse or even embracing the woman's head (and nose) are frequently near the man's armpit. Many say that this physical proximity is essential for the transmission of odors—and pheromones. (Heavy winter clothing obscures these signals, and the frequent scrubbing Americans generally do may wash them away altogether.)

Monti-Bloch believes another pheromone-rich site is the nasal groove that runs from the outside of the nostrils to the corners of the mouth. Kissing, he believes, is a ritual that developed to detect pheromones.

Whether synthetic pheromones alter the way we react to events and people remains to be seen. The human brain is complex, and, as everyone knows, there is much more to sexual attraction than airborne particles. Humans respond to sights and sounds (not to mention societal pressure and fat bank accounts). If they didn't, movie stars would be unlikely to attract fans, pornography Web sites wouldn't keep the Internet financially afloat, and glossy magazines with pretty models on the cover wouldn't sell.

Even so, evidence continues to mount that odors affect our sexual decision-making. Rachel Herz, an experimental psychologist at Brown University who researches the effects of odors on behavior, asked 166 women what makes a man attractive enough to consider sleeping with. The women said that appearance mattered, of course, as well as the sound of a man's voice and the touch of his skin, but scent was ranked as the most important, particularly in deciding whom *not* to sleep with. It's not as if women are jumping out of their clothes whenever they get a whiff of someone who turns them on, Herz explains. "It's more like, 'You don't smell right, I'm not going ahead with this.' "

The preferences of the human nose, of course, are complicated. Researchers at Monell once found that foul odors provoked happy responses in study subjects just as often as pleasant ones. Some people are fond of the smells of animal manure or even dead skunks, at least in passing. And body odor itself is hardly static: it depends on food and genes—and may vary with fear, happiness, or anger.

Science has yet to determine just how crucial the ability to detect odors is to living: to sex and love, to eating and remembering, to inspiring and to bewitching. Nowhere is this more evident than in Patrick Suskind's novel *Perfume*. The book's hero, Jean-Baptiste Grenouille, is born in the slums of eighteenth-century Paris with an uncannily acute sense of smell. Grenouille lacks a scent of his own, which renders him a pariah from birth onward: his mother, disgusted with his odorless body, abandons him in the gutter at birth. Apprenticed to a master perfumer, Grenouille's gift spawns an obsession to create the greatest fragrance the human nose has ever known. But to do it,

Grenouille must actually obtain these odors, the best of which reside in the bodies of beautiful young virgins. He becomes a serial killer, slaying girls in order to possess their scents. Grenouille, this olfactory vampire, has a barbaric triumph as he terrorizes France in the elegant "Age of Reason." He is finally caught and tried in Grasse, the center of perfumery, but once more his freakish acumen assists him: he dabs himself with his concoction, which proves so seductive that the scene for his execution becomes a frenzied orgy.

Suskind's message—that even in the age of logic and abstract thinking, the nose, this "primitive organ of smell, the basest of senses," as a priest in the book put it, held sway in inexplicable ways. *Perfume,* which topped international best-seller lists for months, shows that even the thought of scent's powers captivates us still.

# The Recreational Nose:

# A Glimpse

Nobody saves America by sniffing cocaine, Jiggling
yr knees blankeyed in the rain, When it snows in yr
nose you catch cold in yr brain.

—Allen Ginsberg

The nose has long played a role beyond attracting mates or communing with the gods: since ancient times, it has also served as a vehicle for achieving altered states. The first method of getting high, however, was ingestion. Herodotus observed the Scythians in the fifth century BCE as they inhaled the smoke of burning cannibis seeds. "As it burns, it smokes like incense and the smell of it makes them drunk, just as wine does. As more fruit is thrown on, they get more and more intoxicated until they jump up and start singing and dancing."

Snorting drugs didn't become popular until the discovery and transport of products from the New World, when Columbus noticed American Indians sniffing pulverized tobacco during his second voyage to the Americas in 1494. He returned to Europe with vast stockpiles of the powder, or snuff (the word is derived from *snuffen,* a medieval German term meaning "to inhale deeply"). It quickly became fashionable among the Spanish and French.

English noblemen got hooked after Charles II, who had been in exile in France, returned to London with an enormous supply. Queen Anne so enjoyed the stuff that her entire court took up the habit, and Queen Charlotte, the wife of George III, became so addicted to it that she was nicknamed "Snuffy Charlotte." Her son, George IV, changed his snuff according to the time of day and had a storage room for it in each of his palaces. Commoners, meanwhile, smoked tobacco in pipes because it was a cheaper form of the drug. But in the early eighteenth century they took to snuff, too. It became widely available after kidnapped Spanish seamen ransomed themselves with a huge shipment of snuff. Their British captors then distributed it at ports throughout the country, and it quickly became a fad. Mills and snuff shops became ubiquitous, with more than four hundred stores in London alone.

The drug was so popular throughout the nineteenth century that the period was often called "the Age of Snuff." People carried and exchanged elegant porcelain snuffboxes. Production of the powder far outweighed cumbersome smoking or chewing tobacco. Everybody partook: Charles Darwin used it, Alexander Pope wrote of the "pleasant lift" it gave, and Napoleon sniffed more than seven pounds a month. Doctors used it as a cure-all, prescribing snuff for headaches, insomnia, toothaches, coughs, and colds, and as a general preventative against ailments from tuberculosis to syphilis.

Snuff consumption declined in the mid-1880s, as cigarettes, developed in Spain, became a more popular medium for tobacco. In France, women were particularly fond of the elegant new cigarettes, which were more feminine than pipes and more refined than snuff. Cigarettes soon caught on among both sexes in London, New York, and Boston as sophisticated and "continental."

Tobacco's popularity was soon outweighed by that of cocaine, derived from coca leaves grown in the Andes. Natives of Colombia and Peru had chewed the plant's leaves for centuries; it served as a stimulant and bronchodilator, which was useful for performing physical tasks in such high altitudes. Early explorers returned to Europe with the plant, but it wasn't until the mid-nineteenth century that scientists learned to synthesize it into a more usable powder form. The medical world didn't recognize cocaine's powers as a pain reliever, energizer, aid in sexual performance (as well as a remedy for swollen nasal tissues) until the 1880s, when Sigmund Freud began using it himself. In 1884 he called it a "magical" drug, and was an early advocate of its use as a cure for depression and impotence. He even recommended it for ending morphine addiction (morphine, isolated from opium poppies, became popular in injectable form in the 1850s). Freud changed his mind about the drug's benefits when he spent a night with a morphine-addicted friend trying to wean himself off the opiate with cocaine. The cocaine induced a terrifying night of hallucinations, and afterward Freud cautioned against using it altogether.

## In America: Things Go Better with Coke

Americans, far from Vienna, loved cocaine. From the 1850s to the early 1900s, the American elite used a wide variety of drugs, from cocaine, which they snorted, to opium which they smoked. Both drugs were mixed into drinks: cocaine, of course, was an ingredient in Coca-Cola when it was introduced in 1886 (the cocaine was replaced by caffeine in 1903). Snorting cocaine was the preferred medium for most, though, and few were shy about their habit. Thomas Edison praised cocaine's "miraculous" effects, and Sarah Bernhardt gave glowing testimonials, too. In fact, cocaine became a mainstay of the silent film industry—actors and directors found that with it, they had the energy they needed to meet production schedules.

As use spread—people could get cocaine powder in any drugstore—so did concern about the drug's side effects. The drug so powerfully stimulated the brain that addicts often hallucinated, went days without sleeping, and forgot to eat (or bathe). As the drug's effects wear off, depression sets in, leaving the user feeling tired, jumpy, fearful, and anxious—so anxious that addicts desperate for a fix generated a new phrase for the American idiom: "dope fiend." By the turn of the century, American cocaine consumption had grown to an estimated 350,000 (in a population of 76 million), helping to spawn the foundation of the Food and Drug Administration in 1906.

By then, snorting cocaine was a national pastime. Dockworkers along the Mississippi used it to keep energy from flagging, and soon the habit spread throughout river towns from Louisiana to Illinois. Managers of Southern construction camps used cocaine as a means of increasing production among their employees. Western developers found it useful too: overseers in Colorado mining camps found the drug—it had acquired the nickname "snow"—a helpful tool in motivating tired workers, and even supplied it at company stores. Snow found its way to textile mills in the Northeast, where it took the edge off mind-numbing work.

Temperate lawmakers like William Jennings Bryan denounced the drug as a national scourge. Foreign leaders echoed his concerns, but they were troubled for another reason: the United States lacked drug restrictions, which made it a tempting place from which to smuggle. This eventually led to the passage of the Harrison Tax Act of 1914. Far from a prohibition of the drug, its purpose was merely to collect revenue from anyone who imported, manufactured, sold, or dispensed the drug. As a result, the price of cocaine rose significantly. Social critics were outraged.

> As was expected . . . the immediate effects of the Harrison anti-narcotic law were seen in the flocking of drug habitués to hospitals and sanitariums. Sporadic crimes of violence were reported too, due usually to desperate efforts by addicts to obtain drugs . . . The really serious results of this legislation, however, will only appear gradually and will not always be recognized as such. These will be the failures of promising careers, the disrupting of happy families, the commission of crimes which will never be traced to their real cause, and the influx into hospitals to the mentally disordered of many who would otherwise live socially competent lives.[1]

Six years later, Prohibition was decreed, ironically driving addicts hooked on alcohol to cocaine, a more addictive drug. Cocaine was eventually replaced by much cheaper amphetamines in the 1930s, and didn't resurface until well into the 1970s, once the fads of LSD and pot had reached a peak. In the 1980s, cocaine's use grew to epidemic proportions, as imports from South and Central America flooded American cities. It seemed the perfect drug for boom years. Rejuvenated on the club scene in New York, the city that never sleeps, it was as much a staple as coffee bars in today's Seattle.

Its effects, as they had been at the turn of the century, were legion. Hits, depending on their purity, could cost up to several hundred dollars. Even in a fluid economy, the habit ruined fortunes—as well as hearts, brains, and noses. Cocaine stimulates receptors in the cells to release large quantities of endothelin, a chemical that causes blood vessels to contract. Excessive amounts of the chemical can make blood vessels constrict faster and tighter, choking off the heart's blood supply and inducing an immediate heart attack. Seizures are also common. At the height of the epidemic in the mid-1980s, there were one thousand cocaine-induced deaths per year. (Comedian John Belushi died in 1983 of a cocaine and heroin overdose; in 1986, University of Maryland basketball star Len Bias died of a coke-related heart attack.) The deaths did little to stem cocaine use; by 1988, occasional cocaine users numbered around 6 million, and another 4 million addicts snorted weekly or more.

In the materialism of the 1980s, cocaine's rituals were as telling as the quaint snuff porcelain snuffboxes of eighteenth-century England. Cocaine was poured onto a mirror, chopped, separated into "lines," then snorted off a tiny coke spoon, or through rolled-up dollar bills. But snorting took its toll. The powder burns, and over time can wear through the delicate mucous membrane and even perforate the septum. Stevie Nicks, Fleetwood Mac's lead singer, suffered such an indignity: her septum, she has said, eventually bore a hole "big enough to put a gold ring through."

Cocaine use dropped in the early 1990s, only to be replaced by other narcotics. Today, drugs from heroin to glue to ketamine, an animal tranquilizer, are snorted in clubs and school yards, but in truth, the nose is a poor delivery system. Drugs injected into the veins are carried to the brain most rapidly; smoking, in that peculiar race, is second. This is, in part, why the use of crack cocaine—coke that has been cooked into rock form with baking soda or ammonia—became such an epidemic in the late 1980s. (It is also why "huffing," the inhaling of products like spray paint, butane gas, and air freshener, has become so widespread among teenagers.) When smoked, drugs rapidly penetrate the extremely thin lung tissue, which is constructed to allow gases to pass through, and then proceeds via the heart straight to the brain. A drug that is sniffed first has to penetrate the thick mucous membrane of the nose, travel through the blood to the heart, and then return from the heart to the lungs before it can be transported to the brain, resulting in a considerable dilution. The nose's small surface area leaves it an impractical, albeit tidy, way, to get high.

# seven

# Past Scents: Odor and Memory

Smell is believed to be the most highly developed sense at birth; a crying infant recognizes the unique odor of her mother's breast milk and can be calmed with a piece of her clothing. Without smell, one of life's great pleasures—food—would be scarcely more than fuel, boring and unremarkable. But to understand the importance of smelling, perhaps it's easiest to glimpse life through the experience of one who can't.

Michelle Wood is a trim, active blonde in her mid-fifties with an easy manner, sharp wit, and a hearty laugh—a grown-up tomboy. A professional horse agent, Michelle spends long days outdoors, riding and grooming her charges. She loves the salty air of the Maryland shore near her farm, and cooking—crab-cakes, using local blue crabs, are a particular favorite. Wood takes a special pride in her garden, delighting in the heirloom tomatoes in her vegetable patch and cheery annuals that line her driveway.

At least Wood used to enjoy those things. In the summer of 2000, she got a terrible cold. Chilly and achy on a torpid, hot July weekend, Wood figured she had no ordinary virus. Her nose was so stuffy she couldn't breathe. She couldn't smell, or taste a thing, either. Her family doctor prescribed first one round of antibiotics, then another. Finally, he gave a prescription for steroids, hoping that her post-viral swelling was simply blocking odor molecules from reaching the receptors.

Wood took all the drugs, but nothing helped. Her cold, as it happens, had brought on a malady called *anosmia,* a term forged from Latin and Greek meaning "lack of smell." The disorder is not classified by the Centers for Disease Control, and estimates vary from 4 to 16 million Americans affected. This condition can strike at random, and differs from the gradual fading of the sense of smell experienced by 25 percent of those over the age of 65, called *presbyosmia.* Anosmia can occur after a virus, a bout with sinusitis, years of smoking, repeated chemical exposure, or head injury, which can all destroy the mechanism that fires olfactory information to the brain. In Wood's case, it is likely that the virus attacked odor receptors in such a way that they died off or became unable to bind with odor molecules.

The loss has devastated Wood. She feels, as she puts it, "like I go through the day in a sealed bubble." She still works, traveling frequently to the Netherlands to buy and sell horses. She still tells jokes, and attends to ordinary tasks—cooking, babysitting her baby granddaughter, shopping. But she feels detached, cut off. "Smells have such meaning in my life. As a young girl, I could always weed out boyfriends by whether or not it was OK with them that I smelled like a barn," she says. Now, a dimension is gone from everything. The heady odor of the horses no longer lingers on her boots and hair. Climbing into a bed with clean linens isn't comforting anymore. "I'm there but I'm not," she says. "It sounds crazy to complain when you add it up—I'm walking, breathing, functioning. But that's just it. I'm just functioning."

Researchers believe that the olfactory process helps explain why smell, memories, and feelings are closely intertwined. Odor molecules bind to receptors in the nose, ferrying impulses to the olfactory bulb. The bulb sends messages to the limbic system, the brain's emotional center, and the hippocampus, which is thought to store memory.

For millennia, societies have believed that smell has the power to boost moods and even alter events. In ancient Egypt, embalmers used cedar and myrrh oils to help hasten the mummies' voyage to the afterlife; in ancient Greece, mothers tucked lavender stems in their infants' beds to induce sweet dreams. The scent of a madeleine dipped in lime blossom tea overwhelmed Marcel Proust, launching *The Remembrance of Things Past*. For most, smells usher in powerful sentiments, often for inexplicable reasons.

While science shies away from the term "aromatherapy," some studies show that the effects of pleasant odors are indeed real. Today, Japanese companies circulate the smell of lemon through air-conditioning systems in the morning to help clerical workers stay focused, switching to cedar in the afternoon to boost sagging energy. At London's Heathrow Airport, the scent of pine is sprayed throughout the vast terminals to keep frantic passengers at ease. And doctors at Memorial Sloan-Kettering Cancer Center have found that the vanilla-like aroma of heliotrope, a tiny purple flower with a sweet scent, significantly reduces anxiety for patients undergoing MRI scans.

Yet the ability to smell is perhaps the most underappreciated of all senses. In fact, surveys show that it is the sense a majority of people would be willing to relinquish. Still, current science is showing that the 'Proust phenomenon' is much more powerful than many people realize. Researchers are discovering that smell is vital to memory—and mood.

Wood, for her part, says she doesn't need science to validate her emotional state with research: since becoming anosmic, she has also become profoundly depressed. "What's the mystery?" she says. "Nobody would wonder why I feel this way if I'd suddenly lost my eyesight." Others who have lost their sense of smell report feeling a similar despair. They complain of losing their confidence and becoming paranoid that they stink—many carry around extra stashes of breath mints and deodorants, just in case. They tell of a crushed sense of self—suddenly, they lack clues about how and where they fit in the world. They can't know when the Thanksgiving turkey is done roasting just by smelling, though they've been cooking one for thirty years, or take in the neighbor's freshly cut grass even as he is pushing the mower. They can't smell the skin, or hair, of a loved one. Suddenly, a world of subtlety and nuance becomes altogether flat.

After a while, this sensory isolation becomes self-reinforcing. Many anosmics say that as their illness progresses, they become increasingly secluded. Eating becomes especially unsatisfying. Researchers say that 90 percent of the flavors we enjoy actually comes from a food's aroma: think of a heady sprig of basil, the perfume of an orange, or a thick steak sizzling on the grill. As you take a bite, odors travel up the back of the throat to the nose, where they latch on to odor receptors. (The tongue, meanwhile, savors only sweet, salty, bitter, sour, or a newly dis-covered, hard-to-describe flavor called *umami,* which can roughly be translated from Japanese as "delicious" or "meaty.")

Since most social gatherings revolve around food, meals are simply new opportunities to be reminded of loss. Wood is a per-fect example. Since she became anosmic, Wood, already slim, has shed six pounds—she can't taste anything, so why bother eat-ing? Her withered enjoyment of food mirrors life in her odorless universe: "We went out with friends for crabs not long ago and I became bored very quickly," she says. "Picking crabs is a lot of work and usually a labor of love. But if there is no reward—smell or taste—it is a waste of time." For a time, she and her husband, Wayne, joined friends in restaurants. While others savored their food and wine, Wood would hope in vain for an errant whiff of anything. Before long, though, she realized that she might as well eat burned food at home—she wouldn't notice the difference be-tween it and a twenty-five-dollar steak. She still tries, she says—she loves socializing—but feels that it's senseless to pay for an experience that, in the end, will only leave her bluer than before.

Every so often, Wood will catch a flavor or aroma, but only for a moment. One day she popped a Jolly Rancher candy into her mouth—she can still sometimes distinguish tartness—and was shocked that she could actually taste it. She took it out of her mouth, incredulous, and sniffed the wet red cube as if it were a truffle. "I almost cried, I was so happy," she said. "And of all things, fake fruit!" Instances such as those keep her hopes buoyant, but usually in vain. In December she put up a Christmas tree and lit the bayberry candles she usually enjoys. For a moment, she thought she could smell the candle, but she couldn't be sure. "Was it really the candle, or was I just remembering the smell?" she wonders. The recollection of the pungent pine—or of the loss—is still so palpable, Wood dreamed she smelled a Christmas tree early one May morning, even as lilacs bloomed outside.

When she drives through the Maryland countryside, Wood reminisces about summers she spent on her grandparents' farm: picking strawberries, cranking the handle of the old-fashioned ice cream maker (chocolate was a favorite), or wolfing down her grandmother's chicken and dumplings. On a recent warm day, Wood, her daughter, and granddaughter passed the old farmhouse with their windows down. "There's just something about the air on the Eastern Shore, isn't there? It's different, earthy," her daughter observed. Then she looked at her mother and said, "Oh, God, Mom, I'm sorry. I forgot." Most painful, says Wood, is the link to the past that odors bring. "Maybe some day I will be able to taste and smell my memories again," she says wistfully, "or at least share those experiences through my granddaughter."

At the beginning of her illness, Wood tried to conjure smells. Just after she got sick, she would bury her nose in her husband's neck and take a deep whiff. She could smell—or thought she could smell—his aftershave, the one he'd been using for years. In the beginning, it wasn't so hard: Wood just commanded herself to remember a smell—Wayne, the beach—and she could somehow recall the odor. Now, even that has faded. "I feel like I've lost even my daydreams," she says. "My past—the person I was, and the person I'm trying to remember. You can only go on memory for so long." On a warm day in early summer she was lying on her deck sunbathing. After a few moments, Wood grew restless, and went inside. It just felt too odd. She realized that the fragrance of the sunscreen and the breeze moving off nearby fields was part of what made sunning so pleasant. Without them, she was lost.

Only a handful of researchers actually treat smell disorders, which range from anosmia to "olfactory hallucinations"— smelling odors that simply aren't there. Conditions also include congenital anosmia, being born without the ability to smell, and dysosmia, a condition in which sufferers sense unpleasant smells constantly. Dysosmics report that the stench of garbage, rotten eggs, or a decomposing animal fills their nostrils, driving them to distraction. (Like many anosmics, Wood suffers from occasional dysosmia, and on bad days, she says is overcome by the stink of bacon left in the fridge over a monthlong vacation.) Some, unable to cope with the invasion of horrible odors, commit suicide.

Experts say the small size of their field reflects the fact that smell loss is rarely life-threatening. Every year, however, hundreds of elderly people with diminished smell die in fires or gas leaks others nearby could smell. Many suffer from food poisoning because they can't detect spoilage.

Others, like Wood, suffer much less tangibly. Then there are cases such as Adolfo "Rudy" Coniglio, a pizza chef and restaurant owner from Closter, New Jersey, who in the early 1970s was struck with a heavy cold. A few days later, he returned to work at his pizzeria. But as he settled in among his tomatoes and herbs, he detected a rancid odor. He sniffed the tomatoes: rotten garbage. He sniffed the garlic: rotten garbage. His famous sauce? Rotten garbage. So Coniglio called his suppliers. "Everything's rotten!" he recalls saying. "I was mad, I tell you, I was mad."

"They told me, 'What, you think we'd sell you rotten stuff? You're joking! You're crazy!' It was awful. I couldn't stand it. I went around furious—everything stank. Everyone else says it's fine but I know it's not—it stinks. Even when I cooked in the house it smelled rotten. The vapor from the food, the smells! All I could do was just stand out in the woods with a cigarette. That was the only place I could get comfortable."

Doctors told Coniglio, now eighty-five, that his problem was "in his head"; that he needed tranquilizers; that he needed "rest." In search of respite, he left the country to visit his mother's hometown outside Naples, but the problem remained. "Everything stank. Even in Italy they thought I was crazy. I didn't feel like no crazy guy, but after a while, you got to wonder."

Mainstream medicine has few answers for people like Wood and Coniglio. (Sometimes, smell loss is linked to sinus problems, and can ultimately be treated with steroids. Surgery is also sometimes indicated.) For the most part, there is not even a clear-cut understanding of what causes post-viral anosmia in the first place.

Many anosmics and dysosmics wind up at the Taste and Smell Clinic of Washington, D.C., run by Dr. Robert I. Henkin, a neuroendocrinologist. Coniglio first met Henkin at the

National Institutes of Health in Bethesda, Maryland. Henkin had achieved some renown after he found that tweaking metals in the bloodstream—copper and zinc, largely—could help relieve taste and smell distortions that were the result of viruses or medication. (While hearing and vision tests were commonplace as early as the 1940s, a universal smell test did not exist until 1980. Even its inventor, Dr. Richard Doty, who heads the Smell and Taste Center at the University of Pennsylvania, calls it "an eye test for the nose.")

Henkin tested Coniglio, found his blood serum metals low, and gave him zinc. On the zinc, Coniglio improved dramatically. After his testing, Henkin gave him a placebo with the caveat that he could be on either zinc or a placebo, and asked him to sign a consent form. "But if things get worse," Henkin recalls saying, "call me."

Four months later, Coniglio called. "It all came back," he told Henkin. "Of course!" Henkin said, realizing that the placebo had had no effect. In the meantime, though, Coniglio had sold his business, unable to bear the sensation of rotten garbage any longer. Henkin was horrified. He had just ruined a man's life.

Coniglio, however, shrugs and says it doesn't matter. He had wanted to retire anyway. (He does add, in the next breath, that the net worth of the pizzeria today would be well over a million dollars.) "For a while I didn't know if I'd ever enjoy a bite of veal again! The guy is my hero."

But Henkin isn't a hero to everyone. Doty and Terence Davidson, an ear, nose, and throat doctor at the University of California at San Diego, who also directs the Nasal Dysfunction Clinic there, cautions that none of Henkin's ministrations have received FDA approval—at least for the purpose he employs them. His treatments range from theophylline, an asthma medicine he says helps stimulate enzyme production needed to help olfactory receptors work properly in anosmics, to anticonvulsants and antipsychotic medications for those who suffer from distortions. (Wood visited Henkin, and says that theophylline he prescribed made her anxious and gave her heart palpitations. She stopped the treatment and never went back.)

On the other hand, patients with smell disorders have few places to turn. In the medical community, anosmia is an "orphan disease." There is little research in the area, and drug companies rarely fund the development of medications upon which they can't guarantee profit.

Smell loss is so obscure to many physicians that they simply dismiss it. Those who do seek help are told by their doctors that they should simply "learn to live" with their problem. Furthermore, insurance companies do not often cover treatment for anosmia; consultations and evaluations can cost several hundred, or even several thousand dollars. "There isn't widespread knowledge about a lot of these conditions," says Doty. "And it's not all that hard to understand, really: some diseases have decades of research and understanding—heart problems, vision problems. We're just not in that same place yet."

Many with smell disorders often run through a long string of specialists—ENTs, neurologists, even psychiatrists. "The system doesn't treat them very well," says Doty. "It's like, 'What? I've got a room full of patients with tumors and you're complaining that you can't smell your coffee? Get out of here!' There's a lot of that, I'm sorry to say. But these people are suffering. They have lost a great deal. We spend a day evaluating these people. We can't always help everyone—I'll be honest. And for those we can't, we try to at least help them get closure on what is realistic, and what isn't."

Almost a year after her virus, Wood has high hopes that she will get her sense of smell back on her own; occasionally, odors creep into her nostrils, if only fleetingly. One brilliant spring day she unlocked her trunk to retrieve some horse strapping. As the door flew open her nostrils filled with the smell of warm leather. "I breathed it in and realized it wasn't just a memory, it was the real thing," she says. "You'd have thought I won the lottery."

Anosmics like Wood, who have lost their sense of smell to a virus, often experience a slow recovery, Doty says. Since olfactory neurons regenerate every month or so, one would think that those who lose their sense of smell would recover—or at least notice improvement—within weeks after the initial loss. Instead, it takes months, sometimes even years, for ex-smokers to regain much of their sense of smell. Smokers, Doty points out, suffer mild damage, and are still able to identify many odors. "Obviously, most people with smell loss haven't had their olfactory abilities tested before becoming injured or ill," he says, "so it's impossible to compare." Those whose sense of smell is not completely gone, he says, have a better chance of improvement.

For many years scientists could not explain why we remember smells. Olfactory neurons are constantly being replaced. New neurons have to form new synapses, even when smelling an odor you've smelled daily for twenty years. If that is so, why would the brain remember odor? Buck and Axel, the Columbia researchers who discovered the genes responsible for smelling, hypothesize that memories survive because the axons of the neurons corresponding to various receptors always go to the same place in the brain.

For her part, Wood gets by. "It's really easy to feel sorry for myself," she says. "But then one morning I'll get a whiff of the garbage that didn't get emptied the night before—and I'll just be so thrilled I could scream. Garbage? Rotting banana peels? Wayne's aftershave and horse manure still elude me, and those are two things I long to smell. It's an odd combination, but that is the stuff my life is made of, and I need it back to feel complete."

According to recent studies, brain scans using functional magnetic reasoning imaging (fMRI) among those with a normal ability to smell showed that the brain "activated" when exposed to three different chemical odors. Scans of those who could not smell revealed little or no activation of the brain, including the hippocampus and limbic system. Wood is depressed to hear it. "Good God, I wonder what's happening to *my* brain," she says, laughing grimly. She spurns any suggestion of pharmaceutical help, like Prozac, to "adjust" to her disorder. No pill can help her distinguish grilled salmon from Starkist tuna, so what's the point? Still, some measure of human enjoyment has been drained out of everything—eating, her work, sex. "It's not because I have a lack of interest in my husband," she says. "It's because I can't smell him." Experts draw the same conclusion. Anosmics often have a diminished sex drive. Rats whose olfactory bulbs are removed become disinterested in mating.

\* \* \*

What of the emotional lives of people who cannot detect the scents around them? Are they deprived of full happiness—or even of their capacity to remember? Rachel Herz, the professor of psychology at Brown, says scientists are only beginning to realize the connection among the three. "People who lose their sense of smell for extended periods generally feel as if their emotional lives are blunted," says Herz. "But we can't say for sure why. This is total conjecture, and it needs to be studied, but it is possible that without a constant stream of sensory input the limbic areas of anosmics actually do start to atrophy."

The ability to smell adds an extra dimension to the sipping of wine, a luxuriant bubble bath, a hike outdoors. But beyond the scents themselves, researchers say that smells can help to elicit memories in a way that other sensory stimuli can not. Scent is often said to be the most powerful conduit to memory. "It's much more subtle than that," says Herz, a small woman with green eyes and long auburn hair. When an odor triggers a memory, she says, the emotions that accompany the recollection are often more intense than memories spurred by, say, music or a photograph. "Because your feelings are so strong, they may make you feel more confident that what you are recalling is especially accurate," she adds.

Memory, after all, is more than just an accurate representation of a past event, or a simple recall of facts. Brain scans taken as a person remembers Paris as the capital of France differ greatly from those of the same person reminiscing about a first trip there. Not all memory is emotional, of course, but the recollection of specific episodes often is. "People associate past events with feelings—where they were, what they were eating, who said what," Herz says. "Those feelings can range from a kind of hazy nostalgia to intense emotional responses." That's why vanilla-scented pipe smoke—the very kind of tobacco your grandfather smoked before he died—may make you tear up. Or why you continue to buy the brand of dish soap your favorite aunt used—it reminds you of warm evenings spent at her house.

In a study Herz conducted with Jonathan Schooler, a psychologist at the University of Pittsburgh, subjects were prompted with words for an item—in this case, Coppertone suntan lotion, Crayola crayons, Johnson & Johnson's baby powder, Vick's Vapo-Rub, and Play-Doh. (Herz and Schooler thought these products would be more likely to trigger childhood memories and not recent ones.) The subjects were asked to search for a memory associated with the word for the item, and to rate it for the feelings it elicited, how vividly or in how much detail they could recall the event. After a pause, the researchers presented the sight or the smell of the item, and asked subjects again to think about and rate the episode they had just described. Vividness and specificity didn't vary in the ratings the second time, the researchers found. But when odor was the cue, subjects recalled the same incident with much more intense emotion. "They really felt as if they had been transported back to the original event," Herz says.

In another experiment, Herz showed people a series of emotionally evocative paintings. At the same time, the subjects were exposed to another sensory cue—an orange, for example—in different ways. Some saw an orange. Others were given an orange to touch, heard the word 'orange' or smelled the fruit. Two days later, the subjects were given their sensory cue once again and asked to recall the painting. The sensory cues were all about the same in eliciting recall of the picture, but those exposed to smell not only remembered the painting, but felt a "flood" of emotional responses to it as well, Herz says. This insight, she believes, helps explain a lot about smell and memory. "It's the level of emotional intensity that makes it seem as if a whiff of a former lover's cologne somehow reminds you of him better than just looking at a picture of him," she says.

Smell enhances life's pleasures, but the reverse is also true. Researchers are exploring whether impaired smell in the elderly, among chemical workers and smokers, might affect mood disorders as well. Duke University researcher Susan Schiffman suggests that smell loss in the elderly can lead to unwanted weight loss and deepen depression, which affects about 10 percent of those over fifty-five.

Not surprisingly, there is also a connection between scent and negative emotions. In a project conducted with Gisela Epple at the Monell Chemical Senses Center in Philadelphia, Herz and Epple asked the children to complete a lap-sized maze that was in fact impossible to solve. At the same time, the researchers piped an unusual odor into the room. Twenty minutes later, they gave the children an easy assignment in another room filled with the same odor, a different odor, or no odor at all. The children who were given the simple task in the room scented with the same odor as that of the maze room did significantly worse than the other boys and girls. Meanwhile, there was no difference in performance among children in either the no-odor or different-odor rooms. The researchers concluded that the performance rates were not due to the presence of maze odor, but to the specific associations the first odor triggered—the experience of failure.

So, if you flunked your first exam in a classroom freshly scrubbed with bleach, you might be at risk of repeating your performance in another recently Cloroxed room. Scientists believe that odors not only affect our memories—but how we respond to them. Researchers in France found that newborns prefer the odors of breast milk and amniotic fluid to those of vanilla and baby formula. Certainly, those preferences don't last long, but events certainly help shape whether we like an odor or not. Trygg Engen, a professor emeritus of psychology at Brown, wrote that a person's affinity for or dislike of an odor is determined by his first exposure to it, and is bound forever to the joy, hilarity, or sadness of the experience. Anecdotal evidence of this is everywhere. One woman I know can't bear the aroma of marinara sauce; it was what her mother was cooking the night her father had a massive heart attack and died. For years, the scent of Juicy Fruit or Doublemint gum repulsed my sister, who believed they made her nauseous. In fact, it was, and is, what our father always chews, and he used to go through a whole pack on the winding road through the Cascade Mountains as we went for weekend ski trips. It was only years later, as a driving parent herself, that she realized the *road* made her sick, not the gum.

*e i g h t*

# The Sinus Business

It feels like the most common of maladies, a cold, with its runny, stuffy nose, headache, and general malaise. Most people can treat their symptoms with nothing more than a day or two off from work, a box of Kleenex, and an extra carton of Tropicana. But for the estimated 37 million Americans who suffer from chronic sinusitis, the scratchy throat that marks the beginning of a simple respiratory virus is met with utter dread. It is the start of a cycle that typically leads to visits to the doctor (if not the hospital), rounds of antibiotics, and weeks of misery. For reasons that science has not been able to fully understand, the sinuses of these people never function properly, and collapse at the onset of a case of sniffles. The gaping chasm between what medicine can provide, and what human beings need, can be witnessed dramatically in their sufferings.

The disease has stumped doctors by its sheer numbers. In 1982, the National Center for Health Statistics reported 27 million cases of chronic sinusitis; by 1993, that figure had spiked to 37 million, affecting roughly one in seven Americans. According to the NCHS, chronic sinusitis is the most common long-term disease in the nation, overtaking asthma, arthritis, hypertension, and back pain. More patients are reporting symptoms of the disease than ever before—NCHS records what patients seek treatment for, not doctors' diagnoses—and physicians, armed with new machines like CT scans and endoscopes, are finding increased cases as well. Neither the rise in patients' symptoms nor improved tools for finding the disease can explain the dramatic growth.

Chronic sinusitis differs vastly from allergic rhinitis, but people often confuse the two. When pollen collides with cells called "mast cells" just beneath the lining of the nose, eyes, or respiratory tract of susceptible people, the immune system goes into overdrive. Once disturbed, mast cells go into high gear, producing some 15 inflammatory molecules. One, called histamine, leaps to defend the body against the invader. Histamines attach to receptors on nerve cells, which then lodge on receptors in nearby blood vessels. The vessels become porous and seep with fluid that becomes the most notable feature of an allergic reaction: the ticklish, runny nose, the leaky eyes and scratchy throat. Antihistamine drugs work for allergies, but not for chronic sinusitis. The active ingredient in antihistamines is a molecule that fits the histamine receptor, thwarting the signal that causes the drippy signals. Often, patients and doctors alike confuse the symptoms, but antihistamines do nothing for patients with chronic sinusitis, and can sometimes make the patient worse by drying up the tissues.

The sinuses themselves are something of an enigma. Experts don't agree on their original function. One theory suggests that they evolved over time, in order to make our heads lighter, once we began walking upright; some say they exist to cool, heat, and humidify the air that goes into our lungs. Others say that they're there to equalize barometric pressure changes. One thing is certain: sinuses are the seat of the voice's resonance, acting for a singer much like the chambers of a violin.

The nose, sinuses, and their interconnecting ducts, no bigger than 2 millimeters in diameter, are lined with a mucous membrane, which, when healthy, resembles the lining of the inside of the mouth. The mucous membrane produces between a pint and a quart of mucus a day, which is flushed out of the sinuses, a grapelike cluster of cavities, by thousands of tiny *cilia,* or hairlike filaments. They help pass pollen, bacteria, and viruses out of the nose at the back of the throat. (Many bigger particles, such as dust and pollutants are trapped by visible nasal hairs, and eventually gets blown out.) The mucus, along with any viruses and bacteria it may carry, gets swallowed and then dissolved by stomach acids. These functions go largely unnoticed by most people, but for those who suffer from chronic sinusitis, even breathing and swallowing are conspicuous.

In the late 1990s, a small band of researchers at Minnesota's Mayo Clinic began to question the conventional treatments of the thousands of patients who flooded the clinic's ear, nose, and throat department. They are led by a young German doctor named Jens Ponikau.

A tall, bearish man with a broad face, Ponikau has a crushing handshake, and thinning, close-cropped blond hair. His English is marked by the year—1983—he spent in Minnesota as a foreign exchange student; he says "Awesome!" or "Neat!" when something strikes his fancy. He smiles broadly and claps colleagues on the back as he rushes past them in gurney-filled hallways—a jolly German. Little about his appearance or demeanor reveals that he is a revolutionary in his field, the rarefied world of ear, nose, and throat surgeons.

Born in Halle, East Germany, in 1966, Ponikau's earliest memory is the night he and his mother stowed themselves in a trunk to steal across the country's western border. Acting on a tip from their smugglers, the country's security agents, the Stasi, raided the car. "It is quite something, as a child, to look up and see three AK-47s pointed at your face," he says. His parents were jailed for treason. Young Jens, an only child, spent two years in the care of his grandmother.

Eventually, in 1978, the West German government ransomed a group of highly trained political prisoners; Jens's father, a doctor, and his mother, a teacher, were among them. The family settled in Hamburg, where Jens aspired to be a doctor. In his last year of medical school, he spent some time at the Mayo Clinic in Rochester, Minnesota. There, he met some ear, nose, and throat surgeons with whom he felt an immediate affinity—his father is also an ENT—and he planned to enter the field himself.

For Ponikau the subspecialty is not just the family profession, it is fascinating in itself. The ears, nose, throat, and sinuses, he says, are central to the human experience: hearing, smelling, breathing, talking. Ponikau was especially interested in chronic sinus disease and its precipitous rise. Back at Mayo as a resident, Ponikau found himself under the tutelage of Eugene Kern, a mustachioed New Jerseyan whose skill as one of the clinic's sinus surgeons had earned him a national reputation. Every year, Kern assigns his residents a project. Ponikau's was to look at fungi in the sinuses. He remembers the day he got the assignment—it was a wintry morning in Rochester—because it would touch off his research career.

In sinus surgery, the excised tissue is sent to the lab to be analyzed for bacteria and irregular cells. In rare cases, 4 to 5 percent, patients were found to have a condition called allergic fungal sinusitis, or AFS. Strangely, though, a great many people with chronic sinusitis seemed to have fungal growths lodged in their sinuses. But cultures, didn't usually find anything. What doctors could see—or thought they could see—was not confirmed by lab results.

And yet fungi, like bacteria, are everywhere, Ponikau reflected one evening as he hunched over his microscope and slides. Spores flourish in the air—inside walls, shower stalls, wet basements, under Formica countertops, in the soil; they even are the food we eat—mushrooms, of course, being the perfect example. It seemed perfectly likely that fungi existed in the sinuses as well—the perfect moist, warm incubator.

Ponikau was particularly mystified by the symptoms of chronic sinusitis patients. Their complaints were numerous, and real: persistent congestion, a runny nose, headaches, facial pain, fevers, and other flu-like symptoms that can last for months. Often, like Ponikau himself, they suffer from asthma as well. "Put together, the disease seemed systemic," he says. "There is rarely just a localized problem; sometimes patients come in and say, 'I know the infection is back because my asthma has flared up again.'"

Ponikau trudged back and forth between the lab and Mayo's vast waiting room, equipped with television sets, board games, and an adjacent espresso stand, thinking about the patients symptoms of those who shuffled forlornly into Gene Kern's office. At best, chronic sinusitis patients complain of low energy. But for most, the illness dominates everything, forcing absences from work, school, and social functions. Visits to the doctor's office and the pharmacy become as frequent as trips to the supermarket. Unlike chronic fatigue syndrome or fibromyalgia, maladies the medical community disputes, chronic sinusitis has quantifiable measurements: CT scans reveal diseased tissue, and doctors can see swollen, inflamed mucosa and infected mucus. The disease is also responsible for 73 million lost workdays, according to a 1990 Harvard study. It is rarely fatal, but its complications—meningitis, encephalitis, or pneumonia—can be. "There isn't a single doctor who deals with chronic cases of this disease who doesn't want to throw up their hands," Ponikau says.

Unlike the heart, lungs, kidneys, and immune system, whose function can be evaluated with simple tests, few clinics are equipped with tools to measure sinus function. (Mayo is one of the few places in the United States with a nasal physiology lab. Doctors there can determine how well a microscopic sample of cilia passes along mucus.) Elsewhere, the only test is whether or not patients feel better after one or more types of treatment.

Surgery is a last resort. Many who exceed the ken of their own physicians wind up at Mayo. Most of this group, by this time, has had multiple surgeries—one patient Kern saw had had twenty-five. They also go to remarkable lengths to try to improve their condition themselves: selling a house they think makes them sick, moving across the country to a different climate, buying special machines to change the ions in a room, taking allergy shots for years. On the advice of self-help books, health store clerks, and Internet doctors, patients drink vinegar, swallow acidophilus pills, drop oregano oil under their tongues. "I've talked to patients who go on diets that won't allow carbohydrates or fruit—no fruit! This is religion, not science!" Ponikau says.

Whatever is causing the problem, one thing is for certain: the disease translates into big business, especially for drug companies. The 1990 Harvard study found that the average drug costs for patients with chronic sinusitis totaled $1,220 per patient, per year. Drugs to treat the disease include antibiotics, antihistamines, decongestants, and steroids, either in nasal sprays or pills, or both. That works out to some $45 billion on drugs a year. The same study found that the cost of surgery averaged nearly $7,000 per patient; there are some 250,000 sinus surgeries performed in the United States per year. The Mayo Clinic's business office did a study that found actual costs of sinus surgery were much higher. Once blood tests, anesthesia, and hospital costs were included, the figure neared $12,000. That would make a national total of surgical and hospital costs close to $3 billion. None of those figures take into account the sums Americans spend on alternative or over-the-counter (OTC) care. One study, released at a San Antonio conference on sinus disease, estimated that Americans spend $15 billion on OTC medicine and alternative therapies like acupuncture treating themselves for sinusitis. According to the CDC, in 1998 chronic sinusitis was responsible for 12 million doctor's visits and 1.2 million hospital admissions.

The economic implications are obviously far-reaching, and the rewards for the drug companies are great. According to Kline and Company, an independent market analyst firm in New Jersey, the consumers spent $200 million on OTC nasal drops, inhalants, and sprays, up 10 percent over 1999; OTC sinus medications, such as Sudafed and Tylenol Sinus, accounted for another $150 million. Pharmaceutical companies clearly recognize the size of the epidemic; one study showed that in the mid-1990's, the commercials aired most often during winter on the largest networks, ABC, NBC, and CBS, featured cold and sinus remedies, with combined revenue for the ads averaging $600 million yearly. A book on sinus disease called "Sinus Survival: The Holistic Medical Treatment for Sinusitis, Allergies, and Colds" has sold more than 300,000 copies.

Acute sinusitis, which generally appears after a bad cold or a prolonged allergy season, is easily treated with antibiotics. But chronic sinusitis is much more elusive. For years, doctors have attributed it to a variety of causes: allergies to pollen, mold, or animals; sensitivity to pollution and chemicals; bacteria trapped in the sinuses. Genetic disorders can also play a role. The only constant is the sufferer's diseased, damaged epithelium, which cannot adequately move mucus out of the sinuses. Constant inflammation of the sinus lining can also lead to polyps, small, benign growths that further block the interconnecting passageways.

In addition to medication, doctors have also sought to treat the disease with surgery, by creating larger ducts, removing congenital blockages or scraping away tissue deadened by repeated infections. Surgery for repeated sinus infections was advocated as early as the nineteenth century, but it was a risky and unwieldy procedure. Doctors could only gain access to the sinuses by cutting incisions in the roof of the mouth, or, more drastically, on either side of the bridge of the nose beneath the eyebrow.

In the mid-1980s, Dr. David Kennedy, chairman of the otorhinolaryngology department at the University of Pennsylvania School of Medicine, introduced American doctors to the use of endoscopes in sinus surgery, a technique he had learned from a surgeon in Austria named Heinz Stammberger. Endoscopes, small telescopes attached to a video monitor, allowed surgeons entryway through the nostrils. These gave a magnified view of their tiny operating field. Endoscopes allowed sinus surgery to become commonplace, with large ENT practices advertising happy, easy-breathing "customers" in newspapers and yellow pages everywhere.

Quite literally, the technology opened up a whole new surgical field. Endoscopes allowed easy removal of tissue that doctors suspected was to blame for chronic infections. Surgeons took out turbinates, stripped away membranes, and created new, larger ducts in the floor of the sinuses.

But by the mid-1990s, doctors began to question the wisdom of such aggressive procedures. While many postoperative patients enjoyed a level of health they had never experienced, many others began showing up at Kern's office. Many complained that their illness worsened *after* the surgery, and that their symptoms had increased. Not only did they have chronic infections, they now suffered from bloody noses and had extensive breathing problems. They were also very depressed.

Soon Kern noticed that 157 of his new patients had another thing in common: they had all had their turbinates removed. Looking at their CT scans one day, a Swedish colleague, Monica Stenquist, even came up with the name for the new condition: empty nose syndrome. Scans of normal, healthy sinuses show the turbinates curling from the outside of the nasal wall into the air, like miniature fiddleheads. In the X-rays the doctors were reviewing, all lacked the bony structures.

Humans, in fact, need their turbinates: they are essential for humidifying the nose and keeping disease from traveling to the frontal sinuses, which are separated from the brain by the thinnest of bones. More than 160,000 people had turbinate tissue removed in 1996, the last year for which the Centers for Disease Control and Prevention has statistics. (Kern believes the true number is far higher and that it is rising.) Other radical procedures had proved equally disappointing. The new, bigger ducts created by surgery went unrecognized by the cilia, which just kept using the ones nature had made. Often, stripping the sinus membrane permanently damaged cilia. Technology had given well-trained physicians a boost, but in the wrong hands, it had become a destructive tool.

Even in the best of circumstances, sinus surgery is a difficult procedure. The surgeon, generally a man (83 percent of ENTs are male), must possess fine motor skills comparable to those of a concert pianist. As in art, there are Picassos, and there are journeymen, and the skill required to remove damaged tissue—but leave the delicate cilia intact—is refined indeed.

For the private practitioner, sinus surgery can be a lucrative subspecialty, bringing in as much as $500,000 a year. Doing the surgery itself, many say, is "fun." Part of that fun derives from the arsenal of high-tech medical toys many doctors have at their disposal: fiber optics and micro-cameras, to better peer into the dark, cramped space; giant monitors that magnify the field of action; and three-dimensional CT scans. Some operating rooms are even outfitted with $160,000 global positioning systems that beep when the surgeon is too far off target—or too close to severing a nerve.

In fact, the only thing about which sinus surgery cannot boast is success. In addition to complications from empty nose syndrome, thousands of other Americans undergo repeat procedures every year. While there are no certain figures, the revision rate on sinus surgery is estimated to be anywhere from 20 to 50 percent. One reason the figure is so difficult to track is because patients often switch doctors once one surgery fails them, only to repeat the process elsewhere.

The Harvard study did show that patients require fewer drugs after surgery, but it is possible that those figures disproportionately reflect patients with congenital blockages or too-small ducts.

At any rate, the "simple ambulatory procedure," as the surgery is often described, is anything but. For a painful postoperative week, the patient grits through swelling, bleeding, and the immense pain of having had bone and tissue removed from one of the most nerve-dense regions of the body. Several days after the surgery comes the sensation—and indignity—of having wads of bloody cotton packing extracted from one's nasal cavities: "Close your eyes now, you'll feel a little tug!" (As a veteran of both childbirth without anesthesia and multiple sinus surgeries, I'd choose labor any day.)

"If surgery cured people, we'd all be happy," Ponikau says. "But clearly, it only temporarily helps most patients."

At the beginning of Ponikau's tenure at Mayo, the whole department debated the disease. Many times, it felt like the team was "sitting" on an answer, particularly when postsurgical patients would return just as sick as before. The department held meetings on difficult cases to determine the "right" surgical plan, one that would solve the poor patient's problems forever. But six months later, Ponikau would see him or her looking dejected in the waiting room. "You felt heartbroken just to see them, and know that you'd failed them," he says. "Sorry, Doc, I'm back," they'd say. And you'd say, "What are you sorry for? We're the ones who are failing *you!*"

In many cases, it was easy to lay blame elsewhere. One busy afternoon Gene Kern rushed into the examination room to see a patient. The man had several surgeries behind him, and clutched a new CT scan showing disease in every cavity. "Well, this poor guy had some inexperienced doctor do his surgery," Kern thought to himself.

"When did you have your last procedure?" Kern asked the man.

"Nine months ago, Doctor."

"I see," Kern said. "Who did the surgery?"

The man cleared his throat and flinched for a moment before looking Kern in the eye.

"You, Dr. Kern. You did it last May."

Stubborn cases eventually made Kern question not only the mechanism of the illness, but its accepted treatment. Was constant surgery a crude—and brief—way to ameliorate symptoms? "As a surgeon, your main goal is to help these patients feel better," Kern says. "But when you looked at this objectively, a lot of what we were doing just wasn't really helping."

The department often debated the cause of the disease, at lunch in the cafeteria or at weekend barbecues. At Mayo, where the dozen or so clinic buildings are connected by a series of underground passageways referred to as "the subway," there is an attitude of surprising affection and collegiality. In many other labs, breakthroughs are carefully guarded from everyone except research partners. But at the elite fraternity of Mayo, ideas are currency. If you have an interesting theory, you pick up the phone, and within hours or even minutes have the second, third, and fourth opinions of a staff pathologist, an immunologist, an epidemiologist.

One day Ponikau realized that maybe the department was looking at the wrong thing. Maybe it wasn't the tissue, or a bacterium, or a virus, that was causing the problem: maybe it was the body's own immune system. Together, Ponikau and a surgical pathologist, Tom Gaffey, began looking at patients' tissue under an electron microscope, which can magnify cells up to 200,000 times. They saw something unusual: clusters of white blood cells called eosinophils clumped near the surface of the membrane.

"For a while, we forgot about the fungi," Ponikau says. "My whole life was eosinophils."

Eosinophils normally exist in the bloodstream in minute numbers—the range is anywhere from 1/200 to 1/2000 of white blood cells. They are incompletely understood, but their chief role is thought to be in combating parasites. Eosinophils contain several dense granules comprised of powerful proteins, which they use to destroy invaders. "Stupid warrior cells," Ponikau calls them. "Rambo-like." Gaffey and Ponikau experimented with fluorescent staining techniques so they could better locate eosinophils. Once they had perfected the new stains, they noticed something unusual: the immune warriors were literally lined up in the basal cell wall of the mucous membrane—the meeting place between the body and the outside world. Their concentration had jumped from an average of .01 percent in the blood to 20 percent in the tissue—a 2,000 percent increase.

Until that moment, the conventional wisdom in medicine had been that viruses, bacteria, or chemicals irritate or infect the lining of the sinus. Get rid of the invader, end the problem. Instead, Ponikau realized, the key to the disease might be in what the body was producing itself: the mucus produced by the membrane to moisten and protect it. For surgeons dealing with the disease, mucus was generally an irritation—something to be suctioned out and discarded. But in fact, Ponikau thought, the mucus likely had its own story to tell. The eosinophils had accumulated at the membrane wall and were even entering the membrane itself. Perhaps, he thought, they were even going into the mucus. But why? Clearly, the body had deployed them to destroy something, much as bacteria are attacked by neutrophils, another type of white blood cell. If Ponikau's theory was right, chronic sinusitis patients should be disproportionately those people whose phlegm was full of esosinophils. In order to follow up on his hunch, Ponikau needed vast quantities of mucus.

When surgeons set about operating, the first thing they do is clear the mucus—it blocks the tissue they need to reach. Ponikau had to convince first Kern and David Sherris, one of Kern's partners, that he needed the mucus. But to do that required a reversal of operating room procedure as it had been practiced for decades. Ponikau's strange request for a waste product required the support of some thirty staff members, from scrubs nurses to lab technicians to pathologists, all of whom were accustomed instead to preserving tiny bits of diseased, excised flesh, but not mucus.

Operating room procedure was not the only hurdle. Once the mucus was extracted, Ponikau had to ensure the safety of his samples up to the pathology lab, several floors away. Running through tunnels and hallways in his teal scrubs and clogs, mask dangling from his neck, Ponikau cut an amusing figure. "Don't drop the mucus! Don't drop the mucus!" he would shout as he jogged through the gleaming white corridors.

"It was as if we were carrying some sort of ancient, precious glass," says Karmen McGill, a surgical technician who was among the first of Ponikau's converts. "It was pretty funny. People would look at you as if you had an organ for transplant or something, and here it was just mucus on a slide."

It was a complex process, and it aroused deep suspicions. A pathologist once called him, irate at the strange specimen that had appeared in his lab. "Somebody delivered snot up here!" he shouted. "What the hell are you people thinking?"

Gaffey began reflecting on Ponikau's theory in his off-hours. A tall, affable man with jet-black hair, Gaffey is fond of murder mysteries and jigsaw puzzles, and grasped the possible significance of Ponikau's speculation immediately. For years, Gaffey had sent lab reports back on sinus surgery patients which read: "Evidence of chronic inflammation. No cancer. Tissue marked by 10 percent eosinophilic penetration." Looking back, Gaffey saw a pattern: the higher the penetration of eosinophils, the more intensely the patient suffered from the disease.

Gaffey and Ponikau began to search the mucus under the electron microscope, and found clusters of eosinophils there. Maybe a parasite was in the mucus, Ponikau announced to his colleagues. Sherris laughed out loud. "Now the German's really gone nuts," he said. "Send him back home."

As a control, Ponikau had collected mucus from healthy medical students who had no allergies—no nasal symptoms whatsoever. To their surprise, Gaffey and Ponikau found the common fungi in both patients and healthy controls. At first, it looked like the end of his theory. But then Gaffey started to notice something strange. In the mucus of healthy patients, the fungi were characterized by their branch-like appearance (under a microscope, they look like saguaro cacti). "Textbook," Gaffey says. One afternoon, Gaffey had a "Eureka moment." Sinusitis patients' fungi, under the microscope, looked misshapen and odd-looking by comparison. It looked "destroyed, beat up," he says, "as if it were sitting in a cloud of toxic protein."

Suddenly, Ponikau's fungi assignment for Kern looked like scientific fate. When the two scientists realized that the eosinophils were forming clusters around the fungi, Ponikau wondered if his early, coincidental interest might have an effect on the understanding of the disease. Everyone had fungi in their mucus, but only the sinusitis patients had eosinophils there. Finally, Gaffey and Ponikau understood the meaning of their findings. The eosinophils were crossing the blood barrier—literally leaving the bloodstream in order to search out the fungi and destroy it. The eosinophils were releasing MPB, major basic protein, which is known to be toxic to parasites. Unfortunately, MBP is also toxic to the delicate mucous membrane, leaving it damaged and ulcerated, even destroying cilia. It wreaks havoc on the whole system. Bacteria weren't the problem—studies had long established that they were as rampant in healthy people as in sinusitis patients. But if the tissue gets inflamed or ulcerated—which it does when the MBP is released—the bacteria can penetrate and invade the body. Bacterial infections are common in chronic sinusitis patients, and are known as acute exacerbations of the disease. But the bacteria's presence obscured the fungi. Bacteria are easy to culture, and, absent antibiotic resistance, are simple enough to treat.

Ponikau points to an ugly, swollen gash on his left hand, the result of a scrape with his garage door. "It makes perfect sense. The skin on my right hand is clear—no red, infected-looking scabs. Why? Because the skin is protecting the tissue from all the bacteria that normally live on top of it." Once the skin is cut, bacteria can rush in and multiply. This, he says, is exactly what happens in patients with chronic sinusitis, again and again. The reaction to the fungi is like a cut that never heals— it allows the bacteria to invade.

While the clinic's findings had yet to be published, Ponikau felt confident enough about the fungal link to present his theory at a 1998 conference of rhinologists and allergists in Vienna. The news was met with mixed reactions.

Heinz Stammberger, an Austrian ENT who, along with his mentor, Walter Messerklinger, is largely credited with pioneering endoscopic sinus surgery, listened intently. Stammberger himself had written his doctoral dissertation on fungal sinusitis, and looked on in stunned amazement.

Stammberger, a tall, slender man with a crisp British-German accent, was both surprised and disappointed by the discovery. His own team of physicians at the ENT University Hospital in Graz, Austria, had been looking at fungal disease for years. "I felt that we should've come up with the diagnosis. But we simply didn't have the idea Jens had. He had the right concept, and followed through." Stammberger was almost as astonished by the reaction of other doctors, many of whom did not welcome the new theory. At many meetings over the next few years, people were aggressive and often downright rude. "They simply did not want to hear this," he says. "The findings could spell radically new treatments."

At one conference, a young ENT marched up to Ponikau, arms folded across his chest. He felt that his surgical skills, hard won after years of training, were in danger of being made obsolete. "I am thirty-three years old, and have been waiting for the day I could practice medicine in my subspecialty now for fourteen years. I worked part-time in college, put myself through med school, and, after my internship and residency, am almost $200,000 in debt. I am about to get married. I want to pay off my bills, buy a house. But what you've just shown us might obviate all my hard work. Do you realize that?"

Others took the results—published in the Mayo Clinic's journal, *The Mayo Clinic Proceedings*, in 1999—less personally. Hannes Braun, an ENT at the Graz Hospital, believed Ponikau, but thought the problem was environmental. Braun had always thought that fungal growth was an American predicament, somehow tied to contaminated air-conditioning filters. "I was interested, sure, but I didn't think these results could be duplicated elsewhere—most of the rest of the world doesn't have air-conditioning."

Stammberger and Braun replicated the study with ninety patients, many of whom had never drawn a breath of air-conditioned air in their lives. As controls, they used healthy doctors and medical students. They, too, found eosinophils in the tissue and mucus. They also found fungi in the mucus of more than 92 percent of their subjects. The team could no longer say it was a function of American air conditioners. "Ponikau was right," Braun concedes.

Walter Buzina, a microbiologist on staff at the clinic, showed Stammberger his lab results: a total of 283 positive cultures had grown—an average of 3.2 organisms per patient. As a mushroom lover in the Central European tradition—he hunts for them on weekends—Buzina decided to let the specimens take their course. Some weeks later, he summoned the team into the lab for a viewing: enormous mushrooms had grown from the swabs from subjects' noses. Specimens ranged from huge blooms of *cladosporium,* the black growths typically found in dank showers, to *penicillium,* the soft blue-green mold that appears in forgotten bread bags, to the graceful gills of *tricholoma,* prized by mushroom lovers for its delicate flavor and aroma. "We couldn't quite believe these growths ourselves," Buzina says. "It was quite amusing."

Buzina presented his findings—on slides—at a conference of nose experts in Washington in September, 2000,[1] and the mushroom harvest got a big laugh. Ponikau, for his part, addressed the crowd by saying that the new theory was a "major shift in the paradigm" of understanding sinus disease. Dr. David Kennedy followed up with a talk concluding that many of the field's assumptions about sinuses now appear as "a collection of facts, theories, and fetishes," obscuring multiple causes for the disease—heredity, allergies, pollutants, and stress. Studies from Finland to Turkey link the disease to pollution. Kennedy recommended more studies to evaluate genetic or individual factors, as well as the role of bone inflammation in the disease.

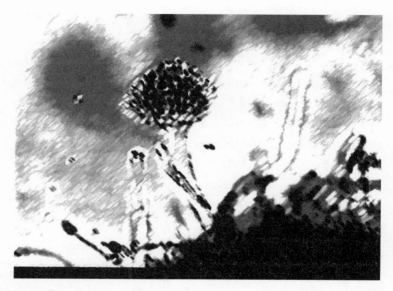

*Aspergillus, one of the nose's most common fungi. (Photo courtesy of Dr. Walter Buzina.)*

Kennedy admits that surgery is not a panacea, but he feels that "it does help resolve symptoms over time." He adds that it can take up to two years to fully recover from the postoperative inflammation and assault to the cilia of sinus surgery. "This is a slowly progressive disease that does not get resolved quickly. It can seldom be reduced to a few simple elements."[2]

Ponikau shrugs. "You know, 500 years ago, everyone thought that the sun revolved around the earth. How could it all be wrong? People saw the sun going up and down every day. The paradigm shifted when Copernicus saw it another way. I'm hardly saying our findings are on par with Copernicus's—but look what happened! He was terrified to publish his theories.

After his death Galileo was imprisoned for embracing them. This is the way it is, in science."

Meanwhile, at the 2001 meeting of the American Academy of Asthma, Allergy, and Immunology in New Orleans, three Mayo immunologists, S-H Shin, Gerald Gleich, and Hirohito Kita discussed a study in which they found that the immune systems of patients with chronic sinusitis reacted to fungi by producing the same kind of eosinophilic inflammation Ponikau and Gaffey had observed. In healthy people, this reaction was absent, even when fungi were present. The study led to a $2.5 million grant from the National Institutes of Health to further investigate fungi's role in sinus disease.

Some speculate that the American diet may supply some answers in the rise of sinus disease and asthma, which are often linked. Massive amounts of antibiotics in the food supply—American cows, chickens, and pigs consume twenty-five tons of antibiotics a year—may be behind the increase. Trace amounts of antibiotic in meat, the theory goes, may kill the bacteria that prevent fungal overgrowth. To test the idea, doctors at Mayo hope to enroll the Amish of southern Minnesota in a study soon. The Amish breathe the same air as the rest of the population, but they grow their own food and raise their own livestock, shunning such "advances" as hormones and antibiotics. According to Ponikau, asthma and sinus disease are virtually nonexistent among older Amish, who maintain traditional ways. For the first time, though, asthma and sinus specialists in Rochester are seeing younger Amish, who have abandoned some conservative customs, as patients. Doctors caution that this study—and findings from it—are a long way off.

In the meantime, Sherris and Kern had started using topical antifungal sprays to kill the fungi, with promising results. In a study of fifty-one patients, all of whom had had repeated surgery, thirty-eight, or 75 percent, reported feeling better and needing fewer supplementary medications, such as decongestants and steroid nasal sprays. Even the doctors were surprised by how much their patients had improved. People who had had five, ten, fifteen surgeries were for the first time walking in for checkups without sniffling or wheezing.

Joanne Meyer, a sixty-eight-year-old piano teacher and mother of three, has struggled with the sinus trouble her whole life. "I lived on antibiotics," she says. "Flat out lived on them." She has been hospitalized for sinusitis, which invariably led to pneumonia (and the threat of meningitis) at least six times. During a three-week stay in an Indianapolis intensive care unit in the 1980s, she asked her doctor what the prognosis was. " 'You'll keep having these infections until one day you die,' " he replied.

In 1996, Meyer went to the Mayo Clinic. As a patient of Kern's, she was scheduled for surgery at least three times in as many years. But by every appointment, her CT scans had cleared a bit, and Kern agreed to put the surgery off. Finally, after the eosinophil discovery in 1999, he discovered a common fungi, aspergillus, in Meyer's nose, and prescribed a spray that used Itraconazole, an older antifungal medication. He told her not to expect immediate results, and when her problems didn't clear up, she was deeply disappointed. The antifungal spray was yet another nostrum in her otherwise loaded drug cabinet: prednisone, asthma inhalers, antibiotics, and decongestants. After a few months, though, Meyer noticed that she felt better, and had more energy—and realized she was cutting down on her other medica-tions. "It's been fifteen months now without a single bad bout of asthma," she says. "For someone like me, that's a marvel."

Now divorced, Meyer says her illness put strains on her mar-riage. Her husband, she says, couldn't understand or cope with her condition. "I come from hardworking people who don't com-plain—that's my heritage—but for years all I could do was make it from the bed to the couch to the piano for lessons." When her children were small, she was sick constantly—so much so that she had to hire help in an era when only mothers took care of their children. "I got so depressed. I didn't wind up in the psy-chiatric ward or anything but you sometimes had to wonder about yourself. Why was I sick all the time? Why did it take me three months on antibiotics to get over a simple cold?"

Carol Van Camp, an airline systems programmer from Kansas, suffered from sinus, ear, and lung infections for years. With three small children in day care, she blamed her illness on her constant exposure to viruses. But when, in the late 1990s, her illnesses became so severe she was routinely hospitalized, she knew something was wrong. "I could never get well, ever," she says. "I'm not a complainer, but this drove me crazy." Her ears hurt so badly she couldn't sleep at night, and during her bouts of insomnia she wondered if she was losing her mind. Eventually, doctors prescribed tranquilizers. Still, she refused to give in to the disease. A lifelong athlete, she continued to break in her horses, or go on her daily four-mile runs. But she loathed the medication, particularly the prednisone. (Irritability is a common side effect.) "If people would cough near my desk at work I'd tell them to get the hell away from me. People thought

I was nuts. 'You don't understand!' I'd say. 'Your little cold will turn into a sinus-ear-lung ordeal for me,' I'd tell them. They thought I was some kind of hypochondriac."

After one sinus surgery, multiple procedures to insert ear tubes, and a move from an old farmhouse she loved to a newer structure where she might "feel better," Van Camp sought help at Mayo. Two years ago, Kern found a colony of fungi in her Eustachian tubes—they had traveled from her nose to the tiny crevice of the ear, causing chronic pain and inflammation. She, too, takes the antifungal medication. "It'll sound like some infomercial for a diet product, but I swear, this has given me my life back," she says. At first she was disgusted by having to squirt medicine into her nose every morning and night. Now, though, it's like brushing her teeth. Van Camp has not been on antibiotics for a year. "The one little cold I got went away *by itself*," she says incredulously. "For me, that's just amazing. That never happened to me, not in fifteen years."

Now a double-blind randomized placebo trial is under way, but anecdotal results are promising.[3] "Folks come in clutching a newspaper article with the findings, having driven three days from Texas," says Sherris. He cautions that it is too early to declare victory. But in an ongoing study of Mayo patients in which disease ranges from mild to severe, mildly ill patients have responded as well as those who have the most difficult cases. Still, many doctors continue to scoff at the new data, pointing out that it has not been proven to be effective.

Stammberger maintains a scholarly resolve along with his cautious optimism. "How this treatment, after it is out of trials, will affect the millions with the disease, we don't know. So far, we have good news. But is it for everyone? We can't say."

Buzina, the microbiologist, makes some dry observations. ("I haven't any patients, only specimens. So I say what I like.") In Europe, medicine is funded by the state. Doctors get paid whether they perform surgery or not. "The situation is very different," Buzina says. "Even so, those who discredit the results will tell you that they object to the science. They are not going to say that they fear for their income." After so many years of training, many surgeons find it hard to believe that topical antifungal agents, applied daily, can alleviate their patient's symptoms. "Look," says Kern, pushing up his surgical glasses as we cross a Rochester street one bitter March day, "the closest thing we can liken this to is the news that *H. pylori*—a simple bacterium—caused ulcers, and could be treated with antibiotics. Ulcers weren't 'in your head' or 'from too much stress' or because of 'bad diet' that was somehow all your fault. They came from a bacterium in the gut. Nobody wanted to hear that news, either," he says, "especially all the heartburn drug makers."

The threat that the discovery will alter the surgical landscape may be more perceived than real. In fact, Kern and Sherris are still in the operating room two to three days a week. Sherris says that the team's revision rate appears to be less frequent than it used to be, but that it is too early to tell. "It's a new way of treating the disease. It's hopeful. But we don't pretend that it's a panacea."

In the continuum of medicine, Stammberger cautions, this is just another new discovery. Doctors don't know when the fungi get there, or when they start to cause problems. In Graz, doctors are even starting to look in the noses of newborns to see if babies are born with fungi they got from their mother's bodies.

"There is so much we don't know," he says. "But as we reflect on medical history and the treatment of this disease, you have to wonder." Like all science of the nose, surgery of the sinuses has undergone its own recent evolution. Stammberger believes that after some initial missteps, the field is now on the right course, with the early, overly intrusive surgical methods giving way to treatments that combine antifungal medicines and antibiotics with more conservative surgery.

"We know now that the old approaches tended to make things for the sick person even worse. Chopping out the innocent turbinates, stripping the membrane—none of this was done with malice. But we kind of had to go through all that in order to get to this point. Discoveries like this put things in a new perspective."

Even those who fully embrace the fungal theory insist that it doesn't mean surgery is obsolete. Polyps must still be removed; deadened, chronically infected tissue must also be excised before sick sinuses can hope to heal. In order for the antifungal treatment to be effective, it has to be able to reach areas that are often covered with scar tissue. "You wouldn't use a topical medication on skin that was coated with a layer of Jell-O, would you?" Kern asks. "Sometimes, there is no way around surgery."

Stammberger agrees. "But certainly today you hope that there is a brain behind the hand that is cutting you," he says.

"As we look back on the history of treating this disease, you come to the painful conclusion that the twentieth century was a century of butchery." Stammberger gives a sigh. "As someone who helped to improve these techniques, I hope I can eventually be someone who helps make them less necessary."

# Part Three

# The Commercial Nose

# nine

# Smells Like Money

W̶hether we like it or not, our noses today are working over-time. The early nose functioned to sniff out danger, but today's nose is bombarded with scents that are supposed to help seduce, relax, refresh—practically everything short of unload the dishwasher. Botanical candles at Pottery Barn vow to transform rooms. Fragrance-doused paper pine trees for the car's rearview mirror are stacked next to Doritos at the gas station. The Gap dis-plays eau de toilette and body lotion called Heaven and Dream right next to the checkout line. From upscale boutiques to Wal-Mart, you can buy an aroma to help set mood or suggest a place (it is not clear who did the research on heaven). But this burst of scent is a recent phenomenon in America. In less than fifty years, fragrance journeyed from crystal bottles behind the glass counter at Neiman Marcus to the street.

The American attitude toward such luxury got off to a slow start. But each epoch and cultural turn powerfully influenced America's relationship to fragrance, from the first transatlantic flight to postmodern sexuality, from dazzling materialism to pared-down simplicity.

Annette Green has seen it all. While many industries see trends and leaders come and go, Green has endured as the scent trade's evangelist for more than forty years. In 1961, Green took charge of the Fragrance Foundation, a nonprofit organization designed to educate the public about the importance of scent, and has served as the industry's chief spokeswoman, historian, and archivist ever since. (She has even established a fragrance museum at her office in downtown Manhattan.) Her mission in life, as she sees it, has been to liberate scent from its imperial perch in fancy department stores to envelop the masses. She has quietly guided the way Americans buy, and use, scent: annual retail sales in the personal fragrance industry—perfume, eau de toilette, and soap—have gone from $250,000 in 1950 to $6 billion in 2000.

Walking into the Fragrance Foundation is like walking into a spectacular restaurant. A pale green carpet hushes noises. Giant backlit bottles of amber perfume glow against the cool white walls of the two-story office in Manhattan's Murray Hill. A scent is pumped into the office daily, so delicate it is all but unnoticeable. Is that the tiniest bit of spilled perfume—those bottles really are everywhere—or your imagination? Green is mum on her own favorite scent, and no one else in the office will say what the fragrance is. The secrecy emits its own mystique. "It's all Annette," says Theresa Molnar, the foundation's executive administrator and Green's right arm. "She thinks of everything."

Green, in her eighth decade, has amazing energy. She is at her desk before eight, and often stays past seven, long after the staff has left. A trim, small woman with short gray curls and impeccable makeup, she wears Ferragamos, knots Hermès scarves around her neck, and sports the hands and ankles of a woman half her age. Her nails are painted a pale pink, her fingers a flash of gold rings.

Where others divulge nothing—industry insiders are as covert as CIA operatives—Green is forthright and bold. She calls women "dames" and "broads," and speaks her mind on trends.

Green's affinity for fragrance began at birth: her mother went into labor as she stood sampling perfumes at a Philadelphia department store. Though luxury was off-limits for most women in the midst of the Great Depression, Green's mother, a milliner, saw perfume as essential. When Green was small, she knew the best way to make her mother happy was to save for a special bottle of the stuff, for Christmas or her birthday. "She just lit up when she'd open it," Green says.

Her mother was the exception. During the first half of the twentieth century, American interest in scent was minimal. Most products were French, and by association so blatantly erotic that they were anathema to rugged American sensibilities. While the French had been using perfume for four hundred years, the Americans had a decidedly different tradition. (As recently as the 1800s, some descendants of American Puritans still viewed body odor—man as God made him—as an outward sign of godliness.)

In 1949, four French perfumers, Caron, Chanel, Coty, and

Guerlain, established a small consortium, which they named the Fragrance Foundation. Its first director traveled the country on the ladies' luncheon circuit, speaking on the powers of scent. But the notion of wearing Shalimar or Joy (launched in 1935 as the "most expensive perfume in the world") seemed an unspeakable indulgence, especially in a period when women were returning from the wartime workplace to the hearth. And as the country set out to Americanize recent urban immigrants, the goal was to get people *not* to smell. Foreign language newspapers from Manhattan to Milwaukee urged new Americans to wash with products that conveniently doubled as both soaps and household cleaners.[1]

The Fragrance Foundation struggled to promote its wares in the United States, but bridging the cultural gap was neither easy nor swift. In the postwar period, scent was a by-product of the ultimate ideal: a squeaky clean image both at home and in person. Perfumed soaps like Tide and Cashmere Bouquet had been around for decades, but after the war chemical companies devised a slew of new cleaning products for their new market of college-educated housewives. In *The Feminine Mystique,* Betty Friedan documents the advertising of new sprays and powders that would allegedly clean better than old-fashioned elbow grease and vinegar. By buying these new cleansers, scented with synthetic pine and lemon, women were made to feel as if they were doing themselves—and their families—a great service. Housewives could put their brains to use, right in their own home laboratories.[2]

Fragrance on the body was another matter entirely. Returning GIs had brought home fancy bottles of French perfume after the liberation of Europe, but for the most part, even years after the war they remained unopened on dressing tables, too intimidating to use.

Meanwhile, Green, an aspiring journalist, had moved to Manhattan from New Jersey, where she hoped to land a job at a fashion magazine. Such work was highly sought after—there were few respectable jobs for young ladies, and editorial assistantships at *Vogue* and *Harper's Bazaar* were chief among them. Instead of waiting for an opening, in the early 1950s Green took a job at a publication called *The American Druggist,* where she soon wrote her own column. One day, one of her bosses asked Green to help dress windows of a New Jersey drugstore. She agreed, and once the task was completed, she turned to studying, and chatting with, the teenagers who passed time at the store's soda fountain. As it turned out, when girls had finished with their flirting and floats, they turned their attention to cosmetics. In those days, such products were kept behind the counter, much as condoms and pregnancy tests often are today. In her early twenties, Green watched the girls with fascination as they giggled and tried on lipstick testers. But only a brave few mustered the courage even to ask for anything, let alone buy an item.

After a few trips to the store, Green suggested to the owner that she might step in as a salesclerk herself. She thought her presence as a young woman would make the girls feel more comfortable—and be more profitable for the store. Her hunch was right, and soon she was a fixture on Saturdays, laughing and joking with the teenagers as she racked up sales of compacts and rouge. Green wrote about the simple logic in her column, deftly suggesting that cosmetics would yield even more sales if they were moved onto open shelves. Girls with crushes on good-looking soda jerks were bound to visit drugstores. If they could legitimize their "stopping in" with a purchase, all the better.

Green earned a reputation as a thoughtful marketer. But writing was her real love—or so she thought—and soon she landed jobs with publications elsewhere. Within a few years, however, a French perfumer, Lenthéric, offered her a job in public relations. She took it. "They paid me a heck of a lot more money than I'd ever made as a journalist," she says. Eventually, she started her own public relations firm, and in 1961 took on the Fragrance Foundation as a pro bono client and soon began serving as its executive director. Green knew that perfume, like cosmetics behind the counter in the drugstore, was daunting to most American women. Yet French women, whether they were doctors or housewives, glided through Paris swathed in scent. "It's as natural to them as breathing," she says. For Green, fragrance was magical. She hoped that one day, Americans could see it the same way. As it was, women only used a tiny drop behind the ears before going out—and then only for special occasions.

But as the country redefined itself in an era of middle-class comfort, women strove to keep up with new pleasures, from cars to TVs. Magazines were more than happy to dispense advice about how to spend money on advertisers' products. Perfumers, of course, paid for many ads, and *Glamour* magazine encouraged readers to be daring with the stuff. A 1957, article advised: "The most important rule in the art of applying fragrance is to apply it. Don't simply admire the bottles on your dressing table. And learn that the only thrifty way to wear perfume is to use enough to count—a touch behind the ears is a lot too little and a waste of this valuable, functional invention."[3]

## A Shift

Just as Green was wrestling with how best to organize the foundation, a new development transformed America: airplane travel. Pan American World Airways had recently completed its first transatlantic flight from New York to Paris, cutting jet travel time in half and creating a huge upsurge in Americans traveling abroad. Films helped deepen the appeal—from *Sabrina* and *Roman Holiday* to *Gigi*. Paris beckoned above all. American women returned from visits with flacons of perfume that they had sampled and chosen themselves. For the first time, they began to wear it regularly. Chanel No. 5, the French sensation (introduced in 1921, it was the first scent to contain aldehyde, a synthetic molecule), enjoyed instant fame on the other side of the Atlantic after Marilyn Monroe told a reporter that it was all she wore to bed. European manufacturers began to recognize the American market, and by the end of the 1950s they had introduced thirty new women's fragrances. In the United States, Estée Lauder launched Youth Dew, a heavy floral scent purportedly worn by Joan Crawford and Gloria Swanson. Avon (which began in the 1880s as the California Perfume Company) became a trusted name by selling fragrance and makeup to housewives directly, with no intimidating sales-

clerks. Saleswomen were peers who went door-to-door proffer-
ing little product samples, so women could see which colors
and scents their husbands liked best.

The packaging of an era's fragrances mirrored its architecture, striving to be both modern and "functional." Even cosmetics companies entered the fragrance market, designing gold or
silver-toned lockets that held a scented wax that could be
smeared across the skin. They were inexpensive, and fairly dis-
gusting, but few women got past Mother's Day without receiving one as a gift.

Green knew that with money to be made, and glamour to be
had, Americans would start wearing real perfume sooner or
later. Using her training as a journalist and her skills as a marketer, Green spoke to society columnists at major newspapers
everywhere. Fragrance, she told them again and again, was as
important in a woman's wardrobe as the proper shoes.

By the early 1960s, companies had even introduced scents
for men. Far from Dad's stodgy Old Spice or medicinal Aqua
Velva, these were uncorked machismo: Aramis, named for the
Third Musketeer, was supposed to evoke the manliness of a bygone era. English Leather, though available at the drugstore, appealed to the proto–Ralph Lauren suburban patrician. And
Brut's celebrity endorsers said it all. In commercials, Joe
Namath and Wilt Chamberlain, totems of American masculin-
ity, slapped Brut liberally on their cheeks as women clustered
nearby. Hai Karate, introduced in 1968, at least had a sense of
humor. It used "Laugh-In"-like ads to show that men who wore
it were so attractive they had to resort to martial arts kicks to
fend women off.

But as art mirrors life, industry reflects culture. As soon as perfumers had established a market, Woodstock and antiwar marches jolted American society. At campuses and protest meetings far outside tidy suburbia, perfume was the last thing on people's minds. Fragrance, however, lingered: its ability to transform image and mood somehow stuck with consumers, no matter how antiestablishment they were. Soon jasmine candles, sandalwood massage oils, and patchouli incense sticks mingled with marijuana as an accessory to the sexual revolution. In the early 1970s, perfumers launched breakthrough scents like Cachet, a woodsy fragrance said to "react" with a person's individual chemistry. (In fact, all scents vary from person to person, reacting differently to each wearer's skin.) Nevertheless, Cachet advertised that it was "as individual as you are."

Scent was now accessible to everyone—in price, location, and packaging. While early French perfumes bespoke elegance and sophistication—Baccarat and Lalique often designed the bottles—vessels were no longer demure and feminine. Now, they were simple, modern, utilitarian, and often downright phallic. Many were cylindrical and topped with large half-spheres of plastic or metal. They could be purchased everywhere—at drugstores, discount outlets, even supermarkets. If the scents of yesteryear had appealed to the inner glamour of a trapped housewife, the fragrances of the seventies appealed to Everywoman, Everygirl, and even Everyman—and their inner desires.

Revlon introduced two fragrances, Charlie and Enjoli, with blatant appeal to emerging feminist sentiments. With its perky pantsuit-clad model, Charlie ads invoked the independence of the new young woman. In one commercial the blonde "Charlie Girl" carries a briefcase, and strides happily along a city street. The spot ends with her patting a male coworker on the behind as she turns to grin at the camera. Enjoli ads had a similar message: You *could* have it all. Its sassy blonde model, in a navy blue suit and pumps, comes home and begins slinging pots around her kitchen while she sings Peggy Lee's classic: "I can bring home the bacon / fry it up in a pan / and never let you forget you're a man." By the parting shot, she has changed into a slinky cocktail dress, and thrusts a bottle of Enjoli toward her viewers.

Suddenly, scent was everywhere, even in snacks and makeup. New candy, such as Starbursts and Tic-Tacs, were loaded with artificial flavorings and potent fruity "aromas." Fragrance permeated toiletries like shampoo; "Gee, Your Hair Smells Terrific" and Herbal Essence were top sellers. Flavored lip glosses borrowed scents from popular culture: Dr. Pepper and Bubble Gum were two favorites with adolescents. Some colognes were specially marketed to teenage girls. No sixteen-year-old's dressing table was complete without a bottle of Love's Lemon Fresh or Baby Soft, a sweet, treacly scent, colored pink, that theoretically bottled innocence. Its ads sent a somehow different message: a young girl, dressed in a low-cut white dress, sat lasciviously licking a lollipop. The box read: "Because innocence is sexier than you think."

But nothing changed the landscape of fragrance like musk. Medieval Arab traders first sold musk as an aphrodisiac. (The word "musk" is derived from an ancient Indian word for testicles; the deer's gland is located right next to them.) Two entrepreneurs, Bernard Mitchell and Barry Shipp, took note of hippies buying vials of the stuff (or rather, its synthetic substitute) from incense and head shops in Greenwich Village, and introduced Jovan Musk in 1972. Rather than use clean-cut blond models, Jovan ads, which ran in magazines from *Playboy* to *Redbook,* left nothing to the imagination. Neither did the bottles. The company introduced his-and-hers gift sets with flasks that nestled suggestively together. One said that it was the "provocative scent that instinctively calms and yet arouses your basic animal desires. . . ." Another promised: "It may not put more women into your life but it'll put more life into your women." And a commercial opened with the question, "What is sexy?" It showed a man ogling a woman in a skimpy dress as she washes her car, the hose squirting suggestively.

Fragrance in the 1970s reflected an open sexuality, but also another feature of the decade: frugality. At a time when people struggled in gas lines and wore buttons vowing to "Whip Inflation Now," the industry was full of affordable colognes and eaux de toilette. Now that more people could afford it, attitudes toward scent had changed dramatically—enough so that Green inaugurated an annual awards ceremony to honor the year's most innovative fragrances. Modeled after the Oscars, she called it the Fifi Awards.

The 1980s ushered in an era of conspicuous consumption. Designer products expanded from clothes to sheets to eyeglasses, and inevitably, to scent. It had taken twenty years, but Green finally had her wish: American women had begun to think of perfume as vital. If you couldn't afford Calvin Klein or Oscar de la Renta couture, you could at least wear status on your wrists and neck—and almost everyone did.

Scents were just as dramatic as the big hair and tight jeans that were in style. Bottles had extravagant designs and bright colors. Even their names evoked power: Poison, Obsession, and Decadence. "It was a voluptuous, egocentric time and fragrances were too," Green says. "People wanted you to be able to smell them from across the room."

One potent scent, Giorgio, achieved just that. Available only by mail order or in trendy boutiques, it had a snob appeal akin to that of clubs modeled after Studio 54. Shortly after its introduction in 1982, Giorgio founders Fred and Gale Hayman gambled on a new technology they believed would popularize their scent like no fragrance counter ever could. With $300,000 of their own money, they invested in a "scent strip" researchers said could deliver a whiff of the fragrance straight to consumers' nostrils—millions of them. Unlike the crude "Scratch 'n' Sniff" technology of the 1970s, the perfumed strips came on double-thick perforated pages that could be bound into glossy women's magazines like *Vogue* and *Glamour*. When torn away and rubbed across the wrist, they gave consumers an actual sample of the fragrance.

The gamble paid off. Within Giorgio's first three years, the fragrance generated $80 million in sales. Soon the heavy scent was so ubiquitous that restaurants in New York and Los Angeles posted signs: "No Smoking. No Giorgio."

For the first time, Green says, masses of people had the opportunity to sample fragrance away from the retail marketplace. Men could try it out in the waiting room of their doctor's office instead of at a counter they were too embarrassed to approach. Within a few short years, every perfumer distributed the scented strips. By the end of the 1980s, you could try seven or eight of them, all for the price of a magazine. For a time, the novelty even boosted magazine sales.

As Green reveled in the success of fragrance in America, she also became aware of the small groups of scientists studying olfaction and behavior. If perfume could make people feel good about themselves, surely scent used on a larger scale had implications for moods as well. Though olfactory science was in its infancy, Green met with researchers at Yale, the University of Pennsylvania, and Georgetown to discuss how the foundation might reinforce the researchers' efforts. At a meeting with the foundation's board of directors, Green asked the industry to support the new discipline.

"Aromatherapy" had been in use in Europe for many years but had only recently come to the United States. Green never liked that phrase, thinking it connoted folklore rather than science. She coined "aromachology" to describe the work she hoped the foundation could support with a new research arm, the Olfactory Research Fund (since 2001, it has been called the Sense of Smell Institute). Green envisioned offering grants to scientists of olfaction, particularly those whose research bolstered the positive effects of scent.

The fund has since sponsored hundreds of studies on smell and behavior, ranging from the role of fragrance in women's sexual fantasies to the sense of smell in space.[4] New York's Memorial Sloan-Kettering Cancer Center found in 1994 that the smell of heliotrope, a vanilla-like scent, significantly reduced the anxiety of patients about to undergo an MRI. Now technicians pump the aroma into the claustrophobia-inducing chamber before loading patients into it. By 2001, the fund had financed 51 projects for $1.3 million.

Indeed, the MRI study helped launch a whole new industry within an industry: helping overworked Americans unwind. By 1997, several companies had introduced a wide range of aromatherapy products. Coty's Vanilla Fields claimed to calm, and Shiseido's Relaxing, a mix of bamboo, tea rose, and cucumber, promised to soothe away stress. Estée Lauder's sporty division, Clinique, launched Happy, and Origins, its upscale bohemian line, released aromatherapy products (including aromatic gumballs) in 1998.

Home-furnishing stores started selling scented candles and room sprays—updated Renuzit. Aromatherapy products—creams, tinctures, shampoos, and lotions—soon crowded the toiletries aisles at drugstores and supermarkets. Smell, suddenly, had overwhelmed the marketplace. An industry trade publication found that home fragrances such as candles, incense, and bathroom soaps increased more than 20 percent in 1998. A Connecticut candle and potpourri manufacturer, Blyth Industries, reported sales of nearly $1.2 billion in 2000. And NPD, a marketing research firm, estimated that aromatherapy products within the beauty industry grew 8 percent between 1999 and 2000.

Green loves the barrage of fragrance, though she sniffs that "a lot of companies have jumped on the aroma bandwagon." New research, she then adds, has simply helped manufacturers to make more and better products.

One would hope. By the mid-1990s, celebrities such as Sophia Loren, Elizabeth Taylor, Cher, and Mikhail Baryshnikov had each put out their own fragrances, but few of these products took off. Cher's Uninhibited seemed anything but. Its claim was offset by its bland scent and detailed Art Deco bottle. Baryshnikov was celebrated for his soaring flights, both artistic and political, but his perfume, Misha, fell flat. Meanwhile, Elizabeth Taylor's fragrances, Passion, followed by White Diamonds, were hugely successful. People wanted to smell like the beautiful icon from *Cleopatra,* but not necessarily like Cher.

Scents in the 1990s tried to evoke simple pleasures. Crabtree & Evelyn Ltd. has a line of "kitchen scents," ranging from Patisserie to Salad Greens. The marketing pitch is domestic rather than seductive. Ads say: "We all love those delicious aromas wafting from the kitchen. Now you can enjoy them anytime—even when the cook's off duty." The reality? Salad Greens smells more like Seven Seas bottled dressing than arugula dressed with balsamic vinegar and olive oil. And a stroll through Sephora, the ultramodern French cosmetics chain with branches worldwide, is almost too much for the nose to bear. There is Fresh Rice Oil ("to unblock 'chi,' "), Brown Sugar Body Polish ("rejuvenating and relaxing"), and Chocolate-Orange-Chocolate bath foam ("bewitching"). But Green approves. "If you're dieting, you want rich aromas," she says. "Sometimes you just want the smell or taste of something you love—not necessarily to eat it." Indeed, a recent institute study conducted by Susan Schiffman, a professor of psychology who specializes in eating disorders at Duke University Medical School, found that inhaling scents can be nearly as satisfying as eating.

The trend doesn't end there. Demeter, a New York company, comes out with new colognes every season. Although they are called "Pick-Me-Up" sprays, some, it seems, are intended more to lift spirits with their wit than with actual scent. Demeter's colognes range from Dirt to Popcorn and Altoids, "the curiously strong mint." (The company even has a collection they call their "Attitude Adjustment" line. Touted as "anti-aromatherapy," the scents range from Gin-and-Tonic for the recently jilted to Brownie for the "Never Happy.")

And in recent years, the notion of scented products has drifted into household cleaning products. Tired of your wooden floors smelling like Murphy's Oil Soap, and your bathroom like Fantastick? The makers of such products as Palmolive and Lysol have launched new scent lines, although it's anyone's guess what "Orchard Fresh" dish detergent and "Spring Waterfall" countertop cleanser are actually meant to evoke (or are going to make you forget you had to clean up after dinner).

Upscale retailers have also introduced new products. Elegantly packaged cleansers—everything from scented water to put in the steam iron to window washer—are sold at high-end stores like Williams-Sonoma and Anthropologie. They smell great, and are, of course, expensive: Williams-Sonoma's special basil and verbena countertop cleaner costs $9.50 a bottle; their chamomile ironing water costs $12. Consumers at Nordstrom's cosmetics counters can now pick up such items as Caldrea's Green Tea Patchouli dish soap ($8), and Jane French Laundry Wash ($16), along with their mascara and lipstick.

Although these products represent a small share of the market, Green expects the niche to grow. She laughs at the innovations. "The nose is individual. Why not pamper it? We now know that the nose can improve our whole quality of life. If popcorn's what turns you on, hey, why not?"

At the beginning of the twenty-first century, Green thinks that people today have reawakened to the significance of their sensory selves, in cuisine, in architecture—and in their noses. She feels it an inevitable humanizing response to the rise of the computer. "We still have primal urges," Green says of the Internet, "and one of the most pronounced is smell." Perhaps both worlds will meld someday—a French cinema company, CanalPlus, is exploring the possibility of a box to deliver scents that correspond to the audiovisuals. Like Smell-o-Vision, the 1950s precursor of the idea, moviegoers may soon be able to see a chef chop and sauté onions on-screen—and smell it as well. (A Silicon Valley firm, DigiScents, enjoyed brief fame in the late 1990s when it introduced a computer device containing a mixture of chemicals that allowed a person to smell certain odors while browsing the Web. It went bankrupt after two years.)

Cyrano, a company in Pasadena, California, is developing a computer chip that can smell. A simple version of the device already exists in smoke alarms, but Cyrano hopes to eliminate the human variations—colds, fluctuating hormones—that can influence a person's ability to sniff out items gone bad, from food and wine to beauty products. Lancôme, the French cosmetics company, and Starbucks, the Seattle coffee giant, have both bought models of what Cyrano calls its "e-nose." The device is capable of distinguishing only a fraction of the 400,000 smells humans can distinguish, but researchers believe that computer advances will yield better results soon.

And then there are the increasing commercial applications for pheromones. Fragrance companies are adding synthetic pheromones to perfumes and colognes. David Berliner, the researcher and venture capitalist in Menlo Park, started a company called Erox; its products include a line of pheromone-laced scents called Realm. A British company called Kiotech now markets a product it calls Sex Wipes, a baby wipe–like tissue soaked with pheromones. It sells them in rest rooms at nightclubs and bars—right next to the tampon and condom machines. Winifred Cutler, the biologist and behavioral endocrinologist, has founded Athena Institute, which manufactures fragrances with chemically reproduced human pheromones. Its men's line, called Athena Pheromone 10X, promises, like the swinging Jovan ads in *Playboy* of the 1970s, to "Raise the octane of your aftershave." The women's version, Athena Pheromone 10:13, conveys more of a *Ladies' Home Journal* sentiment: "Let human pheromone power enhance your sex-appeal and increase the romance in your life."

No scientific studies exist to show whether the products "work" or not. One day, though, on a crowded commuter train to Manhattan, I sat next to an athletic-looking man as I sifted through some material on pheromones, including Realm. My seat partner politely asked if I was a scientist, so I told him I was researching a book. The man, Ted Thomas, turned out to be a dancer with the Paul Taylor Dance Company in New York. He said that he used Realm regularly, and that when he did, women approached him freely to strike up conversations, telling him deeply personal details within minutes of meeting—medications they were on, family histories, job woes. "And they always finish with, 'I don't know why I'm talking so much. I don't even know you,' " he said. To be sure, Thomas is a handsome man—almost intimidatingly so—and, as a professional dancer, he carries himself with uncommon grace. I remarked that he very likely had little trouble attracting women in the first place. Which came first? I asked. He blushed and said, "Well, *more* women talk to me now." For now, there is no definitive answer.

Berliner welcomes such anecdotes. "I am not at all surprised," he says, not at all modestly. He thinks for a moment, then adds: "But Realm is not an aphrodisiac. The same substances which might attract one person may repel another." Still, Realm, which is sold only in department stores and over the Internet, made Erox $20 million in 1996, only a year after its debut. (Berliner won't divulge current company revenues, but a recent *Wall Street Journal* article put the figure at $40 million.)

But from pheromones to Demeter's kitschy Funeral Home scent, there may be some signs that the industry has gone too far. Millions of Americans are believed to suffer from MCS, multiple chemical sensitivity. They experience myriad symptoms, primarily inflammation of the nose, sinuses, and lungs, when they come into contact with low levels of chemicals. Estimates vary, but government statistics show that anywhere from 2 to 6 percent of the population might be affected. A whiff of anything scented, from cigarette smoke to laundry detergent to perfume, can make those with MCS ill.

Now, companies that once spent millions on coming up with the most appealing fragrance for their products make "scent-free" soaps, deodorants, and detergents. Restaurants, doctors' offices, and some corporations now prohibit their employees from wearing scented products. In the heyday of scent strips, so many mail carriers—and subscribers—complained of allergies and headaches that magazines began to limit them. (*The New Yorker* even had a scent strip hotline, for subscribers who wanted odor-free issues.) Some towns are considering banishing artificial scents altogether (Halifax, Nova Scotia, already has).

This backlash against the perfume excesses of the 1980s and the aromatherapy bombardment of the 1990s may be a sign of things to come. Like a laminated menu with dishes numbering in the hundreds, some say there are too many scents—the nose needs relief. Sales of perfume have begun to show signs of sluggishness. While it could reflect a downturn in the economy—clothes, jewelry, and air travel have slowed too—some critics, particularly the scent-free-space advocates, say that people have had their fill of fragrance.

Ironically, some new research points to evidence that sexual attraction—the promise of many perfumes—is actually based on natural odors. Synthetic ones, therefore, might hurt rather than help your chances of attracting the right mate. Isn't the romance and mystery surrounding the fragrance industry, then, just a clever ruse? Might wearing colognes and perfume be actually counterproductive?

None of this seems to worry Green. She has seen many things come and go, and she retains a sunny confidence about the future of perfume. Fragrance, she says, is here to stay. "Look at the changes in the industry in the past forty years," she says. "We've gone from women afraid to wear perfume to now having scented body lotion at the lingerie shop. When you go to pick up a couch, you can pick up potpourri for your car." Green shrugs. "I get a lot of energy from my work—the sense of smell itself. You just have to keep thinking, 'What will people want and need tomorrow?' "

That, of course, is anyone's guess. If aromas can affect sexual fantasies, why not research odors that could minimize aggression, or even combat fear? Scent has held its allure for millennia. "The world moves on," Green says, waving a perfumed hand in the air. Every epoch has its successes, from Nero's rose petals to Giorgio. The future, she says, will come from science, from learning how fragrance affects our moods and our behavior.

Ads and bottles help, but in the end, people will respond to how scents make them feel, dream about, and hope for—or what it makes them remember. Perhaps Proust gave the best explanation for how an industry founded upon the esoteric can flourish. Perfume, he wrote, "is the last and best reserve of the past, the one which when all our tears have run dry, can make us cry again."

# The War on Stink:

# Banishing Body Odor

The flip side of fragrance, of course, is stink. Human beings are naturally pungent. Food particles affect the breath. Women menstruate. People sweat. The average adult body has between 3 and 4 million sweat glands, capable of producing four gallons of fluid a day.

But Americans, in general, loathe the smell of human beings. We do anything to keep from smelling like ourselves—bathing, scenting, and deodorizing more than at any other time in history. Even so, humans are still the most "highly scented of apes," Michael Stoddart writes in his seminal book on human odors, *The Scented Ape: The Biology and Culture of Human Odor.*

Each person has an odor as individual as the whorls on his fingertips. Body odors differ from culture to culture and even among race: they are influenced by genes, environment, diet, and bacterial flora. (While people generally blame perspiration for smelling bad, sweat itself is odorless. In fact, the fluid excreted by the eccrine, or sweat glands, is nearly 99 percent water, but it begins to stink when it breaks down the bacteria that rests on the skin's surface.) The culprit for your most pungent odor is the apocrine glands, which release not only perspiration but also fatty substances that provide the perfect environment for bacteria to multiply. While sweat glands begin working at birth, apocrine glands start functioning only at puberty. The apocrines are concentrated mainly in the armpits and around the genitals, and it's no coincidence that these areas usually sport tufts of wiry hair—hair that soaks up the thick, oily apocrine secretion and disperses it into the air from a vastly increased surface area. The placement and texture of the hair leaves endocrinologists with little doubt about the odor's role as a sexual attractant—at least millennia ago.

Caucasians and Africans have more aprocrine glands than do Asians, and consequently, some experts say, have sharper odors. In fact, having body odor in Japan was once thought to be a sign of poor genes and bad character, and immediately disqualified one from military service. Recently the Japanese concern about stinking prompted a Shiseido researcher to isolate the smell of growing old: in particular, nonenal, an unsaturated aldehyde. While nonenal is a traditional component of body odor, men over forty were found to emit particularly concentrated amounts. Shiseido and other fragrance companies were quick to capitalize on fears of smelling like *ojisan,* a term that literally means "uncle" but also implies a square old man who is hopelessly inept. New nonenal-neutralizing products quickly appeared on shelves of Japanese drugstores and department stores—including a line of antimicrobial men's underwear. Ads for the briefs featured a young woman surrounded by middle-aged men, arms hanging onto subway straps, in a crowded commuter car. Overwhelmed by their odor, she finally screams, wrests her Walkman off her head, plucks the foam ends of her ear pieces off, and stuffs them up her nose.[1]

Elsewhere, it is foreigners who smell the worst. The Chinese, for example, refer to Westerners as those who "stink like butter." Butyric acid in butter and other dairy foods makes Americans and Europeans reek to Asians who eat no milk products. Likewise, odors from garlic, onion, strong-smelling fish, and spices are carried through the bloodstream and excreted through the sweat glands to the pores. In the United States and in Europe, disdain for immigrants who eat such sharply flavored food has often expressed itself as disdain for their objectionable "smell."

Yet around the world, body odors are meaningful in ways many Westerners might find repulsive. In Burma, a common greeting is "Give me a smell" ("Come close enough so I can smell you"). Members of a New Guinea tribe bid good-bye to each other by placing their hands under each other's armpits and rubbing themselves with the other's scent. (By contrast, a German expression for "I can't stand the guy" is *ich kann ihn nicht riechen,* literally, "I can't smell him.")

Americans are often quite disturbed by the smells of others, which poses delicate personnel problems. In offices and factories around the country, managers struggle with the stink that dare not speak its name: the body odors of employees. Whether caused by a diet rich in spices, poor hygiene, or too much perfume, supervisors everywhere wrestle with this most sensitive of issues.

Few executives are even willing to discuss the problem openly for fear of embarrassing colleagues or employees. To inquire about the source of body odor can trigger civil rights liability—if the problem is caused by medical conditions or certain foods in the diet, it is covered under the Americans with Disabilities Act. One Portland, Oregon, manager suggests that employers must first verify if the problem exists—sometimes people are downright malicious. If it does, she says, "proceed with caution." And if the employee volunteers that his or her body odor is the result of a medical problem, she advises, "Shut up!"

## The First Deodorants

The human journey from reeking stench to intolerance for odors was relatively quick. Prior to the nineteenth century, Westerners merely disguised their body odors with strong perfumes, if they bothered to do so at all. (René Laennec, a nineteenth-century cardiologist, found a way to ease the olfactory assault of diagnosing heart problems the old-fashioned way—putting an ear to the thorax—when he devised the modern stethoscope. It put a safe distance between the doctor's nose and the patient.) Baths were weekly, at a maximum, until indoor plumbing became commonplace in the 1920s and 1930s.

Until then, anyone concerned with such a mundane matter as body odor relied on household products—one popular way to fight odors was a mix of ammonia and water splashed onto the tender skin of the armpits. In 1888, a Philadelphia doctor came up with a commercial concoction, a thick, waxy cream made with zinc oxide, a microbial designed to kill odor-causing bacteria. He called it "Mum," and relied on his nurse to sell and spread word of the product. It not only caught on, it worked, and soon many were using Mum and other creams like it. Applied with the fingers, the first deodorants were cumbersome, and contained caustic chemicals that not only stung but ate through clothing.

By mid-century, other inventions, many from the war, led to the development of more practical applications. A pointed tip, loaded with a ball bearing, was able to deliver a controlled amount of liquid through a tube in the first ballpoint pen. (The British Air Force was one of the first wholesale consumers of the pens, once airmen who used them at high altitudes discovered that they didn't leak.) Proctor and Gamble used the mechanism to deliver the first roll-on deodorant, Ban, in 1952. It became a top seller. Now, though, deodorants had an added ingredient: chemicals designed to quell not just odor but sweating itself, by reducing the amount of perspiration that reaches the surface of the skin.

Americans, it turned out, were more than eager not to smell bad. Listerine, for example, produced by the Lambert Pharmaceutical Company, was first used in the 1870s as an antiseptic in hospitals and homes. In the 1920s, it was relaunched as a mouthwash. Ads showed a young woman gazing at her reflection in a mirror. "What secret is your mirror holding back?" it read. The text went on to say: "She was often a bridesmaid but never a bride. And the secret her mirror held back concerned a thing she least suspected—a thing people simply will not tell you to your face. That's the insidious thing about halitosis (unpleasant breath). You, yourself, rarely know you have it. And even your closest friends won't tell you." Paranoia suddenly boosted sales from $100,000 in 1920 to $4 million in 1927. Listerine's ingredients hadn't changed a bit, but its concept had.[2]

During the Great Depression anxiety intensified, and soap companies stepped up their campaigns as well. Lifebuoy soap coined the phrase "B.O.," for body odor, and echoed Listerine's hint with a 1931 ad that warned: "Don't risk your job by offending with B.O. Take no chances! When business is slack, employers become more critical. Sometimes very little may turn the scales against us."[3] A radio ad for Lifebuoy made B.O. sound terrifying. It used a foghorn with a screechy voiceover shouting "Beeee-ohhhh!" The soap became the country's most popular bath soap.

In prosperous postwar America, worries about job security had long since faded. The technological advances that propelled the economy also revolutionized the war on body odor. The new antiperspirants, which contained aluminum salts, were thick and slow to dry, and customers complained that they stained clothes. But a second wartime discovery added another alternative to the list—the delivery of a product through aerosol spray. Though it had been in use since the late nineteenth century, in 1941 inventors Lyle Goodhue and William Sullivan patented the aerosol, which was used to deploy insecticides for U.S. troops at risk for malaria during World War II. By the late 1950s, manufacturers had deployed antiperspirants in cans as well, and by the early 1970s, they accounted for 80 percent of

the market. Heightened awareness of air pollution in the mid-seventies led to a ban on spray cans using aluminum zirconium, a main ingredient in the antiperspirants. Today, some 95 percent of adult Americans use some form of antiperspirant or deodorant, according to the Gillette Company, and most prefer the solid powder or clear gel that glides onto the skin.

Americans go to great lengths to stop sweating—and stinking. Some have a condition called hyperhidrosis, or excessive sweating, and for extreme cases doctors sometimes remove sweat glands or the nerves that stimulate them. The procedure has fallen out of favor since the introduction of a prescription product called Drysol, which, when applied correctly, can reduce sweating for up to a week.

Even cosmetic surgeons have discovered a slice of the sweat-free market: the toxin botulinum, or botox. First they injected it in wrinkles to paralyze the muscles causing them; then they realized the same treatment could relieve migraines. They also discovered that the toxin stopped facial sweating, and began experimenting with injections of the sweat glands in the hands and armpits of excessive sweaters. The procedure works, but requires thirty to sixty injections every three to six months and costs an average of $1,200 per treatment.

Along with rank armpits, millions grapple with "feminine odor" and foul-smelling feet, and a huge industry churns out arsenals for battle. In hygiene-obsessed America, combating malodors has for many turned into a profitable career. Karl Laden, who holds a Ph.D. in chemistry, has advised the health and beauty industry on antiperspirants and deodorants for more than thirty years. He has written two volumes on their use and technological development; they serve as a sort of bible of B.O. for the personal products industry worldwide. Laden now works at a company he cofounded in Israel called InnoScents, which is working to develop new methods of fighting body odor.

Another such entrepreneur is Herbert Lapidus, an industrial

chemist who came up with the idea for Odor-Eaters, the latex inner sole with activated charcoal. Like other sweaty parts of the body, feet begin to reek when bacteria feed on perspiration. Because feet are trapped in socks and shoes all day, bacteria have the perfect conditions in which to grow, especially since each foot contains 250,000 sweat glands and can produce a pint of perspiration in a day.

As the head of research and development for a small company called Combe International, based in White Plains, New York, in the early 1970s, Lapidus was seized with the idea of solving the problem of foot odor. (He demurs at first from saying why, then says that his wife suffered terribly.) He saw a British invention, a paper sole that covered a layer of activated charcoal, which gave him an idea. You couldn't very well put paper inside a shoe and expect it to last, but the activated charcoal was a brilliant notion. Activated charcoal filters chemicals and odors in everything from nuclear waste plants to airport ceilings (the fumes would be intolerable without it). If you put the activated charcoal inside a bed of latex, he thought, it might work.

In order to keep the feet dry, Lapidus designed the latex soles with hundreds of tiny holes, which would act as a bellows with each step, circulating air. The charcoal absorbed the perspiration and the odors, and an antibacterial powder killed the bugs that led to bad smells in the first place. For six months, Lapidus worked around the clock to perfect his new sole.

To test the product, Lapidus put an ad in the *New York Times* advertising a remedy for foot odor. Overnight, he had dozens of willing participants. Each had stories more outrageous than the last. One woman refused to let her husband indoors until he had "aired out" his feet; his shoes had to be kept a certain distance from the family noses at all times. Another woman claimed to use a gas mask when she washed her husband's socks. One desperate wife said she was contemplating leaving her husband if she couldn't find a way to deal with his foot odors. He marketed the product as a one-size-fits-all, with patterns people could trim to fit their own shoes.

Lapidus is retired now, and declined to release sales figures. But he does say that if every pair of Odor-Eaters ever sold were placed toe-to-heel, they would circle the planet twice. According to market analysts, Combe's share of the odor-eating market is 85 percent, which would account for about $50 million a year in sales. Lapidus designed and patented many other products, including Lanacaine, Vagisil, and Just for Men haircolor. "But all anyone ever wants to discuss is Odor-Eaters!" he says. "I'm sure it'll be on my tombstone."

Then there is Mel Rosenberg, a microbiologist in Tel Aviv who is a leading expert on bad breath. Patients visit his clinic from around the world—some are so convinced their breath reeks, they are suicidal. One woman was desperate for help with her halitosis, but Rosenberg couldn't smell a thing. He quietly probed the cause of her insistence. As it turned out, the woman's father had always had foul breath, so she subconsciously assumed that she did, too. Eventually, she brought her eighty-four-year-old father from New York, and Rosenberg treated him. Often, he says, it is those with the least awareness of their odors who smell the worst. Another woman who had suffered from halitosis for decades was found to have a calcified bead lodged in a sinus. It had been there since she was three.

Like bad odors elsewhere on the body, bad breath generally comes from bacteria. If you don't brush and floss daily, particles of food remain in the mouth, collecting bacteria, which can cause bad breath. In addition, food that catches between the teeth, on the tongue, and around the gums can rot, leaving the odor of decay in the mouth. Dentures that aren't cleaned properly can also trap food and attract germs. Other culprits are foods in the *Allium* family, such as garlic and onions, which, once they are absorbed into the bloodstream from the digestive tract, are transferred to the lungs. The odor is expelled with exhalations. No amount of brushing or flossing can help until the body eliminates all traces of the offending food. Dieters, too, can get bad breath from not eating enough. When dieters burn stored fat, it gives off acetone, which has a rank, medicinal odor.

Though Americans spend a fortune on breath fresheners, they don't do anything but mask bad odors, Rosenberg says. "You have to kill the germs in order to get anywhere." Working with dentists, Rosenberg developed a two-phase oil and water mouthwash, which is on the market in Israel and the UK. Bacteria and debris attach themselves to the solution and are discarded.

The topic of body odors, from wherever they emanate, makes people laugh. It also makes them nervous. But obliterating our smells has become a national reflex. Consider the following, from a pamphlet distributed to foreign students at the Rochester Institute of Technology:

. . . Americans have been taught that the natural smells of people's bodies and breath are unpleasant. Most Americans bathe or shower daily (or more often if they engage in vigorous exercise during the day), use an underarm deodorant to counteract the odor of perspiration, and brush their teeth with toothpaste at least once daily. . . . They rinse their mouths with a mouthwash or chew mints in order to be sure their breath is free of food odors. . . . Most Americans will quickly back away from a person who has "body odor" or "bad breath." This backing away may be the only signal that they are "offended" by another person's breath or body odor. The topic of these odors is so sensitive that most Americans will not tell another person that he or she has "bad breath" or "body odor." Some foreign students and scholars come from places where the human body's natural odors are considered quite acceptable, and where efforts to overcome those odors, at least on the part of men, are considered unnatural. Still other students and scholars come from places where personal cleanliness is considered more important than Americans and they may view most Americans as "dirty."[4]

Today more than ever, Americans are urged to embrace diversity, and to accept differences in race, beliefs, and religion. Muslim women may wear veils; Indian women may wear saris. But woe be to the newcomer who smells like one.

# eleven

# From the Bronx to America: Odyssey of a Nose

> I imagined that there was no happiness on earth for a man with such a wide nose, such thick lips, and such tiny gray eyes as mine. . . . Nothing has such a striking impact on a man's development as his appearance, and not so much his actual appearance as a conviction that it is either attractive or unattractive.
>
> —Leo Tolstoy

> A beautiful nose will never be found accompanying an ugly countenance.
>
> —Johann Kaspar Lavater

For as long as he can remember, Richard Garvey has been thinking about noses. Such awareness was born of many experiences. The first was an unfortunate collision between his nose and a stickball bat when he was in first grade (his nose was broken). The second came about a year later, when, one day after school, he sat transfixed before the television. As he watched Superman fly through the walls of a skyscraper to rescue Lois Lane, his mother interrupted to ask if he could go to the corner for some milk. "Sure, Ma," he remembers saying. "Just wait till the commercial." If he ran fast enough, he knew he could get back before the episode restarted.

Inspired by his hero, he bounded down the stairs and onto the street. A huge oak, encroaching onto the sidewalk, gave little Richie an idea. "I was learning in church that faith could move mountains," Garvey says, "and the damn thing was in my path." He thought that if he prayed hard enough, he could soar through the tree, just like Superman. So, clutching his quarters, he started to run. He picked up speed, stretched his arms before him, and flew—straight into the trunk of the oak. A woman waiting for the bus shouted, "Sonny! Didn't you see that tree?" Blood was everywhere—on his shirt, his face, in his mouth. It took a moment for him to realize that it was pouring out of his nose. Sobbing, he limped back home. Not only had he missed part of "Superman," his nose had swollen "like a zucchini," Garvey recalls. "My mother didn't know what the hell happened."

His nose healed, but it was badly broken. Never small, it now had a big hump, right in the middle. He could see it even without looking in the mirror. When you have a large nose, the bridge of the appendage is always within your field of vision, like the emblem of a Mercedes-Benz on the hood of a car.

In time, he grew both to hate, and to love the bump. It wasn't exactly pretty, but it was distinguished, differentiating. And when he felt insecure or nervous, he would rub it with his fore-finger, almost as if for good luck.

Garvey had other reasons to care about noses, and not just his own. The youngest of six children, Garvey helped to care for his sister Valerie, who had spina bifida, lung and heart defects, and severe facial deformities. The two were the closest in age, barely two years apart. When he was very young, his mother took him aside and asked him to help her. "She's a special child," she told him. "She's not going to be with us very long, and God wants us to take extra special care of her."

Garvey's father died when he was two, and an older brother was grown. So he assumed the role of Valerie's caretaker as a boy of five. He drew her blood for tests, and gave her medicine from a dropper at bedtime each night. "Kids at school would make fun of her, call her names, and I would just get furious," he says. The girl's nose was small and misshapen, and her voice was high-pitched. "They'd laugh, because she looked different, sounded different. I would storm out of the house and want to beat up any kid who made fun of her. I even hit somebody once in church." She died at thirteen.

A few years later, Garvey was again watching TV, and as he flipped through channels, he saw a PBS special on plastic surgery called "A Normal Face." He was awestruck. On the show, plastic surgeons repaired cleft palates, aligned asymmetrical eye sockets, and grafted new skin on the cheeks and noses of burn victims. "I always thought plastic surgery was for women of a certain age, or people who were in the federal witness protection program," he says. (His neighborhood was thick with wiseguys.) Now he wondered what Valerie's life would have been like if she had had such an operation. "Maybe we could've helped her have a more normal life," he says quietly. "Maybe people wouldn't have been so cruel." He decided then what he would do with his life, despite other distractions.

And so at fifteen, he started saving for his education by working at a local restaurant near Yankee Stadium. Signed pictures of Joe DiMaggio and Mickey Mantle line the walls. From busboy to bartender, Garvey worked weekends, nights, and summers to put himself through school—first through Columbia University, and then through medical school at Georgetown. Through it all, he says, his work at the restaurant helped remind him who he was, and where he came from.

But for his mother Lorraine, at least some of where he came from was worth forgetting. As the daughter of Sicilian immigrants in the Bronx in the 1930s and 1940s, when anti-immigrant sentiment was high, Lorraine had claimed that her surname, La Forge, was French. Once she married Al Di Piero, though, there was no doubt about her or her family's identity. Still, when Richard was young, she took him to speech therapy in order to take the edge off his Bronx accent. "You have to be totally American to succeed here," she told her son. Richie Di Piero understood that the chance of his somehow metamorphosing into Greg Brady was slim. But some years after his father's death, his mother married Martin Garvey, an Irish-American bus driver. He adopted all the Di Piero children and bestowed, along with love and stability, what was to become an extraordinary gift: an ethnically ambiguous surname.

"You're a real American boy now, Richie," Garvey's mother told him, "with a nice American name."

But still, there were always reminders that somehow he was

not. For one, the nose. Second, his accent, though diminished, remained. And Columbia's wealthy elites did their best to remind him of his origins. "There were guys with Roman numerals after their names, and they'd give me all kinds of shit. 'Hey, here's our smart little wop! Hey, Richie, say sometin'!' " Garvey winces. There is nothing worse, he says, than someone from Connecticut trying to mimic an outer borough accent.

It was hardly as if he were trying to be someone else in the first place. He points to the walls in his basement, covered with its own icons: the all-Italian cast of *A Bronx Tale,* and the nearly purebred crew of *The Godfather.* A signed picture of Robert De Niro hangs above the fireplace. But still, the comments stung. He taps his nose. "They stuck with me, you know."

Training for plastic surgery is long, beginning with four years of medical school and a residency of seven years. But Garvey was determined to enter the specialty even as he enrolled at Georgetown. He knew firsthand how a nose—"a nose!" he says, incredulous at the thought—could mark a person, and before long he was a man obsessed. He became fascinated with their shapes, their anatomy—and how to change them. In his spare time, he watched doctor after doctor sculpt and streamline noses, and he made notes to himself about whose surgical style he would eventually emulate.

What surprised him most, though, was learning about the long history of rhinoplasty, as nose jobs are formally known. As it turned out, people's concerns about "fitting in" on account of their unusual noses went back centuries. Plastic surgery takes its name from the Greek *plastos,* meaning molded or shaped, and while there were reports of repairing wounded features in Asia, the most detailed versions did not appear until the Renaissance in Italy. Most celebrated was the work of Gaspare Tagliacozzi, a surgeon and anatomist from Bologna who described a method of substituting noses lost to injury or disease with the skin of the arm. He published his findings in a book, *De curtorum chirurgia per insitionem* (The Surgery of Defects by Implantation), printed in 1597. The Church was aghast at Tagliacozzi's work—officials believed it to be tampering with the work of God—and excommunicated him. At any rate, his technique was short-lived, as the reconstructed noses tended to freeze in cold weather, or get dislodged during a violent sneeze. But Tagliacozzi knew the benefits of reconstructive surgery were also psychological. While the new features lacked physical perfection, they helped to "buoy up the spirits and help the mind of the afflicted."[1] Elsewhere in Europe, people experimented with other nose replacements. After losing part of his nose in a duel, the Danish astronomer Tycho Brahe fashioned a mixture of metal and wax, which he affixed to his scar.

In India two hundred years later, a British officer noticed the peculiar nose and a large scar on the forehead of an Indian merchant with whom he traded. The officer learned that the man's nose had been sliced off as punishment for adultery. A potter who was trained in crafting new noses had made him a new one of wax, which was placed on the stump. A flap of skin was cut from the forehead and grafted over the prosthesis. The technique, which had been used for centuries on the subcontinent (cutting off noses was a common penalty), was soon reported in the *Gentleman's Magazine of London* in 1794.[2]

The article attracted great attention. Europe was in the midst of a syphilis epidemic, and noses were obvious casualties of the disease. The infection attacked the soft tissue of the nose, causing the bridge to collapse, or worse, leaving a gaping hole in the middle of the face. It was a public marker of private behavior, even branding sons and daughters with the sins of their parents (infected mothers could pass the disease to their babies). A nineteenth-century German surgeon devised surgical tools and materials ranging from wax to gold to rebuild sunken syphilitic noses, and an American plastic surgeon once butchered a live duck in the operating room so he could graft the bird's breastbone to the nasal cavity of a syphilitic man.[3] However, incisions to insert the new materials, which later included ivory and glass, were made on the outside of the nose. They were highly visible, but they could at least help those with disfigured features slip more easily into society.

More than anything, early plastic surgery involved reconstruction of the nose. But by the late 1800s, there was a shift from restorative to cosmetic surgery as immigration—and xenophobia—transformed the modern world. From Jews in prewar Germany to Irish immigrants in England and the United States, noses had a way, much as they did in Lavater's day, of branding—however wrongly—a person's character. John Orlando Roe, a surgeon in Rochester, New York, performed an operation to "cure" the Irish "pug" nose. Borrowing from Jabet's classifications, Roe concluded that the pug nose was the outward sign of weakness and stupidity. Roe crafted straighter, more linear noses, and was the first in the United States to use internal incisions, making cuts on the inside of the nostrils so as not to leave evidence of his work.

Shortly thereafter, an orthopedic surgeon in Germany, Jacques Joseph, made a similar breakthrough. Born Jakob Lewin Joseph to a rabbinical family in Königsberg, Prussia, Joseph changed his biblical name to the more cosmopolitan Jacques as a student in Leipzig and Berlin. During World War I, new explosive devices inflicted facial casualties on a mass scale, but improved hygiene and sanitation helped keep alive wounded soldiers who would otherwise have died of infection. Advances in anesthesia had also helped to make surgery more commonplace.

Joseph reconstructed the faces of countless German servicemen at a Berlin hospital. A dour man who bore dueling scars on his cheeks—a mark of prestige and acceptance into German society, especially for a Jew—Joseph devoted himself to studying the repair of wounds and deformities. He devised tools for many of his procedures, some of which are still in use today.

Like Roe, Joseph also concerned himself with transforming faces that advertised ethnicity—particularly those of his fellow Jews. In 1898, an elegant, wealthy merchant approached Joseph for a consultation. On Sunday afternoons, he customarily drove his family through Berlin in their stately carriage. But something held him back from fully enjoying his outings: his nose. Though he tried to offset it with a thick black mustache waxed into upward curls, the man still believed that his prominent profile drew unwanted attention to his family. They might invite fewer stares if only his nose was smaller. Could it possibly be changed? the patient asked. Joseph assured the man that it could. In surgery a few weeks later he filed down the cartilage on top of the man's nose, which resulted in a new look with "gentile contours."[4] The gentleman returned to the driver's seat of his carriage, his nose transformed. Word of the change spread swiftly through Berlin, and Joseph soon had a burgeoning cosmetic practice.

Indeed, between the world wars, anti-Semitism was a growing feature of life for German Jews. In an increasingly hostile culture, many Jews—some whose families had been in Germany for centuries—began to fear for their jobs and their futures. If altering a small matter—a distinct nose—could make matters easier, such a change was welcome. And since Joseph also made incisions on the inside of the nostrils, he left no trace of his handiwork. (In fact, Joseph thought he was the first to use this method until he learned of papers by Roe.) Many Jews underwent the procedure at the hands of a surgeon they found sympathetic to their concerns, and Joseph later said that he was only too happy to help those he found to "suffer a Jewish nose." He performed many such rhinoplasties free of charge.

Joseph promoted the psychological benefits of cosmetic surgery, writing in his 1931 book *Rhinoplasty and Other Facial Plastic Surgery,* that a person's well-being depends, to a large degree, on his sense of confidence and dignity. Such attributes are enhanced, he wrote, when facial features are in harmony. Joseph's book included a nasal "scale," which touted as its ideal a woman whose nasal tip was no greater than 30 degrees from its bridge. (To some extent, his theory persists today.) Joseph believed that anyone self-conscious about his or her features deserved to feel more self-assured—particularly as Nazism gained currency. If a smaller nose could help a person feel better, Joseph reasoned, it was bound to have some functional benefit.

After World War I, Joseph's reputation as a reparative surgeon was widespread. But, as he performed more and more rhinoplas-

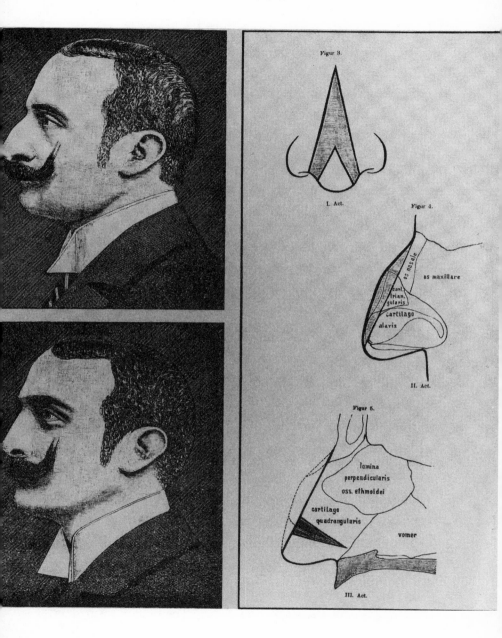

Figur 3.

I. Act.

Figur 4.

os nasale

os maxillare

cavi
trian.
gularis

cartilago
alaris

II. Act.

Figur 5.

lamina
perpendicularis
oss. ethmoidei

cartilago
quadrangularis

vomer

III. Act.

ties, that regard soon slipped to scorn. Medical officials, concerned that he was performing procedures for vanity's sake (or worse, in order to camouflage Jews), revoked his operating privileges throughout the city. Whether in principle or out of fear of increased scrutiny, even Berlin's Jewish hospital barred him from performing surgery. Finally, he opened his own clinic, which drew curious surgeons and apprentices from abroad.[5] A German patriot, Joseph died in 1934, just months after Hitler seized power.

The year after Joseph's death, the Nazis passed the Nuremberg laws, which reserved citizenship in the Third Reich for Aryans alone. Jews were stripped of their German citizenship, forbidden to marry Germans and hire German domestics. More than ever, Jews who remained in Germany felt the need to become as inconspicuous as possible. Nazi schoolteachers began to preach the "principles" of racial science put forth by Adolf Hitler. They measured skull size and nose length, and recorded the color of their pupils' hair and eyes to determine whether students belonged to the true "Aryan race." Jewish and Romani (Gypsy) students were often humiliated in the process. Soon enough, those lacking "Aryan" features sought to change prominent noses by surgeons familiar with Joseph's techniques.

## Postwar America: Joseph's Legacy

In postwar America, where many of Joseph's protégés had taken up practice, plastic surgery flourished. The timing was perfect.

Americans trying to conform to strict standards of beauty sought "nose bobs," as they had come to be known, in huge numbers. Joseph's legacy was to change the shape of the American nose for generations.

Joseph's disciples guarded their techniques carefully, and as rhinoplasties became more popular, this presented a problem: not enough doctors knew how to perform them. Samuel Foman, an anatomist and medical textbook writer, had traveled to Germany before Joseph's death and had a good grasp of his methodology. But in order to describe the procedure in textbooks in as much detail as possible, he needed to observe it. Yet whenever he entered an operating room, American plastic surgeons covered their work. Undeterred, Foman sought to teach the techniques to otolaryngology students, who, he believed, understood the nose as well as plastic surgeons, if not better.

Among his students at Mt. Sinai Hospital was a brash young ENT named Irving Goldman. He shared Foman's interest in the nose's anatomy—so much so that on his honeymoon, he traveled to Germany to study with a Hungarian doctor trained by Joseph, Zoltan Nagel. Eventually Goldman became well known in Manhattan, and refined a rhinoplasty technique known as the "Goldman Tip," which narrowed the bridge of the nose, or *dorsum,* and divided the cartilage that formed a dome over the tip. The result was a pert little nose. Goldman believed his procedure gave ideal support to the new noses he shaped, which, after removing large amounts of cartilage and bone, were radically different features.

The stylish new nose was helped along by another innovation: television. Women were already eager to emulate their perky idols; those who lacked genetic luck could always get a bob to look like Judy Garland, Shirley Jones, and Debbie Reynolds. Between Annette Funicello's years as a Mouseketeer and a bikini-clad sidekick to Frankie Avalon, she altered her wide nose to match her frisky new all-American image. Not only wholesome actresses shared such features. There is great debate about whether Marilyn Monroe had rhinoplasty or not, but at any rate, she bore a small, upturned nose, much like the one Barbie dolls would sport some years later. (Not everyone fit the pattern—or wanted to. Despite the advice of many, Sophia Loren refused plastic surgery, preferring instead to keep her long nose. For a time, American photographers were forbidden to snap her in profile, but the ban was relaxed as her appeal spread.)

But for those of long nose who lacked Loren's curves, the pressure to look a certain way was great. Harold Holden, a Los Angeles plastic surgeon who trained with Joseph, wrote of the gratification he derived from "fixing unaesthetic noses." He describes one patient, a teenager, who was so disturbed by her large nose that she wanted to quit school. Though a talented singer, she nevertheless avoided performing—she was convinced people would ridicule her profile. She despaired that her looks disappointed her parents, who, from time to time, lamented that she lacked a "cute nose" like her older sister, June. "I can't go on. . . . since Dad has become pretty well-known in his field and he and Mother have stepped up our social life, I feel more than ever that I am the scarecrow of the family, and I've gotten to where I just don't want to be seen."

Holden agreed with the girl's assessment of her nose, writing that it was "pretty bad." Such misfortune would surely be the girl's ruin. "This is a situation almost anyone and especially a young girl would find it hard to stand up against. This is a youngster whose whole future is at stake." Holden thoroughly reshaped her nose. "From the moment the final dressing was removed, the girl's happiness was a thing to see. Her deep feeling of inferiority to her sister was both revealed and ended in her first words: 'Oh, Doctor! Now my nose is not in my way! It is even better than June's!'" Holden, too, was pleased. "A life had been weighed down with deformity. 'Burial at sea' under waves of misery appeared to this adolescent personality the sole possibility in life. When the deformity was removed, the girl became able to cope with all the normal currents of her existence."[6]

Another doctor who became well-known for his transformational powers was Howard Diamond, a Manhattan plastic surgeon who perfected a scooped-out bridge and upturned tip that was popular up through the 1960s and early 1970s. According to some of his former students, Diamond was a veritable nose-bobbing machine, performing as many as five operations per morning.

Like Garvey's mother, many second-generation American parents were eager to give their children every possible advantage. Many followed their moves to the suburbs with offers of nose jobs for their daughters, just in time for their bat mitzvahs or sweet sixteen parties. But by the mid-1960s, style—and times—were changing. Revolt overtook conformity from politics to pop culture. Bob Dylan's antiestablishment lyrics, reedy voice, and less-than-classical looks helped underscore his appeal. Though Ringo Starr was dubbed "The Nose," attention to the Beatles focused on their music and spiritual quests, not teeny-bopper beach frolics. Barbra Steisand leapt from her role in *Funny Girl* to leading lady opposite Robert Redford in 1973. Her popularity soared. Beverly Johnson, an African-American model, appeared on the cover of *Vogue,* displacing decades of Grace Kelly look-alikes. Cher, too, became a national icon (although, unlike Streisand, she eventually got her nose fixed. Streisand rejected the idea of altering her nose for fear of changing her voice).

What was essential for parents reared in the 1940s and 1950s—a strict set of rules applying even to appearance—rarely made sense to their children. Outlandish and "natural" replaced the docile and the familiar. From long, free-flowing hair to the Pill and legal abortion, young women suddenly had choices about their bodies that were unimaginable to their mothers. The primer of feminist acceptance, *Our Bodies, Ourselves,* went from an underground publication in 1970 to a paperback tome that ultimately sold 4 million copies—and stood out openly on shelves from college dorm rooms to mainstream bookstores.

The number of people getting nose jobs, meanwhile, dropped precipitously.

By the late 1970s, not only young women were questioning the wisdom of radical rhinoplasties—doctors joined in as well. The procedure was still the most common cosmetic operation, despite the era, and few plastic surgeons were sitting in empty offices. In fact, women who had their noses hollowed out and upturned began showing up with myriad complaints. It can take as long as two years for a rhinoplasty to heal fully, and many noses that had been completely transformed began to look odd once tissue scars settled and skin shrank around the new nose. Some of them were misshapen, even frozen, on faces with otherwise strong ethnic features. Suddenly, doctors began to ask questions:

Why did this occur in this patient but not in that one? What hadn't been done that should have been—or, more pointedly, what had been done that shouldn't have been?

And as the culture of plastic surgery evolved, so did technology. In the 1960s, plastic surgeons had trained by watching their mentors in the operating theater, often with binoculars. But by the early 1980s, young doctors didn't even need to leave their offices—they could watch the greatest practitioners on video. More than anything, this advance changed the profession, says Robert L. Simons, a Miami facial plastic surgeon who acted as president of the American Academy of Facial Plastic and Reconstructive Surgery in the mid-1980s. Students—and teachers—became much more willing to question procedures and outcomes as they stood in front of a VCR than if they were inside an operating room. And suddenly students began learning from people all over the United States, not only the doctors they had observed during their residencies. One doctor's technique for fixing a certain problem might well be incorporated with that of another. Such openness encouraged physicians to be more considerate of their patients, and as a result operations became more individualized. But since the days of Joseph, the general procedure has been roughly the same. The surgeon cuts inside the nostrils and separates the skin of the nose from the underlying bone and cartilage. The bone and cartilage are then reshaped and the skin is redraped over the surface. Occasionally a surgeon will make an incision in the skin between the nostrils, allowing him to more easily see—and reshape—the nasal tip.

By the mid-1980s, most plastic surgeons had dispensed with

the notion that they "knew best," and began asking patients what they, in fact, wanted to change. Doctors stopped turning the noses on angular faces into "cute" features. Even the terminology changed. Cartilage was left in place, and tips were "refined" or "reshaped"—not named for a surgeon who honed a certain technique. "By doing a little," Simons says, "we learned we could achieve a lot."[7]

But elsewhere, a deft touch was not necessarily the rule. By the late twentieth century, cultures from Brazil to Japan pursued perfection from the knife—at any cost. In Rio and São Paulo, where large derrières are a hallmark of beauty, even the poorest of women rounded their rumps with buttock implants. In Tokyo and Seoul, teenagers and young women sacrificed to pay for operations that would dramatically "Westernize" their faces. Two procedures are highly popular: one removes skin from their eyelids, while another raises the bridge of their nose (for those who aren't entirely convinced, removable nasal implants, which slide up into the nostrils, are available).

Social scientists say that beauty everywhere relies on symmetry. Even in the most remote societies, the loveliest woman and the most handsome man have balanced features and shapely bodies. But notions of beauty also depend on the prevailing social mores. Nowhere is this more evident than New York City, where the idea of the perfect nose can vary from neighborhood to neighborhood. In Manhattan, which shares a perch with Los Angeles as the capital of American plastic surgery, there are even a handful of experts for each ethnic group.

Until recently, though, plastic surgery textbooks prescribed the classical noses Da Vinci depicted five hundred years earlier—the "ideal" faces of Northern European noblemen. While many patients still seek the delicate silhouette of Anglo-Saxon features, they simply don't belong on many Mediterranean or non-Caucasian faces—which means the majority of the population in many of large American cities.

Some years ago, Ferdinand Ofodile, the head of plastic surgery at Harlem Hospital, began to worry about some of the requests he was hearing. While many in the African-American community recoiled at the sight of Michael Jackson's whitening skin and ever-dwindling nose, some patients approached Ofodile with pictures of white entertainers whose features they wanted to emulate. "The great majority confessed to hating their noses," he says. "It was as if the negroid nose was something that had to be changed in order to be acceptable. For many, to be born with such a feature is by definition to have something wrong."

An authority on the treatment of black skin, Ofodile traces his roots in medicine in the Ibo country of Nigeria for generations. (African skin can turn black, white, or form fibrous keloid tissue after it is injured or cut in surgery.) But Ofodile was also drawn to the nose, and the rich variations among black features worldwide. Unlike the Jewish and Italian teenagers who got nose jobs a generation earlier, many of Ofodile's patients were Latino, Caribbean, and African-American adults. Ofodile, an elegant man who wears French cuffs and speaks with precise diction, realized that few in the rarefied world of plastic surgery understood the differences in black features—and how to change them subtly.

"It can be distressing for someone to feel trapped inside their body, or their face," he says. "To affect such change in a positive way can be very gratifying. But a face—this is something that must be approached with the utmost sensitivity." And so Ofodile began publishing articles in plastic surgery journals to educate fellow surgeons about black noses. "The history of plastic surgery is seen largely through white eyes," he says.

First, he sought to explain nose structure as a matter of evolution. Because the nose's principal functions are to warm, cool, and moisten the air drawn into the lungs, its shape evolved to reflect its climate. And so, before the dawn of mass migration, the length of noses of those in cold, dry climates became long and had a narrow base, which increased the surface area and the period of time over which inspired air was warmed and humidified. Conversely, in hotter, muggier climates, the nostrils became more circular and had a wider base, decreasing the surface area and the time over which warming and moistening of a breath took place.[8]

Through the volume of patients he saw, Ofodile created three categories of African noses, which other surgeons soon used as a model: African, Afro-Caucasian, and Afro-Indian. Many with African noses sought Ofodile's help for flat bridges and wide nostrils; those with Afro-Caucasian and Afro-Indian noses wanted to change drooping tips or excise humps from the dorsum, the part of the nose that extends from the bridge to the tip. But mostly, Ofodile sculpted new, more defined tips, and performed augmentations: increasing the size of the dorsum by grafting cartilage from elsewhere, usually an ear.

Slowly, as surgeons began using more restraint among whites, those with ethnic patients began to scale back the procedure as well, tailoring it to other features. Since the late 1980s, Ofodile says, rhinoplasty has been the most popular facial plastic procedure among American blacks. African-Americans now make up 7 percent of patients seeking plastic surgery, up from 4 percent in 1992. Latinos account for 10 percent, and Asians 4 percent. Individual procedures are not broken down, so it is impossible to tell the numbers for rhinoplasty itself.

At about the time those categories were published, Richard Garvey was starting his residency in his old neighborhood, at Jacobi Hospital, a public facility in the Bronx across the street from his grandmother's old house. Most of his first cases were reconstructions: burns, trauma, gunshot and knife wounds. Soon he came to the same conclusion Ofodile and Simons had, that plastic surgeons needed to respect the patient's wishes and individuality. "Plastic surgeons weren't God. They had skill. But it was nothing without listening, and looking at your patient."

And Garvey had many patients to listen to, in many different languages. Like other major cities, New York—and particularly the Bronx—was becoming a more diverse place. Gone were many of Garvey's "paisans." Italians and Jews, once the bulwark of the borough, had long since moved to the suburbs, replaced by Latino and Caribbean immigrants who presented challenges unlike those he had encountered in the lush, leafy world of Georgetown, where senators came for "stealth" facelifts.

At Jacobi, most of Garvey's first patients were Latino. Many were gang members, and bore not only slashing scars on their cheeks but whole chunks of tissue missing from the dorsums of their noses, also a result of run-ins with switchblades.

One wintry day Garvey prepared to reconstruct the nose of a seventeen-year-old boy, Ricardo, who had recently dropped out of high school. Ricardo sat nervously in the patient's waiting room, twisting his hands and then wiping his sweaty palms onto his jeans. Deep gashes lined both sides of his face. A scraggly beard covered sore-looking pimples. Garvey had described the wounds on the boy's nose, but from the front, they didn't look that bad. When Ricardo turned his head, however, he looked like the famous painting of the Duke of Urbino that rests in a room of its own in the Uffizi. A finger-sized scoop near the bridge of Ricardo's nose was missing. The sight of it was alarming, to say the least. Garvey mentioned "harvesting" cartilage from deep inside the septum. I had skipped breakfast, and suddenly I was glad I had.

"You doin' OK, man?" Garvey asked. "We're going to fix your nose, pal. You'll breathe better, and you won't be upset when you look in the mirror, OK? You gotta just promise me to stay out of trouble, OK?"

The boy, seventeen, looked on, dazed. "I'll try, Doc, I'll try," he said.

"You clean, man?" Garvey asked. Ricardo nodded and crossed his heart. "I'm clean, Doc, clean." (Cocaine users are at special risk during surgery because the drug can seriously damage the lining of the nose and can cause intense constriction of the blood vessels. "You can hemorrhage," Garvey told me matter-of-factly. "It's bad. In the eighties, sometimes addicts died in the OR.")

In the operating room, Ricardo was stretched out like a dead man, arms motionless at his sides, toes poking through the end of the blankets. Garvey started to inject his nose with a numbing agent; even though Ricardo was asleep, he didn't want to risk his feeling anything. Garvey's partner, Don Roland, reached into Ricardo's nostrils with fine long scissors to snip his nose hairs. Garvey then made incisions alongside the septum with a tiny scalpel, and urged me to peer inside. Blood spurted from each cut, and the doctors moaned knowingly: too much coke in the days before the operation.

Garvey peeled the skin back on the septum, and began to operate. It was stiflingly hot under the lights, and it felt very crowded. Garvey took a minute instrument that resembled a cheese slicer, and muttered what sounded like a prayer. The plan was to take cartilage from deep inside the septum, then graft it onto the hole in Ricardo's nose. Beads of sweat appeared on Garvey's forehead, and even though I'm not squeamish, I felt faint.

With a grunt and a stunning show of strength—Garvey is a big man, with powerful arms—he forced the blade of the device deep into Ricardo's septum. The violence of it was striking, and the room fairly snapped with intensity. Everyone waited nervously to see what he would retrieve. Finally, he held up a small piece of white tissue. It looked exactly like the cartilage on a chicken drumstick.

Garvey tucked it into the hole, and started sewing Ricardo up. Roland clipped the sutures as short as possible. "Otherwise," he said, "they'll itch." Even with tubes in his mouth and his nose still swollen from the force of the operation, Ricardo looked wildly different. His deformed nose had skewed his whole face. Now, he looked handsome—or at least as if he had a chance at it.

For several years, Garvey has practiced in the Bronx, at a suburban New York practice and in an office on Fifth Avenue in

Manhattan as well. His following is large, a fact he attributes to his honesty about his own flaws: a thickened waist, his humped nose. When patients come in complaining about every wrinkle and blemish, he tells them: "Look at me! I'm no symmetrical masterpiece!" His demeanor—and family history—play a role too. "I remember what it was like to be the one asking a doctor for help," he says. "I know all about the anxiety you feel when you're on the other side. You're thinking, 'Will this person be able to help me or not?' "

After seeing hundreds of satisfied patients, he began to consider changing his own trademark: his nose. What's the big deal? he thought. By 2000, rhinoplasty seemed downright routine. It had outpaced all cosmetic procedures in the United States, from liposuction to breast augmentation. Some 389,155 Americans had their noses reshaped that year, at a cost of $1.11 billion. Men accounted for 39 percent of the patients.[9]

The older Garvey got, the bigger his nose seemed (fatty tissue at the tip begins to sag with age). Garvey began to scrutinize his appearance more, and more, and more. He'd look at himself in photographs, smiling with his wife and three children or on the beach with old college friends, and all he saw was his nose. "I swear to God, it looked like a big ugly bird had landed on my face," he says. In his spare time, he once again started studying plastic surgeons—whose techniques he admired, who he thought "listened" well to his patients' requests, and with whom, he says, he felt "simpatico."

Finally, he decided on a surgeon, Mark Erlich. They were acquaintances, not friends. "God forbid I wasn't happy with it—then what would I do?" The day of the surgery, Garvey was nervous, and asked his wife and a friend to help him get home. Once in the holding area before the operation, he fretted. Was he really doing the right thing? Time and time he had counseled his patients: It's not so painful, and you'll be back on your feet in no time. Now, he himself was worried. What if the procedure was more than just "uncomfortable?" He had lived with his nose his whole life. Would changing it be worth it?

Hours later, he awoke in the recovery room, hysterical. He ripped the IVs from his arms, and insisted that he get up and walk. Two nurses and a very large orderly had to wrest him back onto the cot. "Let me out of here!" he screamed. "I want to go to my own bed!" He felt as if he couldn't breathe beneath his splint, and began gulping for air. He couldn't urinate, and he had an insatiable thirst. The sensations gave him a full-fledged panic attack. His heart raced, and he lashed out at everyone—nurses, his wife, his friend.

Once home, he was scarcely better. Clearly, he was having a bad reaction to his anesthesia: it had relaxed his bladder too much, created his thirst, and made him "nuts." He picked up the phone and, groggy, called Erlich, who was still in surgery and was unreachable. Then he dialed every anesthesiologist and urologist he knew in New York City for advice. One suggested taking a warm bath. Another prescribed Xanax, a tranquilizer, to calm him down. Finally, Erlich called. Garvey exploded, he says, sounding off like John Gotti. "If I don't pee in the next hour," Garvey screamed, "your anesthesiologist is going to be in the fucking East River!"

Armed with Xanax and Vicodin, a painkiller, Garvey finally settled down enough to sleep. Through it all, he dreamed of his patients, and the times they, too, had experienced such discomfort. "I felt so trapped and numb. Finally I realized what all my patients had gone through. It was just awful. I had never experienced anything like that—or been so out of control."

The following few days, Garvey was his own worst nightmare. While he gives his rhinoplasty patients strict instructions not to touch the inside of their noses—nostrils are lined with stitches—he couldn't help himself. He picked at the blood clots until the sutures became loose, and one by one, dislodged entirely. Then he began to blow his nose—hard. The more he did it, the better he felt, even though he knew he risked blowing air into the newly stretched skin around the outside of his nose. One day he blew so violently that he felt air travel beneath his eye and cheek all the way up his forehead. He dispatched his wife to the drugstore for Afrin—a topical (and caustic) decongestant that stung the tender, swollen tissues.

Meanwhile, Erlich couldn't believe what he was hearing. "Is this guy insane?" he wondered, and called Garvey's mentor at Jacobi, Bruce Greenstein. "I hope he doesn't manage his patients like this," Erlich told him. Greenstein assured him that as a surgeon, Garvey was as conservative and caring as he had ever seen.

But as a patient himself, he was a "self-destructive machine." One night, unable to breathe, or sleep, he bolted out of bed and pried off his splint—three days before it was supposed to come off. Relieved, he settled down to watch *Goodfellas,* his favorite movie. He still felt constricted, though, and went to the mirror once more. There, he peeled off the tape—again, days away from its scheduled removal.

A week after the surgery, he walked sheepishly into Erlich's office—no splint, no tape, no stitches. Erlich just shook his head. "I hate working on doctors, and operating on plastic surgeons is nothing I ever look forward to," he said. "But you are the worst patient I have ever seen." Indeed, Garvey had subcutaneous air bubbles beneath his nose, which Erlich had to aspirate with a syringe. He ordered Garvey not to blow his nose again for weeks.

But Garvey couldn't help himself. Once in his car, he took a handkerchief and blew, even before realizing he had. Too embarrassed to return to Erlich, he drove instead to his own office, where his partner removed the bubble once more. "Man, you're like a whale with a blowhole," Roland said. This time, the needle's insertion left a tiny scar on the bridge of his nose. "Serves me right," Garvey says.

Two months later, Garvey has had plenty of time to think about his new profile. He is thrilled to have the old bird gone, he says. But at the same time, he misses it. "Just a little bit," he adds. He doesn't feel nostalgic for the broad tip, or the cleft on the end someone once told him "looked like an ass crease." Yet he does miss his bump. "It had a strength to it," he says, with a twinge of sadness. And like today's newly shaped noses, it is, to be honest, scarcely noticeable. Garvey, broad and gruff, with sturdy features and dark, expressive eyes, has a nose that still matches his face—not that of a patrician, or one with an indented bridge. And the experience certainly deepened his understanding—and empathy—for his patients. It wouldn't be such a bad idea if every surgeon had to endure the operation he performs, Garvey says. (In fact, Garvey now describes all postoperative possibilities with his patients, including bad reactions to anesthesia. On the off chance they might react similarly,

Garvey prescribes Xanax. "It's unlikely that anyone will end up like me," he says, "but even so, I want my bases covered. I don't want anyone going through that if it can be avoided.")

Garvey says his new nose makes him feel more at home in the world. He no longer feels *beau-laid,* or "ugly-handsome," as the French would say. "An unattractive nose on an attractive face can be a huge distraction," he says, shrugging. "An attractive nose can take you to another level."

If someone meets him today, he says, they are no longer likely to think, oh, Rick Garvey, Italian guy with an Irish name, big nose. Not long ago, he attended a lavish wedding in the Caribbean, among a wealthy international set who, if they weren't born with perfect features, had certainly arranged to get them. For the first time, Garvey realized, he felt comfortable in a crowded setting of "mixed" people—in other words, not the native New Yorkers he counts as his intimates—Italians and Jews, all. There were wealthy American WASPs and European aristocrats. He could even take a sip of champagne without having to tilt the whole glass back beneath his nose. For the first time, it fit into a flute. "I looked around and realized, hey, man, no one is looking at your nose," he says. "It felt good. I felt, well, American."

But did a new nose really steady his soul? Were Tagliacozzi and Joseph right? Does a new appearance really help a person "fit in" better, or does one's perception of oneself merely change so that it feels that way? "I don't know," Garvey says. "But I can say that I don't miss the end of that big ugly snout one bit."

And yet Garvey realizes that there are certain taboos against discussing such feelings openly. While those opposed to plastic surgery dismiss the very notion of it as vain or "selling out,"

Garvey disagrees. People want beauty everywhere—in art, in their gardens, even their food. "When someone has a gorgeous home, you don't walk out saying, 'Man, what a vain person!' You say, 'Nice house.' As a plastic surgeon, you work on the surface. You fix scars or cut away the bumps or time, is all—it's like changing drapes that don't work. Of course I wish that the outer layer wasn't so important. But look at the Romans! The Greeks. The pursuit of beauty has been around a long, long time."

Mostly, he finds deep gratification in his work, in patients who tell him that he changed their lives. One, a woman in her thirties who was self-conscious of her nose, says she keeps him in her prayers nightly. She believed her nose kept her from having the confidence she needed to meet the right man. And there are trauma victims, such as the little girl whose nose and face were slashed by hundreds of pieces of glass when a tire fell off a truck and into her windshield. "You do everything you can," he says. "You just want people's lives to be easy, you know? Or at least not as hard as they have to be."

There are, of course, the demands of those who expect the impossible—women who have had numerous rhinoplasties and go from surgeon to surgeon in the hope of finding the "perfect" nose. Structurally, the cartilage and delicate nasal bones can only stand so much, and once in a while, a person will come in on their sixth or seventh procedure. "Those are the people you send away. You say, 'You can find someone in this town to help you, but it's not going to be me.'" Garvey looks up, hears his young son crying, and heads up the stairs. "Some people," he says, "think it will change everything about their lives."

That, he says, is impossible.

It will be a long time, of course, before the contours of exotic noses, like Garvey's "birth nose," as a woman I once met called her wide one, are celebrated by mainstream America. Unusual noses are suspect; strange tips and prominent bridges remain as unwelcome as garlic breath and "nervous B.O." An essay by an Orthodox woman in a Jewish weekly in New York went so far as to justify plastic surgery under Jewish law.

It would be nice to believe that in a time of multiethnic supermodels, worries like that of Holden's patient, or Richard Garvey's, or mine, perhaps might someday fade. But to think so would be naïve: studies prove (ad nauseam) that beauty counts, even when we think it shouldn't matter. An ultrasound technician at New York Presbyterian Hospital told me that once expectant parents get assurances about their unborn baby's health, they ask questions about its nose. "They want to learn that the baby is OK, and then they want to look at the nose," she said. "Sometimes people get really upset and say, 'Oh, no, he got your nose!' We're talking about a sixteen-week-old fetus." But it's not so mysterious. Mothers coo more to pretty babies than to plain ones, and we go out of our way to help the better-looking among us. Both women and men admire symmetry; they broadcast good genes—biological safety. As for the nose, well, as anyone with a less-than-perfect one can tell you, there is no such thing as it "not mattering."

If Americans, by birthright, pursue happiness, so too do they pursue beauty. And rhinoplasty—with all its pain, risks, dubious results, and expense—will prevail, as a rite of passage, an icon, and a metaphor.

# *Epilogue*

After nearly three years of living with the nose and its intricacies, one thing, at least, has become as obvious as the nose on my—or anyone else's—face. As little understood as it is, the nose is an organ that is the core of everything imaginable in life. We undergo significant pain and cost to change its appearance. The billions we spend to cure sinus disease testify to our often-fruitless search for good health. We roll deodorant on our armpits and splash perfume on our wrists and necks in an attempt to please it. We tempt it with tantalizing aromas, from vintage merlot to sizzling prime rib. We attract mates with enigmatic chemicals detected by a tiny, mysterious organ lodged deep within it, if pheromone theory turns out to be correct.

The process of writing this book was, in some ways, a gift.

For the first time, I came to truly understand the centrality, and magic, of smells in my world. At some point, it became clear to me that I could continue my research for years, as the recorded history of the nose stretches back to the beginning of time. Even so, its starting point for me is a clear one, snapping into focus on a snowy February night in 1998.

It was my husband's birthday, and my daughters and I were baking an orange cake. I had grated the peel and squeezed out the juice from two huge navel oranges, but to me, the extra flourishes were meaningless. The essence of the fruit was lost, its sunny aroma as silent as a white sheet of paper. Why not just use Betty Crocker? I thought. I stood, sullen as a teenager, as the girls broke eggs and mixed in flour. The dining room table was set; red tulips drooped seductively from a vase, and a fire crackled in the living room. Moisture gathered on the kitchen windows, and the girls giggled as they stirred.

My annoyance mounted to outright meanness. I scolded them for getting flour on the floor—they were five and two and a half at the time—and I snatched the mixer from my older daughter as it clinked against the Pyrex bowl. (Although science has disproved the so-called "Helen Keller theory," my inability to smell seemed only to augment my other senses. Sounds, especially, seemed to grate on me in all sorts of irritating ways. Or maybe it's simply that I concentrated on them more.)

Just as I was putting the pans in the oven, my husband burst through the door and screamed at us to get out of the house. I looked at him, and set the timer. Did he want us to

see the snow? I wondered dully. "The stove is leaking gas!" he
shouted. "I can smell it clear out on the street! Get out of the
house!"

He ushered the girls onto the deck, and shoved an anorak at
me. "Get out!" he shouted. "What's the matter with you?" I
stood, insanely mute, as I watched my family on the whitened
lawn. Finally I went outdoors. I couldn't smell my kids, I
couldn't smell myself, I couldn't even detect danger. I just stood
and sobbed in the snow.

Desperate, I sought help from my allergist, an old-fashioned but up-to-date doctor who listens to his patients. He
theorized that after four surgeries, the trauma to the delicate
lining of my sinuses was so severe that no odor molecules
could possibly make their way to the olfactory epithelium. So
he wrote out a prescription for a very high dose of prednisone,
80 milligrams. I had already tried several go-rounds with lower
doses, to no avail. This time, I was to taper the pills down over
the course of two weeks to 5 milligrams a day. Its unpleasant
side effects are legion, and the main one I experienced—irritability—added to my already sorrowful state. But by the end
of the two weeks, I could smell again. This time, it wasn't just
an errant whiff of garlic—it was everything, sometimes with
excruciating clarity. From bad breath to fake grape bubblegum
to an overheated, overchlorinated indoor pool in a mildewy
1950s YMCA, I could breathe it all in. I felt like Dorothy traveling from Kansas to the Land of Oz. Suddenly my nose had
switched from "seeing" black and gray cornfields to glittering
ruby slippers.

I finished this book while I was pregnant, a time during

which hormones heighten the ability to smell. In a few years, I had gone from not smelling at all to smelling too much. One particularly queasy morning I was convinced I could smell an egg cooked over easy and sprinkled with black pepper from a house nearby. The coffee on my students' breath at journalism school made me want to bolt. During a trip to Paris, a man next to me on the subway platform ate a tuna sandwich from a crisp paper wrapper as he calmly scanned *Le Monde.* Combined with the scent of overheated urine, I couldn't, and didn't, bear it. I love Paris, and I love its smells: melted Gruyère on a Croque Monsieur; chocolat chaud wafting from a café in winter; briny seafood on ice in a sidewalk display. But this time, as I struggled to keep nausea at bay, I found myself longing, ironically, for the isolation of anosmia.

Pregnancy is a misery for me, with nausea and stuffiness filling hours insomnia doesn't. When I can't sleep in normal times, I pop a Benedryl, and as I wait for it to work I come up with crazy lists intended to invite sleep—I alphabetize world capitals, or bodies of water. But in my heightened olfactory state, for a few weeks my mind fastened on smells and wouldn't let go. Had something triggered them, or was my mind—and nose—just playing tricks on me? Was it nerves? Hormones?

Stranger still, the smells that roamed into my brain each night were smells particular to a place and era: Eastern Europe of a decade prior. Perhaps not surprisingly, the odors had been accompanied by intense emotions in real time.

My husband and I were based as reporters in Poland for three years in the early 1990s, and I wasn't particularly happy there. I was especially cross about the weather (winter drags on reliably until mid-April) and the lack of light. (In December, night falls at three in the afternoon.) My husband, a native Bostonian, had no qualms about the short, dark days. In fact, he loved Central Europe, and the juxtaposition of our sentiments created flurries every now and again. But what really tested our contrasting sensibilities, I found, were smells. What drove me crazy—cheap black diesel fumes, ripe body odors on the tram in midsummer, the salty, garlicky odor of open-air butcher shops, where pigs dangled from hooks in full view—he scarcely noticed.

On restless nights a good ten years later, pregnant with my third child in my bed in New York, my nostrils couldn't shake a trip to Slovakia. I wasn't worried about myself (olfactory hallucinations can be linked to schizophrenia), but I was annoyed—the odors were rank. And like dreams, they were uninvited and nonsensical, even rude. I wasn't imagining daphne, sun-dried sheets, or the smell of my husband's hair. My mind somehow stuck on a stinking trip to Bratislava on a hot week in June.

It started out like this. Early one morning after a gulped-down breakfast, we gathered for a "press conference" in the dank medieval wine cellar of an unctuous politician who was doused with cheap aftershave. There are no dictates against drinking early in the day in Central Europe, and a "hostess" in a miniskirt thrust glasses of the sweet, golden Tokaj into everyone's hand. It is considered bad form not to at least take a sip, and the taste I took landed somewhere between Tinkerbell perfume and the red-dyed sugar mix you put in a hummingbird feeder.

Next on the agenda was lunch. The waitress recommended a "light Slovakian appetizer, specialty of Bratislava." She returned some minutes later with a heaping platter of hot, fried cheese. Globs of grease settled on the plate, and to my mind, both then and now, it smelled like a carton of Kentucky Fried Chicken someone had accidentally left in the car.

That evening, my husband suggested a romantic little stroll on the banks of the Danube. By that time, I, and my nose, had had it. "No way," I said. "Why not?" he asked. "The river stinks," I said. He laughed out loud. "What?" "The river stinks," I repeated. "It does *not,*" he said. This conversation deteriorated into one of our most irrational arguments. "That's my whole problem here!" I recall shouting. "The river stinks, and you can't even smell it!"

Modern science has yet to come up with a full explanation for why millions of people like me lose their sense of smell, or why a far smaller and luckier group manage to regain it. (Imagined odors are another question still.) But my journey through smells—lost, regained, and imagined—gave me an unusual appreciation of the secret world of neurons, receptors, and molecules, as well as the scientists who try to puzzle it all out.

My voyage through science, medicine, literature, and commerce has been a humbling one. If one theme seems clear, it is how little we really know. If history is any guide, a large percentage of what we now believe to be true about the nose will turn out to be uninformed or flat-out wrong. The sequencing of the human genome and the understanding of how specific genes affect smell is only in its infancy, as is the true grasp of how odor influences our memories, thoughts, and behavior.

As I learned, I began to sense the truth behind the aphorisms in many cultures suggesting that the nose can be followed to knowledge. The French compliment a person's intelligence by saying, *"Il a un bon nez,"*—"He has a good nose." The Germans have an expression, *"naseweise,"* literally, "nosewise." And in English we have our own maxim: The nose knows. While that may well be true, unlocking its secrets is still beyond us. The nose is aware of far more than we know—yet.

# Notes

## Chapter 1: Memoir of a Nose

1 The Egyptians believed that it was good luck to sneeze after looking at the sun; the Romans and Greeks found it an augur of good fortune as well. In Greek mythology, Prometheus fashioned a clay image of a man, then seized fire from the sun and applied it to the statue's nostrils. It sneezed, and became a living man. Aristotle believed a hearty sneeze was an "emotion of the brain," and was evidence of the brain's vigor. "He who hears it is honored," he wrote.

Saying "Bless you" after a person sneezes appears to stem from an ancient Jewish custom. Today, we say it as a reflexive courtesy, but in ancient Israel, a sneeze was a dire matter. According to the Talmud, from the time that God made Heaven and Earth a person never became ill. There is no mention of sickness in the Bible until Jacob hears of his father Isaac's: "Behold, your father is ill" (Genesis 48:1). Jacob asked God to give man warning of his impending demise, so that he might have time to repent. And so a sneeze, then, came to symbolize a death knell, prompting those who heard the sneeze to call out blessings—"Gesundheit" (to your health) or "God bless you."

This tradition traveled with the Diaspora. By the time the Black Plague struck Europe in the fourteenth century, Pope Gregory VII decreed that healthy people who heard a sneeze—one of the first signs of affliction was a violent sneezing fit—should utter "God bless you" in the hope of staving off the disease. Failing that, the benediction at least granted the sick a chance to repent.

## Chapter 2: Centuries of Stench

1 Morris, Edmund, *Scents of Time* (New York: Metropolitan Museum of Art, 1999), p. 22.

2 Lise Manniche, *Sacred Luxuries: Fragrance, Aromatherapy, and Cosmetics in Ancient Egypt* (Ithaca, NY: Cornell UP, 1999), p. 33.

3 Pilch, John J., *The Cultural Dictionary of the Bible* (Collegeville, MN: The Liturgical Press: 1999), pp. 14–20.

4 Nard, or spikenard, is an aromatic imported from the Himalayas. It is a member of the valerian family, which also includes the more familiar (and heavenly) heliotrope.

5 For more history on the ancient baths, see Mikkel Aaland's book, *Sweat.* Published by Capra Press in 1978, it is out of print, but excerpted at www.cybohemia.com /Pages/massbathing.htm.

6 According to legend, women washing clothes in the Tiber River discovered that the clay riverbed beneath Mount Sapo had special properties—this attributed, naturally, to gods pleased with animal sacrifices made on the hilltop. What is more likely is that the animal fats and alkali, leached out of the ashes by winter rains, streamed into the Tiber, where it accumulated in the soil. The story is likely just legend, but *sapo* is the origin of the word "soap" in many Indo-European languages. Other legends date the discovery of soap to the Roman invasion of England, in 43 CE; there, they learned the art of soap making from Celts, who called it *saipo.*

7 LeGuerer, Annick, *Scent: The Mysterious and Essential Powers of Smell* (New York: Turtle Bay Books, 1992), p. 41.

8 Classen, Constance; Howes, David; Synnott, Anthony, *Aroma: the Cultural History of Smell* (New York: Routledge, 1994), p. 49.

9 This passage by Plautus is noted in *Aroma,* p. 49. The book is a great portrait of smell and its meaning around the world.

10 St. Jerome, *Select Letters,* translated by F.A. Wright (Cambridge, MA: Harvard University Press, 1975), p. 183.

11 Classen, Howes, Synnott, p. 130.

12 *Smithsonian Magazine,* February 1990, Vol. X, p. 66. "How a Mysterious Disease Laid Low Europe's Masses," by Charles L. Mee Jr.

13 *The Florentine Chronicle* was written by Marchione di Coppo Stefani in the 1370s and 1380s. The original appears in *Cronaca fiorentina. Rerum Italicarum Scriptores,* Vol. 30., ed. Niccolo Rodolico. Citta di Castello: 1903–13. A modern translation is available at: http://jefferson.village.virginia.edu/osheim/marchione.html.

14 Defoe, Daniel, *A Journal of the Plague Year* (New York: Signet Classics, 1963), p. 79.

15 *Ibid.*, p. 93.

16 Classen, Howes, Synnott, p. 62.

(The nursery rhyme "Ring Around the Rosy," which originated during the plague era in Britain, notes the custom of protecting oneself with herbs and flowers with the line, "A pocket full of poseys." The ring, meanwhile, referred to the darkened red swellings that appeared on the victims; "Ashes, ashes," is a corruption of "Achoo, achoo." Sneezing fits seized the afflicted— while they still had the strength to emit them.)

17 Suskind, Patrick, *Perfume* (New York: Pocket, 1991), p. 4.

18 Corbin, Alain, *The Foul and the Fragrant: Odor and the French Social Imagination* (Cambridge: Harvard UP, 1986), p. 46.

19 *Ibid.*, p. 44.

20 Hoy, Suellen, *Chasing Dirt: The American Pursuit of Cleanliness* (New York: Oxford UP, 1995), p. 24.

21 The PBS television show "The 1900 House," which aired in the United States during the spring of 2000, gave the following statistics: in Britain in 1900, there were 2,000 scalding deaths per year; in 1999, there were 11.

22 Hoy, p. 35.

23 Hoy, p. 48.

24 Hoy, pp. 171–173.

25 Leopold Senghor, "New York." From Leopold Sedar Senghor, *Selected Poems,* translated and introduced by John Reed and Clive Wake. (New York: Atheneum, 1969).

## Chapter 3: The History of Science

1 Weir, Neil, *Otolaryngology, An Illustrated History* (London: Butterworths, 1990), p. 54.

2 The Digital Lavater, published online by http://www.newcastle.edu.au/department/fad/fi/lavater/lav-intr.htm

3 Charles Darwin, *The Autobiography of Charles Darwin, 1809–1882,* ed. Nora Barlow (New York: W.W. Norton, 1993), p. 72.

4 Jabet, George, *Notes on Noses* (London: Richard Bentley, 1859), pp.2–3.

5 *Ibid,* pp. 9–11.

6 *Ibid,* pp. 121–127.

7 Morantz-Sanchez, Regina, *Conduct Unbecoming a Woman: Medicine on Trial in Turn-of-the-Century Brooklyn* (New York: Oxford UP, 1999), p. 117.

8 Mackenzie, J. R., *American Journal of Medical Science,* LXXXVII, 1884, pp. 360–365.

9 Morantz-Sanchez, Regina, *In Science and Sympathy: Women*

*Physicians in American Medicine* (New York, Oxford: Oxford UP, 1985), pp. 116–117.

10 Ehrenreich, Barbara, and English, Deirdre, *For Her Own Good: 150 Years of the Experts' Advice to Women* (New York: Doubleday Anchor, 1979), pp. 122–123.

11 E-mail with Dr. Steven Reisner, Freud scholar and professor of psychology at Columbia University, March 5, 2001.

12 Masson, Jeffrey Moussaieff, *The Assault on Truth: Freud's Suppression of the Seduction Theory* (New York: Pocket, 1998), p. 57.

13 *Ibid*, pp. 62–66.

14 Mayer, Emil, *Journal of the American Medical Association*, Jan. 3, 1914, LXII:1, p. 7.

15 Obendorf, C.P., *Psychoanalysis* X, 1929, pp. 228–241.

16 Holmes, Thomas H.; Goodell, Helen; Wolf, Stewart; Wolff, Harold G., *The Nose: An Experimental Study in Reactions Within the Nose in Human Subjects During Varying Life Experiences* (Springfield, IL: Charles C. Thomas, 1950), pp. 69–77.

17 *Ibid*, pp. 30–32.

18 *Ibid*, pp. 89–91.

19 *Ibid*, pp. 96–97.

20 Holmes, et al., pp. 120–122.

21 Holmes, et al., pp. 125–135.

22 In fact, informed consent was first implemented in the United States by the U.S. Army at the end of the nineteenth century. Walter Reed, a bacteriologist, was intent on trying to puzzle out the cause of frequent outbreaks of yellow fever in the Southern states and the Caribbean. But it was not until an outbreak in Havana threatened American soldiers during the Spanish-American War that scientists worked in earnest to solve it. And so, with the support of the Surgeon General, Reed headed the Yellow Fever Commission on a mission to Cuba, where an epidemic was decimating both military and civilian populations. While many theories abounded, Reed was particularly intrigued by a fifty-year-old suggestion that insects spread the disease. Cold winds seemed to halt outbreaks, and Reed wondered if the weather interrupted the breeding patterns of mosquitoes. Others, however, believed the disease was spread by the spittle or blood of infected victims.

Since no known animals contracted the virus, Reed asked for healthy volunteers to test his hypothesis. Several Spanish immigrants participated in the experiments, but the majority of volunteers came from nearby troops. Reed was authorized to pay each volunteer $100 in gold apiece, which to a poor Spanish immigrant or an underpaid army private was considerable incentive. In a consent form—possibly the first of its kind—Reed emphasized that contracting the often fatal disease was highly likely. But because his experiment would be in a controlled environment with medical care available immediately to those who fell ill, Reed suggested that the chances of recovery were far greater than those in a remote camp.

One set of "volunteers" slept in a screened chamber on the clothes and sheets soiled with the blood of yellow fever patients. Another was sequestered from the patients' fouled linens and clothing but exposed to the mosquitoes that had been allowed to bite people ill with yellow fever. None of those who slept on the contaminated items became sick; those bitten by the mosquitoes contracted the virus immediately.

Curiously, such consideration was not extended to *sick* patients until after World War II. As the Nuremberg trial got underway, the American Medical Association enlisted Dr. Andrew Ivy, a leading medical researcher, to draft a hasty policy for medical experimentation. Ivy's proposal included the following three requirements: voluntary consent of the person on whom the experiment is to be performed must be obtained; danger of each experiment must be previously investigated by animal experimentation; and the experiment must be performed under proper medical protection and management. At a December 1946 meeting, the AMA voted its approval of Ivy's draft.

According to a report published in 1995 by the Advisory Committee on Human Radiation Experiments (http://tis.eh.doe.gov/ohre/roadmap/achre/chap2_2.html), some 70 percent of American physicians belonged to the AMA. Association members received a regular subscription to the *Journal of the American Medical Association,* but in fact, these rules were not published prominently. They were set in small type along with a variety of other miscellaneous business items in the lengthy published minutes of the meeting. Only an exceptionally diligent member, or one with a special interest in medical ethics, is likely to have located this item.

23 Dr. David Kennedy, the chief of otolaryngology at the University of Pennsylvania, cited Wolff's work on stress and sinus disease at a Washington, D.C., conference called "The Nose 2000," in an address on September 22, 2000.

## Chapter 4: Nagasaki Up the Nose

1 Figures on childhood deafness prior to the late 1950s are impossible to come by, according to the National Institutes of Health and the Centers for Disease Control and Prevention. The 4 million figure comes from the *Saturday Evening Post* article; whether it is reliable or not is debatable. The article was published on August 14, 1948.

2 The Johns Hopkins University School of Medicine and School of Hygiene and Public Health, to Federal Security Agency, Public Health Service, National Institutes of Health, July 1948 ("The Efficiency of Nasopharyngeal Irradiation in the Prevention of Deafness in Children,

Notice of Research Project, Grant No. B-19," ACHRE No. HHS No. 092694-A).

3 These comments were first reported by Molly Rath in a Baltimore *City Paper* feature called "Fair Treatment," which ran on November 4, 1997. It is available online at: http://members.aol.com/radproject/city_paper.html.

4 Proctor, Donald, *The Tonsils and Adenoids in Childhood* (Springfield, IL.: Charles C. Thomas, 1960), p. 18.

5 http://tis.eh.doe.gov/ohre/roadmap/achre/chap18_1.html.

6 This is from the March, 29, 1996, edition of the CDC's weekly morbidity and mortality report: http://www.cdc.gov/mmwr/preview/mmwrhtml/00040719.htm.

7 The musician Frank Zappa, who was born in Baltimore, was also irradiated as a child. He describes the ordeal in his autobiography, *The Real Frank Zappa Book*. He recalled a doctor stuffing "a long wire thing" up his nose. Zappa wondered later if his "handkerchief is glowing in the dark." (New York: Poseidon Press, 1990, p. 20.)

**Chapter 5: What Smells?**

1 Brodal, A., *Neurological Anatomy*, 3rd. ed. (New York: Oxford, 1981), p. 640.

2 Interview, Dr. Barry Davis, director of the Taste and Smell Programs at the National Institutes on Deafness and Communication Disorders, which oversees research and funding for olfaction at NIH, February 5, 2001.

3 Chemosensory scientists study olfaction, of course, but also gustatory, or taste cells, which react to food and drinks. We can commonly identify four basic tastes: sweet, sour, bitter, and salty. In the mouth these tastes combine with texture, temperature, sensations, and odor to produce flavor. These cells, which line the surface of the tongue, send taste information to their nerve fibers. The taste cells are clustered in the tiny bumps on the tongue—taste buds. Another mechanism is called the "common chemical sense," which contributes to smell and taste. In this system, thousands of nerve endings—especially on the moist surfaces of the eyes, nose, throat, and mouth—are responsible for the sensations we get when we feel the sting of rubbing alcohol, the burn of Scotch, the cool of peppermint, or the irritation of hot peppers.

4 Classen, Howes, Synnott, pp. 98–100.

5 Sacks, Oliver, *The Man Who Mistook His Wife for a Hat and Other Clinical Tales* (New York: Harper Perennial, 1990), pp. 156–158.

6 Richard L. Doty, the director of the University of Pennsylvania's Smell and Taste Center, developed a multiple-choice smell test—an eye exam for the nose—in the early 1980s. The test, which is called the University of Pennsylvania Smell Identification Test, is used to determine a number of

disorders, including degenerative neurological diseases such as Alzheimer's and Parkinson's.

7 Rodriguez, Ivan; Greer, Charles A.; Mok, Mai Y.; Mombaerts, Peter, *Nature Genetics*, September 2000, Vol. 26, No.1, pp. 18–19.

8 Jacob, Suma, and McClintock, Martha, *Hormones and Behavior*, Vol. 37, No. 1 (Feb. 2000): 57–78.

## Chapter 6: The Recreational Nose

1 "Mental Sequel of the Harrison Law," *New York Medical Journal*, 102 (May 15, 1915): 1014.

## Chapter 8: The Sinus Business

1 At the Washington conference, a faculty disclosure sheet listed the companies for which various speakers served as consultants. David Kennedy was listed as a consultant for three pharmaceutical companies, as well as for two companies, which use the global positioning systems in operating rooms. He receives royalties for one of them as well. Sherris is a consultant for Bayer; Ponikau advises for Schering; Kern does not consult.

2 While stress is clearly a factor in illness, in sinusitis, unlike heart disease, it is all but impossible to quantify. Only anecdotal evidence links the two. And as for pollution, Ponikau and others point to the landmark study done in the early 1990s by Dr. Erika von Mutius at the University Children's Hospital in Munich. Von Mutius compared asthma and allergic rhinitis rates of 5,600 children in polluted Dresden to that of state-of-the-art clean Munich, and found that the asthma rate among West German children was significantly higher than it was in East Germany. Von Mutius was so surprised at the results that she checked and double-checked all the data entries. She was convinced they had made a mistake, but again and again the numbers were the same.

Indeed, between 1975 and 1995, asthma rates in children doubled in many parts of the world, and the rates for adults also rose sharply. But pollution does not appear to be the culprit: when people from the Polynesian island of Tokelau move to New Zealand, their chances of getting asthma double. Similar increases have been seen among Filipinos moving to the United States, and Asians from East Africa moving to Britain. Chinese people in Taiwan, who have stayed in the same place, but gradually adopted a Westernized lifestyle, now have eight times more cases of childhood asthma than they had in 1974. In Ghana, wealthy urbanites have more asthma than do the poor in the same cities; in remote villages, there is little or none of the disease. Asthma researchers say that "Westernized life" is to blame, but that does not account for high rates of asthma in Brazil and Peru, where it strikes all socioeconomic groups. In his book called *Asthma: The Complete Guide,* Dr. Jonathan Brostoff, a professor of Allergy and Environmental

Health at University College London Medical School, says that air pollution is usually blamed, but the case against it "simply doesn't hold up." Although it can make asthma worse for people who already have the disease, and may produce a *small* increase in the number of people developing asthma, there is no way that air pollution is the major cause of the asthma epidemic. Some places with extremely clean air, such as New Zealand, have very high rates of asthma. (Healing Arts Press, Rochester, VT, 2000, pp. 78–85.)

3 Mayo has received patents on the two antifungal medications it prescribes to patients.

## Chapter 9: Smells Like Money

1 Hoy, Suellen, *Chasing Dirt: The American Pursuit of Cleanliness* (New York: Oxford UP, 1995), p. 146.

2 Friedan, Betty, *The Feminine Mystique* (New York: Bantam Doubleday, 1984), pp. 209–219.

3 Green, Annette, and Dyett, Linda, *Secrets of Aromatic Jewelry* (Paris: Flammarion, 1998), pp. 137–138.

4 Many of the smell researchers interviewed for this book have received fund grants.

## Chapter 10: The War on Stink

1 Mark Magnier, "The Smell of Aging," Los Angeles *Times*, p. 1, July 14, 1999.

2 Classen, Constance; Howes, David; Synnott, Anthony, *Aroma: The Cultural History of Smell* (New York and London: Routledge, 1994), pp. 182–183.

3 Classen, Howes, Synnot, p. 184.

4 From a pamphlet distributed to foreign students at the Rochester Institute of Technology, Rochester, NY, 2002.

## Chapter 11: From the Bronx to America

1 Gilman, Sander, *Making the Body Beautiful: A Cultural History of Aesthetic Surgery* (Princeton: Princeton UP, 1999), p. 68.

2 Holden, Harold M., *Noses* (New York: World Publishing Company, 1950), pp. 203–204.

3 Gilman, p. 57.

4 Simons, Robert L., *Coming of Age: A Twenty-fifth Anniversary History of the American Academy of Facial Plastic and Reconstructive Surgery* (New York: Thieme Medical Publishing, 1989), pp. 2–3. It is unclear, Simons says, whether the patient described here was indeed Jewish, but scholars conclude from Jacob's wording that he was.

5 *Ibid*, pp. 3–6.

6  Holden, Harold M., *Noses* (Cleveland and New York: World Publishing Company, 1950), pp. 106–108.

7  Interview, Robert L. Simons, June 19, 2001.

8  Ofodile, Ferdinand, *Annals of Plastic Surgery,* Vol. 32, I (Jan. 1994): 25.

9  These figures were provided by the American Academy of Plastic Surgery in Arlington Heights, IL. Statistics from previous years are not appropriate comparisons, because 2000 was the first year the organization tracked figures from all doctors who perform the procedure. It can be performed by an ENT, a general plastic surgeon, or a facial plastic surgeon. In 1992, for example, the academy listed 50,175 rhinoplasties, as reported by facial plastic surgeons. But officials in Arlington say that the overall figure has remained fairly steady throughout the decade.

## Epilogue

1  During World War I, American cotton companies endeavored to create a gas mask that would protect soldiers from poison gas attacks. Eventually, they did, using a supply of crepe-like cotton as a buffer allowing the soldiers to breathe. Once the war ended, the companies had a surplus of the soft cotton that they pondered how to use.

At first, product designers used the cotton for the first commercial sanitary pads. Wartime nurses were the first to use the cotton for menstrual blood; they discovered that it was much easier than the traditional flannel rags, which had to be washed and reused. Prim mores of the era were a huge impediment to selling the pads, however: magazines refused to advertise them, and stores balked at carrying them.

By 1919, an answer for the surplus arrived in the name of the automobile. Americans owned 6 million cars, which were mostly open-air "touring automobiles." While men wore goggles and mustaches, women got windburn on their noses and cheeks, and began to use cold cream nightly as a remedy for their red skins. In the morning, however, they needed something to remove the oily residue. Towels were an obvious choice, but since few homes had modern washing machines, the idea of disposable tissues made perfect sense. Officials at Kimberly Clark, the cotton giant, instantly saw a market. Soon, American drugstores were filled with ads—and boxes—of Kleenex tissues. The name, Kleenex, derives from its intended use, with an "ex" added to cement brand loyalty.

Meanwhile, Ernst Mahler, a Kimberly Clark executive who suffered from hay fever, began filching his wife's tissues for his own runny nose. The handiness of the tissues, combined with lingering fears of the flu epidemic of 1918–19, helped spawn an instant product: nasal tissues. By the late 1920s, the company began to market its "cleansing" product as a hygienic one. Ads for Kleenex showed a sneezing child spewing mucus into a tissue:

"Colds fill handkerchiefs with germs—boiling water fails to kill them! A handkerchief used once during a cold is unfit to be used again. Avoid Reinfection! Use Kleenex disposable tissues."

Today, Americans go through 200 billion Kleenex a year. Puffs, Kleenex's top competitor, in 1990 introduced an improved version of disposable tissues, laced with lotion and aloe for sore noses. Together, they account for some $1.2 billion in revenues.

# Acknowledgments

This book, no ordinary project, took advantage of many talented souls. Thanks are due the following physicians for their patience with a layman: Joseph Gogos, Richard Axel, Richard Garvey, Ferdinand Ofodile, and Robert Henkin; at the Mayo Clinic, Jens Ponikau, David Sherris, Eugene Kern, Thomas Gaffey, and Thomas McDonald, as well as their Austrian colleagues, Heinz Stammberger, Walter Buzina, and Hannes Braun.

Thanks are also due Rachel Sarah Herz, Stewart Farber, Tyler Lorig, Luis Monti-Bloch, David Berliner, Richard Doty, Annette Green, Theresa Molnar, Mike Norwood, Adolfo Coniglio, and Rabbi Lawrence Perlman. My own doctors, Clark Huang, James Pollowitz, Michael Tom, and Scott McNamara, have been exceedingly tolerant of a know-it-all patient. Thanks to Miriam Reinharth, Diane Solway, Rita Beamish, Michelle

Jackson, Jon Jackson, Mitchell Glaser, Wendi Glaser, Nina Martin, Jane Gross, and Edward Engelberg for their highly capable eyes.

My agents, Glen Hartley and Lynn Chu, played an important role in creating this book, from the initial idea to the galleys. They are deeply loyal and decent human beings. Rosemary Ahern is an old-fashioned book editor who actually reads and edits manuscripts. Thanks to her lyricism, this book read much better after she got done with it. My husband, Stephen Engelberg, read—and improved—this book in many drafts, even when he was on deadline with his own. He is, in all senses of the word, a mensch—and a brilliant one at that. And while book writing gives you time with your family, it also often takes away: from bedtime, from soccer games, from swimming dates (made and broken, made and broken) on summer afternoons. Thanks to my older daughters, Ilana and Moriah, for understanding.

Mostly, though, I'd like to thank my parents, Steve and Virginia Glaser, and my grandmother, the late Violet Claypool, for creating such a lively world of smells. It travels well.